KEY CONCEPTS IN DRAMA AND PERFORMANCE

Palgrave Key Concepts

Palgrave Key Concepts provide an accessible and comprehensive range of subject glossaries at undergraduate level. They are the ideal companion to a standard textbook making them invaluable reading to students throughout their course of study and especially useful as a revision aid.

Key Concepts in Accounting and Finance
Key Concepts in Business Practice
Key Concepts in Criminal Justice and Criminology
Key Concepts in Cultural Studies
Key Concepts in Drama and Performance (second edition)
Key Concepts in e-Commerce
Key Concepts in Human Resource Management
Key Concepts in Information and Communication Technology
Key Concepts in International Business
Key Concepts in Language and Linguistics (second edition)
Key Concepts in Law (second edition)
Key Concepts in Leisure
Key Concepts in Management
Key Concepts in Marketing
Key Concepts in Operations Management
Key Concepts in Philosophy
Key Concepts in Politics
Key Concepts in Public Relations
Key Concepts in Psychology
Key Concepts in Social Research Methods
Key Concepts in Sociology
Key Concepts in Strategic Management
Key Concepts in Tourism

Palgrave Key Concepts: Literature
General Editors: John Peck and Martin Coyle

Key Concepts in Contemporary Literature
Key Concepts in Creative Writing
Key Concepts in Crime Fiction
Key Concepts in Medieval Literature
Key Concepts in Modernist Literature
Key Concepts in Postcolonial Literature
Key Concepts in Renaissance Literature
Key Concepts in Romantic Literature
Key Concepts in Victorian Literature
Literary Terms and Criticism (third edition)

Further titles are in preparation

www.palgravekeyconcepts.com

Palgrave Key Concepts
Series Standing Order
ISBN 1–4039–3210–7
(outside North America only)

You can receive future titles in this series as they are published by placing a standing order. Please contact your bookseller or, in the case of difficulty, write to us at the address below with your name and address, the title of the series and the ISBN quoted above.

Customer Services Department, Macmillan Distribution Ltd, Houndmills, Basingstoke, Hampshire RG21 6XS, England

Key Concepts in Drama and Performance

Second Edition

Kenneth Pickering

palgrave
macmillan

First edition 2005
Second edition 2010

Published by
PALGRAVE MACMILLAN

Palgrave Macmillan in the UK is an imprint of Macmillan Publishers Limited,
registered in England, company number 785998, of Houndmills, Basingstoke,
Hampshire RG21 6XS.

Palgrave Macmillan in the US is a division of St Martin's Press LLC,
175 Fifth Avenue, New York, NY 10010.

Palgrave Macmillan is the global academic imprint of the above companies
and has companies and representatives throughout the world.

Palgrave® and Macmillan® are registered trademarks in the United States,
the United Kingdom, Europe and other countries.

ISBN 978–0–230–24147–3

This book is printed on paper suitable for recycling and made from fully
managed and sustained forest sources. Logging, pulping and manufacturing
processes are expected to conform to the environmental regulations of the
country of origin.

A catalogue record for this book is available from the British Library.

A catalog record for this book is available from the Library of Congress.

Contents

Acknowledgements

I wish to express my sincere thanks to Paul Allain and Patrice Pavis at the University of Kent and to my former Trinity College, London colleagues Mark Woolgar and Eunice Roberts for their inspiring and helpful conversations, lectures and seminars; to Charlotte Emmett and Anushka Magan at the Institute for the Arts in Therapy and Education for their support; to Suzannah Burywood, Karen Griffiths and Jenni Burnell at Palgrave Macmillan for their constant help and encouragement and to my wife, Irene, for her care and patience.

KENNETH PICKERING

Introduction

The aims and approaches of this book

The aim of this book is to provide students with an informative and accessible guide to the study of drama and performance and to equip them with an appropriate vocabulary for discussing these areas of human activity. I hope, also, to be able to demonstrate the inter-relatedness of the concepts that are key to understanding the subjects.

I am assuming that a *concept* is not only an idea but also the embodiment of that idea, and that it may be subject to variable perceptions. Thus, for example, we all understand that the term 'actor' describes a person who engages in a certain craft but our *concept* of what is meant by the term extends to our beliefs concerning the nature and purpose of that craft. Concepts, says Alan Read, 'are useful in identifying and discussing transient phenomena, and theatre is the transient *par excellence*' (1993, p. 12). The transient nature of theatre can also mean that the definition of drama itself can be slippery and I am perfectly aware that there is considerable current debate concerning the status of scripted plays in this field of discourse. I am using the term 'plays' to mean stories told by actors through the medium of theatre or the recorded media of radio, film or television. However, for the purposes of this book, the emphasis will be on the live theatre and I am taking drama to mean: 'Plays performed in a particular way in a designated space to a defined group of spectators'. This definition will, in fact, provide the structure for the entire book but it will also be one of the few definitive statements that I make. I hope that your basic approach to this book will be deductive and that you will construct your own definitions from the information, descriptions and discussion offered. I certainly encourage any reader to disagree with any conclusions I may have reached and to challenge the inclusion or omission of certain concepts as being *key*.

Let me say an important further word about the usefulness of developing a vocabulary for discourse. In the late 1950s the college where I was a drama student presented one of the first English productions of Ionesco's *The Lesson*. Those of us who were involved in or saw that production were acutely aware of experiencing something strange and new; but we had few terms of reference. None of us had ever heard of the Theatre of the Absurd let alone Postmodernism or liminality. Within a few years, however, Martin Esslin had published his famous book *The Theatre of the Absurd* (a term he appears to have invented), in which he developed that concept from a close observation and analysis of a number of contemporary plays. The book provided insights into such plays as *The Lesson* and even a vocabulary for discussing a short and disturbing play by the obscure playwright Harold Pinter, *The Room*, that my college had given its second English production. Each successive generation of drama students has benefited from the development of more concepts that have been created in an attempt to make sense of what seems to be a fundamental human activity: the devising and presenting of performance events. All of us involved in the study of drama must also acknowledge that there are many possible approaches to this process and that these are constantly evolving and changing. Some approaches will focus on the primacy of the text while others will explore the nature of the theatrical event or the cultural pressures and factors that affect performance. We must remain open to the many facets of our subject. It is likely, however, that you have come to study drama because of some involvement as spectator, reader or performer of plays and this book is rooted in that premise.

This is not another book of drama theory: there are plenty of those and some are unspeakably dull. However, the theory that underpins practice will be evident. When I was first planning this book a colleague remarked that he hoped I would, at least, 'retain a whiff of the greasepaint' and, although this way of indicating the live theatre may be something of an historical cliché, it is important to remember that we are discussing a vital and constantly evolving art form. That is why there are four principal theoretical sources of whose presence you will be aware throughout this book, all of which reflect practical involvement in the act of performance.

The first of these books is the *Poetics* of Aristotle, the first and probably still the most influential book on the theoretical basis of drama ever written. If that seems hard to believe consult an account of the contemporary theatre director Augusto Boal's reaction to Aristotle. The *Poetics*, dating from the fourth century BC, is a descriptive rather than a prescriptive text, based on the author's observations in one of the most prolific ages and situations of Western drama: Ancient Athens. The book became the basis for classical dramaturgy and particularly for concepts relating to the development of tragedy. We do not have to make the mistake of Renaissance thinkers who sometimes saw Aristotle's descriptions as formulaic, in order to benefit from the concepts he developed.

Whereas Aristotle laid the foundations for a theory of drama and performance from his observations as a member of the audience, the remarkable Russian actor and director Constantin Stanislavsky (1863–1938) used his experience to develop a system of acting and the training of actors that has provided much of the theoretical basis for the study of this art since the early years of the twentieth century. Some of the concepts we shall consider have their origins in the record of Stanislavsky's work preserved in his books *My Life in Art* (1924), *An Actor Prepares* (1936), *Building a Character* (1950) and *Creating a Role* (1961), which together probably represent the most systematic approach to acting yet to be devised.

Bertolt Brecht (1898–1956) developed theories of drama and performance in the process of directing and playwriting. The discourse he developed in his reflective writings, of which the *Messingkauf Dialogues* (first published in English in 1965) are a particularly interesting example, added significant new concepts that you will encounter in this book. The fact that Brecht was determined to depart from what he labelled 'Aristotelian Theatre' illustrates the diversity of influences that can shape our perceptions. Although the fashion for performing Brecht's plays may have waned somewhat, his sense of a strong ideological commitment reflected in a certain style of performance ensures that his influence and the importance of his conceptual framework for understanding drama remain as strong as ever.

It is also appropriate that I should acknowledge the unseen presence of the great Polish director Jerzy Grotowski throughout much of this book. Ten years since his death, students, teachers and practitioners of theatre continue to debate and draw inspiration from his ideas. His remarkable book *Towards a Poor Theatre* came as a life-changing and liberating force when it first appeared in the late 1960s and even those many who had never actually worked with or met him found themselves adopting a whole new approach to thinking about their work, the nature of drama itself and the meaning of 'research' in that context.

A further source of theoretical material from which I shall be drawing is the relatively new discipline of 'Performance Studies', which initially emanated from New York and has been embraced by universities and colleges over the last twenty years or so. Some of the impetus for the development of this subject, together with its attendant concepts, came from Richard Schechner's 'Performance Group'. Schechner has remained a key figure in this movement through his writings and his editorship of the *Drama Review*. For students of Performance Studies the kind of performances generated by the types of drama discussed in this book fall somewhere towards the middle of a continuum that has 'informal processions' and 'karaoke bars' at one end and 'grand opera' at the other. For such students, the interest lies less in the nature of the works presented and more in the nature of the performance *event* itself. Thus, their judgements are more anthropological than aesthetic and they acknowledge no hierarchy of 'great plays'. For this reason Performance Studies sits fairly comfortably with the work of structuralist critics and that set of aesthetic and philosophical ideas we label 'Postmodernism'.

Performance Studies has sometimes attempted to disengage itself from Theatre Studies. Although I shall be drawing liberally at times from the concepts of Performance Studies I shall nevertheless maintain that it has something very useful to contribute to the study of drama, not least a reminder that performance is an essential element in the understanding of drama. The fact that there are other forms of performance beyond the scope of this book and that concepts related to dance or public ceremonies may illumine the study of drama merely illustrates the inter-relatedness of aspects of our subject.

There is one final source to which I shall make frequent reference and for which I make no apology – that is Shakespeare. Writing in 1987, the most influential of modern British theatre directors, Peter Brook, said, 'We need to look to Shakespeare. Everything remarkable in Brecht, Beckett, Artaud is in Shakespeare. For an idea to stick, it is not enough to state it: it must be burnt in our memories. *Hamlet* is such an idea.' You may wish to substitute your own favourite Shakespeare play but we cannot escape the fact that the London of Elizabethan and early Jacobean England was the most prolific and, in many ways, most significant influence in our theatre's history.

The structure and content of this book

For the purposes of this book, I have defined drama as 'plays performed in a particular way in a designated space to a defined group of spectators'. If we break this statement down it will provide us with the five remaining chapters in the following way:

> **Plays** – Textual Concepts
> **performed** – Performance Concepts
> **in a particular way** – Production Concepts
> **in a designated space** – Staging Concepts
> **to a defined group of spectators** – Critical Concepts

Each chapter will begin with a reminder of this definition and a brief introduction to the concepts it embraces and will then contain alphabetical listings of those concepts. All key concepts that have their own entry are printed in **bold** so that it is clear when a concept has further discussion and explanation elsewhere in the book. Other concepts are printed in *italics*, as are the titles of books for reference and further reading.

All the key concepts are listed both in the General Index and the Index of Key Concepts so that cross-referencing is a straightforward matter. The fact that a single concept is mentioned in several sections illustrates further the inter-related nature of the study of drama. On the performance continuum that moves from the 'cultural', through 'cultural/aesthetic' to 'aesthetic', I have taken 'drama' to mean 'staged plays and theatrical events', as part of the 'aesthetic' category. The book ranges over a subject that includes dramaturgy, text and discourse, genres and forms, staging, structural principles and aesthetic questions, performance styles, reception and semiotics.

Using this book

There are many ways in which this book can be used but I would strongly advise taking some time to browse through its contents, beginning with the list of concepts that precedes this introduction and then becoming familiar with the book's scope and layout. You may have a particular topic that you wish to look up or revise; in this case you may find that, in addition to a specific entry, they will be referred to other entries that deal with related topics. Where I recommend further reading in the text I shall initially give either the author's name and the date of publication or the title of the book together with the author's name and date. If I then refer to the book again I shall simply refer to it by author and date, e.g. Thomas (2001). Full details of all books mentioned will be given in the Bibliography following Chapter 5.

1 Textual Concepts

This chapter focuses largely on the written playtext because that is where the vast majority of people begin their encounter with the study of drama. It would be helpful to read this introduction in conjunction with the entry on **Postmodernism** in Chapter 5.

One of the most famous photographs in the history of Western theatre shows a group of actors from the Moscow Art Theatre together with their director, Stanislavsky, gathered round the playwright Anton Chekhov as he reads from his play *The Seagull*. The 'first reading' of a play is a familiar event to anyone involved in the creation of performances and this celebrated photograph reminds us that it was the *process* engaged in by Stanislavsky and his actors that transformed the written text of *The Seagull* into an event widely acknowledged as an artistic landmark.

The term 'playwright' implies a maker rather than a writer of plays but the written text occupies a unique position in the practice of drama. As I hope to demonstrate, the text is far more than words for speaking – a playwright's text encapsulates an entire image of a potential performance and many playwrights remain adamant that their suggestions are integral to the future life of their play. In a television interview, the distinguished American playwright Edward Albee drew attention to the detailed stage directions in his most recent play *The Goat* (2003) and insisted that these were as important as the words themselves. Of course, the word 'text' is now also a verb and even this transition has been acknowledged by at least one playwright, Patrick Marber. In his play *Closer* (1998) he has an option for some scenes to be presented as text messages.

The written text shapes the form, content and discourse of a play: there *are* other ways of arriving at these but those processes remain experimental and frequently transient. Until recently, the written text remained the sole recognised means of preserving a play for future performance and there are still thousands of playtexts written and hundreds published every year. The use of DVD recording techniques has, however, enabled the devising process to be documented and preserved and can include elements of written as well as performed text. This may indicate the way forward for both the generation and the study of drama but, for the time being, it is difficult to see any diminution in the importance of the published play as the only means of access to the works that constitute the rich resources of Theatre.

It is frequently said, particularly in academic circles, that the primacy of the written text has now been challenged and that we may have to let go of our dependence on it. Let's think for a moment about the reasons that underpin this kind of assertion. I have already alluded to the growth of Performance Studies – a discipline that takes a largely postmodernist stance both in its attitude to the whole concept of a text and in its refusal to place any work of art on a higher level than another. Drawing also on structuralist critics, postmodernist scholars and theatre directors have insisted that all performances have to be 'read' and that therefore the various elements of a theatrical performance (words, action, lighting, costume etc.) are all part of a text. For this reason, they prefer to refer to the original piece as 'the work'. They also claim that, once a 'work' has been created, the author or playwright abdicates all rights over what happens in the process of translation into a performed text. This has led to some notorious disputes with playwrights like Arthur Miller or Edward Albee who assert that their intentions as communicated in the written text must be respected.

However, the unease with the reliability of the written text stems from deeper concerns, articulated by such philosophers as Jacques Derrida, because it is argued that the essential discourse is between the text and the 'reader' and that the text is not a conduit linking the writer to the reader or spectator. I shall be exploring many of these ideas at intervals throughout this book but, for the moment, it is important to be aware of one further set of ideas that have changed attitudes towards the written text.

Drama, Theatre and Performance Studies have successfully struggled to throw off the shackles of English Literature. There are still situations where a play is simply another 'set book' and it is also possible to meet writers who create plays without any concept of how these plays might be realised in performance. However, this does not devalue the written text as an integral part of the study of drama. There most certainly has been a perceptible shift in the approaches to generating performance in the theatre. Actors and directors now search avidly for the physicality of a character or situation even in established stage classics, sometimes to the detriment of the spoken text. What one colleague described as 'through the teeth naturalism' has, to some extent, also replaced projected and articulated speech. In a conscious reaction against the 'stage voice' and what was sometimes thought of as a 'proper handling of the text', the spoken word may have been relegated to a point where little if any meaning is communicated. This is not to deny the intense excitement and creativity of much recent physical theatre but such theatre pieces can rarely be re-created, and remain firmly embedded in the conditions of their creation.

This book invites you to take the study of the written text and the canon of dramatic literature past and present seriously. It is not a question of *if* the text or work is studied but of *how* to study it. Directors and actors continue to find their most satisfying moments in the theatre by delving into the text. Repeatedly, in rehearsal, I have watched directors urging actors to return to the text. Harold Pinter as playwright, director or actor always insisted that the text was non-negotiable and that it states no more nor less than is set down. What emerges from considering and working with a playtext is invariably surprising and rewarding.

Absurdism/Theatre of the Absurd

The term 'Theatre of the Absurd' was first used in 1961 as the title of a book by the critic and one-time head of BBC radio drama, Martin Esslin. In this work he considers the plays of Samuel Beckett, Jean Genet, Eugene Ionesco, Fernando Arabal, Arthur Adamov, N. F. Simpson, Harold Pinter and Edward Albee (whose very recent play *The Goat* provoked considerable anger and protest), all of whom came to prominence in the 1950s and 1960s, and to which list it is reasonable to add the name of the frequently overlooked but widely performed David Campton. It is extremely dangerous to assign playwrights to a category and expect their work to conform to certain characteristics and some critics would argue that the more recent plays of Pinter or Albee are not of the 'absurdist' kind. However, Esslin identified a movement in the theatre that appeared to respond to a view that any belief in a rational universe is an illusion and that humanity is out of harmony with its surroundings in such a way as to suggest a lack of meaning. We might now recognise in this the language of **Postmodernism**, which was not being widely used to discuss theatre when such plays as Ionesco's *The Lesson* or Pinter's *The Room* were premiered by drama students. However, we can trace the concept of the Absurd to movements in late nineteenth- and early twentieth-century atheist and Christian existentialist philosophy and theology and to such artistic concepts as **surrealism**, *Dada*, or the work of Alfred Jarry whose play *Ubu Roi* (originally written in 1896) became popular with those seeking an alternative to **realism** after the Second World War.

The influential Danish philosopher and theologian Søren Kierkegaard (1813–55) had already laid the foundations for the later work of the French philosophers and writers Sartre and Camus when he said

'Credo quia absurdum est' (I believe because it is absurd). Stunned by the horror of the Second World War, and particularly its impact on their native France, Jean-Paul Sartre in *Being and Nothingness* (1945) and Albert Camus in *The Myth of Sisyphus* (1942) reflected a feeling of total abandonment by God, of uncertainty, anxiety, purposelessness, and of mankind's inexplicable relationship with the universe, which was reflected in their later plays and novels. It was in this intellectual and spiritual climate that, what has become the emblematic play for the Theatre of the Absurd, Samuel Beckett's *Waiting for Godot*, was written. It was first produced in England by Peter Hall in 1955.

More has probably been written about *Waiting for Godot* and its impact on the post-war theatre than about almost any other modern play and it would be beneficial to become acquainted with both the play and the many subsequent critical reactions to it; it is constantly revived and revisited and remains one of the most uncomfortable, provocative, bleak yet sometimes comic stage metaphors ever created. Decoding its meanings and creating their own may well lead students to seeing the play as depicting the nobility of the human spirit or the hopelessness of existence; or they may see it as exposing the fallacy of any divine dimension to the universe or the futility and difficulty of communication in language. Audiences may well continue to be struck by the fact that, in performance, the play can be comic and touching. Whatever the response, the effect of this single play on the shape of subsequent plays and modes of production has been profound: Peter Brook, for example, when directing Shakespeare's *King Lear* in 1962, described that play as 'the prime example of the Theatre of the Absurd'. Although the influence of Beckett may have been subconscious, his work released a creative energy in a number of playwrights about whose work we can make some useful collective observations.

Theatre of the Absurd works by cheating and frustrating the expectations of its audience. In performance the laws of logic and of cause and effect appear to have deserted the language and action. Characters inhabit a world in which there are few explanations: a crowd awaits the arrival of a headless leader; two tramps await the coming of a mysterious figure who never appears; the stage slowly fills with furniture; a huge corpse or a 'dumb waiter' from another room intrudes into the space occupied by the characters; actors may be almost buried in dustbins or have paper bags over their heads for the entire play. In place of conversation that moves a story forward there may be huge passages of silence in which characters carry out repetitive actions; there may equally be prodigiously long speeches or shorter speeches that seem to have no reference to what has been said before – indeed, whole passages of dialogue may employ the *non sequitur* (a speech that does not follow in meaning) so as to give the impression that neither character is listening to the other. However, language may equally be used to intimidate, confuse, fill the void of silence or time, or to indicate the presence of some unspecified external threat. It has often been said that the Theatre of the Absurd is about the breakdown of communication, but Pinter, by far the most impressive and influential British writer in this mode, frequently asserted in interviews that his characters are communicating only too well; it is what and how they communicate that is explored in his plays. Most plays of the 'absurd' are written in forms that were certainly unexpected in the 1950s and 1960s: whereas a few may be 'full length', others may be of no more than a few moments' duration; some end as unexpectedly as they begin, others have no obvious shape or climax, no **denouement**, no **exposition**, and provide no sense of development. Characters reveal little or nothing about themselves and may either behave in strange ways or spend large parts of the play in total stillness. Action may be punctuated by comic routines and, to use an expression of David Campton's, there is an uneasy blend of 'laughter and fear'.

Although the main energy of the 'absurd' may now be spent, audiences continue to be fascinated by the plays of Beckett and Ionesco. It is the inner landscapes of the mind that remain so potent in their work and how those psychological maps spill out into relationships, politics and codes of communication remains the central concern of the concept of the 'absurd'.

Martin Esslin's *The Theatre of the Absurd* (1961) and John Russell Taylor's *Anger and After* (1962), along with *Changing Stages* (2000) by Richard Eyre and Nicholas Wright, remain the best introduction to this topic. Kenneth Pickering's *Studying Modern Drama* (2003) places the absurd in the context of other modern plays, and there are now many important studies of the individual playwrights.

See also the Introduction *and* **comedy**.

Act

The division of plays into sections known as 'Acts' has both a practical and an artistic purpose. An Act is a manageable unit for a two- or three-hour rehearsal and has a shape that enables a director to work towards its climax. For the seventeenth-century French dramatist Molière, an Act lasted as long as one of the large candles used for lighting the stage, and the space between the Acts was used to refurbish the relatively crude form of artificial lighting. By the late eighteenth and early nineteenth centuries, in plays, operas and ballets, an

Act provided an opportunity to cater for the growing demand for elaborate spectacle, so that each of four or five Acts might represent a different location and the curtain would be dropped between each of them. The complex scene changes might take place to the accompaniment of music: the 'entr'acte' (see **incidental music**). The curtain would then rise to reveal more wonders; indeed, the habit of applauding the new setting has not entirely vanished today. The writers and producers of melodrama became adept at building the climax of the action to the drop of the curtain and this technique was absorbed by the exponents of the **well-made play** and writers of the **naturalistic** school, such as Ibsen (1828–1906), who used three-, four- and five-Act structures, and Chekhov (1860 1904), who preferred four Acts, although he also wrote a number of one-Act plays. For Ibsen or Chekhov the change of Act is not necessarily a change of location: it is a change of rhythm and almost like a musical structure, provides opportunities to break or suspend the tension during the theatre 'interval'. Chekhov's *The Cherry Orchard* resembles a symphony with 'movements': an early morning opening movement of excitement juxtaposed with weariness; a 'slow' movement set in a late summer afternoon, when characters make unhurried movements and desultory conversation; a third movement of increased agitation and tension, full of dancing; and a final movement mingling despair, hope and a sense of finality. The play moves from May to October, each Act enabling that passage of time to be accomplished to shifting rhythms and counterpoints.

Such crafting of a play into Acts and sometimes into component 'scenes' appears to have derived from the division of Ancient Greek tragedies into *epeisodia* interspersed by five **choruses**. The Roman poet Horace insisted on the use of such divisions, in his *Ars Poetica* (The Art of Poetry), which, along with Aristotle's *Poetics* and illustrated editions of the plays of the Roman comic dramatist Terence (190–159 BC), became the principal sources for those neo-classical theorists who were attempting to establish rules for drama in sixteenth- and seventeenth-century France. These ideas were brought to England by Ben Jonson (1572–1637), the first English playwright to have his 'complete works' published in his own lifetime. Therefore, the familiar division of Shakespeare's and other Jacobean plays into five Acts was often the work of later editors and does not always serve the plays' structures well. However, this can still be a useful mode of reference when studying or rehearsing a play.

Many modern dramatists have abandoned the Act in favour of a more episodic structure of short scenes, or of an entirely different form (as, for example, in the **Theatre of the Absurd**). We would probably no longer feel the need to describe a short play as being a 'one-Act' play and it is worth pondering as to why that is significant.

See also **Epic Theatre; Naturalism; realism** and **well-made play.**

Action

See Chapter 2.

Actor-generated text

Any form of theatre that relies to some extent on **improvisation** will invariably contain elements of **text** created by the actors themselves. We know from Shakespeare's *Hamlet* for instance, that Elizabethan 'clowns' added to and embellished the written text and we can see their modern counterparts doing the same in traditional British Pantomime. Evidence suggests that the actors of the sixteenth-century **commedia dell'arte** companies generated their own texts from agreed episodes and incidents and, in a rather similar fashion, the contemporary theatre and film director, Mike Leigh, allows the text to emerge from a series of intensive improvisations. Such actor-generated texts are now seen as an essential aspect of **devising** for the theatre.

The results of actors creating texts may eventually be fixed and written down in a permanent form or they may remain extempore, changing with each performance and, perhaps, feeding off varying **audience responses**. In either case, the activity is an aspect of what the theatre practitioner Eugenio Barba describes as the **dramaturgy of the actor**. This process has now been recognised as an integral part of actor training and is best exemplified in the **autobiography**. The creation of an autobiographical piece, where the text is exclusively actor-generated, provides students of acting with the opportunity to explore and confront some of the episodes and influences in their lives that have brought them to the 'now'. As an exercise in introspection and honesty, the autobiography enables the student **actor** to recognise where they have 'come from' and, more importantly, where they are 'hoping to go'. It provides an arena in which issues that have remained unspoken can be addressed and these may be presented through the medium of stage images and metaphors.

An autobiographical piece will usually take the form of a **monologue** or monodrama and may be developed into a substantial performance. It is now quite common for actors to create autobiographical pieces in the role of an historical or even fictional character and to tour these as 'one-person' shows. This activity demands extensive research, often using such primary sources as letters and diaries and the results have become a familiar feature of small-scale Arts Festivals, cultural events and spaces.

Allegory

The term 'allegory' comes from the Greek for 'speaking otherwise' and describes a narrative in which the events and characters stand for something other than their literal interpretation.

For Patrice Pavis (1998), allegory is the 'personification of principle or an abstract idea' adding that 'in the theatre this is done through a character with well defined traits and characteristics' (p. 19). However, in their excellent *Medieval Drama* (1991) Christine Richardson and Jackie Johnson warn us against so narrow an interpretation of the concept. Referring to the medieval English Morality Play, the most obvious allegorical form in our drama, they suggest that modern 'readers' tend to concentrate solely on the issue of personification (characters such as Strength or Beauty in the play *Everyman*, for example), whilst failing to recognise that 'Allegory is metaphorical in its basis and consists of a complex web of metaphors arranged in narrative form' (p. 98).

Allegory is very often associated with religious belief and myth, as is a good deal of drama. This has come to be of interest in a variety of relevant fields of study: for example, the technique of Dramatherapy known as the 'Sesame Method' and taught at the Central School of Speech and Drama is based on Jungian psychology with its concern for archetypes, and uses 'myth' as a major feature in its methodology. Furthermore, scholars now investigating an early form of Christianity known as Gnosticism (Gnosis = 'to know') argue that the Gnostics did not believe literally in the events of the life of Jesus but regarded his virgin birth, death and resurrection as an extended allegory for human existence in relation to Consciousness, probably pre-figured by the Osiris/Dionysus myths of ancient Egypt and Greece. When the Christian myths were presented in dramatic form in the **Mystery Plays** of medieval Europe they were both literal and allegorical. The most substantial of the fifteenth-century Morality Plays, a form of didactic, dramatic sermon, is *The Castle of Perseverance* and it employs many allegorical features. The castle itself is the central allegory and is surrounded by a moat which protects the soul from the attacks of the Seven Deadly Sins, who are marshalled by the World, the Flesh and the Devil. A siege ensues in which the Vices fight against the Virtues and, at a later point in the play, there is a significant journey (a favourite device of allegory) and a debate between the Four Daughters of God. The combined effect of the various allegorical elements is to create an illustration of the means of salvation for humankind.

The use of allegorical personifications also characterised some of the pageants of Elizabethan and Jacobean England. Records show that the first anniversary of the accession of James I to the throne of England in 1604 was celebrated by an elaborate procession, pageant and presentation through the streets of London employing hundreds of artisans and craftsmen in the making and a huge company of 'performers', including the great actor Alleyn, who spoke dramatic orations scripted by Ben Jonson, full of allegorical references to royalty. The entire 'performance', which was largely conceived by the dramatist Thomas Dekker, included an enormous arch displaying allegorical figures such as 'the Genius of the Citie', with his six daughters, 'Gladness, Veneration, Promptitude, Vigilance, Loving Affection and Unanimity'. Such events are now recognised as part of the continuum that makes up the gamut of performance and there is a useful consideration of the 'pageant' as performance in Michael Bristol's *Carnival and Theatre* (1985). Bristol points out that 'Allegory is considerably more than a mere technique or instrument of representation in official pageantry; the nature of the allegorical symbol is an essential part of truth about nature and society' (quoted in Counsell and Wolf (2001), *Performance Analysis*, p. 213). What he is implying here is that the allegory is demonstrative of a wider world view so that, for example, an allegory that operates to show a hierarchy of God, the angels, mankind and the animals in descending order may also reflect a similar structure of society itself in which the monarch is at the apex of a fixed order and peasants are at the bottom.

Pavis (1998) maintains that the use of allegory waned as characters became 'more bourgeois and anthropomorphic' and that it then re-emerged in **Agit/Prop**, **Expressionism** and Brechtian parables. In all such cases the narrative signifies more than its literal meaning. In any play that employs a 'dreamlike' technique there is the possibility of allegorical interpretation: Freud, whose work on dreams was a major factor in the fascination with and understanding of the unconscious mind in the late nineteenth century, interpreted most dreams as a form of allegory. The irrationality of dreams also has something in common with the images of the Theatre of the Absurd and it is tempting to place allegorical significance on many of the plays in this genre. Remember, however, the story of the dramatist Terence Rattigan saying to Harold

Pinter concerning his play *The Caretaker*, 'it's about the Old and New Testament'. 'It's not, you know,' replied Pinter, 'it's about a tramp and two brothers.'

See also **Epic Theatre** *and* **ritual**.

Anti-hero

See **hero**.

Aristotelian (or neo-classical) unities

The concept of the unities of 'action' (no subplot or irrelevance), 'time' (events occurring within a single revolution of the sun) and 'place' (a single location) is key to much of the classical **dramaturgy** that appeared in the sixteenth and seventeenth centuries, and influenced the structure and form of drama for many years. Aristotle, to whom (along with Horace) the neo-classical scholars turned for their insights into drama, advocated in his *Poetics* (VII and VIII) a unity of 'plot' or 'action' for tragedy, but a number of commentators and translators, including Castelvetro (1570), D'Aubignac (1657) and Boileau (in his *Art Poétique*, 1674), wrongly assigned to Aristotle the two other unities, of 'time' and 'place'. The English dramatist Ben Jonson (1572–1637) adhered to the three unities, in such plays as *The Alchemist* (1610), and in what is often said to have been his last play, *The Tempest* (1611–12), Shakespeare makes some play of keeping to the unities of time and, to some extent, place and action as if to demonstrate his awareness of the 'rules'. However, it is generally thought that the first play written to accord with this set of principles was Jean Mairet's tragedy *Sophonisbe* (1634) and thereafter the plays of Racine (1639–99) in France and of Dryden (1631–1700), Congreve (1670–1729), Goldsmith (1730–74) and Sheridan (1751–1816) in England adhered fairly rigidly to the neo-classical 'rules' of subject matter and form, including the 'unities'.

In 1765 Dr Johnson, in his *Preface to Shakespeare*, was defending Shakespeare from the attacks of the French intellectual Voltaire (1694–1778), who found the English playwright's works crude and barbaric and only likely to be tolerated in a country as uncivilised as England. For Voltaire, it was Shakespeare's inability to comply with the rules of neo-classicism that damned him but Johnson counter-attacks with a mocking assault on the limitations of the 'unities'. It is relatively easy to discern the strain that is placed on the quality and content of dramatic writing by the artificial imposition of the unities. They have, in fact, put a serious restraint on experimentation, and modern drama has tended to demolish them. However, we need to recognise that the writers of the sixteenth- and seventeenth-century 'Enlightenment' were looking to preserve a sense of order in the human mind and that dismantling the more genuinely Aristotelian unity of 'action' in a play can lead to such fragmentation that audiences derive nothing from their experience. It is also worth considering what other forms of integration and unity are possible and desirable in drama. Brecht contrasted his **Epic Theatre** with what he called 'Aristotelian Theatre' and Augusto Boal draws heavily on Aristotle (see 'Boal on Aristotle', in Milling and Ley, *Modern Theories of Performance*, 2001).

See also **Act; catharsis** *and* **forum theatre.**

Autobiography

See **Actor-generated text**

Chronicle history play

The chronicle history play reached its peak of popularity in England during the reign of Queen Elizabeth I (1558–1603)) when a significant proportion of the population of England developed an almost insatiable appetite for new plays. This passion led to a period of productivity and creativity unparalleled in the history of the theatre. A relatively small number of the plays have survived in performance, but this is not unusual: a glance at those plays enjoying popularity in any period will show just how ephemeral the theatre can be.

The demand for new plays was largely fuelled by the increasing number of professional companies in their newly licensed, purpose-built or adapted permanent playhouses based in London at a time when the capital was seeing a growing cosmopolitan population. As a centre for world trade and influence, London was rapidly expanding and its population sought entertainment. When the plague or inclement weather closed the London playhouses, the actors took to the road and brought live theatre to most of the major towns and cities of the country; using and adapting every conceivable space as a performance venue and setting up their stage wherever an **audience** could be guaranteed.

Plays dealing with the history of England seem to have reflected and contributed to a growing sense of national identity but they also derived much of their fascination and relevance from the threat and later defeat of the Spanish Armada and the uncertainty concerning the succession to the throne. Events culminating in Elizabeth's becoming Queen had included periods of civil war, intrigue, treachery, military expeditions, international diplomacy through marriage and religious turmoil and these are all chronicled in plays from the period. Much of the popularity of chronicle history plays was no doubt due to their pageantry, spectacular battle scenes, dramatic deaths and moments of high emotion, all of which exploited the physical facilities and shape of the new theatres with their various levels, entrances and large central stages. The plays also provided a vehicle for some of the greatest and most popular actors of the day.

It has been estimated that around 220 plays written during the Elizabethan period were drawn from incidents in British history and approximately half of this number have survived. During the period 1558–1606 almost a quarter of all new plays were based on British history: six of them included the character of King John, seven featured Henry V and Edward III, Richard III appeared in eight and Henry VI in ten.

The majority of these plays appear to have used either Edward Hall's *The Union of the Two Noble and Illustrate Famelies of Lancastre and Yorke* (1548) or Holinshed's *Chronicles of England, Scotlande and Irelande* (1577) as their major source although there is some evidence to suggest that the work of Sir Thomas More may have been among other sources.

The fact that the majority of chronicle history plays revolved around the lives of monarchs reflects the views of Tudor historians that 'kingship' was an element of the Divine order. In fact, many of the plays seem almost formulaic: as Alvin Kernan (1973) puts it:

A weak or saintly king makes political mistakes and is overthrown by rebellious and arrogant subjects; the kingdom becomes a wasteland and society a chaos in which every man's hand is set against his fellows; after a period of great suffering, reaction against the forces of evil occurs and a strong and good king restores order. (p.264)

Such a pattern is reminiscent of the concepts of the Fall and Redemption of mankind set out in the Biblical narrative of the Garden of Eden and in the doctrine of Christ as the 'Second Adam' who comes as redeemer. Even if this set of ideas is challenged in some of the plays, the chronicle history plays were invariably an exploration of the activities of tyrants and good monarchs in the light of Providence.

Scholars frequently cite John Bale's *King John*, written just before the middle of the sixteenth century as the first chronicle history play but, although the play contains characters from 'real' history it is also peopled by many **personifications** of abstract virtues and vices. Early history plays, such as the anonymous *The Life and Death of Jack Straw, The Misfortunes of Arthur* and *The Troublesome Reign of King John* all date from around 1558 and deal with almost legendary incidents and characters in British history as does *The True Chronicle History of King Leir and his three daughters, Gonoril, Ragan and Cordelia*, (a forerunner of Shakespeare's *King Lear*) dating from almost the same time. A fascination with tyrants and foolish kingly decisions permeated Norton and Sackville's *Gorboduc* and Preston's *Cambyses King of Persia* both of which appear to have been popular in the late 1560s but were performed either at court or in college situations. It was not until Marlowe's huge play in two parts *Tamburlaine the Great* was performed in 1587, the year before the Armada, that London Theatre audiences were enthralled by a story of exotic cruelty and tyranny finally overthrown by its own arrogance and divine judgement.

There seems little doubt that the defeat of the Armada in 1588 acted as a trigger for the production of much patriotic and conflict-based drama in the form of history plays. Every major playwright of the day attempted the genre and there were clearly many collaborative ventures. However, A.D. Wraight (1993) argues convincingly that it was Marlowe, having been involved in clandestine activity and intelligence concerning the Spanish threat ,who turned to English history in writing the play *Edward III*, producing the first true English history play and providing a means of celebration through the play's parallel incident of a great naval victory. However, Sams (1996) argues with equal conviction that this play, first published anonymously in 1596, was written by Shakespeare. Other scholars consider that it was the appearance of the first part of Shakespeare's *Henry VI* that provided the model for subsequent developments.

What is without doubt is that by far the most substantial body of work in this area is the collection of history plays attributed to William Shakespeare covering a vast sweep of almost two hundred years of British history from the reign of Richard II to that of Elizabeth's father Henry VIII. This period covers the so-called 'Wars of the Roses' and the reigns of the Plantagenet and, finally, Tudor monarchs. The popularity of these plays remains undiminished to this day and they have frequently been compressed into 'cycles' or otherwise adapted for the stage or screen. Laurence Olivier's film version of *Henry V* was used to boost national morale toward the end of the Second World War and a highly successful television adaptation of the plays *The Wars of the Roses* together with John Barton's compilation *The Hollow Crown* brought Shakespeare's chronicle 'histories' to new audiences.

The continued popular **reception** of Shakespeare's plays has, however, tended to obscure the qualities of many other history plays from the same period. The plays of Marlowe, Peele and Greene, for example, all offer rich performance and production material. It is important, none the less, to stress that none of the so-called 'chronicle history plays' provides an accurate or unbiased account of history. Many of them were written with an eye to royal favour and patronage or to anti-French, Spanish or Catholic sentiments. We have only to compare Shakespeare's treatment of the character of 'La Pucelle' (Joan of Arc) in his *Henry VI part 1* with that of the later German dramatist Schiller in his play *The Maid of Orleans* to make the point. In the former play she is shown driving the English soldiers before her with demoniac power until she is captured and derided as a witch. In the latter she is shown dying heroically on the battlefield. The line between fact and propaganda is, in fact, very fine.

Although the concept of the chronicle history play belongs to the Elizabethan period the use of history as a source of and inspiration for drama remains. The German playwright Brecht in his time and the contemporary British dramatists David Hare and David Edgar, for instance, have chronicled events from recent world history in powerful and sometimes shocking plays. They illustrate Hamlet's belief that it is actors and the theatre that are 'the abstract and brief chronicles of the time' (Act II, sc.ii).

Frohnsdorff and Pickering (2010) provide a useful source of examples from chronicle history plays in their *Great Neglected Speeches from the Elizabethan Stage* and A.D. Wraight, whose work has not always been well received in academic circles, certainly uses her extensive experience in the theatre to create a vivid picture of such plays in their original performance in her *Christopher Marlowe and Edward Allain* (1993). A fascinating insight into performance in History plays is given in *Exit Persued by a Badger* (2009) by Nick Asbury who appeared in the most recent complete Royal Shakespeare Company cycle of History Plays.

Climax

The concept of 'climax' derives from the Greek word for 'ladder' and represents the highest point of tension in a **scene**, **Act** or play. At that point, the audience's attention is focused with particular intensity, either by action, word or some ingenious aspect of staging. The climax is most relevant to the **well-made play** or similarly structured play, where each Act or scene may lead to a climax that ensures the audience's interest in the following scene. This technique is now used regularly in television 'soap' drama.

We sometimes refer to the moment or incident in a play that encapsulates the climax as an 'obligatory scene'. This is a scene that the audience is actually expecting, and they would be frustrated by its absence.

It invariably grows from the motivations, interests and passions of the characters. One of the earliest English translators of Ibsen, William Archer, considered (*Playmaking*, 1912) that the five factors that make a climactic scene obligatory are: the internal logic of the theme; the obvious requirements of a specific dramatic effect; the fact that the playwright appears to be leading inexorably to it; the need to justify character development or a change in determination; history or legend requiring it.

The fact that some plays of the **Absurd** or in the traditions of **Expressionism** or **Epic Theatre** may have no obvious climax is, of course, a deliberate device relating to the purpose of the play. It is also important to recognise that a climax is not necessarily defined by the spoken text and may emanate from the psycho-physical aspect of a play in performance.

Comedy

In his very engaging book *The Crafty Art of Playmaking* (2002), Britain's most commercially successful modern playwright, Alan Ayckbourn, has set out a number of 'Obvious rules'. The first of these, significantly, states: 'Never look down on comedy or regard it as the poor cousin of drama.' Ayckbourn goes on to say that he feels that the English have a problem with taking comedy seriously and that 'unless they have had a thoroughly miserable time' they feel that they have somehow cheated themselves. This sense of unease with comedy and the tendency to 'downgrade' it permeates a great deal of our critical approach. I vividly recall watching a performance of Shakespeare's *The Tempest* by a French company and marvelling at the relaxed and accomplished ease with which they handled the comic scenes, using techniques clearly derived from **commedia dell'arte**, and how this compared with the many laboured versions I had seen from English companies. It is almost as if we have forgotten a strand of our theatrical heritage, which we are only re-discovering through a renewed interest in forms of comedy that directly engage the audience, such as 'stand-up comedy'. Indeed, at least one British university drama department now offers a course in this aspect of performance. At every level of experience there is a tendency to give less attention to comedy than to its opposite: **tragedy**. A number of recent books on the study of drama and performance make no mention of comedy at all. Beginning with Aristotle, even the theoretical writing has been less substantial and certainly less impressive; ironically there is little in the study of drama and performance more arid than a conference or volume of criticism on comedy!

The concept of comedy covers a broad category. Its name derives from *komedia*: a ritual song used during a procession in honour of the Ancient Greek god Dionysus, and it is traditionally deemed to have characteristics that contrast with those of its sister, **tragedy**. The characters are of humble origin, there are happy resolutions and endings and the purpose is to induce laughter. Much of the critical debate about comedy centres around *what* makes people laugh, and what we are laughing at: always remembering that laughter, tears and fear are often related. At this point, however, we should look at some tentative definitions and descriptions of the varieties of comedy, bearing in mind, however, that many plays have comic elements without being defined as comedies. Alan Ayckbourn insists that all plays need the light of comedy to create the shadows of darker drama.

- *Greek Comedy.* This is sometimes divided into 'Old Comedy', which is the label given to the eleven surviving plays by Aristophanes (c. 448–c. 380 BC), and 'New Comedy', a term used to describe the work of some sixty-four writers in the period after 336 BC. Only one entire play and some other lengthy fragments by Menander (c. 254–c. 292 BC) have survived from this period. Contemporary characters or gods and abstract figures, in combination with a **chorus**, act out fantastic situations that explore topical, social or political issues using burlesque, invective, parody, verbal wit, obscenity and argument, and culminate in revelry.

- *Comedy of Intrigue.* This concept is based on the Aristotelian idea of *peripeteia* (sudden reversal or change). A variety of stock characters such as an irascible father, young lovers, witty servants, and a marriageable widow or 'shrew' are embroiled in a crisis that probably involves money, a secret or a clandestine relationship, and enables the actors to give a virtuoso display of physical and verbal dexterity and wit. The main action may be punctuated by singing and dancing from the chorus and leads to reconciliation and celebration: the resolution of the intrigue or conflict is invariably a marriage. It is generally thought to be related to the Comedy of Character.

- *Comedy of Character.* A group of characters who are individually portrayed in great detail as to their psychological and moral make-up are involved in a situation where their motivations are made clear and their behaviour is a source of amusement. The plot is not complex and the action may be fairly static.

- *Comedy of Manners.* Human behaviour in society, often ridiculously exaggerated, is presented through a narrative that involves intrigue and verbal elaboration. Differences in class, milieu and behavioural characteristics are often highlighted.

- *Comedy of Menace.* This ironic derivation from the Comedy of Manners was used in the 1960s to describe the drama of Harold Pinter and David Campton, in which the characters appear to exist with a constant suggestion of an obscure threat from an unidentifiable source from outside the main action of the play. Good examples would be Pinter's *The Dumb Waiter* or Campton's *Then* (*see also* **Absurdism/Theatre of the Absurd**).

- *Romantic Comedy* and *Musical Comedy* (remember that 'Musical Comedy' was the term used in the early and mid-twentieth century for what we now simply call 'the Musical'). In such comedies a narrative, very often with a love interest, provides the context for lyrical speaking and singing and for dance, by individuals and, in some cases, a chorus. A subplot is concerned with topical incidents, speciality acts and rich humour. The young and beautiful protagonists are frequently required to relate to and circumvent villains and other difficult and unattractive characters and the entire action is played in an exotic setting and an atmosphere of magic or escapism.

Within the genre of comedy we should also include **farce**, but I have allocated a separate entry for this later in this chapter.

Comedy is usually deemed to have developed from the Greek 'Old Comedy' of Aristophanes, to the 'New Comedy' of Menander and thence into the Roman comedy of Plautus and Terence. The Renaissance saw a fusion of those classical and other comic traditions into the **commedia dell'arte** and on into the plays of Molière (1622–73), through the eighteenth-century Comedy of Manners and the nineteenth-century French Farce, and into the commercial and 'Black' comedies of the twentieth and our current centuries. Another line of influence is the popular comic tradition which inspired Shakespeare and became the stuff of the comic routines of Music Hall and stand-up comedy, which, in turn, infused the work of Beckett, the **Theatre of the Absurd**, and Brecht's technique of **alienation**.

Comic theory has evolved from the brief references of Plato and Aristotle to the concepts of 'playful malice' and the 'ludicrous'. A group of theorists from late antiquity known as the 'grammarians' (*circa* fourth century AD) produced the significant *De Tragoedia et Comoedia*, often quoted in introductions to early editions of the comedies of Terence. Its most important contribution to the theory of comedy was the belief that comedy is instructive and teaches 'what is of use in life, and what must be avoided'. This idea was developed into the neo-classical view of comedy as 'corrective laughter'. In the time that elapsed between the writings of the grammarians and the reintroduction of classical ideas, the theories of comedy tended to focus on poetry and narrative and saw comedy as a celebratory activity.

The first true English comedy, Nicholas Udall's *Ralph Roister Doister* (c.1534), was written largely in imitation of Roman comedy and celebrates the concept of 'mirth' as something that cures ills and gives moral instruction. However, it was the publication of Sir Philip Sidney's *An Apology for Poetry* (1595) that typified the Renaissance view of comedy. He saw the purpose of comedy as the exposure of evil and the 'beauty of virtue'. 'Comedy', he wrote, 'is an imitation of the common errors of our life, which he representeth in the most ridiculous and scornful sort that may be.'

Neo-classical ideas emphasised the observation and imitation of Nature and this gave rise to the use of the concept of 'humours' as the basis of comedy such as those of Shakespeare and Ben Jonson, for example, *Everyman in his Humour* (1598). According to early theory the human body was constituted of four fluids: black bile, phlegm, blood and yellow bile. When mixed, these constituted the four human temperaments: melancholic, phlegmatic, sanguine or choleric, according to which was dominant. These became the basis of comic character types for drama and had much in common with the 'stock figures' of ancient comedy. Thus the *Comedy of Humours* is another recognisable type of comedy, in which characters behave in predictable ways according to their personality types. In our present age both Mike Leigh and Alan Ayckbourn have made use of this formula.

Modern comic theory begins with the work of Henri Bergson (1851–1941). In his famous essay *Le Rire* (1899) he describes laughter as a 'sort of social gesture' and reckons that it is 'an inelasticity of character, of mind and even of body' that will arouse the suspicions and provoke the mockery of society. A certain autonomism on the part of characters will provoke an idea of the ludicrous. Comedy, according to Bergson's 'superiority theory' mocks those whose behavioural patterns have become predictable, fixed and obsessive and targets those who are greedy, proud or lazy. Those who are greedy, proud or slothful are held up for particular mockery and, according to Bergson, the laughter of an audience arises from a perception of 'the mechanical encrusted upon the living'. Thus, any stereotypical behaviour brought on by repeated gesture and verbal slogans will be the stuff of comedy. It follows that any reversal of expectation or anything incongruous will cause amusement and laughter.

Of course, Bergson's attitude is somewhat limited: there are many other forms of comedy besides those that appear to ridicule forms of behaviour with a view to moral improvement. Freud, for example, put forward the theory that comedy and joking arise from a need for 'relief' deep in the unconscious mind. Comedy thus exhibits what the repressed and 'civilised' self does not wish to confront, hence its obsession with sex and other disturbing subjects. For Freud, therefore, comedy is a healthy activity. On the other hand, the philosopher Kant (1724–1804) had argued that comedy and laughter emanated from moments when two lines of logic conflict and produce incongruity.

Writing to John Addington Symonds in 1889, the great English novelist Thomas Hardy said 'All comedy is tragedy, if only you look deep enough into it.' I suggest that you reflect upon and discuss this statement in relation to your experience of drama.

The Bibliography lists a number of sources that will enable you to take your investigations into comic theory further. This might include the consideration of such issues as the **actor–audience relationship** or the importance of 'timing' in the performance of comedy.

Denouement

The denouement of a play is literally the 'unknotting' or 'unravelling' of the strands of the plot in a final moment when various revelations and disclosures are made or the action is resolved in some fashion. In classical and neo-classical attitudes to drama the denouement followed the 'reversal of fortune' known as the *peripeteia* and the play's climax. Classical dramaturgy required that plays should conclude in a realistic and natural manner and should only involve the *deus ex machina* (the descent and intervention of the gods) when there was no possibility of a human resolution. On the other hand, the well-made play would usually unravel in a series of revelations and relationships to provide a sense of fulfilment and satisfaction for the audience.

In some plays, the denouement may be a catastrophe that nevertheless provides a resolution. Shakespeare's *Romeo and Juliet*, for example, culminates in a catastrophe on which the characters left living must reflect; by contrast, Shakespeare's comedy *A Midsummer Night's Dream*, which has many plot similarities and the potential for catastrophe, culminates in a denouement of harmony.

Shakespeare and English Jacobean writers of 'Revenge Tragedy' consistently ignored the 'laws' of classical drama in their denouements: *Hamlet* concludes with a stage littered with corpses, as does John Ford's *'Tis Pity She's a Whore*, whereas neo-classical French dramatists such as Corneille tended to employ a final narrative to preserve decorum.

The concept of a neatly resolved plot and the sense that every aspect of a protagonist's fate is explained is, of course, anathema to the writers of **Epic Theatre** or of the **Absurd**. In Epic Theatre the resolution of problems is in the hands and minds of the audience, whereas the whole notion of the Absurd is that there are no resolutions, explanations or disclosures.

Devising

The concept of 'devising' belongs to a more democratic and less hierarchical form of theatre than is common in the commercial world. It is a mode of creating plays and theatre pieces that do not emanate directly from a pre-existing **text**, and instead involves a company of actors in creating their own texts. The traditional roles of director and playwright are replaced by a collective although, finally, a work may become scripted and may even be subject to the direction of one particular member of the company. 'Devised' pieces are usually, but not invariably, developed through **improvisation** and even Mike Leigh, the most famous of modern theatre and film directors to use the devising process, would claim that he acted as facilitator rather than director or playwright. Devising challenges the primacy of the dramatic text and has evolved as a means of working during the last thirty years or so: a period in which there has been more intensive discussion about the nature of theatre, who it is intended for and who should create it, than at any time in our history. It has grown out of the desire for politically committed theatre, small-scale touring theatre, a sense of disenchantment with the power of theatrical managements and of established playwrights, and a search for relevance and new modes of expression.

Devising is, in itself, an act of defiance of the status quo in theatre and draws on the entire range of performance skills. Early devised pieces, such as those of the 'Living Theatre' in the USA of the sixties, included every conceivable method of shocking and arousing an audience by unconventional means. James Roose-Evans, himself a leading experimental theatre director, describes one performance, *Frankenstein*, as 'a collage of Grand Guignol, shadow play, Yoga, meditation, gymnastics, howls, grunts and groans' (*Experimental Theatre*, p. 142). This assault on the audience is fairly typical of the approach of a number of exponents of the collective means of working but there is an increasing tendency for companies to employ multi-media, physical theatre skills and **intertextual** references in their techniques. University, 'alternative' and 'fringe' theatre remain the most common settings for devising, but there are now very strong links between such theatre and modern dance and it is significant that the choreographer is giving way to the 'deviser' in the work of a number of new dance companies.

In modern theatre, the boundaries between 'writing' and 'devising' have become imprecise. A recent example is the production by the Trestle Theatre company of a play about the artist Marc Chagall 'written' by Darren Tunstall in collaboration with the company's director, Toby Wilsher. This play, in which the character of Chagall is the only speaking character, utilises masks, puppets, live music, narrative and direct address to the audience, mime, and flexible and inventive scenic devices. For those familiar with the production style of this particular theatre company it is obvious that far more than that has been evolved in rehearsal. The play is, in one sense, a **monologue** yet the scenes in which the central character works with the other characters, who are represented by grotesque, larger than life-size masked figures, are, in another sense, **dialogues** because there is a mimed response. Many figures in the production play live music to act as a counterpoint to the action, and the entire approach to this piece of theatre seems to reflect the images and distinctive quality of the artist. This is more than 'writing' or 'direction' and, in its totality, seems to have been 'devised'. For extensive discussion of the devising process, see Alison Oddey, *Devising Theatre* (1994).

See also **actor-generated text, environmental theatre** *and* **improvisation**.

Dialogue

The most common understanding of the concept of 'dialogue' in drama is that it consists of the verbal exchanges between two or more characters and provides one of the most distinctive and important elements of any play. Even given that the written **text** may no longer have the primacy it once enjoyed (*see* **devising**), few theatre-goers would disagree with the nineteenth-century German philosopher Hegel when he said: 'The complete dramatic form is the dialogue.' Inter-personal communication has been shown to be a fundamental human need and activity so 'dialogue' is an essential feature of reality as we know and perceive it. We become keenly aware of the consequences when dialogue breaks down.

Students of Communication Studies have pointed out that all verbal activity is in some way dialogic and this has implications for our study of drama. Certainly, it could be argued that even in a **monologue** or **soliloquy**, some form of dialogue is actually taking place. There is a constant dialogue between actor and audience in any performance (see **Aside**); some scholars have also maintained that there is also constant dialogue between author and audience. Dialogue may also take place between a character and an unseen presence or it may be wholly, or in part, non-verbal (see my illustration of a devised piece; see **devising**), and it is fairly certain that the soliloquy was employed by its creators in the Renaissance as a dialogue with the seen audience at the same time as being an inner dialogue between a number of aspects of a single character's consciousness.

Dramatic dialogue can take many forms, but it usually seeks either to *represent* or *simulate* some aspect of everyday language, be it formal or informal. In classical antiquity, dialogue was both a philosophical and a dramatic tool: the philosophical dialogue was a device used by Socrates and made popular in the writings of his student Plato; whereas, in drama, the dialogue first appears in the tragedies of Aeschylus, Sophocles and Euripedes and the comedies of Aristophanes. We may no longer consider that dramatic and philosophical texts have a common root but in the fifth century BC they were aspects of epistemology (the understanding of the ways in which we acquire knowledge). In Aristotle's *Rhetoric* there is consideration of drama and in his *Poetics* there are references to philosophic methods employed in *Rhetoric*. In some senses the use of dialogue in the tragedies of the classical period was an integration of the needs of philosophical debate and narrative. The form of dialogue in plays was reminiscent of the traditional disputation in which characters holding opposing views made persuasive speeches as a means of resolving an argument. Longer speeches would be interspersed with a series of short exchanges between alternate speakers, known as *stychomythia*, in which conflicting ideas were presented. These, however, though representing 'everyday' speech, retained the formality of a philosophical argument. In the **comedy** of Aristophanes particularly, we find a form of dialogue known as *agon*, which derives from and virtually becomes the conflict between enemies that is the essence of the play. Thus the verbal and dialectic conflict between the protagonists in a play is sometimes said to employ the 'agonistic principle'.

Although many later plays were based on the classical model, for English theatre-goers the most remarkable fact is probably that during the sixteenth century the dramatist Christopher Marlowe brought to the London stage a strong and engaging form of verse dialogue based on the 'iambic pentameter': each line of the verse consisting of five alternate weak and strong stresses. These five metrical 'feet' formed decasyllabic (ten syllables) lines of verse that, with subtle variations and perfected by William Shakespeare, represented spoken language in such a way that it seemed capable of sustaining any dramatic situation imaginable. This phenomenon has profoundly influenced the way in which the writing of dialogue has been perceived ever since. For instance, Henrik Ibsen's abandonment of writing verse dramas in favour of the 'very much more difficult art of writing the genuine, plain language spoken in real life' is often seen as a key moment in the development of **realism** in the European theatre.

Now, consider for a moment the following statements concerning dialogue, made by playwrights, and what our expectations for dialogue might be.

Avoid 'choice' diction. The language should be simple and forceful. The lackeys should speak simply. (Anton Chekhov, 1889)

... there must perforce be another dialogue besides the one that is superficially necessary. And indeed the only words that count in the play are those that at first seemed useless, for it is therein that the essence lies. (Maurice Maeterlinck, 1896)

The dialogue! Good dialogue again is character, marshalled so as continually to stimulate interest or excitement. (John Galsworthy, 1909)

The actor masters his character by paying critical attention to its manifold utterances, as also to those of his counterparts and of all the other characters involved. (Bertolt Brecht, 1948)

That is why one of our problems has been to search out a style of dialogue which, while utterly simple and made up of words on everyone's lips, will still preserve something of the ancient dignity of our tongue.... It seems to us that we shall recapture a little of the pomp of ancient tragedies if we practise the most rigorous economy of words. (Jean-Paul Sartre, 1946)

In regard to the dialogue, I have departed somewhat from tradition by not making my characters catechists who ask stupid questions in order to elicit a smart reply, I have avoided the symmetrical, mathematical construction of French dialogue, and let people's minds work irregularly, as they do in real life, where, during a conversation, no topic is drained to the dregs, and one mind finds in another a chance cog to engage in. So, too, the dialogue wanders, gathering in the opening scenes material that is later picked up, worked over, repeated, expounded and developed like the theme in a musical composition. (August Strindberg, 1888)

With a modesty, in no way inferior to Mr Shaw's I realised that I could not write dialogue, a bit. (William Archer, 1893)

I urge you to engage in discussion concerning these statements because they highlight some of the issues that need to be kept in mind when evaluating or analysing dialogue in plays. What emerges, in general, is that the creation of dramatic dialogue is a demanding and difficult craft and that it is constantly linked with the problem of **character** and with 'reality'. Before we examine some of the features of dramatic dialogue we need to think what this form of language does in everyday life. We use dialogue to argue, to establish relationships, to intimidate, to achieve our goals, to conceal or reveal our feelings or intentions, to comfort, to persuade, to charm, to discipline, to chastise, to learn, to influence, to exchange information and opinions, to pray, to think, to alienate or to encourage, to elicit or conceal the truth, to move towards understanding or deliberately confuse. These are only some of the uses of dialogue. Its form may vary from heated exchanges of a few words at a time, disjointed fragments of utterance punctuated by silences and pauses, hesitant and incomplete sentences padded out with 'ums' and 'ers', to more eloquent pronouncements that are difficult to interrupt. In all cases, there is a close affinity between the way in which we use dialogue, and the **context** in which it is used and the kind of character we are, or are talking to. All I have said here is, of course, relevant to the dramatist's task of the representation of human dialogue in plays.

Recent Linguistics and Communications Studies have provided a terminology that enables us to analyse the dialogue of plays in a number of useful ways. Think first of the particular 'voice' and characteristics of the dialogue of any one character in a play. The particular way of speaking of any individual is known as their *ideolect*, and this is a feature that an actor needs to recognise. This may well be combined with a *sociolect*: a pattern of speech shared by a certain social or regional group. Both a character's ideolect and sociolect are part of their personality and may be a source of apparent eccentricity, distinctive utterance or the cause of stereotyping. Without perhaps using this terminology, the playwright Alan Ayckbourn has regularly insisted on reading aloud all the parts of his characters as he dictates drafts of his plays for word-processing so that he can be sure of the various characters' 'ideolects'. Within any play, however, we can also read the author's 'signature': that distinctive quality by which we might recognise the work of Shakespeare, Wilde or Pinter, for example.

The twentieth-century British philosopher J. L. Austin recognised a quality of language and dialogue that has always been implicit in drama. In his book *How We Do Things with Words* (1962) he postulated the theory of 'speech acts', which concerns the concept that a form of action is embedded in language. The basis of Austin's theory is that there are fundamentally two kinds of utterance: the **performative** and the *constative*: both are present in the dialogue of plays. Constative utterances state facts and describe the world as it is perceived by the speaker. They tend to assume that there are verifiable realities about which it is possible to make definitive statements. However, the degrees of success we might achieve in the use of such statements are labelled by Austin as 'felicity' and 'infelicity', although some theorists prefer to use the terms 'happy' and 'unhappy'.

Performative utterances contain the essence of an action; examples would include commands, promises, vows, oaths. These do not describe an action you intend to carry out, they are *themselves* the action. A statement like 'I am determined to ' is typical of a performative utterance because it embodies both a passion and a determination for action. Austin went on to further analyse the speech acts of performative language, identifying: '*locutionary* acts' as the formal components of a statement irrespective of the context in which it is made; '*illocutionary* acts', which embody the intentions of the speaker; and '*perlocutionary* acts', which are what happens as a result of the '*illocutionary* act'. We can see that these concepts establish that dialogue in a play is far more than people talking; speech acts are occurring all the time in a play's text and they are what provides the tensions and resolutions within any situation. Speech acts are always part of the social context in which language is used, and both implied and overt forms of such speech acts are found in most drama because of the dialogic nature of play texts.

There is a very helpful discussion of the analysis of dialogue in Wallis and Shepherd's *Studying Plays* (2002).

See also **exposition; monologue; naturalism; performative, realism** *and* **subtext.**

Dramatic irony

In his *Notes for an Effective Play* (1902) the playwright Strindberg wrote:

> An effective play should contain or make use of ... a secret made known to the audience either at the beginning or toward the end. If the spectator but not the actors know the secret, the spectator enjoys their game of blindman's buff.

The playwright here is advocating the use of dramatic irony: a situation in which the audience is able to perceive aspects of the plot that are hidden to the characters, who are, thus, unable to act with full knowledge or understanding. Much dramatic irony depends on the fact that characters who may think themselves to have free choice, are, in fact, subject to the control of the playwright, and the spectators are always in a more powerful situation than those characters. This may be reinforced by the playwright's finding ways to address the audience directly and commenting on the action and its interpretation as it unfolds. As Patrice Pavis (1998) puts it: 'Irony ... invites the spectator to see the unusual aspects of a situation, not to swallow anything without examining it carefully.' Spectators are the only people who can hear ironies in the **text**. They may, for instance, be aware that something said echoes something said by another **character** earlier in the play. The **audience** alone knows when a husband is cuckolded or when what a character says about another is totally inaccurate, because only the audience has witnessed other scenes which gave a different impression of the loyalties or behaviour of the characters being trusted or spoken of. Dramatic irony is so powerful that it can even cause audience members to cry out to the characters on stage 'Don't do it', or 'Can't you see what is happening?' The painful and harrowing experience of watching Shakepeare's *Othello* is based on this kind of dramatic irony, which builds almost unbearable tension in actors and audience alike. Conversely, dramatic irony is often the foundation of **comedy** or **farce** as the audience witnesses characters blundering into amusing or compromising situations because they lack a vital piece of knowledge revealed only to the audience.

A particular sophistication of dramatic irony, alluded to in the reference to *Othello*, is *tragic irony*, sometimes called the *irony of fate* or *Sophoclean irony* because the most frequently cited example is in Sophocles' *Oedipus Rex*. In this play there is a tragic reversal of what the main **protagonist** thinks will happen, leading to what the audience has known from the outset. The **hero** is completely deluded about his own situation and moves swiftly towards his end, thinking he will be able to escape. Oedipus accuses the blind prophet Teiresias of being corrupt and lacking understanding; yet by the end of the play he discovers (as the audience have known all along) that it is he who is mentally blind and guilty of corruption, while the prophet sees and has true knowledge. It is, in fact, the audience who accordingly become aware of the dangerous ambiguity of language and of the moral and political dilemmas and insights of the play. However, at times the audience may be forced into an awareness of issues, perhaps involving guilt, suffering, deceit or death, which they would rather not confront. In *Oedipus Rex* the audience is conscious not only of Oedipus's ignorance but of the consequences and moral dilemma resulting from his discovering the truth. Audiences may well feel an empathy with the protagonist and yet be reminded of truths they have repressed or refused to face. Irony seems to be at the very centre of tragic conflict and has engaged the thoughts of leading philosophers, such as Søren Kierkegaard (*The Concept of Irony,* 1841).

See also **tragedy.**

Dramaturg

In Brecht's *The Messingkauf Dialogues* one of the four major characters is the *dramaturg* who speaks eloquently about the nature of plays and playwriting. The concept and term *dramaturg,* which has its origins in the German theatre and language, is widely employed in Europe and the United States but remains relatively unfamiliar in the British theatre. Lessing (1729–81), who was attached to the National Theatre in Hamburg, is generally considered to have been the first *dramaturg* and his perceptive critical reflections published as *The Dramaturgy of Hamburg* (1767) established a body of dramatic theory and ideas for **praxis** (doing) that has been used to underpin the staging of plays in the German tradition ever since.

A *dramaturg* is based at a professional theatre and will be responsible for preparing **texts** for performance. This may involve research, translation and adaptation and s/he will advise the **director** and discuss the context of the play's original writing or its likely impact on potential **audiences**. A *dramaturg* may also be required to contribute to the selection of plays for performance during any one season, write copy for publicity or programme notes or attend rehearsals to provide fresh insights to the **actors** and director.

In some cases, the writing of a play and the preparation of the **text** for performance will be carried out by the same person. Brecht, who subjected his own plays to rigorous analysis prior to production was the supreme example of this dual role, but it is more common for the *dramaturg* to act as a literary adviser to a theatre. The most productive partnerships between directors and *dramaturgs* are usually built up over a substantial period of time and such collaborations frequently result in productions of great integrity and depth.

Dramaturgy/dramaturgy of the actor

It might seem logical to assume that 'dramaturgy' was the exclusive function of the ***dramaturg*** but this is not necessarily the case. In its classical origins the concept of dramaturgy simply meant 'the art of writing for the theatre' and in this sense any playwright could be said to be participating in dramaturgy. But even in antiquity the search for rules and principles by which successful plays could be written had extended the concept to include an analysis of the process of playwriting. Scholars and early **dramaturgs** following in the traditions of classical learning in Europe concerned themselves with the creation of **texts** and not with issues of performance. However, the German playwright, director and **dramaturg** Bertolt Brecht (1898–1956) used his discourse and writings to extend the concept of dramaturgy to include all those factors involved in making a text 'work' in performance. Not only did he consider the *mise en scène* (the entire process of staging a play) but also the philosophical, aesthetic and political considerations by which a performance might be framed.

The idea that dramaturgy can involve both an analytical and creative process lies behind the concept of the 'dramaturgy of the actor' expounded by the contemporary Italian theatre practitioner, Eugenio Barba. Influenced initially by his work with the Polish director Grotowski (see **poor theatre**), Barba created his 'Theatre Odin' in Norway and described aspects of his practice in his *The Paper Canoe* (1997). For Barba the entire process and product of an actor's work constituted a contribution to the **text** and performance. Factors that shaped that text and performance would include the actor's initial research, the inner energy brought to his or her work and what Barba termed the 'score and subscore' that are constructed through the actor's response to the **director's** stimulus and material through **improvisation.** Barba's method of working enables the actor to develop a physical score that is distinct from a vocal score. Working initially alone and then with others the actor, under the director's guidance, creates actions rather than movements. The resulting **text** is the product of the dramaturgy of the actor finally shaped by the dramaturgy of the director.

Patrice Pavis (1998) provides a comprehensive survey of the development of dramaturgy and Jane Turner's *Eugenio Barba* (2004) is an excellent source for exploring the concepts of the dramaturgy of actors and directors.

Episode

As with so many terms and concepts used in drama, the episode has its origins in Greek **tragedy** long before the introduction of **Acts** and **scenes**. The *epeisodia* were the segments of **dialogue** between the songs of the chorus following the 'prologue' and before the final exit of the chorus known as the *exodus*. These dialogue sections either consisted of *'stychomythia'* (*see* **dialogue**) or 'tirades' (see **monologue**). In contemporary drama we tend to associate the concept of episodes with radio or television 'soaps' and it is helpful to consider the characteristics of such episodic works before we return to think about stage plays. An episode has its own unity although it exists within a larger narrative structure. It may not, necessarily, be linked temporally or causally to the episodes that precede or follow it. This is because the type of drama involved does not have a single **plot** or even a plot and subplot, as many stage plays do: instead, it is as if each character has his or her own story or narrative, which may or may not intersect with the narrative of others. An episode may, therefore, choose to focus on a part of the overall design of the work that deals with a particular character or group of characters. The total unity of the work is more likely to be thematic: all the characters involved, for example, may live in the same general location or illustrate an aspect of a work situation or profession. At times, we, the **audience**, agree to put our interest in one set of characters 'on hold' while we catch up with the lives of another set.

The use of episodes in stage plays adopts a similar approach to the narrative. In medieval **Mystery Plays** we see events taken from the Old and New Testaments of the Bible enacted. Although there is some importance in the chronology, the thematic progression is even more important and there is evidence to suggest that audiences in medieval times witnessed the succession of short plays in a variety of orders of events. At least one recent production in Canterbury Cathedral demonstrated that, at certain points, the order in which the audience saw these short plays was immaterial: the episodes have a completeness in themselves. Such episodic drama was made possible both in its original and in more recent productions by a form of staging that permitted a multi-focus space to contain episodes in various locations, or a mobile staging in which either the actors arrived on a wagon, performed and moved on, or the actors simply took the audience with them in a 'promenade'.

The emergence of the division of plays into Acts and their subdivision into scenes gradually produced a rather formulaic approach and it was not until the discovery of Georg Buchner's remarkable play *Woyzek* (1836) that modern playwrights became aware of an episodic alternative. *Woyzek* is, in fact, an incomplete fragment consisting of 25 short scenes. A good deal of controversy has surrounded attempts to produce the play because of uncertainty as to the intended final order of these scenes. Although the play has a unifying theme and a story line of a kind, it also contains many characters who only appear in one or more 'episodes' and the effect of the play in production is more cumulative in demonstrating a theme rather than providing a straightforward narrative. I would strongly recommend you to obtain and read John Mackendrik's extensive introduction to and translation of *Woyzek* in the Methuen edition (1987), to gain an insight into one of the most fascinating plays in Western drama.

A structure of scenes of the kind employed in *Woyzek* was used by Piscator and Brecht in their development of what came to be known as **Epic Theatre**: events are not causally linked and may move episodically across huge sweeps of time and space. Once again, this envisages a very flexible form of staging, and the use of sophisticated lighting has enabled directors to 'frame' episodes on various parts of an otherwise bare stage.

The writing of plays in episodes has become very popular in the contemporary theatre. Playwrights such as Caryl Churchill (e.g. *Fen*) and David Edgar (e.g. *Mary Barnes*) write plays as a succession of short scenes. The use of the episode enables playwrights to move back and forward in time, to juxtapose events from the past with those of the present, to move swiftly between imagined locations and to present delicate fragments for consideration rather than huge slices of experience.

See also **Epic Theatre.**

Exposition

During the course of any performance an **audience** needs to decode a great deal of aural and visual information. Even in the relatively straightforward process of reading a script it becomes obvious that large amounts of information are imparted by a playwright to enable the reader to evaluate the dramatic situation, comprehend the background and follow the complications of the **plot**. In broad terms, this process is all part of the 'exposition'. However, in more specific terms and reflecting classical dramatic practice, the exposition usually occurs at the beginning of a play, particularly in plays structured along the lines of the **well-made play** and presenting realistic situations.

The exposition or *protasis* aspect of a play is frequently achieved through the exchanges of information in the **dialogue**. In the case of the plays of Ibsen this is often initiated by the arrival of a 'protatic character', perhaps someone who has been absent for some while and has now returned. Such characters subtly elicit information so that the audience is unaware of the technique being employed. As the eighteenth-century French critic J. F. Marmontel wrote in 1787: 'The art of dramatic exposition consists of rendering it so naturally that it contains not the slightest hint of art.' By the time these early stages of the play have been completed, the audience has become aware of the context of the unfolding action and further information can be imparted in a more fragmentary way. Strindberg's *Notes for an Effective Play* (1902) include 'a secret made known to the audience either at the beginning or toward the end' (*see* **dramatic irony**), and if this advice is to be followed it requires the playwright to consider the mode and means of exposition. But as I have already indicated, this need not necessarily involve dialogue or verbal clues because the entire framework of a production provides information and this may include the physical setting or the unspoken behaviour of the characters.

The great nineteenth-century actor Henry Irving used to speak of the importance of the audience's understanding 'expired events'. In many of Ibsen's plays the playwright permits the audience to accumulate such information and achieve understanding gradually. In this way, tension and suspense are built, and the process of exposition may include revelations and discoveries.

Every audience is presented with a series of potential questions in any performance. What is the significance of what is seen and heard? Who are the characters and what are their intentions and motivations? Where, when and in what context are the actions of the play carried out? It should be possible to add other, similar questions. In every case, it is the exposition that enables these questions to be answered or frustrated. If we consider some of the plays of the **Absurd**, for example, we can see how the dramatists have set up the expectation of an exposition that provides explanations or revelations, but which, in fact, proves false.

See also **well-made play.**

Farce

Farce is a form of comic drama that exploits the foibles of humankind and relies for its humour on placing characters in compromising situations. It has remained one of the most popular forms of drama in Western theatre. Any theatrical management knows that a farce will usually attract larger audiences than any other production except a Musical. In our own age, Alan Ayckbourn (*Bedroom Farce*), Dario Fo (*The Devil in Drag*), Michael Frayn (*Noises Off*) or Christopher Durang (*Beyond Therapy*) have exploited the form and some people still recall the famous 'Aldwych Farces', mainly written by Ben Travers, presented in London between the wars. Farces such as Brandon Thomas's *Charley's Aunt* (1892) have remained part of the British theatre repertoire and such plays cultivated a taste for the early farcical films of Charlie Chaplin, the Keystone Cops and the Marx Brothers.

With its combination of knockabout, buffoonery, improbable and embarassing situations, sexual innuendo and risk, lewdness, intrigue, stock or gross characters, quarrelling, cheating and scheming, human imperfection, mockery of pomposity or authority, and fast action it is little wonder that Patrice Pavis describes farce as 'an indestructible genre'!

The term farce was first used in fifteenth-century France although we generally consider the first farce to be the thirteenth-century French play *Le Garçon et l'aveugle* (The Boy and the Blind Man), written in a Flemish dialect and telling the story of a trickster who deceives a blind man through ventriloquism. The literal meaning of 'farce' is 'stuffing': the spiced food used to stuff meat and add flavour. **Mystery Plays** of the time included farcical elements to provide 'comic relief' from the seriousness of the main matter: hence some 'spicing' of the material. The laughter and release of tension provided was later emulated by Shakespeare in such plays as *Macbeth*.

Although we can certainly see the antecedents of farce in the comedies of Aristophanes, it is in an early Italian form of the genre known as *fabula Atellana*, dating from the first century AD, that we see its characteristics emerging most clearly. Emanating from Atella, a town situated between Naples and Capua in southern Italy, these short plays based on scenarios handed down by oral tradition, became very popular in imperial Rome and appear to have been about trickery, cheating and tomfoolery, spiced with obscenity. They featured a number of 'stock' characters, such as 'Maccus' – the foolish clown; 'Bucco' or 'Fat Cheeks' – the simpleton; 'Pappus' – the foolish old man; and 'Dossenus' – the cunning swindler. Although the *fabula Atellana* seem to have disappeared after the first century AD, these characters, or some similar to them, survived into the **commedia dell'arte** and on into the modern Italian farces of Dario Fo.

It is reasonable to speculate that the type of drama I have described, with its strong improvisatory element, brevity and modest staging requirement, remained popular in early medieval Europe with the *jongleurs* and 'troupes' of itinerant performers. Although the major creative energy in drama was centred on the cycles of Mystery Plays, which told of Mankind's Redemption, they were already becoming increasingly secular and included a good deal of clowning in the plays of Noah and much practical joking, farting and knockabout by devils and comic humanity. The *Second Shepherds' Play* from the Wakefield Cycle contains a complete farce as a counterpoint to the events of Christ's Nativity and it is tempting to see the Old Testament play of *Balaam's Ass*, with its talking and obstinate donkey as a source for Shakespeare's Bottom.

At some stage, short farces (most of them no longer than a few hundred lines) were created independently and around 150 of their scripts, written in verse, have survived from the fifteenth and sixteenth centuries. The most complete and satisfying is *La Farce de maistre Pierre Pathelin* (*c.* 1465), which, like the *Second Shepherds' Play*, focuses on sheep-stealing and which proved so popular that it had already gone through thirty editions by 1600. Remember that sheep-stealing was an offence punishable by death, so we see here one of the essential qualities of farce: risk.

The traditions of farce throughout Europe built on various kinds of folk tale and improvisatory performance by companies of committed players like the 'Basoches' – an association of clerks and lawyers in France. Variations on the form, such as *sotties* and *sermons joyeux*, became popular and were presented, as are their modern equivalents, by students and other groups wanting to present burlesque, political and religious satire, but, invariably, having a strong physical element with such recognisable visual symbols as the fool's parti-coloured costume or a hood with ass's ears.

French farce became popular throughout Europe and we see its development clearly in the plays of Molière and the English dramatist Thomas Heywood (1497–1580), whose best known play *Johan: Johan* (1533), portrays a hen-pecked husband who is mocked by his wife and her priest lover and eventually ejects them from his house. The name most people associate with farce in theatre even today that of Georges Feydeau even though his most famous farce, *A Flea in her Ear*, was written in 1907. Feydeau brought the ingredients we have seen into a sophisticated formula, mainly centring on bedrooms and secret assignations and using the structure of the 'box set' with its opening doors and hiding places. Such plays have kept their appeal in a quite remarkable way.

The reasons for this continuing popularity lie in the concept of farce itself. Characters, although caught or nearly caught in compromising situations, rarely suffer serious physical harm or total humiliation. They exhibit a degree of naïvity and are oblivious to the feelings of others. They remain essentially youthful and, in order to survive, their **action** and that of the play moves quickly. An **audience** is caught up in amusement at the situations and senses the tension arising from the risks of discovery or the possibility of physical jokes. There is inevitably a resolution of the chaos which is part of our dreams and imaginations.

There is a good discussion of the nature of farce in J. Davis, *Farce* (1979).

See also **comedy**.

Flashback

The concept of a flashback is more familiar to film and television than to stage plays but, since the advent of the age of film, dramatists have used the idea to considerable effect, particularly in conjunction with an episodic structure. When a dramatist employs flashback it is important that the play establishes the convention within which it operates so that the audience is aware that it is seeing time manipulated in this way. For example, in Jean Anouilh's play *The Lark*, we see the figure of Joan of Arc at her trial. In answer to questions she takes the on-stage audience of her accusers through the events that led to her hearing voices and the subsequent results. At times she acts in her own flashbacks, and throughout the play, she serves as a narrator to the events so that there is no confusion as to the time frame: we know when we are in the past and when in the present.

The American dramatists Arthur Miller and Tennessee Williams employ a more physical and filmic mode of flashback in their plays, utilising stage technology but still needing to establish the conventions clearly. Miller's *Death of a Salesman* (1949) deals with the imaginings of the **protagonist**, Willy Loman, and whenever he lapses into memory and the action is cited in the past, the characters step out of and through the conventional **'fourth wall'** of the realistic set onto a forestage area. Williams's *The Glass Menagerie* (1948) is also much concerned with memory, but here a narrator/**chorus** figure both addresses the audience directly and participates in the action. The convention of a 'fourth wall' is also utilised, but in this case the scenes that take place in the 'past' are seen through a haze created by a stage gauze: a device that allows the scene to become visible or disappear gradually. Because, in the **stage directions**, Williams maintains that 'memory is seated predominantly in the heart', he instructs that the 'interior is therefore rather dim and poetic'.

The ability to move backwards as well as forwards in time has attracted a number of playwrights. Some of the most significant experiments in this area were undertaken by the English dramatist J. B. Priestley in the 1930s and 1940s as a result of his general interest in the nature of time and his explorations of the ideas of 'cyclic' or circular time proposed by P. D. Ouspensky (*The New Model of the Universe*) and J. W. Dunne (*An Experiment with* Time) in particular. Priestley's 'Time Plays', such as *Dangerous Corner* (1932), *I Have Been Here Before* (1934), *Time and the Conways* (1937) or *An Inspector Calls* (1948), all use elements of the concept of flashback as a way of investigating the effects of time on individuals. Both *Dangerous Corner* and *Time and the Conways* are structured so that Act I takes place in the present, whereas Act II shows events in the past that contributed to the events of the first Act. Act III returns to the present. These plays, along with *An Inspector Calls*, which appears to end where it began, have retained a great fascination among modern audiences.

More recent dramatists have used smaller units for flashbacks or have structured their entire play in the frame of a flashback. Pinter's *Betrayal* (1980) shows the course of a relationship in nine short scenes that move progressively backwards from 1977 to 1968; Hugh Whitemore's *Pack of Lies* (1983) is framed by the narration of one of the main characters, Bob, who talks directly to the audience and takes them back through the events of the play. In Charlotte Keatley's *My Mother Said I Never Should* (1988), the lives of four women from four generations are presented in a series of short scenes that take place in various time frames, defined by the costumes of the characters; and Shirley Gee's *Reach for the Moon* (1986) juxtaposes the life of women in a modern 'sweat shop' with that of women in an 1840s lace factory. Significantly, the playwright prefaces her work with a quotation from Eugene O'Neill's *A Moon for the Misbegotten* (produced posthumously in 1957), 'There is no present or future – only the past, beginning over and over again – now.' The flashback can always produce the effect of the present caught in the past.

Hero

Our cynical age is uncomfortable with the concept of the hero, and since the late nineteenth century the anti-hero has predominated in writing for the theatre. Through the plays of Ancient Greece, those modelled upon them and the drama of Shakespeare and his contemporaries, we retain the concept of the tragic hero as the central **protagonist** of a drama and a good deal of influential criticism has examined the role of the hero in the light of classical **dramaturgy**. The early nineteenth-century German philosopher Hegel set out, systematically, to explore the nature of the hero in his *Aesthetics* (1832) and proposed three categories of hero: (a) the *epic* hero, who struggles against natural forces and is crushed by fate; (b) the *tragic* hero, who contains within himself 'hero': the passion for action, which will be fatal because it 'misses the mark'; and (c) the *dramatic* hero, who adapts to the world and avoids catastrophe and destruction.

Before we examine these categories in some detail it is worth pointing out that a substantial amount of early twentieth-century literary criticism of the kind associated with A. C. Bradley in his book

Shakespearean Tragedy (1904), took Aristotle's word *hamartia* to mean a 'fatal flaw' in the character of the hero. Generations of students found themselves trying to find 'fatal flaws' in the heroes of Shakespeare's plays but more recent scholarship has established that *hamartia* is a term from archery that means 'to miss the mark', and we can see that a flawed 'action' of this kind or a fatal error of judgement is not the same as a personality defect. The hero of Ancient Greece was originally mythological: a demi-god who had qualities and performed deeds that set him apart from normal mortals. To some extent, this concept extended to drama, but in plays the hero was a **character** of greater stature than other characters, though also fallible. The hero of a play was the character whose actions and fate evoked the 'pity and fear' that Aristotle considered essential to the experience of witnessing **tragedy** and by that process the **audience** sensed **catharsis**. The classical hero was not only of noble or princely status but also imbued with noble potential, which made his ultimate fall all the more poignant.

By selecting significant figures from history as the heroes of tragedy, dramatists were often flattering their wealthy patrons by showing how the higher ranks of society influenced the course of history. However, tragic heroes demonstrate by their political importance that they embody important cosmic ideas on behalf of humankind. The Shakespearean hero reflects an 'Old Testament' view of history in which Divine Providence acts through rulers but then intervenes to bring judgement when the actions of the ruler go against the Divine will. This, of course, implies the breaking of a set of pre-ordained laws of moral conduct and for the **Postmodernist** this is an unintelligible concept. Since the collapse of confidence of the Enlightenment, critics have increasingly portrayed the world as an essentially violent entity in which people are largely engaged in wielding or being subjected to power. For the Postmodernist there is no set of absolutes, no hierarchy of aesthetic or moral principles and, certainly, no outside transcendent God. In this context the classical or Shakespearean hero has no particular qualities that mark him or her as 'noble' nor any set of eternal principles by which actions can be judged. The hero simply struggles like anyone else, and their elevated political status is neither a source of greatness nor of particular interest to most people.

The modern world has become acutely aware of the danger of making heroes out of individuals whose sole aim is the pursuit of power. Thus, in modern drama, we have the rise of the anti-hero: a central character who is the product of historical and social forces and has few noble ambitions except to survive. The plays of Beckett or Brecht are inhabited by such characters. The forerunners of such anti-heroes were the merchant and middle-class protagonists of such plays as Lillo's *The London Merchant* (1731) and the bourgeois men and women in the works of Ibsen (1828–1906) and Strindberg (1849–1912), where power is exercised in the family, locally and in business. Many of these figures are concerned with the loss of power, and, in some cases, it is the women who eventually gain it. Perhaps we can regard Willy Loman in Arthur Miller's *Death of a Salesman* (1949) as the last hero because he retains some of the essential, uncompromising nobility and inability to compromise that ensures his destruction rather than his survival. The anti-hero must often make moral choices but will sometimes take on the role of fool simply in order to survive. Life for the anti-hero has no governing purpose and little sense of self-image or personal destiny.

Melodrama

You would probably have little difficulty in describing behaviour or a performance that you would consider to be 'melodramatic' but might find the whole concept of 'melodrama' rather more slippery to define. An attempt at a definition might include excessive or exaggerated emotion in performance style, elaborate structures and affected speech in the **dialogue**, gestures employed to expand meaning and moments of 'freezing' in **action** to highlight pathos. Other characteristics suggested might be elaborate scenic effects and simplistic moral sentiments. All this is true of a genre that emerged in France, Britain and Germany towards the end of the eighteenth century and whose label literally means 'music drama'. We see the concepts of melodrama in the early plays of Goethe (1749–1832) and Schiller (1759–1805), in a new form of post-Revolutionary French drama that showed obviously 'good' and 'bad' characters in frightening or touching situations, and in early pantomime in Britain. In all cases, the action and dialogue was supported and heightened by the use of music and we can feel the spirit and ingredients of melodrama in the popular Gothic Novel. It built on domestic drama and yet was, to some extent, a parody of classical **tragedy** with its heroic sentiments, startling moments of revelation and recognition, strong sense of duty and destiny, love, betrayal, judgement and the triumph of virtue .

Those moments that we know as *coups de théâtre* were greatly embellished by the gradual development of stage technology, which was eventually to lead to the construction of realistic waterfalls, ships tossed at sea by steam engines that rocked the stage from beneath, startling lighting effects, appearances and disappearances achieved by sophisticated gas lighting and gauzes, heroines tied to railway tracks or rescued from swirling waters, and horses galloping across the stage on invisible rollers. The characters of melodrama were clearly defined and easily recognisable: they are either good, bad, or comic; the situations they inhabited were equally clearly drawn: extreme oppressive poverty, total joy, virtue rewarded, villainy punished, disaster averted at the eleventh hour; the setting might have been fanciful or exotic but the characters enjoyed 'homely' virtues.

A number of different types of melodrama developed in the nineteenth century. The early 'gothic' variety with its robbers, ghosts, haunted castles and wicked barons was joined by a more domestic kind such as the nautical *Black Eyed Susan*, based on life in the seaside town of Deal, or *Maria Marten, or Murder in the Red Barn*, dealing with a contemporary local crime. In all cases the **audience** was assumed to be largely unsophisticated, illiterate and economically deprived although the development of the railways was leading to a new middle-class, urban audience having access to theatres.

Melodrama was a major influence on the nature of theatre-going during the nineteenth century and up until the First World War. Even the plays of Shakespeare were greatly altered and adapted to allow productions to focus on special effects, the introduction of horses, or the particular talents and 'moments' of the actor/manager, who would both direct the production and take the leading role. Great insights into these theatrical conditions and attitudes are provided by a study of surviving playbills. These show that a single evening at the theatre might include several short melodramas together with a major tragedy or ballet. Huge amounts of music were composed and played for such evenings, much of it to cover the extensive scene changes that took place with the lowering of the curtain. Make-up worn by the actors was virtually 'painted' onto the face and could create a 'fixed' expression (Strindberg rails against this in his Preface to *Miss Julie*); gas light created a miasma of rising heat so that the stage was seen through a wavering film; actions on stage were large, facial grimaces and enounced syllables would strike us as unnatural but, unless it is understood that an audience for a melodrama brought to the theatre a totally different set of expectations from those of their modern counterparts, it is impossible to appreciate the original power of melodrama.

A specialised form of the genre, *Grand Guignol*, developed in the cabaret theatres of Montmartre and, deriving from the puppet figure Guignol (a French Punch-like puppet), used melodramatic techniques to show short stories set in tense and horrific situations: a figure staggering on stage with his hands chopped off; a wife enticing her husband to place himself in the guillotine at an exhibition, with the constant possibility that the blade will fall, and so on. The *Grand Guignol* enjoyed some brief popularity in England in the 1920s and demanded an intense and detailed physical performance: its appeal lay in the dilemmas and possibilities that confront the characters and the ever-present underlying tension. Such plays appear to cater for the same needs as a horror movie or fairground ghost train and, in this sense, the concept of melodrama is alive now in film and TV soaps, where characters also lack complexity and acquire the status of 'good' or 'bad', heroine or villain or comic.

Monologue

The monologue is usually a substantial piece of **text** for a single voice: a long speech delivered by one **character** that may be heard but not interrupted by others. It may be spoken directly to the **audience**: in many older plays this would take the form of a 'prologue' or 'epilogue'. The speech might exist within the flow of the action of the play, as with Iago's speech at the conclusion of Act I in Shakespeare's *Othello*, or a character might step out of the world of the play to address the audience directly, as happens in Brecht's *Caucasian Chalk Circle* and at the conclusion of the same playwright's *The Good Person of Setzuan*. In modern, especially late, twentieth-century drama there has been a marked increase in the use and variations of the monologue.

A number of playwrights have written plays that are an entire monologue or have structured their plays around a series of monologues that 'freeze' the rest of the physical action. Of the first kind, the best known examples might be Dario Fo's plays for a single female performer, collected under the title of *Female Parts*, or Alan Bennett's very popular monologues originally written for television, *Talking Heads*. These plays have been highly successful as stage performances. Fo's plays, however, sometimes presuppose another figure on stage to whom words are addressed, and the stage monologue has increasingly been developed as a mode in which the **dialogue** is with the audience or, in the case of the soliloquy, with the inner self. Eve Ensler's *The Vagina Monologues* (1998) concentrates far more on the idea of direct address to the audience, but probably the most fascinating example of the use of the monologue as an entire play in recent times is David Hare's *Via Dolorosa*, a play about the injustices of the situation in Palestine, performed by the author himself. Hare also published a diary of his experiences in this play.

The idea of the 'solo' performer in theatre is by no means new: medieval *jongleurs* clearly developed performance skills that engaged audiences with ballads and narratives. The extensive rediscovery of such skills has resulted from the economic situation in the theatre and a growing awareness of the potency of the solo performer as a means of exploring contentious social issues. The solo text is a very personal response to contemporary social issues and, in both the UK and USA, has been used as a way of addressing the collective conscience of the nation. One of the major exponents of this minimalist form in the USA has been Spalding Gray, a former member of Richard Schechner's Performance Group in New York (see the Introduction, and **environmental theatre**). Gray's devised pieces, which he named 'talking pieces' or 'epic monologues', consisted of improvised memories, reminiscences of childhood, personal emotions and action supplemented by projections, sound recordings and photograph albums. Working for small audiences he refined the performances through discussion until the text was set. Throughout the 1980s and 1990s Gray explored almost every facet of American life through his stage monologues, with such titles as *Sex and Death to the Age of 14*; *Booze, Cars and College Girls* and *Swimming to Cambodia*, establishing the monologue as a major new dramatic structure and theatre event.

British plays structured around a series of monologues include John Godber's *Bouncers* (1977) and Debbie Isitt's *The Woman Who Cooked Her Husband* (2002). Both plays employ a similar technique: the **action** on stage is suspended and other characters 'freeze' while a single character describes an aspect of their predicament or explains some part of the narrative. This technique is foreshadowed in Pinter's *The Caretaker* (1960) and Beckett's *Waiting for Godot* (1953) when one character launches into a massively long solo speech while the other characters remain still and silent. Beckett's monologues and narrative voice technique together with his minimal staging are rather like the 'stream of consciousness' novel and present the conscious and unconscious thought processes of the speaker. One of the most remarkable is *Rockaby* (1980), which is a fifteen-minute 'monodrama' in which a woman, seated in a rocking chair, rocks herself towards death. The performer only speaks one word: 'more', four times, and this single word is punctuated by a succession of other words from a recording.

The use of the monologue as a stage device in modern drama owes more to the influence of performers in cabaret, nightclubs, Music Hall and revue than it does to mainstream commercial theatre. The monologue is an art-form in itself in the hands of a skilled stand-up comic. For example, in the café culture of early twentieth-century Berlin, the comic monologues of the comedian Karl Valentin, the best known of which was *Das Aquarium*, had a profound influence on Brecht and the development of his concept of **alienation** and are still examined by students of Performance today. It is now understood that any performed text has an element of discourse; in the case of the monologue, even though this may include such devices as the **aside** and the soliloquy, the discourse may omit other characters and be conducted directly with the audience. One of the most effective and elemental forms of theatre is the single figure speaking. More economical modes of staging, the need to convey substantial narrative or information, as in documentary drama, an awareness of intertextual references, the use of non-theatrical venues with minimal technology and a far more flexible attitude to what length and form constitutes a play, together with a desire to involve audiences in a dynamic way, have all contributed to the development of the monologue as a potent means of communication. It requires considerable focus and inner energy from the actor together with the ability to employ the voice with clarity and flexibility of pace, pause, volume and pitch.

See also **dialogue; documentary drama** and **political drama.**

Montage

The concept of 'montage', as introduced by Piscator and Brecht in the 1930s as an element of **Epic Theatre**, is derived largely from the photographic techniques of the German designer John Heartfield (1891–1968) and the cinematic techniques of Eisenstein, Griffith and Pudovkin. In film, the process involves the cutting of already filmed sequence shots into longer sections of film, thus giving the finished product a rhythmic narrative structure determined by the editing. In theatre, Brecht, who used the term in his notes to Mahagonny (1930), employed a sequence of disparate yet autonomous scenes following quickly from one to another in order to produce a number of juxtapositions that provide an overall picture of life rather than a narrative plot-line.

Elements of this technique are used in Shakespeare, Buchner, **documentary drama**, Music Hall and Revue, but we see it most clearly in Caryl Churchill's *Top Girls* or Brecht's *Galileo*. Examples of montage in drama would include: (a) a sequence of tableaux in which each visual image forms a scene that does not lead into another; (b) a series of sketches that constitute a 'revue'; (c) a selection of material, either thematic or apparently random, that is presented in a documentary drama; (d) incidents in the life of a **character**.

In Galileo the protagonist is shown in different lights in different scenes: at times dishonest, avaricious, heroic or cowardly and constantly changing so as to adapt to circumstances. The playwright creates a montage of impressions and images rather than a story line. This is Eisenstein's 'montage of attractions', employing the juxtaposition of apparently disparate images by 'cutting' from one to another and shocking the **audience**. This achieves the sense of **alienation**, in which the spectator is constantly aware of the progression of images rather than becoming absorbed in the fictional narrative.

The contribution of the German director Erwin Piscator (1893–1966) (see **Epic Theatre**) to the use of montage has sometimes been overlooked. In the 1920s he expressed his disillusionment with the degree to which the theatre had lagged behind the technical and industrial developments of his day; remarking to the effect that, with the exception of electric light and the revolving stage, the theatre remained virtually unchanged since Shakespeare's indoor theatres. Thus, in Berlin, Piscator made bold experiments with the combining of stage techniques with a montage of film and slides of historical material: an approach seen much more recently in Howard Brenton and David Hare's British play *Pravda*.

There is a most useful discussion on montage in the work of Piscator, Hare and Churchill in Peter Buse's *Drama and Theory* (2001).

See also **alienation**; **Epic Theatre** *and* **documentary drama**.

Mystery Play (Mysteries)

The term 'Mystery Play' probably derives from the idea of the mysteries of craft or trade but has since accumulated the added meaning of the Holy Mysteries with which these short plays deal. Many medieval towns in Europe are known to have had their own series or 'cycles' of Mystery Plays but in Britain only those of York, Chester, Wakefield (Towneley) and an unknown Midlands town known as 'N' town have survived, along with some fragments from Coventry, Newcastle, a 'Brome' manuscript and a very recent fragment from Canterbury. The last recorded complete performance of a Mystery Cycle in the Middle Ages took place in Coventry around 1580 but, for at least two hundred years prior to that, the Mystery Plays had been a very popular form of entertainment and religious teaching, which influenced the work of many subsequent playwrights. Some of the plays, such as those by the so-called 'Wakefield Master', were clearly the work of a single genius but there is plenty of evidence to suggest that many of these plays, which tell the stories of the Scriptures, were constantly changing and being adapted to new performance conditions. Medieval playwrights tended to group plays thematically rather than strictly following the chronology of the Bible. Plays about Jesus's temptations, for example, are placed together. The original productions, like many recent revivals, must have enabled the **audience** to see the plays in a number of possible sequences because it is their theme rather than their chronology that is important. They present a **montage**, which, viewed as a whole, offers a cosmic drama in intensely human terms.

Although the dramatic presentation of biblical incidents had its origin in medieval church services, the full cycles of Mystery Plays (very often of nearly 40 plays) were the responsibility of the crafts guilds. The bonds between the guilds and the Church were close: each guild had its own patron saint and would often undertake the production of a play appropriate to its own trade; thus the Shipwrights or Mariners would present *Noah* or the Butchers or Pinners *The Crucifixion*. Only the medieval Crafts and Trades Guilds had the organisation, personnel and resources capable of dealing with the costly and elaborate business of staging the plays regularly: usually at the festival of Corpus Christi. Records show that no expense was spared in the productions and any idea that these were crude and amateurish is entirely inaccurate. As much effort and care seems to have gone into the construction, costuming and special effects of the Mystery Plays as would be made by a modern trade looking to make an impact with a float at the Lord Mayor's Show. So much time was devoted to the production of the plays that a high level of expertise in acting was probably the result and the plays themselves were clearly the work of scriptwriters with a thorough knowledge of working theatre. However, trades guilds were not the only form of guild to sponsor play production. Many parishes had Church guilds dedicated to saints and to the maintenance of altars in places of worship. Such Church guilds appear also to have supported the presentation of plays, although these were probably individual plays rather than cycles and they may well have been performed inside the church building or in the churchyard.

The staging of cycles of plays took place either on pageant wagons, which would be hauled from one location to another (an extension of the tableaux set up in processions for holy days that we can still see in predominantly Catholic or Orthodox countries), or in 'mansions' representing different locations for **action** in a fixed but multi-focus form of staging. Modern revivals of these plays, notably those at the Royal National Theatre and at Canterbury, Coventry, Chester and Birmingham Cathedrals, have often employed a 'promenade' form of production to enable the audience to gather around the action, or have mounted the production on scaffolds that provide a series of locations and levels for the episodic nature of the plays.

The medieval Mystery Plays are among the great treasures of dramatic writing in English and anyone involved in the many modern productions of them finds it difficult to accept that the written playtext is to be eroded. Like the scriptures that inspired them, they present a tapestry of memorable characters: tyrant kings, pompous prelates, eccentric prophets, talking donkeys, rough shepherds, loose women, beautiful people, and criminals – and at any moment a life can be transformed by an encounter with God, His Son or an Angel. The plays appear to have been written by playwrights who never allowed piety to swamp their humanity and they abound with humour, music, pathos, dancing, tension, refinement and vulgarity. They show the story of Divine Creation as understood by the medieval mind, and of the subsequent involvement of the Divine in that creation in acts of redemption and judgement. At some point in the Reformation, particularly in England, the plays were suppressed and it was not until the twentieth century that they were rediscovered as a vibrant art form (see **audience** and Chapter 5). Similar plays exist within Islamic cultures and a recent production of 'epic stories from the ancient world retold for the 21st century', toured by Chalkfoot Theatre under the title of *Miracles*, included a play in which a group of Muslims were preparing to present one of their sacred plays. For details of the revival of interest in medieval drama in recent years, see Robert Potter's *The English Morality Play* (1975) and Kenneth Pickering's *Drama in the Cathedral* (2001).

Many of the modern productions of the Mystery Plays adopted the title of *The Mysteries* and this can be confusing because of recent interest in the 'Mysteries' performed at Eleusis in Ancient Greece. Scholarship has tended to give little attention to these performances, largely because their precise nature and content is still unknown. We do know, however, that by the fourth century BC, 30,000 Athenian citizens would walk barefoot to the fortified coastal town of Eleusis to celebrate the 'Autumn Mysteries' in honour of the Mother Goddess of fertility, Demeter, her daughter Persephone and the god Dionysus. In what was an initiation ceremony that had probably been practised for over 11 centuries, people danced to a frenzied beat of cymbals and tambourines while masked figures moved amongst them. After ritual naked bathing a small number of chosen 'initiates' were permitted to enter into further secret rituals that admitted them to the cult, most probably the cult of Dionysus. Scholars differ considerably in their accounts and interpretations of these 'Mysteries'. One of the most fascinating ideas is developed by Freak and Gandy (1999) in their *The Jesus Mysteries*, in which they present the argument that the Eleusian 'Mysteries' were the origins of Greek **tragedy** and that they were mainly in honour of Dionysus, the 'dying and resurrecting Godman', thus linking the myth of Dionysus with that of Jesus Christ, about whom the Mystery and **Passion Plays** of medieval Europe concerned themselves. For a more conservative view compare Freak and Gandy's daring thesis with that set out in the Joint Association of Classical Teachers' *The World of Athens* (1984), used by the Open University as a course book. The concept of 'Mysteries' involves the dramatic representation of a set of beliefs, very often in the form of allegory, which enable audiences both to participate in a shared act of worship and to learn what are considered to be holy truths.

See also **allegory; episode; Passion Play** *and* **tragedy.**

Passion Play

A Passion Play is most likely either to be derived from a cycle of **Mystery Plays** or to be part of the tradition of religious procession or ceremony. A Passion Play is concerned with the death of a major religious figure. The Passion – that is, the arrest, trial and crucifixion of Jesus – is probably the most frequently re-enacted event in the tradition of Western theatre and performance. Passion Plays are part of the celebrations of belief on 'Good Friday' in many Catholic countries and will often take the form of re-echoing the 14 'Stations of the Cross', which represent in painting, carving or some other visual form, the incidents along the journey of Jesus Christ from the judgement hall to his place of execution. Throughout the Christian world there seems to have been a constant need to reflect on the 'passion' in a dramatic way. Even in the Puritan or Reformation tradition, which tended to eschew drama or visual art, we see the emergence of the great musical 'Passions' of Bach, and in the nineteenth and early twentieth centuries, various simpler sung forms of the 'Passion' became enormously popular. Building on that tradition and taking advantage of the abolition of stage censorship in 1968, Andrew Lloyd-Webber and Tim Rice created their rock-musical 'Passion' *Jesus Christ Superstar*, the composer's father, W. S. Lloyd-Webber, having written his musical 'Passion' *The Saviour* some years previously. In the meantime, many new Passion Plays were written for performance in churches and cathedrals; some of the most spectacular being in the 'Crystal Cathedral' in California, and the Passion of Christ has continued to attract writers for the stage, film and television.

By far the most celebrated Passion Play is that staged in the Bavarian village of Oberammergau in fulfilment of a vow made in 1633 that a play would be performed every tenth year provided that the village was spared the effects of the plague. The earliest productions of the play took place in the parish church but, as interest in the Oberammergau Passion Play grew and the railway from Munich made it possible for the production to become a tourist attraction, a number of more permanent structures were built, until the present theatre was constructed in the 1930s. The production still involves the entire population of the village and the event has grown to international proportions. The text originally derived from a Passion Play from Augsburg written around 1450; a new version was made around 1750 but the text now used dates partly from 1810, when it was completely re-written by Ottmar Weis, and also uses some of the adapted work of Alois Daisenberger from 1850. A number of composers have contributed musical scores because the play is highly operatic in flavour and makes considerable use of lavish spectacle and huge crowd scenes. The essence of the production is pictorial representation and there are some critics who consider that the play comes nearer to Hollywood than to the profound **allegory** of Mystery Plays. However, the Oberammergau play had considerable influence on those who were determined to reintroduce medieval drama and its sense of ritual and immediacy to Western theatre. Vernon Heaton's *The Oberammergau Passion Play* (1983) gives an honest overview of the project.

See also **Mystery Play** *and* **ritual**.

Peripeteia

This is one of several concepts drawn from Aristotle's *Poetics* and the term is used to describe a sudden and unexpected change in the fortunes of the **hero** or **protagonist** in a **tragedy**. This reversal is often, though not inevitably, a change from good to bad, prosperity to deep adversity, and is often made more poignant by the original state of contentment or prosperity in which the protagonist is shown. However, it is perfectly possible for the change to be from bad to good and it is the unexpected quality of the peripeteia that alters the course of the action so significantly. This turning point or 'tragic moment' sets the protagonist and the main **action** of the play in a new direction and, according to Aristotle, is at its most potent when combined with *anagnorisis*: a transition from ignorance to awareness. Such a shift in the perception of the protagonist may well be anticipated by the **audience**, who already have a knowledge of the situation. In this case, the moment of peripeteia and anagnorisis constitutes a complex and powerful form of **dramatic irony**.

Examples of painful revelations of the truth in drama are not difficult to find, and inevitably one of the best examples comes from Greek tragedy. In Sophocles' *Oedipus Rex* (*c.* 430 BC) a messenger brings news to King Oedipus concerning the true circumstances of his birth. This moment reverses the motives and expectations of both characters, and the audience witnesses the decline of Oedipus into rage and despair. A similar descent is seen in Shakespeare's *King Lear* (1605), but here, the reversal of fortune of the king and the growing awareness of the truth of his situation are more gradual although punctuated by shocking moments of revelation and misfortune.

Shakespeare's play also illustrates another key aspect of peripeteia and that is the simultaneous fall and rise of contrasting characters. In this play's multi-layered imagery, it is those who initially 'see' who are blind and those who become blind who 'see', those who have everything who have nothing, and those who have nothing, have everything.

See also **dramatic irony; hero; protagonist** *and* **tragedy.**

Play within a play

The play within a play, or 'in-set play' as it is now frequently called, is a device whereby some of the on-stage cast take on the roles of actors presenting a play to other members of the cast who have taken on the roles of **audience**. It is now seen as an aspect of *meta-theatre*: theatre that concerns itself with the nature of theatre, and it is interesting to explore just how frequently the theatre has both examined and celebrated its own nature in various ways. The first surviving example of a play within a play is found in Medwall's *Fulgens and Lucrece* (1497), to be followed by Kyd's *Spanish Tragedy* (1589) and Shakespeare's *A Midsummer Night's Dream* (1595). The most famous example of all, the *Murder of Gonzago* or *The Mousetrap*, appears in Shakespeare's *Hamlet* (1601) but there are also examples in other Jacobean plays such as *The Knight of the Burning Pestle* (1607) by Beaumont and Fletcher or the puppet play in Ben Jonson's *Bartholomew Fair* (1614). An example from another period is the play in Act I of Chekhov's *The Seagull* (1896). In more recent years there have been many plays that have been set within the framework of the nature of theatre itself, Pinero's *Trelawney of the Wells* (1898), Tom Stoppard's *Rosencrantz and Guildenstern are Dead* (1967), Timberlake Wertenbaker's *Our Country's Good* (1988), or Ronald Harwood's *The Dresser* (1980) are good examples.

The concept of the 'in-set play' in the early theatre derived from the underlying metaphor of the world as a stage. This was shown to its ultimate in the Spanish dramatist Calderón's play *The Great Stage of the World* (1645), in which God appears as a stage director, humankind as the cast, to whom he refuses to give a script. Improvising, the humans interact with a number of **allegorical** figures and make 'their entrances and their exits', as Shakespeare puts it in the well-known speech from *As You Like It*. This self-conscious awareness of the concept of life as a play or a dream is reflected in the many images of theatre that permeate such plays as *Macbeth* but it also provides a sense of 'playing' whenever characters are dissembling or attempting to be something other than they really are. Thus Rosalind, in *As You Like It*, is constructing her own 'in-set' piece when she disguises herself as a man and goes into the forest. Modern critics would also, of course, refer us to the growing understanding of the roles we play in everyday life, as explained by Goffman (1969) (see **frame analysis**).

The precise effect of a play within a play is worth lingering over for a while. Let me give you an example. In Shakespeare's *A Midsummer Night's Dream* a group of amateur actors meets in a wood to rehearse a play that they hope will be selected for performance at the Duke's wedding. Their rehearsal encounters various problems that will be familiar to anyone who has ever put on a play: the egos of the actors, the inexperience of some of the cast, the use of the physical space, the nature of the **text**, the behaviour of the **director** (or 'teller' as he would have been known) and the style of performance. A major point of debate centres on how the information that part of the play takes place by moonlight can be conveyed; or to use recent terminology, how that information can be 'encoded' for the audience. At one point the group decides that they will look in an almanac to see if the 'real' moon would actually be shining on the night of the performance so that they can simply leave the casement open and allow the moon to shine onto the stage. As an audience with some experience of theatre witnessing this debate, we might be tempted to shout out 'There are many ways to evoke the idea of moonlight and having a "real" moon isn't necessary!' We will, of course, know that the original audience watching the play would have been aware of far fewer options than we have today, but it is almost certain that, when the cast decide that what they really need is a character 'representing' the moon and carrying certain symbolic objects that could be 'read' as signifying 'moon', the original audience would have appreciated this discourse on the nature of illusion and reality in the theatre.

However, Shakespeare has more tricks to play on his audience because, in a later scene, we see the amateur performance of the play for which we have witnessed a rehearsal. A group of 'lovers' who have been through a number of traumatic experiences and illusions in a wood, gather with the Duke and his court to form the 'on-stage' audience. In order to watch the play they have to sit on the side of the stage itself, and from this vantage point they make various witty comments about the performance. So the 'real' audience is watching an 'on-stage' audience watch the same play that they are watching. As a member of a 'real' audience, I have invariably found the comments of the 'on-stage' audience extremely irritating: their attempts at wit seem laboured and pretentious and I cannot help thinking that that is precisely what Shakespeare intended me to feel. We have to remember that in the live theatre of his day, prosperous members of the public could, indeed, sit on the edge of the stage and comment, and that the tradition in which we generally receive a performance in silence, however provocative, was not established. Audiences attending a performance now at the Globe Theatre in London, which has attempted to re-create the physical performance conditions of Shakespeare's theatre, will almost certainly find that the most obvious element lacking is the rowdy and verbal nature of their Elizabethan counterparts! In *A Midsummer Night's Dream*, therefore, we have a clear example of the way in which a playwright manipulates an audience to examine its own role, the **liminality** of the concept of performance, in which the boundaries between reality and illusion are difficult to define, and the fusion of the fiction of the play with a mirror image of the audience members themselves.

Heightened reality is achieved when the audience watches actors in the process of creating a play: this double theatricality draws attention to the *meta-theatrical* nature of the activity and investigates the states in which it is no longer possible to discern life from art. When we see a play within a play it is as if we were putting the concept of theatre itself under a microscope.

Many of the themes I have touched on here are expanded in Ann Righter's *Shakespeare and the Idea of the Play* (1967), Lennard and M. Luckhurst's *The Drama Handbook* (2002), and R. Nelson's *Play within the Play* (1958).

See also **frame analysis** *and* **liminality**.

Plot

In the concluding section of their magnificent survey of British theatre in the twentieth century, *Changing Stages* (2000), Richard Eyre and Nicholas Wright remind us that we expect the theatre to tell us stories, and if it does not it will die. Even if little appears to happen in a play and the **action** seems minimal, we none the less expect the events to have a recognisable sequence but also a causality that we know as the **plot.** The series of events that constitutes the narrative element of a work is sometimes referred to by the Latin term *fabula* but it is the various developments of the *fabula*, the way in which the various characters deal with their various reversals, challenges and conflicts, that is described as the plot. We can distinguish between the external events, the complications and circumstances of which the plot consists, and the deeper, internal movements that make up the action of a play. Concepts such as **exposition,** *anagnorisis*, **peripeteia** or **denouement** are stages of the unfolding of a plot and given that the theatre has been constantly concerned with the presentation of narratives in dramatic form, it is hardly surprising that there have been a good number of formulae for the creation of plots and many analyses of the process of their construction.

Aristotle in his *Poetics* makes *mythos* central to his discussion of the nature of **tragedy.** Most critics have accepted that *mythos* is synonymous with 'plot' although some have asserted that it approximates more to *fabula*. The difference is immaterial for the purposes of study because, in stating that the *mythos* must have a beginning, middle and end, Aristotle is clearly speaking of what would commonly be accepted as the **plot**: a causal sequence of events that forms the framework of the play. Remember that Aristotle's writings were based on his having seen many plays in performance and his observations bring him to suggest that the plot should have a certain *unity*, and in tragedy such features as reversal in fortune, revelations, or recognitions will lead to the emotions of pity and fear and culminate in the purging of the emotions that he calls **catharsis**. So we can see that, for Aristotle, the plot is probably the most important single element of the drama.

The structure of a play has usefully been described by Schechner (1988) as being either 'closed' or 'open'. His first category describes the plot structure of the **well-made play** with its careful **exposition,** development, complication and **denouement**. In this case there are usually two ideas, or people, that are in conflict at the start of the play and eventually move towards some kind of resolution. The outcome may be either happy or tragic; discord, for example, may resolve itself into concord or the resolution may involve the death of one of the **protagonists.** In the 'open' structure, nothing significant happens to change the initial contradiction. There may have been what Schechner calls 'explosions' but these do not fundamentally change the situation. The plot determines whether the play's structure is 'open' or 'closed'. Aristotle considered that the plot of *Oedipus Rex* by Sophocles (see **peripeteia**) was exemplary; we can see that it is an example of a 'closed' structure. His ideas on plot have formed the theoretical basis of much subsequent criticism but he fails totally to recognise the power of having more than one plot or multiple strands to a single plot. Particularly, but not exclusively, in **comedy** there may be a **sub-plot**: that is, an element of the story line that runs alongside the main **action**, sometimes providing an ironic comment upon it. If students look back to the section on **farce** they will be reminded of the *Second Shepherds' Play*, a medieval Nativity Play that shows both the birth of Christ and the comic activity of a sheep-stealing shepherd and his wife, who attempt to pass off a stolen sheep as a baby in a cradle. As the shepherds gather round the supposed 'baby' they ironically foreshadow the scene in which they visit the infant Christ. You may also recall the complex subplot of Shakespeare's *The Tempest,* in which a drunken butler, a jester and a strange creature, Caliban, plot to overthrow Prospero, the magical 'ruler' of an island. Issues of power, usurpation, colonisation and government are all reflected in the counterpoint to the main plot, and the final resolution is brought about by the convergence of the two plots.

The critic Northrop Frye identifies four kinds of plot in *The Anatomy of Criticism* (1957), each relating to a different season. The 'Spring' and 'Autumn' plots are of opposing natures: Spring shows a comic pattern that involves a progression from restriction to freedom and love triumphant whereas in Autumn movement is hindered by obstacles, and opposing forces or characters gain revenge rather than achieving reconciliation, which is postponed for another world. 'Summer' plots involve a quest for the **hero**, who achieves an exalted position through struggle and peril, whereas the 'Winter' quest is unsuccessful and the only escape is through death or madness. Just how useful Frye's linking of the concept of plot to the natural year might be is a matter of opinion but you will almost certainly be able to think of examples of each type.

So far I have confined our consideration to the Aristotelian and Anglo-American traditions of criticism in considering plot, but we can gain other insights from different approaches. The Russian formalist critic Victor Shklovski (1968) identifies plots that have different forms of movement and focuses on the psychological effect on the **audience**. He distinguishes between those plots that: move from one kind of relationship between characters to its opposite; move from a prediction of fear to the realisation of the prediction; progress from a problem to its solution; move from a false accusation or some kind of misrepresentation to a rectification of the wrong. The audience's need for a sense of closure can be satisfied by such devices as an epilogue or further appendage to the main action which might show the subsequent progress of the hero.

By contrast, the French structuralist critic Roland Barthes (1915–70) considered that a plot involved the creation of a 'hermeneutic programme' and that the stages of the plot were 'a statement' followed by 'stages of arrest'. The primary statement establishes the narrative and poses various problems that remain open. Barthes divides his 'statement' into sub-stages: 'thematisation', in which the existence of an enigma is hinted at; 'position', in which the existence of the enigma is established; and 'formulation', in which the enigma is made explicit. The second 'phases of arrest' then suggest that the enigma is not insurmountable and indicate possible false trails, ambiguities, and admissions of defeat, before a partial and finally full disclosure. Like many French thinkers, however, Barthes has remained in many ways within the classical mode of operations and his formula for a plot has echoes of Aristotle.

Perhaps one of the most sobering thoughts is that with the exception of Scribe (see **well-made play**) or Strindberg (see **disclosure**), virtually no proponent of a formula for a plot or for its essential ingredients has ever written a successful play. Playwrights may begin writing with a plot outline in mind, they may base their play on an existing story from which they must structure a detailed plot, or they may, like Harold Pinter, establish some characters and a situation and allow the plot to emerge. It is doubtful if, in devising a piece of theatre, the majority of practitioners begin with a plot outline but this does not mean that the concept of 'plot' is outmoded.

Wallis and Shepherd's discussion of 'Plot and Action' in *Studying Plays* (2002) is very helpful.

See **devising; denouement; disclosure; exposition; peripeteia; structure** *and* **well-made play.**

Political drama

For the accession of the Catholic Queen Mary Tudor to the English throne in 1553 the playwright Nicholas Udall wrote his play *Respublica*, in which a **chorus** figure proclaims:

Joyne all together to thank god and Rejoyce
That he hath sent Marye our Soveraigne and Quene
To reforme thabuses which hithertoo hath been.

This is an early example of an overtly political drama, in which the writer promotes a particular set of beliefs or ideology. (see **Chronicle History Play**) We tend to associate such characteristics with the **Epic Theatre** of Piscator and Brecht and their many followers or with the **Agit/Prop** theatre of the twentieth century but, in fact, politics have always been an essential ingredient of drama. The comedies of Aristophanes, for example, mocked contemporary political figures; the plays of Marlowe, Shakespeare and the Jacobean theatre explored issues of political power and how society was shaped by ideology. Literally speaking, all drama is in some sense political because it presents characters who are forced to interact with a social order shaped by political forces. Furthermore, the act of theatre itself is political in that the performance takes place within a society espousing certain beliefs and political systems. The extent to which a dramatist may consciously exploit or explore the political implications and societal forces at work will vary considerably. Certain plays, such as David Hare's recent *The Permanent Way* (2003), which exposes the machinations that have accompanied the erosion of Britain's railways, are a deliberate response to contemporary social and political issues and in many such plays the predominating attitudes and relevant institutions are attacked and the underlying political ideology may be obvious. However, as we see in many of Brecht's *Parables for the Theatre*, it is equally possible that overtly political drama may take the form of fable or **allegory**, in which the **audience** is enticed to draw parallels between the fiction and the contemporary world order.

Much of the political drama of the twentieth century had a strong Marxist ideology and, at this point, you may wish to turn to the entries on **Epic Theatre**, **documentary drama** and **Agit/Prop** to gain an insight into the origins of left-wing theatre in the Weimar Republic (1919–33). Political motivation also lies behind what I have listed as **Intervention Theatre, Theatre of Testimony**, and 'Theatre of Resistance'. Much of the work of Augusto Boal (see **forum theatre**) is permeated with his ideas of political therapy and there is a political basis to many of the ideas of **environmental theatre** and to the rise of the talking piece and one-person show (see **monologue**). A great deal of political drama has emanated from the United States since a number of workers' theatre groups grew up after the Wall Street Crash and Great Depression. The same energy continued to make theatre in response to the Vietnam War, the whole proliferation of nuclear weapons, AIDS, feminism and issues of race.

In Britain, since the 1950s a considerable number of playwrights with strong personal political convictions have used Brechtian forms. John Arden's *Live Like Pigs* (1958), interspersed with earthy ballads as a mode of **alienation**, is an example of a play that still has relevance. However, it was in the 1970s that Howard Brenton, Howard Barker and David Edgar all presented a socialist standpoint in a setting so violent, colourful and multifarious that they were labelled the 'New Jacobeans'. David Edgar has remained the most prolific and effective of the playwrights who have consistently analysed political systems. His most recent plays, *Daughters of the Revolution* and *Mothers Against* (2004), performed together as *Continental Divide*, investigate the machinations of the Democratic and Republican parties in the USA. Like many of his previous plays, these are on a massive scale and reveal a sense of disenchantment with party political processes. In Edgar's *The Shape of the Table* (1990), which considered the emergence into democracy of a former Eastern European Communist state, the tension between the old communists and the new democrats is reduced to a dispute as to the shape of the table around which negotiations took place. Many of Howard Barker's plays reveal an impatience and anger with social institutions that appear to perpetuate the attitudes he opposes: his book *Arguments for a Theatre* (1989) is a provocative and eloquent exposition of politics and theatre.

During the 1980s, with the exception of Edgar, David Hare, Howard Brenton and Howard Barker, the political agenda for drama moved away from explicit socialist ideology towards the more personal politics of gender, ethnicity and environmentalism. The new, alternative theatre attempted to democratise the processes through which work was created and responsibilities were decided by developing collaborative methods of devising and production and by seeking new audiences, making theatre relevant to sections of the community, such as minorities or those who felt oppressed or exploited and whose interests had not been adequately represented in the mainstream theatre. There had, in fact, been an increasing feeling among theatre practitioners since the 1970s that the largely male-dominated, hierarchical and commercially driven theatre was, itself, a microcosm of society and of the political agenda of the Conservative government of the time. This, together with the growth of playwriting as an undergraduate option, contributed to the emergence of a substantial number of important women writers.

Plays that explored sexual politics also became the basis of the work of the gay collective 'Gay Sweatshop', and by the time Kevin Elyot's *Coming Clean*, with its explicit scenes of gay sex, had been produced in 1984 the latent problems of another disadvantaged section of society had become the stuff of new drama.

Many of the political plays of the last 30 years or so have been based on real, historical incidents or on an evocation of the actual social conditions of a specific time. Playwrights like Barry Keefe, Steve Gooch, Shirley Gee, David Hare, Caryl Churchill, Trevor Griffiths and John McGrath have immaculately researched aspects of social history and events where there has been an abuse of power or deep injustice in order to create plays that disturb, challenge and focus the attitudes of the audience. There has been a renewed interest in more unusual forms of political drama too, with the publication of such collections as *How the Vote Was Won* (1985) – a series of 'suffragette plays' – and with the work of such groups as the San Francisco Mime Troupe (a mixed-race company prominent in the USA in the 1980s). Interestingly, as the Bibliography shows, most of the best critical writing about political drama, such as Itzin's *Stages in the Revolution* (1980), belongs to the 1980s, and Patrice Pavis, one of the most influential thinkers in the contemporary theatre, accords the topic only a few lines in his *Dictionary of the Theatre* (1998) whereas he gives three pages to **gesture**. The move from the verbal and didactic to the physical could not be more obvious.

Philip Auslander (1997) provides a fascinating debate on the possibilities for political drama in a **postmodern** age in his *From Acting to Performance* and Joe Kelleher's *Theatre and Politics* (2009) is a clear and refreshing debate on the whole topic.

See also **Agit/Prop**

Protagonist

From what we can conjecture about the origins of Western theatre in Ancient Greece, it appears that, at some stage, a single actor detached himself from the chorus to make a new kind of performance (see **actor**). This person was traditionally said to have been Thespis of Icaria in the sixth century BC and he was, literally, the 'first actor' or protagonist. The original protagonist may well have been the leader of the chorus, who began to impersonate a character in the *dithyramb* being performed. Thus, 'the protagonist' became the term for the leading actor although, in the fifth century BC, using masks and changes of costume, the protagonist sometimes played several roles. In the drama of Aeschylus a second actor, the *deuteragonist*, was added and the playwright Sophocles added a third, the *tritagonist*. These two latter terms are hardly used today but the concept of the 'protagonist' has developed to mean the central character or characters of a drama, who are at the very heart of the **action** and its various conflicts. Identifying the protagonist's predicament is an essential stage in understanding a play: this character frequently undertakes some form of emotional, spiritual or perceptual journey that constitutes the 'through line' of action.

See also **motivation.**

Scene

Playwrights of the Renaissance and Restoration periods thought of the scene as a unit that consisted of a meeting between a number of characters, or of a solo speech. Once a new **character** was added a new scene began. Thinking of plays in this way can be very helpful because it enables students, actors and directors to select suitable units for rehearsal or study. However, since the nineteenth century, most plays have been printed or conceived in **Acts** and scenes, the latter being a subdivision of the former. The introduction of more spectacular scenery in the early nineteenth-century theatre and the habit of lowering the curtain between scenes in order for changes to take place, shifted the emphasis of the concept of a 'scene' from the characters involved to the location represented. Theatres vied with each other for the elaborateness of the physical settings that might constitute the next scene and it was even common for the audience to applaud the scenery at the rise of the curtain. Such was the complexity of the scene changes, it was often necessary to have lengthy pieces of music to cover the process. With the advent of the **well-made play**, the more substantial Act became the usual basic unit, although subdivision into scenes was not uncommon. In more recent theatre there has been a move towards a more **episodic** structure in plays and it is quite usual for a play to consist of a very large number of short scenes, sometimes consisting of only a few lines of **dialogue**. In such cases, a change of location is usually indicated and the advent of more minimalist and economic forms of staging, together with the ability to isolate small areas of the stage by **lighting**, have enabled a succession of short scenes to be presented in an almost cinematic way.

Script

This term, meaning the written pages of **dialogue** and **stage directions** of a play or film, tends to have been replaced by 'text' or 'playtext' in the world of drama and performance study. There is a tendency to think of a script as something less permanent and it is certainly true that in radio and film, where the word 'script' is still used, changes can be and are made, up till the last minute or even as a result of rehearsal or performance. In the introduction to this section I have indicated that, in recent Performance Studies, the idea of 'text' includes something that involves a continuous act of creation through performance, and that, accordingly, some scholars prefer to refer to the original script or text as the 'work'. There are a number of ways in which a script for a play may come into being: it may be written by a single playwright and sent to a company in the hope that they will perform it, or it may be commissioned by a theatre company from a group or individual playwright. It might be devised through research, **improvisation** and rehearsals by a group of actors either collectively or using a 'playwright in residence', or it may be written as part of a university course in playwriting. Any one of these possibilities may result in a play's being published so that it can be performed by other groups but every year thousands of plays by aspiring playwrights are written and never performed, and only a small proportion of those performed are subsequently published. One leading publisher in the USA and Britain claims to publish about one in six hundred of all the scripts received. If you are reading a play published in book form you can be virtually certain not only that it has been performed somewhere, but that the playwright will have included revisions and additional ideas developed in rehearsal or as a result of the play being seen in performance. The script of a play is not necessarily static, even when published; the playwright Harold Pinter, for example, continued to make changes to the published version of his play *The Caretaker*. Perhaps we should remind ourselves that someone who writes plays is known as a play*wright*: a 'maker' of plays, and that there are many elements to the process that are certainly not all written. The script or text has to function as a type of blueprint for performance.

See also **stage directions**.

Soliloquy

See **Conventions**.

Stage directions

When actors and students think of a **text** or script they tend to think mainly about **dialogue**: the words that are given to the characters to speak. But, in fact, a good deal of the material consists of stage directions, usually printed in a different typeface. If, rather than skimming over the stage directions, students study them carefully it is possible to discern initially that stage directions: (a) tell us *where and when* the action is taking place; (b) provide *details of the way in which the play might be staged*; (c) give instructions to the actors about *where and when the characters move and how they look, behave or speak*. It is, however, important to give a word of caution here. Many relatively ancient texts survived without any stage directions at all and those that have been added are the work of subsequent editors and may well be the result of the performances of famous actors. Some scholarly editions make clear the origins of the stage directions but others may be less transparent. Some so called 'acting' editions of plays may contain the stage directions that were given by the director at the play's first production and so it is very important to establish precisely which stage directions were provided by the playwright. These latter will carry far more authority than those added by stage managers and directors, which are best ignored.

Stage directions will often be very specific: let us look at some possibilities in each of the categories I have suggested.

(a) *Where and when.* Stage directions may tell us:

- Precise details of the room or rooms, buildings or outside locations where the play is taking place and an indication of the structure and furniture of the stage environment.
- Precise details of the positions in which the action is taking place or the characters are located, e.g. 'in an upstairs room'.
- The exact year, day or time of day, or the time that has supposedly elapsed since an earlier scene.

(b) *Details of the way in which the play might be staged.* Stage directions may tell us:

- How the stage is to be constructed in order to represent the required locations.
- How the quality, intensity, direction or colour of lighting might achieve certain desired effects such as different times of day.
- What musical or sound effects are needed or what type of staging the play requires.

(c) *Where the characters move, etc.* Stage directions may indicate:

- Where and when characters enter and exit.
- Instructions for movements of characters and their positions on stage, e.g. 'Upstage', 'Crossing', 'Down Left', 'Near the Door'.
- How the lines should be spoken, e.g. 'whispering', 'slowly', 'exclaiming'.

- What the characters are wearing and how they move.
- Clues to the non-verbal behaviour and body language of the characters, e.g. 'laughing', or details of facial expressions and gestures.

These lists are by no means exhaustive and it is important to look for further examples and possibilities, using the examples of printed texts that are available. This can be a somewhat confusing process, mainly because plays from different periods have come down to us in a variety of forms. In some modern plays, for example, it is possible to find instances of almost all the kinds of stage directions I have identified but in a play by Shakespeare or Marlowe there may well be very few in comparison, and some of these will probably have been added by a later editor. There are three further areas of information that we can deduce from stage directions: they may tell us a great deal about the theatrical conditions for which the play was written; they will inform us about character; and they enable us to understand **motivation**.

Let us consider some examples. The stage directions for a scene in Marlowe's *Tamburlaine the Great*, Part Two (a great popular success in 1587), give an impression of a play written for an **audience** that enjoyed violent spectacle. The governor of Babylon is hanged and shot, and we can deduce that there was some upper level which could be reached by an off-stage access that enabled this scene to take place. The shape of all the scenes suggests a stage that projects out into the audience with entrances and exits from the rear of the stage. With actors virtually surrounded by the audience the emphasis seems to be on a three-dimensional performance with colourful action and an expansive style of acting, in the open air.

If we compare the stage directions in Tamburlaine with those in the popular nineteenth-century melodrama *Black Eyed Susan* by Douglas Jerrold we find that in Jerrold's play the emphasis is on the various panoramic scene changes and the mechanics by which these are achieved. Constant reference is made to 'grooves' in which the 'flats' or 'shutters' on which the scenes were painted would run. Instructions are quite specific, showing the 'groove' in which the flat would slide, e.g. L.U.E, which indicates the position of the groove on the left, upstage. On such a stage, closely resembling the kind of toy theatre you can still buy, there was really only one direction for the actor to face: downstage, to where the audience was looking through a 'picture-frame' proscenium arch (see **theatre form**). There may well have been gas **lighting**, which caused a slight shimmering effect through which the scene was watched.

If we then turn to Ibsen's *Ghosts* (1891) we can see that the stage directions presuppose a **box set** constructed to give the realistic impression of an interior with a view from a window and various gradations of light. This is nineteenth-century stage technology at its most sophisticated, involving the introduction of electric lighting. The instructions to the actors are minutely detailed as to their movements and positions and it is clear that they are intended to create the psychological tension that watching a slice of 'real life' through the frame of the proscenium can achieve.

In assisting the actor to achieve a convincing character and sense of motivation, playwrights have tended to follow Ibsen in providing great detail. The British playwright George Bernard Shaw, who introduced Ibsen to British audiences, prefaced many of his plays and scenes with copious biographical details of the characters and their situations. A very good example is found in his *Candida* (1895), in which Act I opens with three and a half pages of stage directions, many of them biographical. Arthur Miller (who was also much influenced by Ibsen and adapted some of his plays) used a similar technique in *The Crucible*, where, before anyone speaks, Act I opens with two sets of stage directions separated by a short essay on the historical context of the play, focusing largely on the character of the Revd Parris, and providing insights into his attitudes and beliefs.

In Strindberg's *Ghost Sonata* (1907) the opening stage directions are so complex that they create a whole series of images without a word being spoken. There is a great deal of material relating to the sounds to be heard and to the physical appearance of the characters, and the overall effect is to create a dreamlike quality in this **Expressionist** piece. There are many examples of how playwrights provide characters with clues as to the nature of their performance. Ibsen was particularly adept at providing movements at key moments to enhance the sense of motivation; notice, for example, how in *A Doll's House* he has Nora, the wife who is trying to hide the truth from her husband, 'turn away' as if she cannot bear to look at him; or look at the lengthy stage directions in Pinter's *The Caretaker* as Davies begins to explore the junk-filled room in which he finds himself.

Structure

The concept of 'structure' has wide applications in the study of texts or performance. The structure of a play as a *work* or *performance* is its detailed architectural shape, which may be rooted in tradition or some ritual structure related to the performance event. For the written play

text, structure is the design and shape that emanates from the decision to adopt a certain *form*. So, for example, a *one-Act play* (a specific form) may well consist of a number of clearly delineated sections, including a *complication* and a **denouement** (elements of its structure). We have considered Schechner's concepts of *open* and *closed* structures for a **plot** but there are other ways of considering the process of shaping a dramatic narrative. One of the most common structures is for a play to begin with the simple presentation of some **characters** in a situation. Even at this stage, however, the situation will have a certain element of balance that has the potential for becoming unbalanced: we might say that it is *poised* rather than simply balanced. When something significant occurs, the balance is disturbed and the major dramatic question, the source of conflict, is introduced. This event is sometimes termed the *inciting incident* or *attack* and it sets the plot into motion.

The introductory material is the **exposition** and most of the information must come from the **dialogue** and **action** together with what the **audience** will decode from the physical setting (see **well-made play**). The skill of the playwright lies in ensuring that, for the audience, the characters mainly speak only to and for one another, unless some form of **monologue** or *direct address* technique is deliberately employed.

The dramatic conflict intensifies through the *rising action*, often in a series of complications, until a turning point: a **peripeteia**, **climax** or *crisis* is reached. From this point onwards, the outcome may seem inevitable but it marks some kind of reversal. In a traditional **comedy** the **protagonist** is usually a loser until the climax but then becomes a winner; in **tragedy**, the reverse is probably the case. The nature of the tension following the turning point is somewhat different from that which preceded it: the play may be more exciting prior to the crisis but more absorbing afterwards.

In the structure we are considering, the climax is followed by a section of *falling action* that is sometimes called the *untanglement*, which in turn culminates in the denouement and a section of *conclusion*. The idea of structure I have described is pretty standard fare in manuals of playwriting and it may well seem too simplistic to serve for the multi-layered nature of performances that might include a complex subplot, but it is a helpful way of exploring the concept, none the less. Many performances have a similar structure even if they begin life as devised pieces. These structures are frequently represented in diagrammatic form because, as I have indicated, they have an architectural quality. Auslander (1997) refers both to 'the overall structure of the performance process' and to 'individual structures of performance' in his discussion of the evolution of various devised theatre events but he also acknowledges that drama often concerns itself with 'structures of knowledge' and 'structures of authority'. You can see, therefore, that this is a key term and concept in the vocabulary of performance.

Sub-plot

I was recently struck by a newspaper play review with the headline 'When Two Plots are Worse than One'. The review went on to describe a new play in which the two **plots** never seemed to converge nor appear to have much relationship. Clearly, at least in the eyes of the reviewer, the playwright had failed to appreciate the concept of a sub-plot that both enriches and comments upon the plot.

A sub-plot (sometimes known as a *by-play*) was quite a frequent feature of Elizabethan and Jacobean drama but was also an aspect of classical and medieval theatre: I have already described a powerful example in the section on **Mystery Plays**, where, as in most of these early forms of drama, the performance style of the sub-plot contrasts sharply with that of the main plot. In some plays, the sub-plot was a parody of the main plot, and in the majority of cases there was a convergence of the two layers of plot into a final section of resolution. Generally, the sub-plot contained fewer **characters** than the main plot and, in terms of the overall structure and themes of the play, they were of less importance.

The effect of a sub-plot may be to distance the **audience** from the intensity of the main plot and, by a series of parallel events, comment upon it. It also offers an alternative view of humanity from that of the dilemmas of the **protagonist**, particularly when the characters of the sub-plot move on a more mundane level.

Subtext

'Subtext' refers to a concept rather than a concrete reality and was developed by Stanislavsky as a way of describing the discrepancy between the spoken text and those **motivations** that result in particular **actions** and modes of behaviour on the part of a **character**. The subtext may be conveyed by staging, acting style or body language and provides a means whereby the **audience** can *read* the character's inner state, whereas the spoken *top text* may, in fact, be all about concealing it. It may never be possible to grasp fully the nature of the subtext and it may be necessary to deduce its significance. It may be conveyed by silence or strange ritual and repetitive acts, as in the plays of Pinter, or reveal itself in a **gesture** or tone of voice, providing a glimpse of what remains largely unexpressed.

Stanislavsky's training enabled actors to work with and discover the hidden life of the characters by challenging them to explore the imaginary world that existed beyond the play. Indeed, he is often credited with having said that 'the playwright writes the text; the actor writes the subtext'. The pressure behind words that constitute the surface **dialogue** of a play was an aspect of Stanislavsky's approach to the production of Chekhov and Shakespeare. In his productions he sought ways to have actors communicate the unsaid from this hidden text through facial expression, modulation of the voice, and body language in the form of movement, posture and gesture. The subtext was therefore created through rehearsal and performance in a complex transaction between the **text**, **actor**, **director** and audience.

Theatre language

Drama is not a branch of literature: when we read a story or play we understand it first, and only as we begin to understand it do we begin to visualise it. Drama works through the language of theatre and in the theatre this process is reversed: a play witnessed in performance is seen first and only then is it understood. The importance of this is enormous: it means that theatre communicates in a way that is radically different from either everyday speech or the written media. It follows that the language of this kind of communication has its own grammar and syntax, which require **analysis** and practice like any other language.

Analysing theatre language is not particularly easy and there are several reasons for this. The most important is that plays performed in theatres are ephemeral: they cannot be fully recorded without changing their nature in important ways. Yet it is clearly necessary for students of drama to be able to study certain plays irrespective of whether they can see them in performance and it is equally obvious that for every performance given, a vast number of other, different performances could be imagined. For these reasons students often have to deal, or at least begin with, the printed **texts** of plays. Therefore we must distinguish between what is conveyed by a dramatic text and what is conveyed by a performance.

A printed text consists of only two **codes of communication: dialogue** and **stage directions**. The stage directions may be explicit or simply implied but they are present in the text of every play, at least in the minimal form of who is speaking and where. The experience of seeing a play performed in a theatre, on the other hand, is very different: a variety of codes of communication present themselves to the spectator, all competing for attention. The **settings**, **costumes**, **lighting** and physical aspects of performance, as well as the words, all offer to the spectator their peculiar sequence of **sign systems**.

In using terms like 'codes of communication' or 'sign system' we are borrowing from the school of criticism usually termed 'structuralism'. (All the highlighted terms and concepts in this section are expanded in other parts of the book.) Applied to literature, this method has demolished the traditional assumption that a text can function like a transparent screen between the writer and reader. The identity of both the reader and writer and the meaning of the story had previously been assumed to be fixed, in a sense just *there*, waiting to be discovered. Structuralist critics have shown that the identity of the reader and the writer are constructed by and through the process of exchange of communication. So, if meaning in literature is constructed rather than found, then the theatre is doubly complex because meaning is constructed both by performers and by **audience**. The traditional view, which was that the text alone could be reliably preserved, has been called into question and some scholars have argued that the process of *reading* a text is no more reliable than the process of reading (i.e. constructing a meaning for) a performance.

Theatre language is both visual and aural in the way in which it manipulates the perceptions of the audience. By using such terms as 'reading' a performance we are accepting that the language used is something we both hear and see. In determining the form of the spoken aspect of a play the playwright will select a language that either simulates everyday speech, represents everyday speech, or employs complex prose or poetic devices to provide the images or formality that are appropriate to the situation. Conventions enable the audience to accept a wide range of spoken texts but many playwrights have sought to create new and vital forms of theatre language that either enable the writer to engage with transcendent issues or reproduce more accurately the way in which language is used in certain **realistic** situations (see **poetic drama**). However, even the most elaborate soliloquy in a play by Marlowe or Shakespeare has its own reality consonant with a world unlike our own. Theatre language belongs to the characters and the life of a play and expresses feelings and ideas or may be used to cover up motives, intimidate or gain power over others, or simply to provide information. We are so used to equating the concept of language with the *word* that it is easy to overlook the fact that in the theatre it is but a small element in the overall communication that must take place.

Words in the theatre are reinforced and extended by aspects of non-verbal communication such as **gesture**, posture and facial expression together with more overt aspects of the theatrical: lighting, **design concepts** or costume. Performance itself seems to give birth to language, which must express the thoughts, attitudes, motives, intentions and emotions of **characters**, but in the theatre, unlike 'real' life, language is highly shaped and selective; the level of communication must be more intense than in a random conversation. Every aspect of theatre language is integrated to convey meanings.

In the written **script** the words are what are called in communication theory 'signs and symbols', which have the capacity to generate physical or emotional action in the theatre. A sign has a direct physical relationship with its *referent*: the thing it represents. The requirement for a particular quality of light in a play by Ibsen will be a direct sign of the time of day, but equally, a blaze of sunshine in his play *Ghosts* will be a *symbol* of truth and enlightenment. The theatre uses both verbal and non-verbal symbols and signs to enhance our **perception** of the living presence of the actors in performance. Plays are full of examples of the way in which both verbal and non-verbal symbols and signs reinforce one another in conveying aspects of their meaning. Consider also the concept of **gestus** as a form of theatre language, and the implications of what I have said about structure as an aspect of such language.

Many recent theatre practitioners have been concerned to create an expressive form of physical language based on ancient techniques that enable actors to enter their roles through their senses: research into ancient Oriental texts has led to the appropriation of techniques described in unfamiliar and archaic terminology. Others, such as the designer Josef Szajna in Poland, have attempted to establish not only new forms of theatre and theatre language but also a discourse that would create a formal language in which the art of theatre can be described.

Directors such as Peter Brook and his major source of inspiration, Antonin Artaud, attempted to create a universal theatre language that moved beyond linguistic literalism and the *word*, to ritual sound, incantation, explosions and grunts. J. Grotowski (1969) proposed the abandonment of reliance on the spoken word in the theatre, preferring an 'elementary language of signs and sound – comprehensible beyond the semantic value of the word even to a person who does not understand the language in which the play is performed' (p. 24). It is clear, therefore, that the search for new forms of theatre language appears to be ongoing, and attempts to revitalise existing forms are a constant feature of the most innovative work in drama and performance.

Theatre of the Absurd

See **Absurdism/Theatre of the Absurd.**

Tragedy

Probably the most discussed of all dramatic genres, tragedy had four major periods of pre-eminence and development: Athens in the fifth century BC, Elizabethan England, seventeenth-century France, and nineteenth-century Scandinavia. There have, however, always been plays that have some of the characteristics of tragedy. There have been many attempts to define the concept of 'tragedy' and you are encouraged to arrive at your own definition. It is not totally simplistic to say that a tragedy is concerned with human suffering and, because of some disastrous action, ends in unhappiness, and often in death. It is the first of the great and significant forms of Western drama and explores human fallibility. Characters are shown as sometimes weak and vulnerable and at other times almost invincible. Greatness is contrasted with total defeat and the heroes of tragedy, exercising their free will, fight against forces embodied in the other characters or in their environments or, most painfully, in their inner selves. The audience witnesses and empathises with the suffering and inevitable defeat of the **hero** or admires the personal tenacity in the face of disaster and begins to make sense of the paradox of pain and human existence. Tragedy may be a search for meaning and justice in what is supposed to be an ordered world, or a protest against the sense of meaninglessness in an irrational world.

Aristotle's writings on tragedy have been profoundly influential and have provided many of the terms and concepts employed to discuss or write tragic plays. In the *Poetics*, Aristotle speaks of tragedy as:

> an imitation of an **action** .... concerning the fall of a man whose **character** is good (though not pre-eminently just or virtuous) ... whose misfortune is brought about not by vice or depravity but by some error or frailty ... with incidents arousing pity and fear, wherewith to accomplish the **catharsis** of these emotions. (Aristotle, *Poetics*, 1449b)

Aristotelian tragedy was characterised by a number of concepts that I have discussed elsewhere: *hamartia* (see **hero**), **peripeteia**, *anagnorisis* (see **plot**), as well as *hubris* (the stubborn pride of the **protagonist** in refusing to admit defeat in spite of warnings). The **structure** of classical tragedy is summarised by Pavis (1998, p. 414) as follows: 'the tragic story imitates human actions in which the prevailing note is suffering and pity, until the moment of recognition by the characters of one another, or of realization of the source of the affliction'. You may wish to assign technical, classical terms to these stages. The moment of recognition or anagnorisis that follows the hero's struggle frequently takes one of two paths: either recognising that, in spite of suffering and disaster, there is evidence of a world order and of eternal laws (what postmodernists would term a meta-narrative) and that suffering may be instructive, or acknowledging that, in an apparently indifferent, hostile, capricious and mechanical universe (Samuel Beckett's view, perhaps), human acts and suffering are futile, but the protagonist's protests are to be celebrated.

The term 'tragedy' comes from Ancient Greece and literally means 'goat song', almost certainly taking its name from the prize goat, for which the **choruses** competed in *dithyrambs* performed in worship of Dionysus. As I have indicated in the entry on **Mystery Plays**, some scholars believe that the origins of tragedy lie in the secret initiation rituals of the Eleusian Mysteries, which involved ecstatic behaviour of the kind suggested by Euripedes in his tragedy *The Bacchae*. We do, however, know that tragedy played an important part in the Spring Festival known as the *City Dionysia* and that, during these five days of celebration of Dionysus, the god of wine, there were competitive performances of new tragedies, of which the majority, we suspect, have disappeared. The surviving plays of Aeschylus, Euripedes and Sophocles are all that remain of a body of work that was witnessed at dawn by anything between 15,000 and 20,000 male members of the population. You should remember, however, that it was the Roman dramatist Seneca whose tragedies were employed as a model during the Renaissance.

Modern tragedy from Ibsen to Eugene O'Neill and Beckett has continued to explore humankind struggling against societal, moral, political and cosmic forces. Human vulnerability in the face of such pressures seems, inevitably, to lead to destruction or self-destruction. The twentieth-century Marxist critic Raymond Williams asked, in *Modern Tragedy* (1966), what we now mean by 'tragedy' and went on to consider the various dramatic forms that have expressed the basic notion of the *tragic* in the past. His approach is to explore the cultural definitions of the 'tragic' in relation to the historic forms that have been employed to express that concept in drama. In medieval society, for example, tragedy gives a role to Fortune and Providence, whereas neo-classical tragedy, emanating from a more secular, merchant-based and less feudal society, takes a very different view of the fall from greatness of the noble protagonist. Williams finally attempts to narrow down the concept of the 'tragic' to a single, universal definition that would embrace the fundamental experience of all audiences witnessing a tragedy. It is, he says, 'the bare, irreparable fact' – whatever the form of the *tragic* drama, audiences experience a sense of profound and irreversible loss.

Despite the fact that not all tragedies have followed the Aristotelian model, his ideas on tragedy have remained central to any discussion of the concept. Augusto Boal (*see* **Forum Theatre**) finds these ideas coercive and restricting. In his famous book *Theatre of the Oppressed* (1979), he offers a strong critique of Aristotle, whose ideas are considered in more detail under **catharsis**. However, it is important to evaluate Boal's views from personal experience. Milling and Ley (2001) offer an excellent appraisal of Boal's response to Aristotle in their *Modern Theories of Performance*.

Units

This concept was originally articulated by Stanislavsky as part of his system of actor training. He liked to have his students think of acting as a series of problems to be confronted and solved and to understand that many of these would arise from the **text** of the play. He insisted therefore that the play be divided into small sections or 'units' to facilitate close study and the identification of the problems that the play poses. To enhance this process of careful study Stanislavsky suggested that each unit be given a label beginning with the words 'I want to'. In this way actors would be able to gain an understanding of the needs and wants that would determine the behaviour of their **characters**.

The concept of a unit of a play has come to include the idea of a section of a play that appears to have some form of unity and which might constitute a suitable section for close study or rehearsal.

Verbatim theatre

When the British playwright David Hare wrote his play *The Permanent Way* (2004), he used the precise recorded words of real people involved in enquiries and debates surrounding the reorganisation and, some would say, dismembering of Britain's rail system to provide a disturbing drama. This was an example of 'verbatim theatre' a form of drama that is based on documents, transcripts, court records and other sources of words actually spoken. Verbatim theatre demands extensive research and a high degree of selectivity. It is frequently used in **community drama** as a means of bringing history to life or to dramatise events that have far-reaching consequences. Hearing words spoken by officials, victims of disaster, government spokesmen, politicians or industrialists enables audiences to form their own opinions on the events, decisions and actions that those words may reflect or seek to distort or disguise. Verbatim theatre may, therefore, be a powerful form of **political drama**. For a very full and helpful discussion of verbatim theatre see Will Hammond and Dan Steward's *Verbatim Verbatim: Techniques in Contemporary Documentary Theatre* (2007).

See also: **theatre of testimony**

Well-made play

This concept is taken from the French writer Eugène Scribe (1791–1861), who insisted people went to the theatre to be entertained rather than improved and gave his popular **farces** and **melodramas** the label *pièce bien faite*. His simple formula for the **structure** of a play had five stages: **exposition**, complication and development, *crisis*, **denouement**, and *resolution*. These elements were to be arranged in **Acts** and **scenes**. The pattern was followed by other popular dramatists such as Labiche (1815–88), Sardou (1831–1908) and Feydeau (1862–1921; see **farce**), and this construction, in a far less contrived way, was also employed by Ibsen. The concept of the 'well-made play' originally depended on maintaining the **action** in a series of curves and ups and downs, leading to what became known as a *scène a faire*: a scene towards which all the other scenes build, and which was awaited eagerly by the audience; this scene would almost certainly contain a *coup de théâtre*: an event that transformed the dramatic situation. The basic principle was to keep the audience fascinated, often by lowering the curtain at a moment of **climax** or suspense.

Ibsen's use of the form exploited its potential for a **naturalistic** portrayal of events, but it has subsequently been associated with predictable and shallow drama. George Bernard Shaw (1856–1950) attacked the form as leading to trivial characterisation and contrived and over-elaborate plotting; but it is an approach to playwriting, and particularly to the writing of 'soap' drama on radio or television, that refuses to die: see Taylor (1967), *The Rise and Fall of the Well-Made Play*.

Women's Theatre

It is tempting to associate the development of a specific kind of Theatre writing by women with the latter half of the twentieth century, but there had, of course, been a number of significant women playwrights in earlier periods. The medieval German nun, Hrosvitha, whose collection of liturgical plays was published in 1501, and the seventeenth-century Mrs Aphra Behn, writer of *The Rover* (1677–80) and other popular plays and the first woman to make her living as a playwright, are good examples. There had also been a strong challenge to the male domination of the theatre and its agenda in the 1950s by the young Shelagh Delaney with her daring play about mixed-race relationships, homosexuality, prostitution, depressing living conditions, motherhood and the tensions between mother and daughter, *A Taste of Honey* (1958), and by the play's remarkable director, Joan Littlewood. 1958 also saw the London production of Ann Jellicoe's *The Sport of My Mad Mother*, and the following year *A Raisin in the Sun* was the first play by a black woman writer to be produced in New York. Even in 1982, however, the eminent Professor of Drama, John Russell Brown, was listing only Delaney and Jellicoe as women writers in his *Short Guide to Modern British Drama*.

The revolution had actually begun in the 1970s when the two feminist theatre collectives Monstrous Regiment and the Women's Theatre Group had created the conditions for the emergence of such playwrights as Caryl Churchill, Pam Gems and Susan Todd (who collaborated with David Edgar on *Teendreams* (1979)). These playwrights explored the role and identity of women in a male-dominated society often obsessed by image and manipulation and placed issues of gender and sexuality firmly into the political spectrum.

A glance at the scope of the stage plays presented by the Women's Theatre Group between 1975 and 1983 listed in *Plays by Women*, vol. 3 (1984), with its excellent introduction by another leading playwright, Michelene Wandor, reveals the scope of the issues with which the new generation of women playwrights engaged: sexual exploitation, franchise, pregnancy, contraception, media pressure, the idea of 'home', relationships, dress, work, careers and sport are all exposed to perceptive scrutiny.

By the 1980s the British theatre saw more fine women playwrights developing: among them Louise Page, Debbie Horsefield, Timberlake Wertenbaker, Paula Macgee, Michelene Wandor and the overtly lesbian Sarah Daniels. Some of these writers also moved into film and television. Many of the topics dealt with were deeply personal: breastfeeding, organ transplants, violence, abuse, drugs, and the traumas of breast cancer. These topics, together with a view of an increasingly disturbing society based on violence and exploitation, continued to occupy the minds of playwrights in the 1990s and into the current century. It is rewarding to explore the work of Diane Samuels, Josie

Melia, Judy Upton, Winsome Pinnock and Sarah Kane (whose suicide in 1999 robbed the theatre of one of its most powerful young voices) and, perhaps, to compare their view of the world with that of Tony Kushner in his profoundly disturbing two-part, seven-hour play *Angels in America* (1992) with its picture of lurking fascism, fundamentalism, racism, faith and AIDS.

Further Reading

Giles Auckland-Lewis and Ken Pickering (2004) *Thinking About Plays* (London: Dramatic Lines).

Toby Cole (ed.) (1982) *Playwrights on Playwriting* (New York: Hill R. Wang).

Richard Eyre and Nicholas Wright (2002) *Changing Stages: A View of the British Theatre in the Twentieth Century* (London: Routledge).

Steve Gooch (2001) *Writing a Play,* 3rd edn (London: Writing Handbooks).

Robert Leach (2009) *Theatre Studies: the basics* (London:Routledge).

John Lennard and Mary Luckhurst (2002) *The Drama Handbook* (Oxford: Oxford University Press).

Mick Wallace and Simon Shepherd (1998) *Studying Plays* (London: Edward Arnold).

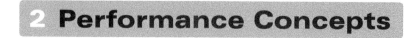

2 Performance Concepts

This chapter reflects the second key item in my initial definition of drama and is a recognition of the fact that drama is an activity rather than a branch of English Literature. That activity involves a number of processes, all capable of being subject to analysis and that culminate in and invite reflection upon an event we describe as 'performance'. Considerable physical and intellectual skills are integral to the processes of drama and these depend upon the understanding and mastery of some key concepts, which I shall be introducing and considering.

Because drama is an activity, I hope that your response will also be active as well as reflective. I have attempted to strike a balance between the kind of study that confines itself to the staging of written playtexts and the more recent investigations of the anthropological, social and aesthetic aspects of the phenomenon of performance, of which drama, as I have defined it, is but a part. It is, however, important to grasp that the skills that are necessary for the creation of a piece of theatre are now drawn from a far wider spectrum than has often been the case. For example, Sir John Gielgud was one of the most skilled and respected actors of the twentieth century, but in a moving television interview at the peak of his career he acknowledged that it was no longer sufficient for an actor simply to be able to speak, move and sing well. Skills drawn from Music Hall, stand-up comedy, circus, street theatre, contemporary dance, classic and traditional Oriental forms of performance, or from puppetry and mask-making have now blended with ideas of Carnival, improvisation, celebration or 'Happenings' to create the raw material from which theatre performances can be made. Studies in performance have also included consideration of style in relation to spaces and audiences.

This chapter will help to reinforce the fact that performance does not take place in a vacuum – it is performance: (a) Of what? (b) By whom? (c) Where? (d) To whom? (e) How? (f) With what results?

All these factors are inter-related and it will be virtually impossible to read one key concept without being aware of how it impinges upon another or others. Underpinning this entire chapter is a belief that a play cannot be said to exist except in the moment of performance. The 'work' *Waiting for Godot* or any other playtext can only begin to create the potential for meanings to be made, images to be constructed or parables to be told when it becomes an aural and visual experience. It is true that a 'theatre of the mind' may enrich a reading or radio production but even this is a form of 'inner performance' that involves artistic and imaginative choices. The point is that a play must 'take place' somewhere, and never suffer the fate of the Greek plays that were once enthusiastically introduced to a class by a nineteenth-century school Classics teacher as a 'positive treasure house of grammatical peculiarities', as if this was the only positive quality they possessed.

Acting styles

In Act III, Sc. 2 of Shakespeare's play *Hamlet* we find one of the best known expositions of the nature of acting. In this play, set in the Danish royal palace at Elsinore, the young prince and student, Hamlet, has been told by his father's ghost that his uncle Claudius, the present king, had obtained the throne by murdering Hamlet's father and marrying his mother. When a group of actors arrive at the palace, Hamlet is determined to use their performance as a means of confirming the king and queen's guilt. In one scene Hamlet himself addresses the company of actors, who are preparing to perform a play that includes some lines that he has inserted. He seems particularly concerned that they avoid an overblown acting style, which is obviously common in his contemporary theatre (the play dates from about 1600), and he makes reference to 'strutting' and 'bellowing' and 'sawing the air' as elements that would run contrary to the 'purpose of playing'. According to Hamlet, 'that purpose is' to 'hold, as 'twere, the mirror up to nature', and he also suggests that a good acting style involves 'imitating humanity'.

Although this speech in *Hamlet* is much discussed and quoted, students often miss the key concepts embedded in it: that the 'style' of performance is largely dictated by the fundamental 'purpose' of acting and that acting involves a substantial degree of 'imitation'. Hamlet appears to be advocating a much more natural style of performance than is customary and this may seem strange to us because it comes from the end of the sixteenth century rather than from the nineteenth. Acting style is notoriously difficult to pin down on account of the nature of our sources: theatre historians rely heavily on contemporary accounts and illustrations together with deductions from the text, to re-create the acting styles of the past. However, if we compare some material from the nineteenth century with Hamlet's speech we find an intriguing pattern emerging. Henry (later, Sir Henry) Irving became particularly famous for his role of Matthias in Leopold Lewis's *The Bells*, which was first produced in 1871. Working from eye-witness accounts, his grandson Laurence wrote a careful reconstruction of Irving's performance and, particularly, of one momentous scene, detailing every movement, facial expression, vocal inflection and nuance of the performance. What emerges is an attempt by Henry Irving to provide a degree of natural and real behaviour unknown in the theatre of the nineteenth century, and the discovery in the 1960s of a wax-cylinder recording of Irving's voice merely reinforced the idea that he was pursuing an unusually 'natural' approach to acting. Yet, within a few years of Irving's death, his style was regarded as hopelessly old-fashioned and out-moded.

Diderot, writing his *The Paradox of Acting* at the end of the eighteenth century, also appeared to be arguing for a more natural and ordinary acting style: 'never try to go beyond the feeling you have; try to find the true point'. As Diderot was attempting to write a new and more democratic form of drama, he found the exaggerated techniques of actors trained for classical drama incompatible with his needs. Our contemporary theatre has been greatly influenced by the search for a style that is as similar to everyday life as is acceptable within the expectations of a theatre audience but this creates almost as many problems as it solves.

We have seen that style is linked to purpose but there are a number of determining features for acting styles. These may be usefully grouped as the *physical* and the *conceptual*. Physical factors will include the shape and design of the performance space, the **lighting** and acoustics in the theatre, **costumes** and **properties** used by the **actors**, and the nature and behaviour of the audience. For example, modern actors performing 'in-the-round' and wearing contemporary costumes in a relatively intimate theatre space, and seen under spotlights that isolate them from the audience, will adopt a very different style from that of eighteenth-century actors moving around wearing swords, in a noisy theatre where the audience is in full view.

The physical aspects of style tend to emphasise the 'craft' of acting, involving, as it does, such features as **vocalisation**, movement, **gesture** and general use of the stage, whereas the conceptual bases of style are more associated with the 'art' of acting, although there is little agreement that these are separate issues.

Conceptual influences on style will revolve around the nature of the **text** and of the performance event itself. A text, for instance, may operate within certain recognised **conventions**, be taken from a particular historical period, use a particular form of language or conform to a certain genre. The text and nature of the performance event will, in turn, determine the idea of the whole purpose for which an actor is engaging in the task, and, as students will see when considering the work of Stanislavsky, Brecht, Meyerhold or Artaud, the underlying philosophy and rationale of any approach may vary considerably. For Meyerhold, for example, the actor was a 'tribune' who acted 'not the situation itself, but what is concealed behind it and what it has to reveal for a specific propagandist purpose'. The 'ensemble' work of Brecht, Joan Littlewood or Monstrous Regiment, with their strong commitment to political ideologies, would provide a different acting style from that of a company seeking to present a 'truthful' picture of life in an Edwardian middle-class home. Thus, 'the purpose of playing' determines much of the style.

The concept of 'imitation' has resonance of Aristotle's description of tragedy as an 'imitation of an action' (see **mimesis**, **tragedy**, **Aristotelian unities**) and it has profound implications for the actor as observer of human behaviour. Many of the key concepts deriving from this idea are explored in later sections of this chapter.

> See also **action; alienation; character; gestus; given circumstances; motivation; Naturalism; personal presentation; realism** and **subtext**.

Action

The action of a play is what engages the interest and attention of an **audience**. However fascinating the **characters** or attractive the staging, a play without action is dead. 'Action' is, therefore, an absolutely fundamental concept in drama but its definition is slippery and the term is used in a number of ways. You may well need to arrive at your own final definition but, in the most general terms, action is what is *happening* in a play and what the actors actually *do*. When Shakespeare had his character Hamlet tell a group of actors (see **acting style**) to 'suit the action to the word and the word to the action', or had Henry V tell his soldiers to 'imitate the action of the tiger' (note the concept of *imitation*), he clearly had a physical process in mind, but in all drama, action is also psychological. There may be total silence between two static characters on stage, but a great deal may still be *happening*. Significantly, a short form of event designed to interrupt performances to make a political or aesthetic point was known as an 'action' by the Futurists and Dadaists of the early Modernist period (*circa* 1910–20), and their rediscovery in the early Postmodernist theatre of the 1950s and 1960s led to the creation of a series of *Happenings*, most notably those devised by Allan Kaprow.

For Stanislavsky, the concept of 'action' had a quite specific meaning. His system of actor-training was designed to enable the actor to create a complete inner life for a character and this involved the building of a continuous stream of feelings and thoughts: an unbroken line of mental processes corresponding to those of the hypothetical 'self' of the character. This complex exercise, in which thoughts, words and deeds represented the character's inner life, is what Stanislavsky referred to as 'action'. Accordingly, an **actor** working with Stanislavsky would initially plot the character's journey through a series of experiences and significant turning points through the play. These would constitute the **through line** of the action. At this stage, the actor must decide the character's main motivating force and 'Super-Objective': the ultimate conscious or unconscious goal that sustains the character through the events of the play. Such a process also required that the actor should investigate more manageable 'Units', and finally compare the intensive research on these smaller sections with the through line of action of the entire play.

Brecht's approach to acting and character led to a contrasting concept of 'action'. For Brecht, action showed human behaviour determined by the pressures or nature of society and not by a personality made up of individual drives and motives. In order that the actor could encode and communicate the various social and political issues arising from the action of the play, the characters were to be created through their *social actions*. To facilitate this process, Brecht developed the concept of **gestus**, through which the 'gist', or underlying attitude of a narrative, could be conveyed in action.

Psychological realism or social determinism as the basis of action are by no means the only way of approaching the concept. Modern Performance Studies tends to take a more phenomenological line, examining what Alice Rayner calls the 'thickness of action' and its quality of 'giving shape and making visible' *in a performance*. Whereas the approaches of Stanislavsky and his followers and of the exponents of Brechtian Theatre both involve the creation of a fictive world outside the actual events of the play, it is also important to consider the *activities* (moving, sitting, standing, laughing, smoking, etc.) that make up the actual physical performance of a play and encode meanings for the audience.

We owe some of the major concepts of action in drama to the Ancient Greeks and, particularly, to Aristotle. (See the introduction to this chapter, **Aristotelian (or neo-classical) Unities**.) In the seventh chapter of the *Poetics*, Aristotle makes crucial use of the term 'action': 'tragedy is an imitation of a whole and complete action of some amplitude. Now, a whole is that which has a beginning, a middle and an end.' The problem with this statement is that scholars continue to debate the precise meaning of 'action' in this context and this is a debate in which you should continue to engage. Aristotle appears to mean at least a deed with all its repercussions and ramifications; indeed, we could be talking about the entire story line as 'action'. From this, and a number of other statements concerning the nature of drama, neo-classicists in the seventeenth century deduced that Aristotle had created the concept of 'Unities', one of which was 'unity of *action*'. Aristotle had probably wished to convey a sense of organic unity for a play, but, solidified into a rigid formula that greatly affected the nature of playwriting, particularly in France and Italy, the principle of 'unity of action' insisted that there be no sub-plot or double plot.

Actor/acting

It is usually thought that the idea of an actor began with the Greek poet and dramatist Thespis, who around 534 BC had a solo performer separate himself from the chorus in a *dithyramb* (see **tragedy, Passion Play, chorus**). The individual was a chorus leader, but he represented a distinct response to the matters of the drama distinguishable from that of the chorus or of himself. He represented, embodied and personalised a set of values and attitudes. Whilst it is likely that performers in other rituals had done something similar before, the Thespian theory identifies the essential characteristics of a single impersonating factor and an audience.

As a result of your practical work you might wish to develop your own definition of an actor but, though we may be able to define the role of the actor itself, its esteem and place in society have vacillated enormously. It has been variously described as 'immoral', 'insane', 'holy' and 'sublime'. It has been associated with both mysticism and dishonesty, seen by some as a job and by others as a spiritual medium. Its association with drama and the theatre has also varied: often the script, the ideology, or the poetry of the play, or even the set, have attempted to supercede it as the audience's dominant concern. Edward Gordon Craig, for example, was one of the most influential figures in the early twentieth-century theatre and yet wanted to do away with actors altogether.

What then is the nature of this role and activity that you wish to explore? It is well known that to act is to do, but the idea of acting also has connotations of performance and unless we believe that all behaviour is theatrical, such an all-embracing definition is not particularly helpful. For the purposes of this investigation I would suggest that you confine your consideration to the behaviour of people in theatres or performance situations, and accept that actors are people about whom there is an agreement that they are to be watched. A simple definition of actors might be that they are 'people who appear before audiences, pretending to be someone or something other than themselves'. The last few hundred years of our own theatrical history have tended to reinforce this idea, for, in spite of evolving beliefs concerning the determinants of human behaviour and each new generation's tendency to reject the theatre forms of its elders, it is versions of human **impersonation** which have provided actors with their basic tasks, and spectators with their satisfaction. However, if you consider the full range of possibilities demonstrated in primitive and traditional theatre forms, human impersonation represents only a small part of potential acting demands.

See also **actor-audience relationship, design concept, lighting; Naturalism and realism.**

Alienation

Alienation is the normal translation for the German *Verfremdungseffekt*: an approach to theatre and to acting in particular rediscovered by Brecht and sometimes translated as 'distanciation'. Alienation is a key concept in what might be termed 'Epic Acting' and is discussed most helpfully by Brecht in the *Messingkauf Dialogues*, where he refers to it as 'the A-effect'. In this imaginary conversation, the philosopher says:

The main reason why the actor has to be clearly detached from his character is this: if the audience is to be shown how to handle the character or if people who resemble it or are in similar situations are to be shown the secret of their problems, then he must adopt a standpoint which is not only outside the character's radius but also at a more advanced stage of evolution. (p. 76)

For Brecht, this 'distancing' from the **character** on the part of the **actor** required a 'demonstration' rather than an 'impersonation' of the role, commenting on the character being portrayed and revealing the relationship between motives and constraints. How this is to be achieved in practice is perhaps best illustrated by 'the actress' in the *Messingkauf Dialogues* when she says that a good example of 'the A-effect' can be seen when you watch children playing at being adults. What we observe is the highlighting of certain characteristics of adult behaviour, sometimes even a caricature, and a *presentation* rather than a *representation* of character.

An **acting style** is determined by the purpose of the drama, and Brecht had a clear didactic purpose. In Marxist terms he aimed to re-create on stage a *dialectic*: a society comprising a number of forces that collide and struggle against one another, and his object was to make the **audience** adopt an attitude of enquiry and criticism. The implication for the actors was that Brecht demanded a performance style in which the emphasis was not on psychological **motivation** or the apparent 'truth' of the character's imagined inner life, but on the way in which the character's actions were influenced and determined by social forces. The characters *presented* might, therefore, be archetypes, caricatures, masked figures or recognisable authority figures with recognisable behavioural traits. The actor, as it were, stood outside the character, inviting the audience to join in a process of evaluation and reflection. In order to achieve this, Brecht sometimes combined simple narrative language with action so that the performer both described an action and demonstrated it simultaneously. Other features of alienation included the punctuation of the **action** by songs and the use of the stage as a 'platform' that made no pretence of resembling an imaginary location. These characteristics are explored more fully under **Epic Theatre**.

I used the term 'rediscovery' in relation to Epic Acting because its origins lie at least in the raw and primitive acting style of the Middle Ages. The great classical plays of Ancient Greece with their attendant highly developed acting style had disappeared, and during the latter days of the Roman Empire both Church Fathers and barbarian invader had, in their separate ways, suppressed the surviving spectacles and farces of Roman Theatre. In medieval Europe, however, drama re-emerged as an amateur, folk activity and on 'holidays' and festivals of the Christian year, ordinary and largely untrained people presented the tenets and stories of their faith on wagons, on platforms and in a variety of locations not primarily intended for drama. In this context, actors presented such figures as the biblical Pharaoh or Herod as strutting tyrants, a both benign and angry God, Balaam's talking Ass, a variety of Devils or, in more sophisticated Morality Plays such as *Everyman*, allegorical figures such as Strength or Beauty. The traditions of these plays, and the acting style they require, can clearly be seen in the work of Marlowe and Shakespeare, even though these dramatists could use the services of professional actors. Significantly, Brecht selected actors well before they had completed their training at conventional acting schools, and trained them by working on productions. He insisted on a clear, energetic and emblematic acting approach: an ability to demonstrate a clear story line and sudden changes of fortune and to overlay acting with Spass – a sense of sport, fun and vitality. These are precisely the qualities that must have characterised the actors of the medieval **Mystery Plays**.

See also **Mystery Play.**

Aside

The 'aside' is an important theatrical convention that was developed during the Elizabethan period but came to particular prominence in Restoration Theatre: it remained a popular device in Victorian **melodrama**.

An aside is a short speech by one character that is not intended to be heard by another, and is, in fact, a form of direct address to the audience. It is still widely used in British Pantomime, which is a theatre form that relies very heavily on a sense of interaction between performer and audience and derives from seventeenth- and eighteenth-century theatre.

There are a number of forms of the aside: there is the direct, almost conspiratorial address to the audience who accept that this is inaudible to the other characters on stage; there is the remark directed at a single other character but inaudible to the rest of the characters and there is the overheard thought, a kind of miniature **soliloquy**.

In order to gain an insight into the development of the convention it is helpful to study the use of asides in Shakespeare's *Macbeth*, most notably Act I, Sc. 3 and 5. Students will see how Macbeth reveals his thought processes in response to events and words on stage. Clearly, the other actors could hear Macbeth, but it is far easier to believe that they do not, and that the words are heard by the **audience** only, when the actor is virtually in the middle of that audience and able to see that audience as in the Elizabethan playhouse. In such a situation it is possible for the aside to be a source of profound psychological insight.

We can compare Shakespeare's use of the aside with that of Middleton and Decker in *The Roaring Girl* (1608) or George Farquhar in *The Beaux Strategem* (1707). Students will see that these playwrights insert the **stage direction** 'aside' into the text and use it as a means for creating comic comment on the **action**, and, indeed, that they peg that action on the quick-fire use of the brief aside. Here, though, we see much more artifice in the required mode of performance and Farquhar's play presupposes an audience to which the actor must turn in order to deliver the aside: a style we can still see in Pantomime. This development was brought about by the construction of new, indoor theatres with forestages and perspective interior and exterior painted settings behind them. This form of staging brought the actors very close to their audiences in what was virtually a 'shared space' and enabled them to treat them as a confidante: maintaining a constant dialogue with them through gestures, nods, winks, whispers or speeches delivered from behind a hand. In fact, the aside could be delivered 'in character' or as a chorus figure commenting on the action by briefly stepping out of character. For an actor trained in modern methods of **personification** this would provide particular difficulties.

Beats

Students may recall that Stanislavsky insisted that his trainee actors divided the text of a play into units, but some more recent actor-educators have subdivided the units into even smaller components as they explore the shape of a play's action. The first of these consists of the individual interactions between characters, and these are often referred to as 'moments' (see **in the moment**) but these, in turn, combine to form 'beats'. A number of beats constitute a 'scene'. One of the most distinguished and successful actor teachers to employ such terminology is Robert Benedetti, and his *The Actor at Work* (first published 1974 and frequently reissued) has influenced several generations of American students and actors. He has demonstrated that a 'scene' constituted from several beats will have a number of momentary transactions between characters and that as actors explore these they will discover how the moments help to fashion a 'beat crisis'. A scene will also have a 'beat change' at some key point and this, in turn, will lead to the 'scene crisis'. Benedetti's main idea is that once students/actors have grasped the concept of a 'beat' they would be able to develop each beat to link with the others in the scene to create the 'scene crisis' and that the total shape of a play would emerge when the scenes had been developed to lead to the 'main crisis' and 'main event'.

Benedetti jokingly remarks that there is a rumour that the word 'beat' was a mishearing of someone with a Russian accent saying 'bit'. This reminds us that many ideas concerning actor-training were introduced into the United States by individuals who had originally worked with Stanislavsky and the form of close scene analysis described here has tended to be more popular in the USA than in the rather more pragmatic theatre in the United Kingdom. The important point to grasp is that the beat is the smallest unit of action and may contain several interactions between characters. Each beat has its own unique shape comprising a central conflict and crisis and these characteristics will derive from one character encountering some form of resistance or contrary behaviour from another. Several such interactions will contribute to the beat crisis or beat change and this is a moment when one or other of the characters will change the direction of the scene by adopting a different line of action. The whole analysis of the beat structure of a play is usually known as a 'breakdown'. It may be obvious that this form of analysis is more suited to some kinds of plays than others and actors and students who can only approach their roles and study through such a method are limited when confronted by many recent **texts**.

The concept of the 'beat' is somewhat complicated by the fact that some playwrights use the term to indicate a momentary cessation or pause in the **action** or **dialogue**.

See also **Units**.

Carnival

Although this book has concentrated largely on the performance of plays, there is an area of work that has many dramatic features that may not entirely fit our rather limited definition. Students of Performance Studies have widened their horizons to embrace a number of events that appear to include aspects of both performance and of theatre/drama. One such area has come to be known as 'carnival'. Processions, pageants, parades, some ceremonies and rituals, demonstrations, fairs, street celebrations, South Asian Melas and even protest marches are examples of what we may term carnival.

One of the major contributions to the debate concerning carnival was made by the Russian literary critic, Mikhail Bakhtin (1885–1975) who developed his theories in a book concerned with early Renaissance literature *Rabelais and his World*. Bakhtin argued that the term carnival could embrace the event, its environment and the behaviour of the participants. He pointed out that medieval feasts and festivals were often characterised by bawdy humour, colloquial language and generally unconventional conduct and even the **Mystery Plays** contained a rough mixture of vulgarity and piety. Bakhtin's thinking on the nature of carnival centred on its social function and he considered this to be ambivalent. On the one hand, carnival was irreverent, challenging to authority and organised outside the immediate influence of the predominant secular or ecclesiastical authorities; on the other hand carnival was permitted through licensing and the declaration of 'holy days' and thus was never a dangerous challenge to the status quo. Bakhtin's ideas were developed from his study into the strange blend of foolishness, grossness and anarchy that accompanied celebrations of profoundly held religious beliefs and his key observations were:

- carnival images closely resemble the artistic form we term 'spectacle' because of their sensuous nature and strong element of play

- carnival belongs to the border between art and life: in reality it is life itself but shaped according to a certain pattern of play

- carnival acknowledges no distinction between actors and spectator
- while carnival lasts there is no life outside it
- carnival is not a spectacle seen by people; they live in it
- carnival celebrates temporary liberation from the established order
- there is no rank or hierarchy during carnival
- a special kind of communication is possible during carnival because of the suspension of rank
- carnival laughter is the laughter of all the people
- a major feature of carnival is grotesque realism

See Counsell, C. and Wolf, L. (2001) *Performance Analysis*: 216–20.

However, the influential Brazilian theatre director and teacher, Augusto Boal (b. 1931) has argued strongly against Bakhtin's view of carnival. For Boal, all such events are an instrument and device for oppression conceived by the status quo to ensure that the public remains passive. Carnival, he argues, may act as a 'safety valve' for the release of tension but does not empower in the way that he believes the theatre can and should. Boal's own particular approach to empowering communities through theatre has been his development of the technique he calls **forum theatre**.

See also **Forum Theatre**

Character

Actors continue to consider the creation of 'character' as a major constituent of their craft. They speak of 'character parts' when the role they are playing has more than functional interest, and 'finding' or 'getting into' their character as an essential part of the acting process. The concept of 'character' is complex but initially depends on an interpretation of words and instructions written by the playwright. From these two rather sketchy components the **actor** begins an investigation that culminates in a 'rounded' performance. This performance, however, is also affected by the variables of **audience perception** and the elements (such as voice and movement) of the physical embodiment of the character undertaken by the actor. Character, therefore, is a transaction, the reality of which arises from a juxtaposition of the author's **text**, the actor's embodiment and the audience's recognition. Character has become almost the staple ingredient of television drama, and recent surveys have shown that large sections of the British population are more familiar with the fictitious characters of television drama than with, say, living politicians. By contrast, many of the leading practitioners and theorists of the modern theatre, with the notable exception of Stanislavsky, have had very little to say directly about the concept of 'character', preferring to consider what Meyerhold called 'the basic laws of theatricality itself'. Indeed, Meyerhold, who worked with and admired Stanislavsky, wrote somewhat disparagingly of 'his notorious system for a whole army of actors, psychologically "experiencing" the parts of all those characters who do nothing but walk, eat, drink, make love and wear jackets'. However, it has often been such actors who have written most engagingly about the creation of character.

Of the six ingredients for drama identified by Aristotle in the *Poetics*, it is character that he places second only to **action** because, he argues, it is only through or in response to **action** that character is revealed. So important did Stanislavsky consider character to be that it occupied the second year of the curriculum in his imaginary training academy, as discussed in his writings, including *An Actor Prepares* and *Building a Character*. In the second of these two books Stanislavsky places great emphasis on the concept of the **subtext** as the predominant feature in an approach to character, and elements of this remain in the 'Method' school of acting and in much that is still written by actors. Peter Barkworth, for instance, suggests that asking 'What does my character *want?*' is a vital aspect of understanding a role. Just how an actor goes about creating a character probably remains the most vexed question about acting. Even the most fundamental question of what a **character** is, is by no means easy to answer. Plays as diverse as *Hedda Gabler*, *Hamlet*, *Galileo*, *Mules* or *Guys and Dolls* seem to offer totally different answers. Critical and acting theories themselves appear equally diverse. The nineteenth-century critic A. C. Bradley, who influenced generations of students with his writings on Shakespeare, saw the dramatist's tragic characters as real people with pre-play, post-play and off-stage lives and an overriding passion. F. R. Leavis argued that Shakespeare did not invent people but 'put words together', thus allowing the actor the task of creating the character. Stanislavsky insisted that characters must have a consistent objective; and Strindberg, as if he were a Jungian analyst, that they must vacillate, be 'out of joint, torn between old and new ... conglomerates, made up of past and present stages of civilization'. Some actors work from externals like gait, feet, or gesture. Some imitate behaviour from people they know, and others work from their own personalities in the belief that they have a number of people inside them. Brecht's characters must reveal their contradictions, whereas Grotowski's actors are asked to use an 'inductive technique of eliminating external effects in a search for their own psycho-analytical language of sounds and gestures'. There are so many acting models that anyone is likely to become confused, but certain key concepts appear to lie at the root of any approach to **character**; of these, *intention* and **given circumstances** seem to be especially helpful.

In its heart, drama does not deal with abstract ideas, but with ideas made concrete in terms of *human interaction*. The abstraction of **character** merely reduces the complexity of the influences on behaviour, it does not obviate them. What holds our interest in a story is the **plot**, an element congruent with our notion of 'action'. Of course, if an actor's sole concern is with the sound of poetry or the quality of ideas in a play then this may not be the case, but it is arguable that s/he would then be using the wrong medium. Character is a function of values, intentions and desired appearance. Action is the playing of strategies to achieve and maintain these three elements in the context of problems ensuing from particular social and material circumstances, and the actor's prime concern is to sustain coherence between the character and the character's 'action'.

Chorus

The concepts of a single chorus figure and of a chorus in which a group of performers act with a sense of unity both have their origins in ancient forms of performance but are still important features of contemporary theatre. In the Prologue to Shakespeare's *Henry V*, a single **character** addresses the **audience**, establishing a context for the **action** and inviting them to use the conventions of theatre to create a drama. Marlowe uses a similar device in *Dr Faustus* when his chorus figure provides essential information and guides the audience through the changes in the **protagonist's** life. Renaissance dramatists were, in fact, taking their model from the Roman playwright Seneca, but the effectiveness of the device of the chorus lay in the ease with which their theatre architecture and conditions facilitated direct address to the audience. Whenever the design of theatres has confined the actors within the picture frame of the **proscenium arch**, direct address has become less common, and it is significant that many of the modern uses of the individual chorus figure have resulted from experiments with more flexible staging forms. One of the most interesting examples of this was Charles Williams's play *Thomas Cranmer of Canterbury* (1936), which included a chorus figure in the guise of an animated skeleton, weaving in and out of the action, commenting to the audience and also addressing the protagonist. This character, 'Figura Rerum', was rather like a medieval 'Vice' figure and derived much of its effectiveness from the fact that the play was written for performance in the Chapter House of the Cathedral at Canterbury with an 'open' stage and entrances through the audience, who were visible to the performers throughout. Robert Bolt's 'Common Man' in *A Man for All Seasons* has a similar function and relies again on a mediating role between actors and audience, made possible by a sense of shared space.

The concept of a single figure addressing the audience, giving information, moving the action onwards through description, providing a narrative commentary and then reverting to participation in the physical events of the play has become a familiar aspect of recent performances, particularly those based on lengthy novels or substantial documentary sources. In this way, the **actor** stands outside the action, drawing the audience into a sense of community with the performers. Theatre companies with clear political, didactic or 'issue' intentions may use this technique to great effect in any variety of venues and with provocative material.

A similar range of functions lies at the root of the concept of a chorus, made up of a small, or large, number of individuals who perform with a sense of unity. It is probably in the modern stage Musical that we see the greatest affinity with the dancing, singing and speaking chorus of the Ancient Greek theatre. Indeed, the demand for performers who combine these skills has increased significantly since Agnes de Mille's choreography for *Oklahoma!* (1943) achieved an unprecedented parity between the music and dialogue in a stage Musical. This led to the concept of what has become known as the 'triple threat' performer: a performer with equal facility in singing, dancing and acting, and this, in turn, has contributed to the growth of theatre works such as Michael Bennett's *A Chorus Line* (1975), in which the chorus is, itself, the protagonist.

The concept of a chorus always contains a fundamental tension between the need for the chorus to act as a unified entity and for the individuals in the chorus to preserve an identity and dramatic function of their own. There have been and still are times when the chorus in Western theatre, usually composed of attractive young men and women, has served a purely decorative function. However, we owe a great deal to the nineteenth-century playwright and librettist W. S. Gilbert for developing a more balanced use of the chorus. In the 'comic operas' he wrote with Arthur Sullivan, which became among the most successful creations for all time in the British theatre, Gilbert insisted on absolute discipline in the chorus. Where movements demanded synchronicity he evolved elaborate and carefully rehearsed patterns, and at times the chorus appeared to act and move as one. At the same time, Gilbert insisted that each chorus member react and focus as an individual in relation to the events taking place on stage. This tradition has survived into a period in which the chorus has become increasingly central to the structure of Musicals.

Similar concerns have been evident in the work of recent directors of opera, where the chorus usually acts as a 'crowd' that comments upon and contributes to the action of the main characters. Opera chorus members have many roles: soldiers, nuns, peasants, townsfolk, ship's crew, dancers, to name but a few, and it has become modern theatre practice to imbue these roles with individuality and 'real' lives. Protests arose in 2003 when the opening male chorus of an opera staged in London were revealed sitting on toilets reading newspapers, but the growing trend to adapt opera for television has also added impetus to the idea of the chorus as an important group of actors who happen to be 'on stage' at the same time. Undoubtedly, the existence of a chorus can greatly add to the spectacle of any stage event: this is not only true of Grand Opera or Musicals but also in such productions as Max Reinhardt's massive version of Vollmoeller's *The Miracle* (1911) at Olympia, or in the Peking Operas of the Cultural Revolution in China (1960s and 1970s), where groups of healthy-looking and optimistic workers filled the stage with their propagandist dramas, moving, speaking and singing with prescribed accuracy and unity.

Whereas opera directors have worked for more individuality in their choruses, writers and directors of plays have tended to favour the eradication of the individual. This was particularly true of the **Expressionist** experiments of Maurice Maeterlinck in such plays as *The Blind* (1890) or of Sean O'Casey in *The Silver Tassie* (1928). In these plays the chorus became a series of ghostly voices creating a soundscape of sometimes terrifying intensity.

However, it was the revival of interest in the production of Ancient Greek drama in the early years of the twentieth century that led to the most extensive use of and experimentation with the chorus in modern theatre. Between 1910 and 1920 the Austrian director Max Reinhardt staged a number of spectacular productions of translations of Greek plays in Europe and Britain. Fortunately, we have extensive eyewitness accounts and in several cases the *regiebuch* (prompt copy) of these productions, and can gauge their considerable impact. One critic wrote of the production of Sophocles' *Oedipus Rex*: 'When Reinhardt's chorus was let loose, it was unanimously reported that several housemaids screamed and went into hysterics!' When Reinhardt came to London he insisted on finding a theatre with a circular arena to contain his chorus, and it was the new translations of Gilbert Murray (who appears, thinly disguised, in Shaw's *Major Barbara*) to which he was attracted. Reinhardt was uninterested in authenticity: he simply strove for the intensity and spectacle that he believed were the essential ingredients of the Greek chorus, but from his, and Murray's, work there sprang up a movement in the theatre and arts education to explore and promote both choral speaking and Greek dance, together with efforts by such composers as Gustav Holst to create suitable music for choric speech and singing in the context of Greek plays.

Awareness of the potential of choral speaking as taught in the new drama schools led T. S. Eliot to write his two experimental verse theatre works *The Rock* (1933) and *Murder in the Cathedral* (1935). The latter was written for the Canterbury Festival and featured a chorus of women played by students from the Central School of Speech Training and Dramatic Art. The play transferred to the Mercury Theatre in London and has since had thousands of performances. Its chorus of 'Women of Canterbury' continues to tantalise directors and fascinate audiences and has probably yet to receive an entirely satisfactory treatment. Although the twentieth century saw many plays inspired by Greek drama, it was only Jean-Paul Sartre in *Les Mouches* (based on the *Agamemnon* of Aeschylus) who achieved a convincing equivalent, in a modern play of what must have been the integration of movement, music and speech employed by the chorus in Ancient Greece.

What *do* we know of the chorus in the theatre of Ancient Greece and of fifth-century BC Athens in particular? According to Aristotle, drama came into being when a *dithyramb*, a choric form of worship of Dionysus using dance and music, evolved into a **dialogue**. Archaeology has discovered the *orkestra*: a circular area in the middle of the theatre, which appears to be the place where the chorus performed. The earliest play we possess from the period is *The Suppliants* (490 BC) by Aeschylus and this opens with a choric song from the daughters of Danaus, of whom there were reported to be fifty. There is no evidence, however, that there were fifty members of the chorus. In this play, the chorus is, in fact, the main **protagonist** but in later plays the chorus comments upon the protagonist's predicament and on the cosmic significance of the action, to which it sometimes contributes in role.

The Choruses in Greek drama were written in metres which differed from the language of the main action, and were apparently chanted in strophes and antistrophes. The direction of the chorus was undertaken by the *coryphaeus*, who, we must speculate, enabled the chorus to achieve a subtle blend of unison chanting, singing, speaking and dancing, and role play that is a lost art today. Our knowledge of the composition and function of the chorus is based on interpretation of various sources, but mainly of the plays themselves. In the early tragedies the chorus was dominant, often being assigned more than half the lines of dialogue, but after the time of Aeschylus the chorus diminished in importance until in the plays of Euripedes it seems at times only to comment on the action with a series of meditations. Scholars continue to argue over the size of the chorus, and you would do well to follow the debate in Oscar Brockett's *History of the Theatre* or a similar reference book if this is of particular interest. The traditional view is that there may well have been a chorus of fifty in *The Suppliants* but that during the career of Aeschylus this was reduced to twelve. This is supported by the fact that Aeschylus's *Agamemnon* contains a twelve-lined choral interlude. It is also asserted that the chorus was increased to fifteen by Sophocles and that it remained at that size for the plays of Euripedes. Whatever the actual size of the chorus, we can be sure that many of the finest Greek plays relied heavily on its initial entrance and its ability to group and re-group both physically and vocally and to relate to the protagonists and events in an impressive ritualised mode of performance.

It is significant that it was the rediscovery of another **ritual** form of theatre, the Japanese '*Noh* play', in the early years of the twentieth century, especially through the translations of Ezra Pound and Ernest Fenelossa, that led to the other significant experiments with the chorus. These were the works of the 'Georgian' playwrights Lascelles Abercrombie and Gordon Bottomley in the 1920s and 1930s and, most importantly, of the Irish poet and dramatist W. B. Yeats. Yeats's *Plays for Dancers* (1917) remain one of the most challenging modern attempts at a ritual theatre built around the ideal of poetry in performance, of which the chorus is a key concept.

See also **catharsis; tragedy** *and* **vocalisation.**

Commedia dell'arte

The tradition of 'Commedia' (as it is usually known) was the product of Renaissance Italy. It was a non-scripted, improvised form of drama and known as 'Commedia dell'arte' because it was performed by professionals rather than by the amateur gentlemen of the court. The form emerged sometime before 1550 and was at its height during the early seventeenth century. Although its influence is still very evident today, commedia performances seem to have largely died out during the eighteenth century. Like **farce**, the commedia probably had its origins in the crude comedies that emerged in the southern Italian town of Atella (see **farce**) in the first century AD but also in the performances of groups of wandering minstrels. Some scholars claim that elements of the commedia are also clearly evident in the comedies of Aristophanes and Plautus. We know, however, that by the sixteenth century, the commedia had become a sophisticated art form.

Commedia actors performed without a **script**. They were, instead, provided with an outline **plot** known as a *sogetto*, which gave brief descriptions of the **scenes**. The actors were then required to invent **dialogue** and **action** to elaborate the bare **structure** that was their starting point. Dialogue was sometimes totally improvised but actors also acquired a repertoire of memorised speeches that might be inserted at appropriate moments. These stock speeches, or *concetti*, were also in keeping with the particular stock **character** that had been assigned to the performers. Additionally, the **actors** drew upon a range of comic actions or business, known as *lazzi*, which had been handed down by generations of performers and which, again, could be inserted into the **plot** to provide a dimension of knockabout humour or excitement. From what we can tell, commedia performances were very physical.

Much of the more obvious form of humour was provided by the *zanni*, the clowns of the company, who usually played the parts of servants to the main characters. We can see the influence of this tradition in Marlowe's *Dr Faustus* or Shakespeare's *The Tempest*. The zanni characters, such as Arlecchino (Harlequin), Pulcinella (Punch) and Scaramouche, were not only vitally important in their own context but developed into recognisable figures in a wide range of performance situations. The other stock characters of the commedia (collectively known as **masks**) were more serious in style and demeanour and the *zanni* highlighted their predicaments. The typical commedia characters were: two *zanni* (one clever and one stupid servant), Il Dottore, (a pompous scholar), Pantalone (a henpecked husband and foolishly inept lover), Il Capitano (a boastful Spanish soldier) and the two unmasked figures, Amoroso and Amarosa, who provided the serious love interest in the drama.

Commedia actors appear to have selected their mask and **costume** at the start of their careers and, bringing their own characteristics and eccentricities to the **role**, developed them into something unique. Particular performers popularised different characters just as nineteenth- and early twentieth-century Music Hall artists became known for their catch phrases, strange costumes and distinctive modes of moving and speaking. Illustrations of commedia characters suggest that they were sometimes grotesque and deformed. The performances exposed stupidity, moral depravity and pride. They were direct, athletic and, at times, brutal, and their influence apparently indelible.

Gassner and Allen (1992) provide the best and most comprehensive set of sources for an understanding of the topic but Mel Gordon's *Lazzi: The Comic Routines of the Commedia dell'Arte* (1983) is also very informative.

See also **comedy; farce** *and* **improvisation.**

Conventions

In order to release the potential energy of any dramatic text there must be a tacit agreement between the performers and intended **audience**. Such agreements or contracts form the 'conventions' of drama. The most basic convention is that an audience watches and listens in a designated space while actors perform in another designated space, even if, at times, the play deliberately breaks or challenges this convention. It is another convention that an actor pretends to be somebody else and that the audience accepts that his or her **dialogue** represents everyday speech. Conventions are governed by fashion, theatre design, technology or cultural tradition and may be established by habit, or even by the playwright or director for a particular play. There are various language conventions, such as the use of verse to represent ordinary speech; conventions of time, such as the agreement to imagine that Dr Faustus's final speech in Marlowe's play lasts an entire hour; and conventions of space, in which the audience accepts that a 'stage' space represents another space or that they can see into several rooms simultaneously (see Kenneth Pickering, *Studying Modern Drama*, pp. 10–19).

Some conventions, such as the use of a **chorus**, belong specifically to the process of performance, and of these, the **aside** and the **soliloquy** are, perhaps, the most interesting and illustrative of the influence of theatre design and **actor–audience relationships**.

Cultural performance

Many activities in everyday life contain elements of what we might recognise as performance, drama or theatre. When friends are sharing anecdotes or stories, for example, it is obvious who takes 'centre stage' at any one time and who constitute the 'audience' even though the intention of such personal narratives is not to give a performance. However, when we attend sporting events, weddings or any of the activities I have discussed in the entry on **carnival** we may be aware that they have more characteristics in common with a theatrical performance. There may for instance, be a designated space for the 'performers' and 'spectators', special **costumes** for the performers, certain clearly understood **conventions** and, in some cases, even a **script.**

There is, in fact, a continuum of what is termed 'cultural performance' with very informal, unscripted activity at one end and something more akin to a formal theatrical performance at the other (see **liminality**). Indeed, the boundary between some forms of cultural performance and theatrical performance can be very imprecise and some activities may contain characteristics of both. We can see this demonstrated in some forms of religious worship: I have often heard Church services described as 'pure theatre' and it is common for people to speak of the 'drama' of the 'Mass'.

Cultural performance, however, has certain general characteristics: firstly, it is often, although not invariably, spontaneous and unscripted and as we have seen, it is only when it is approaching the boundaries with theatrical performance that there may be an element of the more formal and predictable. Secondly, it has a more flexible attitude to **durational** issues than theatrical performance. A cultural performance, may, for example, be very brief and arise from a spontaneous gathering or it may continue for an entire afternoon and spectators may come and go as they please or view some form of happening as it passes by (see **durational performance**).

Thirdly, and most importantly, a cultural performance can only be understood within the context of a certain cultural environment. Let me provide a number of examples. In the city where I live I am aware of an Anglican priest who goes out in his car very early in the morning wearing a long black garment (a cassock) under his coat. Because I happen to have grown up with an awareness of what happens in churches I understand that this priest is going to 'celebrate' early morning communion in a rural church. His dress **code** tells me that he is a priest about to fulfill a priestly function. However, were I to be entirely ignorant of that aspect of my culture I might mistake him for a transvestite wearing a long black frock leaving home to take part in some gathering! Similarly, in the same city I am very aware that late on Friday and Saturday evenings, however cold the weather, there is an area thronging with scantily dressed young people. This fact has baffled and even shocked some of my visitors from other countries but, because I have lived in this city for many years and absorbed its culture and, perhaps, because much of my working life has brought me into contact with students, I know that these young people are all about to take part in the ritual of attending a night club. Cultural performances will, therefore, arise naturally from a cultural milieu and may well have **ritual** elements.

Precisely because they are embedded in a particular culture the 'performances' do not easily transfer. Recent attempts to introduce the razzmatazz of basketball to English cricket grounds, for example, have largely been a failure and you may well wish to consider situations in which such cultural performances as a group of 'cheerleaders' would be totally misunderstood.

Stern and Henderson (1993) provide a most helpful survey of the phenomenon of cultural performance in their *Performance: Texts and Contexts.*

See also **carnival.**

Energy

Actors need to consider and apply energy in terms of its effect upon character behaviour. Essentially, they need to ask whether their character is using energy economically and dynamically in pursuit of a goal or whether he or she is being obliged, through the influence of internal or external forces, to block energy. There is a physiological and anatomical dimension to this problem, but when it comes to action the energy factor determines at least the following elements of human behaviour:

(a) the determination with which he or she pursues a goal;
(b) the degree of influence such blocks have upon the dynamic of goal-striving activity;
(c) the control that the **character** maintains in spite of external blocks.

The questions are: whether the character is centred in terms of energy and personality; and whether he or she is positive in pursuit of goals. The answers to the question will provide the rhythm and tempo of a character's behaviour and will also determine the character's predominance or otherwise in any scene.

Frame analysis

The concept of 'frame analysis' was developed by the social psychologist Erwin Goffman and is now seen as making a significant contribution to understanding the idea of performance. Frame analysis is the process by which we attempt to make sense of what we perceive in human behaviour, given that people are invariably engaged in playing a role of some kind. These roles enable us to negotiate relationships and various kinds of transaction but they only have meaning if they are 'framed' to enable others to read what is actually going on. Goffman's work on **role** is especially important in exploring the acting process, and I shall turn to that later, but, at the outset, it is important to establish how 'framing' works and is facilitated. This will enable us to see the relevance of frame analysis as a means of analysing the performance event.

Let's take a couple of examples. Imagine you, as a student, are attending a lecture given by one of your tutors as part of a course of study. You may know that your tutor is a world authority on the topic and you will expect to sit in a lecture room, listening and taking notes. The room will be arranged in a certain way and the lecturer will behave in an appropriate and predictable fashion. All these factors are part of the *frame* that enables you to accept and understand the event. Of course, you take them for granted because they are so familiar to you. The role that the lecturer plays makes sense to you because it takes place in a recognisable frame. Now imagine that you also attend a comedy club for an evening of 'stand-up' comedy. What will be the aspects of the new frame that enable you to accept the role of the comedians and make sense of the experience?

Another concept concerned with frame analysis is that of the *key*. Again, an example will serve to illustrate. Imagine that you are in town when you witness a bank raid. You will know from the attire of the robbers, the reaction of other people, the expressions on faces, the screams or shouts, the reckless driving and so on that this is for real and that the robbers are playing their role in deadly earnest. However, if you noticed that the event was being filmed and that there were refreshment facilities for actors and a whole group of supporting crew, you would realise that this activity involved a set of transitions into a fiction. In order for this to happen, a number of conventions would be needed, based on the 'real' event, but then transformed into something realised by the participants and onlookers to be something quite different in nature. This process of transformation is described as 'keying'. The fact that onlookers at our imaginary bank raid realise that the actors are 'only pretending or playing' is brought about by their ability to recognise 'keys': the way the activity is repeated for rehearsal or the pause to adjust costume, for example. Indeed, it is part of the frame and the keying process that we recognise that in the 'real' bank raid the participants are wearing 'clothes' but that actors wear '**costumes**'. Frame analysis, then, enables us to recognise and discourse upon an act that is not purely literal or functional.

The implications of Goffman's work for an investigation of the task of performance in the theatre are considerable because 'acting' is invariably based upon, even if it is not an imitation of, human behaviour.

His basic thesis is that each of us is always in some sort of role, but that the role is not our complete selves. We have, in addition, the controlling self which endows all of the roles with particular characteristics. He states: 'Behind many masks and many characters, each performer tends to wear a single look, a naked unsocialised look, a look of concentration, a look of one who is privately engaged in a difficult, a treacherous task' (*The Presentation of Self in Everyday Life*, p. 228).

The task is to negotiate satisfactorily and perform the myriad rituals and multiplicity of roles which social existence demands, in order that we survive socially and physiologically. This task is bedevilled by a need to sustain a recognisable self, persistent in these roles; a self which is itself a construct drawn from the behaviour of admired models, themselves subject to the vagaries of changing perceptions and attitudes. These many problems would be difficult enough in a constant world, but individuals are continually being presented with new information, new ideas and new problems, which they may feel the requirement to adapt to and accommodate.

It must also be borne in mind that the feedback, accommodation and modification of behaviour which an individual undergoes in the course of an encounter are simultaneously being undergone by those with whom he or she is interacting. The idea of an encounter carries with it the principle that people enter into it with the intention of gaining something from it, with the concomitant possibility of failing to achieve this. The drama ensues from our doubts and anxieties about the outcome. In using the term 'drama' here, we are employing it both in the sense of something dramatic and in its association with theatre, for according to some social psychologists the behaviour of people entering into an encounter is stage-managed or 'presented' in much the same way that the performance of a play is presented. Goffman elaborates on the point. He says, 'The self then is not an organic thing that has specific location, whose fundamental fate is to be born, to mature and to die; it is a dramatic effect arising diffusely from a scene that is presented' (p. 245).

The details of this interpretation of affairs are comprehensive. Goffman gives examples of the various staging aids which the individual employs to support the performance, dividing them into 'setting' and 'personal front'. 'Setting' involves furniture, décor and the general physical layout of the environment. This may be very elaborately organised in the case of, say, a VIP reception lounge or a police interview room, or it may be hastily got together to accommodate an unusual or unexpected sort of encounter. Obvious and humorous examples will arise if someone important arrives to conduct formal business in a home when the place has been organised for informal pleasure. Interactants may have to adapt to a new and inappropriate environment, so they will improvise with features available and employ spatial distances to reinforce different stages of the interaction. A 'borrowing-money encounter' can be carried out on the tennis court or in bed rather than in a bank manager's office, but it will involve similar behavioural signs.

Within the idea of 'personal front' come all those elements through which we design our appearance for the occasion. Some are formal and relate very clearly to social status. Within this category would come any uniform of office or rank and associated properties like a baton or a whistle. Others are less precise, but the suggestion is that we organise our clothes and our properties as part of presentational strategies. Other features, such as sex and age, shape, posture, speech patterns, facial expressions and all the body signs which we continually emit, are all available as material for our 'appearance'.

It is perhaps best to separate the ideas of 'personal front' into two categories, *manner* and *appearance*. The latter refers to what Goffman calls the individual's 'temporary ritual state'. Thus we will adopt a certain appearance to conform with our desired image as a senior civil servant, or a sportsman, or a teenage rebel. At the same time, we will also adopt a manner which informs others about the role we expect to play in an encounter. Someone appearing as a senior civil servant may present a manner of meekness in order to suit his purpose in a particular situation. A known autocrat may go to great lengths to appear democratic on television, or a tramp may use strategies to suggest authority when confronted by a police officer.

A person is at least two entities: being a 'self' anxious to maintain credibility and respect; and performing a vast variety of roles within a succession of encounters. Any study of human behaviour or any attempt to create or interpret behaviours must bear in mind the possibilities, the purposes and the pitfalls endemic to the self, the role and the encounter itself. Little has been said so far about the encounter as separately identifiable from the people who take part in it. The critical features of an encounter are that it is perceptible, it has shape, with a beginning and an end, and that persons taking part in it usually give it a common definition. The most obvious examples of this tend to be known as **rituals**. Weddings, funerals, public meetings, receptions, interviews are all more or less rituals in that the roles are clearly defined and separated, the codes of conduct, even the language, are constrained towards a certain conformity, and a general outcome can be anticipated. Expectations from the rituals are precise and they are recognised. Behaviour within them falls into known patterns which cultures go to some trouble to perpetuate. At their most formal they are sacred, and inappropriate behaviour would be shocking, perhaps bringing disgrace and punishment to the offender. However, the least formal of them, such as a casual conversation between strangers, tend to fit into a known pattern with participants choosing known roles. This is not to say that all casual conversations will be the same, but that interactants will choose from a finite number of modes of mutual behaviour that might come within a category of 'encounters between strangers'. There is an initial uncertainty until the participants either separate, or find a shared definition of the situation. If they take the latter choice then they will quickly accept unwritten rules of tact and role behaviour. Of course they may fail, and such playwrights as Harold Pinter or Mike Leigh frequently explore the behaviour of characters constantly on the threshold of encounters, but unable to define a satisfactory ritual.

We have seen that both the self and the role are always at risk, but it is important to remember that the encounter itself can also be jeopardised. If the self cracks up and shows its weakness or inappropriateness, or the role is not sustained, then the encounter is threatened. A drunken priest doesn't only lose face himself, but damages the wedding. The effects can be worse. A drunken anaesthetist may not only upset a surgical-operation encounter, he may also kill the **protagonist**.

It is the potential discrediting of self and role that generates the greatest fear in social life and the greatest drama on the stage. It is the very stuff of both comedy and the thriller. Goffman associates the discredit with the ideas of 'face' and 'front'; with discredit stemming from loss of these through what he calls 'incidents', or those dramaturgical errors which result in the audience seeing the man behind the mask. Examples of such incidents would include unmeant gestures perceived by the wrong person, inopportune intrusions, social *faux pas* and unbridled emotion of the sort we associate with 'scenes'.

Of course, objective perception of these incidents may not necessarily be one of shock or embarrassment. Anyone uncommitted to the encounter, particularly if they disapprove of the encounter's purpose and meaning, will probably be amused. It is funny for the objective observer when the party line or the strategy or the performance fails. We are likely to laugh if the music conductor lets his baton fly out of his hand, or a model breaks her high heel on the catwalk. The oldest gag is for someone to get caught with his trousers down.

If we are to accept the ideas of Goffman then it would appear that most human behaviour is acting, and an inability to act would severely inhibit the capacity of a person to operate in society. In order to act, an actor has to draw on the facility he has, relating it to the particulars of a context or scene. **Audience** pleasure stems from vicariously participating in the characters' social risks without suffering the outcomes.

Gesture

Gesture is one of the principal non-verbal **codes of communication** available to the performer. It encompasses all movements of the arms or hands in relation to the stance and other parts of the body and may be mimetic – calling attention to what it copies; highly stylised; or an 'echo' gesture – reinforcing a point made in speech. The nature of gesture will be affected by the size of the theatre, the overall style of a performance, the **costumes** worn by the **actors**, any fashion appendages, such as fans or swords, and a range of cultural issues, which may include specific meanings attached to certain physical movements. Gesture, as in a number of ancient, traditional theatre forms, may have become codified into a language which stands independent of **dialogue**. For example, the ancient Sanskrit drama of India, dating from around the third century AD, had codified movement and gesture, although based on natural behaviour, into a series of prescribed signs preserved in some Hindu writings. Based upon the emotions and the parts of the body involved, there were thirteen movements of the head, six of the nose, six of the cheek, seven of the eyebrow, nine of the neck, seven of the chin, five of the chest, thirty-six of the eyes, thirty-two of the feet and twenty-four of the hand.

It was the study of such ancient forms including those of Bali, China and Japan, often transmitted for generations, that inspired Brecht to evolve his system of 'the A-Effect' (see **alienation**), and Artaud to prescribe methods of performance for his **Theatre of Cruelty**. Brecht recommended the 'noting of gestures' as part of the curriculum for an acting school, insisting that 'special elegance, power and grace of gesture bring about the A-effect', and that 'everything to do with emotions has to be externalised, that is to say, developed into gesture' (*Versuche* 3, Berlin, 1931). When Artaud saw a troupe of Balinese dancers in Paris in 1930 he determined to create a theatre in which the actors were like 'moving hieroglyphs', the whole appearance one of 'theatrical conventions' with profound symbolic meaning too deep for 'logical discursive language'.

Where gesture has not been passed on as a convention in performance we immediately come up against the problems of reconstruction. Studies such as Peter Arnott's *Public Performance in the Greek Theatre* (1985), Alexander Leggatt's *Jacobean Public Theatre* (1992) or Bertram Joseph's classic *Elizabethan Acting* (1951) all highlight the difficulties of using sources such as contemporary accounts, **stage directions** or illustrations to establish precisely what gestures were used and how, in any given theatre period before means of mechanical recording. By means of informed speculation we can, however, come somewhere near to understanding the gestures that might have been used. Such movements as tearing the hair, holding the head in the hands, kneeling in supplication or raising the arms in triumph have a fairly universal significance and, in the huge theatres of Ancient Greece, we can be fairly certain that Arnott's statement that gesture was 'unambiguous, instantly and vividly evocative and could be seen at a distance' is accurate.

In the increasingly naturalistic theatre of nineteenth-century Britain, Europe and America, it was the emergence of two main concepts that contributed to the most thorough study of gesture for which we have documentation. The first was the concept of methodical training for the **actor** and the second was the developing study of oratory and elocution. The first textbooks (as we would understand the term) to deal with aspects of performance and voice in acting appeared at the very end of the eighteenth century and by 1806 the Revd Gilbert Austin's *Chironomia* included rules for 'the proper regulation of the voice, the countenance and gesture together with a new method for the notation thereof'. The dominant figure in the development of a scientific understanding of gesture and acting, however, was a remarkable French musician, teacher and inventor, François Delsarte (1811–71). Having ruined his voice by faulty training and usage, Delsarte forsook the stage in order to establish a scientific means of training actors that would result in a more natural style of performance. He hoped to achieve this by formulating rules of elocution and gesture that, because they were derived from an exact observation of human behaviour, would culminate in a reproduction of Nature. Delsarte aimed for unity between the body, the voice and the spirit and regarded the voice as invariably linked to gesture: 'The artist should have three objects: to move, to interest, to persuade. He interests by language; he moves by thought; he moves, interests and persuades by gesture.' Indeed, he considered gesture to be more potent than speech. 'The soul of speech is gesture', he wrote (François Delsarte, *The Delsarte System of Oratory*, 1893, p. 486).

Delsarte's system was introduced into the United States by the actor Steele MacKaye (1842–94) and became far more widely used and venerated than in Britain. Nevertheless, it was through application of a modified version of Delsarte's work that actor training became established at a number of new academies in London. Typical of these was the London Academy of Music (which eventually became LAMDA), where what we would now term 'acting' was taught by Gustave Garcia, the author of *The Actor's Art: A practical treatise of stage declamation, public speaking and deportment, for the use of artists, students and amateurs* (1882). Garcia's book began a steady stream of other manuals dealing with voice and gesture, based on the original work of Delsarte. Gesture was analysed according to three radii: the Epic Radius, in which the arm prescribed an arc above the head; the Rhetorical Radius, in which the arms moved in a horizontal arc at eye level; and the Colloquial Radius, which operated between the centre of the chest and the lower hip. Such prescriptions eventually had precisely the opposite effect to their intended outcome as they led to an artificial style in which gesture seemed to be an extraneous addition to language, when in fact, the object of such classifications was to create a sense of naturalness. For this reason 'gesture' has been increasingly shunned as an aspect of naturalistic acting in favour of a more holistic approach. However, the study of nineteenth-century manuals of acting and elocution can provide fascinating insights into the first attempts to devise scientific methods of performance and training, and can throw light on acting in **melodrama**.

Gestus

It is in *Versuche 2* (Berlin, 1930), a relatively early theoretical writing by Brecht, that we first encounter his concept of 'gestus': an important aspect of **Epic Theatre**, and of his concept of **alienation**. The term 'gestus' appears to have first been used by the German dramatist Lessing in his *Hamburger Dramaturgie* (1767), and later by Brecht's collaborator, the composer Kurt Weill. Brecht, however, continued to use and develop the concept of gestic acting throughout his career. You will find a very helpful discussion of gestus in Colin Counsell's *Signs of Performance* (1999) but it is important not to consider the idea in isolation or away from the implications for practical performance. In essence, gestus is an attitude or single aspect of an attitude, expressible in words or actions. It is an amalgam of the physical **gesture** and the underlying *gist* of a **scene** or episode: the **gesture** arising from the gist. For example, if the gist of a scene is that the **protagonist** is in a subservient position to another **character**, the gesture may well involve doffing of hats, bowing, averting the eyes and so on. Physical action and modes of speaking derive from and are shaped by social conditions and structures. In Epic Theatre, the **actor** must discover and develop the *gest* that encodes the social relationships in which the character operates. A *gest* may involve a single movement, gesture or tone of voice or may extend to entire modes of behaviour that reflect the play's depiction of a world of social pressures and relationships: the play's *Grundgestus*.

Brecht was determined to pose questions concerning the situations in which he placed his dramatic characters. In order to demonstrate the *gist* and essence of a situation, he demanded an objective and detached acting style which could both isolate and clarify a character's emotions and social attitudes. Rehearsal would involve a search for a means whereby this process could be achieved through vocalisation and physicalisation. Using methods adapted from the Chinese actor Mei Lan Fang (1894–1961) and involving elements of caricature that he developed during his work on Gay's ballad opera *The Threepenny Opera*, Brecht created a clear gest for each episode in his plays.

In attempting to demonstrate his concept of 'gestus' and gestic acting, Brecht provided a model in a detailed verbal and photographic record of the performance of his wife, Helene Weigel, in the role of Mother Courage (1949). Here we see a highly manipulative character who hauls her canteen wagon across Europe at the time of the Thirty Years' War, living off whatever army happens to be nearby and losing her sons and daughter in a series of tragic events. Weigel's approach was to demonstrate, rather than inhabit, key emotions and to establish codes for conveying her character's relationships and means of dealing with crises through voice and **gesture**. Some of the most significant moments were almost frozen to enable the **audience** to read the signs and reflect upon the cause, injustice or inevitability of the events. The moment when Mother Courage refuses to recognise the body of her dead son in order to survive herself was a particularly memorable example of gestic acting.

Students are often perplexed because the concept of gestus is neither easily recognised nor easy to achieve in practical exploration of a text, but I would draw attention to the section on acting styles, where I have indicated how style consists not of a series of physical or vocal attributes appended to a text, but of something which grows out of the underlying purpose which the drama serves. Elements of detachment and caricature exist in such contrasting situations as Music Hall, stand-up comedy and Shakespeare, as well as in a number of ancient oriental approaches to performance, but where episodic narrative with comment is the form and intention of the theatre work, gestus is a most helpful approach to acting.

See also **acting style.**

Given circumstances

This is a concept developed by Stanislavsky around the year 1934 as part of the detailed analysis and preparation process through which he insisted every actor must go (see K. Stanislavsky, *Creating a Role*, trans.

Elizabeth Hopgood, 1961). There are two elements to 'given circumstances': the first is the fictional content of the play's **action**, the study of which must include an understanding of the play's *line*; and the second is the set of circumstances surrounding performance and emanating from the designer, **director** and others who shape a production, including those circumstances imagined by the other **actors**.

For actors, the first form provides the modifying elements that will influence the behaviour of their character. Whilst they may always be character A, they will also be character A talking to his wife, or at the top of a mountain, and so on. Character is therefore not a stable factor; we behave according to our circumstances, what we wish to achieve from those circumstances and how we intend to achieve this.

The possible elements of given circumstances in this form are almost infinite: a list would have to include every factor influencing human behaviour. However, there are some categories of circumstances which provide guidelines for the actor to work from. The list which follows was first compiled as a result of working with Performing Arts students and is provided as a checklist for acting and as a source of acting exercises:

The material world
   (a) Is the scene outside or in?
   (b) Is the environment known or unknown to the character?
   (c) Does the environment induce feelings of security or insecurity in the character?
   (d) Where are the objects and furniture?
   (e) What is the climate?
   (f) Are there any totemic or taboo objects with particular resonances for the individual character? What are these?
   (g) What is the immediate off-stage world? Where are its accesses into the stage environment? Are there associations of freedom or restraint, fulfilment or deprivation?

The character's psychological world
   (a) What has just happened to him/her?
   (b) Where has s/he just been?
   (c) What was his or her last experience of the material environment?
   (d) Is s/he in a hurry?
   (e) How near the surface is his or her intention?
   (f) Is s/he being threatened in terms of achieving a goal or in any other terms?
   (g) Is s/he anticipating a future event soon to happen?

The character's social or interactional world
  (a) How will the other characters potentially affect the achievement of his or her goal?
  (b) What was the outcome of the previous encounter with the other characters?
  (c) Does the character know anything about the other characters?
  (d) Does the character need to be perceived to have particular qualities by the other characters? Is there conflict between one expected appearance and another?
  (e) What events are taking place simultaneously with the action of the scene?

All of the facts suggested above serve as either a constraint or a resource for the character in pursuit of his or her goal. Some will help, some hinder. We can therefore think of behaviour, in part, as a response to the constraint/resource qualities in the world around us, but which category an element belongs to is determined by how the character sees it in terms of his or her objectives. Prison, for example, whilst most obviously a constraint, can provide satisfaction for needs of security, or sex, or status, or companionship. A limp may only be a partial constraint, for it can also serve as a resource for gaining attention or sympathy.

Constraints and resources
In a way, defining this element we are merely interpreting given circumstances in terms of a character's perception. However, if we assume that the principal logic of a character's behaviour is defined by the objective he or she is working towards, the given circumstances become tools or blocks, available to help or hinder progress. They are also there to be evaluated by the character and used or avoided according to their capabilities or needs. All objects and people are necessarily dynamic and play an active role in the play's action. Frequently they will provide essential tensions, they will determine the character's emotional state and oblige him or her to move in particular ways. It might be argued that emotion is derived from the satisfaction or otherwise that the character is achieving. We are happy because we are secure and successful according to our own criteria. We may cry because we are being thwarted from achieving our ends.

Our spatial patterns are also determined by our relations with people and objects in the space. In a way this is self-evident, but many actors and directors seem to create their moves with only a rudimentary acknowledgement of the potential spatial tensions which can exist between every element of the stage world. Any movement calls for a re-adjustment of these tensions. In any scene there is a finite number of tensions, determined by the **plot** at that time, so for one character there may be a tension between him and another because the latter represents a threat, or there may be a door which represents escape and a hammer which is on the sideboard. Directing entails manipulating the tensions between those various elements. Ibsen's plays abound with such tensions, almost every object in, say, *Hedda Gabler* having resonances far beyond its instrumental value and providing varying tensions throughout the play.

Again, it must be reiterated that external circumstances and objects have only the significance that we give to them. No element is constant or neutral. We weigh up what personal resources we have and use them accordingly, either putting **energy** behind them and creating a forward dynamic or losing confidence and setting up our own energy blocks. The need, for the actor, is to decide what is in the given circumstances for his or her **character** and how it affects the use of energy.

See **energy.**

Impersonation

As drama has moved away from its roots in pagan or Christian **ritual** there has been a strand in its development that has tended towards impersonation rather than **personification**: the representation of ideas or powers in human form. Impersonation, the process of pretending to be someone else, appears to be a fundamental human activity, with its basis in the creative *play* of childhood, but its significance in the development of drama was recognised by Aristotle in the *Poetics* as part of the concept of **mimesis.** This was the difference between rituals re-enacted by a priest before a congregation, and the 'imitation of an action', performed by an **actor** before an **audience** (see **actor, action, ritual**). Impersonation probably originally involved the imitation of a god, creature or person through dance, **gesture** and facial expression.

The concept of 'impersonation' is fundamental to drama: indeed, it could be argued that it is an essential part of the dramatic process. Impersonation not only involves the imaginative act of taking on another persona; it may operate at a number of levels. For example, in a celebrated version of the medieval **Mystery Plays**, at the Royal National Theatre in London (at a time of major conflict between the miners and the Thatcher government), the cast pretended to be miners taking on the roles of God, angels, Jesus and so on. This double level of **role play**, in which a **character** impersonates a character, is particularly effective in **comedy,** where, perhaps, a rogue will don disguise to dupe another character. In **tragedy** also, the element of impersonation that might involve the adopting of disguise may contribute to dramatic irony if the audience is aware of the motives of the disguised figure. At times, the audience members' appreciation of a character's skill in disguise and dissembling may be at odds with their moral outrage at his behaviour. With its origins in the play of childhood, impersonation involving disguise seems always to have elements of a game, albeit sometimes vicious, but observing this in the theatre is already part of an elaborate game, with rules clearly understood by all participants. In plays such as Shakespeare's *As You Like It* or *Twelfth Night*, in which the entire drama hinges on 'cross dressing' and disguise, the audience suspends disbelief to allow the drama to function. Impersonation may range from a mere indication to an attempted exact replication of another human being.

See **acting style; aside; character.**

Improvisation

The concept of improvising is central to all the Performing Arts and its importance in drama was firmly re-stated in the middle years of the twentieth century. Improvisation might include the 'ad lib' line within a fixed **text**, an extended extemporisation around a basic text or outline, the spontaneous invention of a piece of stage 'business' or the creation of a complete text through experimentation and **role play**. Improvisation lies at the heart of most modern schemes of actor training; much of the most creative work in Drama in Education; the 'pyschodrama' of Jacob Moreno, the 'Sesame' method of drama and movement therapy with its emphasis on the work of Jung and Laban; much of the best 'devised' theatre work and the plays and films of Mike Leigh. Improvisation is used in management training; the '**forum theatre**' technique of Augusto Boal; and in pioneering work with clients with learning and emotional difficulties. It probably has the widest sphere of application of any technique or concept derived from the theatre.

The appearance of spontaneity is constantly attractive in the Arts, and improvisation has long been used to achieve this. It is almost certainly older than recognisable forms of drama, but during the history of theatre as we understand it there have been significant periods when improvisation has been especially important. Primitive rituals, from which most theatre has evolved, contained strong improvisational elements; ancient epics in many cultures were probably presented initially as improvised narratives. Greek and Roman comedy and the Renaissance **commedia**

dell'arte were built around the improvisational skills of actors, and Shakespeare had Hamlet insisting that the clowns resist the temptation to extemporise. *Lazzo*, the element of comic fooling in the commedia, has remained an essential ingredient of staged comedy in theatre, film and television and Brecht used similar activities for rehearsal.

We owe much of our modern interest in improvisation to Stanislavsky. Exercises to develop truth and spontaneity and for probing the inner life of characters, as described in *An Actor Prepares*, were assimilated into the training programme of the Actors' Studio (founded 1947), where Lee Strasberg created what became known as the *Method* school of acting. Generations of American actors have been influenced by the Method and this influence has been extended via Hollywood to an almost universal **audience** so that it has become the single most recognisable modern approach to acting. Central to the Method was the requirement for actors in training to research their characters in minute detail and re-enact incidents and imagined meetings outside the scope of the play's text. Indeed, the focus on what became known as the **'scene'**, in which the students presented improvisations of their characters in simple or very complex circumstances, seemed at times to take precedence over work on the text itself. The aims of such improvisations were and remain the total absorption into the **character** and situation, and an openness to other stage **action**, so that reaction can be truthful and spontaneous.

Improvisation has now become established with actors as a means of working, in their training in Britain, America and much of Europe. It is used to obviate blocks to creativity, to sensitise and release the imagination, to establish a unity of body, emotion and **vocalisation** and to enable actors to undertake a wide variety of roles on the basis of observation and inner exploration.

Expressions like 'laboratory' (especially associated with the work of Grotowski in Poland), or 'workshop' (and we think of Joan Littlewood in Britain in the 1950s), indicate the experimental approach to acting that was popularised in the middle years of the last century (see 'Myth and Theatre Laboratories' in Christopher Innes's, *Avant Garde Theatre 1892–1992*, 1993). Joan Littlewood's work at the Theatre Royal, Stratford East has become part of the mythology of British theatre but is surprisingly little documented, although it is possible to argue that the ephemeral nature of improvisation cannot be captured in written or pictorial form. During the late 1950s and early 1960s she worked with a group of actors on plays by Brendan Behan, Shelagh Delaney and Bernard Kopps, using improvisation to achieve a sense of spontaneity and risk-taking, to deepen and enrich understanding of the context of the material and to develop the **script** (of the work of very inexperienced writers). These approaches culminated in employing '**documentary drama**' techniques, Pierrot comic business, Brechtian staging, episodic structure and alienation techniques in *O What a Lovely War*, scripted by Charles Chiltern but devised in considerable degree through improvisation. The idea that a text could be created from a variety of sources through improvisation became established as a way of working for a large number of small-scale theatre companies in the second half of the twentieth century. Some such companies worked in community touring, exploring issues relevant to particular geographical areas or social groups, others took their work into schools and colleges, creating a substantial Theatre in Education (TIE) movement, now, unfortunately, much diminished from its peak in the 1970s and 1980s. Towards the end of the century, playwrights like Ann Jellico and David Edgar turned their attention to creating plays for entire communities through improvisation. Much of the impetus for this grew out of a growing awareness of the value of oral history and the potential of simple documentary sources: diaries, court records, press reports etc.

The establishment of improvisation as a tool for **actor** training led to intensive and carefully researched approaches to character in leading drama schools and in theatres promoting new work. Employing a technique whereby actors worked alone on developing their characters for a considerable period of time before meeting the other characters, Mike Leigh created a series of disturbing plays for stage, TV and film. The works are described as 'devised' rather than written and the entire text appears to have evolved from improvisation. The somewhat reticent and evasive nature of many of Leigh's interviews gives few clues as to his precise mode of working, but it is clear that the method depends on the trust and openness of a relatively small circle of actors who are comfortable with the approach. The experience of improvising under Leigh's guidance is very demanding of concentration, imagination and physical and emotional energy.

It is precisely these features of improvisation that have enabled it to become both an educational and a therapeutic tool. A number of seminal books on improvisation appeared to promote its use by teachers, theatre directors, tutors of amateur drama of all kinds, facilitators and trainers. No texts had ever explored this area of drama before and they comprise a very significant corpus of understanding. Among the most influential are Peter Slade's *Child Drama* (1954), Viola Spolin's *Improvisation for the Theatre* (1963) and John Hodgson and Ernest Richards's *Improvisation* (1963). As the demand for new starting points, stimuli, trust exercises or games increased, these were joined by an extensive number of source books, of which Keith Johnstone's *Improvisation* (1981) and Augusto Boal's *Games for Actors and Non-Actors* (1992) were probably the most widely used by teachers, directors, therapists and actors.

Peter Slade's work as Drama Adviser in Birmingham in the immediate aftermath of the Second World War led to his articulating a concept of an improvisatory art-form that he called 'child drama': a type of play that he categorised as 'personal' or 'projected'. Through such play, he argued, children grow, learn, explore relationships and enrich their imaginations and emotional lives. Role play, **devising**, **ritual** and a physicalisation of ideas and emotions are all central to Slade's approach and, as you can see, involve key issues in theatre and performance. Many practitioners, of whom Dorothy Heathcote is probably the best known, have followed Slade's pioneering approach in using improvisation as a tool for learning and personal growth.

There is, of course, considerable difference between using improvisation as an educational method or as a preparation for performance and employing it as a *vehicle* of performance. The element of spontaneity was central to many of the *Dadaist* performances of the early twentieth century and to the *Happenings* and *events* I have discussed in the section on **action**. Alan Kaprow's essay 'The Happening is Dead, Long Live the Happening' highlights this: once a 'Happening' or 'event' of the kind devised in the America of the hippie era had taken place it could not be repeated: in no sense could such an event be rehearsed and the improvisation extended to include elements of indeterminacy. The experimental and avant-garde work of such groups as the Living Theatre or the Bread and Puppet Theatre, all deriving from forms of improvisation, is well documented in James Roose-Evans's *Experimental Theatre* (1970), but you should also consider those forms of theatre in which improvisation is an element of performance: these will range from commedia to devised pieces in which the text remains fluid.

See also **applied drama.**

Incidental music

Music is, and probably always has been, an aspect of **theatre language**; but the precise meaning of the term 'incidental music' is problematic and you may well wish to work towards your own definition. We can identify a number of types of music in drama: the most obvious is what we might call 'representational music', which would include trumpets and drums as fanfares or as indications of war. Shakespeare's *Macbeth*, for instance, has many 'alarums', 'sennets' and 'flourishes': all forms of trumpet call making a statement about the dramatic situation. Secondly, we would identify 'textual' music: music that is or accompanies a song or a dance. As this use of music in the theatre has developed we see the emergence of opera and the musical, in which the music is, in itself, an element of the **text**. This leaves us with a more nebulous area in which music underscores **action**, is specified for some particular effect or mood, or enables an imaginary change of time or location to take place. Much of this might be termed 'incidental'.

In order to examine this concept we might consider some of the principles that seem to underpin the use of music at certain points in drama. Our knowledge of music in the Ancient theatre is largely limited to speculation based on a few vase paintings and the innate musicality of surviving texts. However, we do know that in the Middle Ages music was used to symbolise God, Heaven and the supernatural events that appeared to shape human life. This usage was derived from the medieval philosophy of world 'harmony' and the concept of the harmonic proportions of the universe reflected in humankind, drawn from Plato and Pythagoras. The clearest statement of the nature of music in early medieval times comes from the philosopher Boethius (480–524), who identified three aspects: *musica mundana* (the music of the spheres), *musica humana* (the music of man's body, spirit, soul, and of human affairs), and the lowest of the hierarchy, *musica instrumentalis* (actual music of instruments and voices). These ideas and those of Ancient Greece entered Renaissance thinking largely through the writings and translations of the fifteenth-century Italian scholar Marsilio Ficino and there can be little doubt that such beliefs greatly influenced the use of music in late Medieval Drama and eventually permeated the drama of Marlowe and Shakespeare.

Although medieval texts give some indication of the use and type of music envisaged, it is in early English tragedy written in imitation of the Roman dramatist Seneca that we discover the specificity we need in order to re-create performance, including music, with some accuracy. In Norton and Sackville's *Gorboduc*, the first Senecan tragedy in English, the *dumb shows* are accompanied by music and the tone colours and instruments are detailed in the text. The first dumb show is accompanied by 'the musicke of Violenze' (stringed instruments usually represented the harmony of the universe) and the action 'signified that a state knit in unity doth continue strong against all force'. Other parts of the dumb show are accompanied by cornets (for royalty), flutes (for a funeral) and hautboys (oboes, to represent supernatural spirits from hell, presaging murder). Other specified music is more 'representational', such as drums and flutes for battles.

We can trace the influence of these **conventions** governing the choice of instruments in Shakespeare's *Macbeth*. In Act I, sc. 6, King Duncan enters the castle of Macbeth, where he will soon be murdered by his host, to the sound of 'hautboys'. In a moment of **dramatic irony**, the King comments on the sweetness of the air. The hautboys also introduce the following scene, in which Macbeth contemplates the act of murder, and underscore a further scene in the play when Macbeth visits the 'weird sisters', whose dark prophecy has initiated the tragic stream of events. The association of the sound of the hautboy with darkness, evil, murder and approaching disaster is an example of the integral part that can be played by music in performance. In such plays as Shakespeare's *A Midsummer Night's Dream*, *The Winter's Tale* or *The Tempest* there are constant references to music as a source of magic, transformation and healing. Images of discord, resolution and harmony abound and we sense that the evidence we have that these plays were probably first performed indoors, and were benefiting from modes of staging associated with the court *masque*, is a clue to their richer and more elaborate use of vocal and instrumental music as well as their metaphorical references to *musica humana*. It would appear that the entrances of gods or goddesses together with some of their dialogue would have been accompanied by music in lavish masque-like performances.

By the later sixteenth and early seventeenth centuries there was a considerable demand for incidental music in the English theatre. Composers were expected to produce new music for each production and this now included four 'act tunes' to be played between each of the five Acts, 'first' and 'second' music to be played during the arrival of the audience, and an 'overture', usually in the French style, to be played before the rise of the curtain. It is from this period that we have the earliest surviving examples of original settings in manuscript form: Matthew Locke's 1674 music for *The Tempest* or Henry Purcell's music for thirteen plays published posthumously as *Ayres for the Theatre* in 1697.

The relatively small instrumental ensembles for which much early theatre music seems to have been written dictated much of its style and form. However, by the early nineteenth century, especially in Germany, France, Italy and Russia, theatres were beginning to maintain large orchestras, and this profoundly affected the development of incidental music. Composers of the Romantic tradition: Beethoven, Mendelssohn, Berlioz or Grieg, were frequently attracted to the prospect of writing for large orchestral forces and by the ideas contained in poetic drama, including Shakespeare. Their 'incidental' music, such as Beethoven's score for Goethe's *Egmont* or Mendelssohn's music for

A Midsummer Night's Dream, later achieved lasting fame in the concert hall but may well have been inappropriate as an accompaniment to theatrical action. A particularly striking example of such a mismatch is Edvard Grieg's score for Ibsen's verse play *Peer Gynt*. For Norway's most celebrated dramatist and composer to combine on a project would seem to be an ideal situation, but in fact, although Ibsen probably owed the initial performance success of his verse drama (which he had never originally intended to be staged) to Grieg's music, he nevertheless found the music to be a great disappointment. It is possible to consider why this was the case by comparing the demands of the **text** with the surviving music. Grieg's music has, of course, become a classic concert item, but the survival of so many pieces of incidental music by 'great' composers as concert items probably tells us a good deal about the actual needs of theatre music. The performance of incidental music in the form of orchestral 'suites' tends, however, to obscure some of its original intention. In a recent imaginative reconstruction of a nineteenth-century production of Shakespeare's *A Midsummer Night' Dream*, for example, actors, audiences and critics were surprised to hear some of Mendelssohn's famous music being played at the same time as the **text** was spoken. This 'underscoring', which has become familiar to us through film, has, perhaps, become less common in the contemporary theatre. The practice of underscoring **dialogue** is still widely used in the Musical: characters will frequently speak over music before moving into a song. In the nineteenth century, particularly, music was also used to underscore **action**, indeed, as the entry on **melodrama** indicates, this popular form of entertainment actually means 'music drama'. Again, we are now more likely to have become aware of this factor through its survival into early silent film where the entrance of a villain or the desperate plight of a heroine is accompanied by appropriate music on a piano. 'Hurry' music is only one form of underscoring that both heightens tension and emotion: the difference between **dialogue** spoken over music or spoken over silence is very considerable as is the difference between **actions** undertaken to the accompaniment of music or without it. The decision to use music adds a layer of performance which requires careful integration of several art forms.

Ironically, it is often composers little known outside the theatre, such as Norman O'Neill (1875–1934), who have produced the most effective and easily integrated music for plays. London theatres still contain collections of huge quantities of incidental music, often in manuscript form, from productions that, like the music, were ephemeral and functional. It is an area of research that has been considerably neglected.

I began this section by suggesting that a precise definition of 'incidental' music is difficult. One recent definition suggests that 'it is specifically written, but does not form an integral part of the play' (*Cassell Companion to Drama*). Clearly, any play *can* be produced without music, even if it is specified. Directors also have the power to select precisely which music they use. What, then, are we to make of the opening **stage directions** of Arthur Miller's twentieth-century classic *Death of a Salesman*: 'A melody is heard, played upon a flute. It is small and fine, telling of grass and trees and the horizon. The curtain rises'? Throughout the play this flute plays at key moments. The precise melody is never specified, and thus becomes a major directorial decision, but, certainly, this 'incidental' music would appear to be absolutely integral to the action. We can find pointers to the nature of this use of music if we look at the idea of **melodrama**, literally, 'music drama'. The use of music as a permanent, ongoing accompaniment to the action of plays served to heighten the emotional impact and led, through its transfer through the early 'silent' films, to the current major use of 'incidental' music in the cinema. Considerable degrees of ignorance and resistance have characterised many attempts to integrate music and drama in genres other than opera or the Musical. Creating music that serves a text demands a thorough understanding and appreciation of that text and an awareness of the possibility of creating an inter-textual **dialogue** through music. Miller's play is one of several modern pieces that make that demand.

For a good example of research into a specialised area of theatre music, see Mary Chan, *Music in the Theatre of Ben Jonson* (1980). For more information on Renaissance ideas on music, see Thomas More, *The Planets Within* (1980). For a discussion of music in the theatre, see Peter Mudford, *Making Theatre: From Text to Performance* (2000).

See also **melodrama.**

In the moment

It would be difficult to imagine a more subtle concept than that of an actor's being 'in the moment', but it is a term that is now widely used with and by students of drama as an aspect of their practical work. We have seen (see **beats**) that, particularly in the United States, acting and drama students are encouraged to analyse a **text** in preparation for performance and that the 'moment' is the smallest **unit** for consideration. Even though a 'moment' is a very small element something significant takes place within it and it is the accumulation of such moments of drama that creates tensions and shapes of **beats** and **scenes.**

The ability to be totally engaged by and focused upon what is happening in a moment of **action** is one of the characteristics of a successful actor, and its achievement will include complete mastery of the **text** and **subtext** and an intensive focus of **energy.** Most students and audiences will be able to recognise when an actor is 'in the moment' but may have some difficulty in defining the concept.

Mask

The mask is a covering for the face, worn as a separate solid appendage or as **make-up**. It is now profoundly connected with theories of the personality and, because drama is also deeply concerned with ideas of '**character**', it is a central concept and major aspect of practice in the theatre. The opposing masks of **tragedy** and **comedy** have become popular emblems for drama. Concepts of the 'persona' developed by the Swiss psychiatrist Carl Gustav Jung (1875–1961) drew on the idea that all humans wear 'masks' as aspects of their behaviour, but the entire modernist concern with the fragmentation of the self, which is explored by such dramatists as Pirandello (1867–1936), often finds expression in the image of the mask. Erwin Goffman, famous for his idea of **frame analysis**, often portrays everyday behaviour as if it is characterised by duplicity and façades, thus making it almost impossible to recognise an individual's true identity and 'self'. Social psychologists now tend to demonstrate that our social selves are often more masks than selves, reminding us that the original word 'persona' meant a mask initially worn by participants and probably representing a deity in the Eleusian 'Mysteries' and subsequently in the Greek theatre.

Masks were in use in rituals before the beginnings of drama as we understand it and remain a central feature of celebratory performance events. Early use appears to have been connected with hunting, and both Greek vases and medieval illustrations show dancers in animal masks. Masks are of particular interest in the study of performance because they are a recurring feature in the continuum from public ceremony and **ritual** to more private acts of theatre. Their transforming power has associations with **impersonation** and **shamanism** and their application has been explored in attempts to reinvigorate Western theatre through the use of ancient Oriental forms.

Masks have very specific textures, forms, size and colour and they often function as symbols, projecting a meaning through a number of associations that take us beneath the surface appearance to another set of meanings. In ceremonies such as the Notting Hill Carnival, the Mardi Gras or Chinese festivals, masks are 'culturally encoded' with meanings specific to the event and its origin. They function in a number of multi-faceted ways: they are 'multi-vocal' (speaking in many voices), 'multi-valent' (simultaneously conveying different meanings) and 'polysemus' (open-ended and subject to many interpretations). Often, the wearing of masks in a ritual will enable a group to suppress individual identity in favour of a system of shared beliefs.

It is not difficult to see why the mask was an essential feature of theatre in Ancient Greece: theatres were vast and masks project a visual image in a large space, enhancing the role of the performer, enlarging the dimensions of the performance and exaggerating its qualities. Character types can be quickly established and vocal projection through the mouthpiece may be supported. Use of these features passed on to the Roman theatre, with its passion for spectacle; the **commedia dell'arte** employed masks to identify its stock characters, but by the time of Shakespeare masks were generally used as a mode of disguise. With the rise of humanism and a resultant increasing interest in the idea of **naturalism**, the mask became a less popular device in Western drama because it inhibited individual expression. The mask tends to assign formal and stereotyped roles and can reflect rigid attitudes and formal structures of society. The powerful economic and social changes that swept away the feudal system of Europe and aspects of medieval thought led to more complex views of human possibility and, as Terry Hodgson puts it, 'The inflexible mask was then removed to reveal the flexible human countenance' (*The Batsford Dictionary of Drama*, 1988).

The continuing use of masks in such forms as the *Noh* and *Kabuki* drama of Japan led to their reintroduction to the West by such writers as W. B. Yeats (1864–1939) and Bertolt Brecht. Yeats was one of a group of writers advocating a return to the idea of ritual in the theatre and the use of verse as the main form of **theatre language**. Working in small, private theatres, he and his colleagues introduced performance ideas drawn from the *Noh* plays, including the ritual designation of the space by the unfurling of a cloth. In his *Plays for Dancers*, the main figures are masked in order to acquire an alternative personality. By contrast, Brecht used masks as a means of showing people acting out stereotypical social roles. In his play *The Good Person of Setzuan* (1938–41), the main character sometimes wears a mask in order to become another character: forced into the ruthless and inhuman other role by her economic situation. As inner impulse and outer pressure gain ascendancy the mask is discarded or donned, accordingly.

Although masks have always been in use in the theatre, they came to be used in actor training in more recent times when Jacques Copeau began his work at the Vieux Colombier in Paris in the 1920s. Michel Saint-Denis, who worked with Copeau, wrote:

> To us, a mask was a temporary instrument which we offered to the curiosity of the young actor, in the hope that it might help his concentration, strengthen his inner feelings, diminish his self-consciousness and help him to develop his powers of outward expression. (*Theatre: The Rediscovery of Style*, 1960, p. 103)

Geraldine Page, who worked with masks as a part of her training, sums up the impact of this work:

> Sometimes the character comes out in ways which surprise me. ... If I do something, and a bell rings somewhere in me, and it feels right, I have a tendency to repeat what I did and find other pieces that fit in with it. ... When you take the character and use the character, you wreck the fabric of the play, but you can be in control of the character without the character taking over. When the character uses you, that's when you're really cooking. You know you're in complete control, yet you get the feeling that you didn't do it. You have this beautiful feeling that you can't ruin it. (Quoted in Hayman, *Techniques of Acting*, 1969, pp. 46–7)

See also **character** *and* **ritual**.

Mimesis

'Mimesis' is best translated from the Greek as *imitation* (in the sense of re-presentation) and forms one of the central concepts for discourse on the Arts, including drama. It is first found as an aesthetic consideration in the writings of the fourth-century BC philosopher Plato. He tended to take a fairly hostile view of performance and it is worth spending some time considering his premise. Describing the emergence of the art of dance, which for Plato seems to have been almost synonymous with acting, he wrote: 'That is why, when representation [mimesis] of what was being spoken first came into being, it produced the whole art of dancing' (*LAWS VII*, 815e–16a). For Plato, the concrete world that we perceive through our senses is not the 'real' world. The 'real' world is a world of ideas and 'ideal forms' created by some Divine force, and what we perceive as 'real' is actually a pale imitation of that higher world. That *imitation* or 'mimesis' is fundamental to existence as we experience it. It could also be argued that, at a personal level, we reflect the cosmic model by having a conceptual world that enables us to make judgements on the perceptual, particularly if we believe that, by some mystery, we are part of the supreme Consciousness we call God.

When it came to discussing artistic creativity, Plato embraced the almost universal belief of the Ancient world that the function of art was to imitate Nature, and therefore argued that, because what we perceive as 'nature' is already an imitation of the 'real' world of perfect forms, artistic creation is a double imitation. The creative artist is therefore twice removed from the truth. In Plato's view then, **actors** are engaging in a morally dangerous activity by deviating from their own personality in order to present, for example, bad men and women. On the basis of this assertion, Plato excluded actors, poets and dramatists from his ideal Republic!

Aristotle refined his master Plato's concept of 'mimesis' to embrace the issues of imitation we have already encountered as a facet of **action** and **impersonation**. He maintained that drama came to exist when **ritual**, in which participants such as priests or dancers were involved in presentation of ideas in symbolic **gestures**, moved towards the representation of characters and actions through the process of mimesis. The process of theatre for Aristotle was, to adapt a view of Eric Bentley: 'A impersonates B while C accepts the pretence', and he maintained that mimesis was produced by 'rhythm, language and harmony, singly or combined'. The organisation of these elements became an essential feature of performance and Aristotle referred to this as their being schematised: '... dances imitate character, feeling and action by means of schematised rhythms' (*POETICS*, 1447a). The criterion by which performance should be judged was 'plausibility', a 'plausible impossibility' being preferable to an improbable possibility. You may wish to consider whether this remains the case. For Aristotle, however, mimesis implied more than individual performance: it extended to the entire drama, which, he maintained, should reflect the movement and mutability of life.

The emphasis in meaning of mimesis shifted with neo-classical writers, who saw it as a description of imitating classical art forms, including drama. The function of art became the mimesis of art. It was only with the more socially and politically conscious drama and literature of the eighteenth and nineteenth centuries that there was a re-emergence of the concept of mimesis as an accurate imitation of life. We can see this particularly in the development of a new and more serious form of comedy in the latter part of the eighteenth century. The German dramatist Gotthold Lessing (see **alienation**) stated that it was the misfortunes of those whose circumstances most resembled those of the **audience** that would make the deepest impression. An intellectual climate emerged in which the capacity to empathise with the plight of fellow human beings regardless of their social status became a measure of one's humanity and, in the arts, this led to a more realistic representation of reality. Erich Auerbach, in his book *Mimesis: The Representation of Reality in Western Literature* (1946), speaks of a movement in literature and drama in which familiar events of ordinary life are treated 'seriously and problematically', and this is seen in such plays as George Lillo's *The London Merchant* (1731). The French novelist Stendhal (1788–1842) insisted that the purpose of the novel was the mimesis of life, and a similar concern shaped the early experiments in **naturalism** in the theatre, with their concentration on surface human behaviour, verisimilitude of settings and natural speech. The plays of T. W. Robertson (1829–71) established a fashion and taste for realistic scenery, plausible speech and credible plot-lines in the English theatre that came close to Aristotle's concept of mimesis, but it was precisely that attention to realistic detail that led to more recent scepticism towards the idea.

For Antonin Artaud (1896–1948) (see **Theatre of Cruelty**), the theatre 'is not mimesis of an event, but the event itself, not a representation of life but a way of living'. In many forms of modern theatre the underlying belief is that art creates its own reality; such reality may well be achieved by deliberate distortion, as in the grossly non-realistic, puppet-inspired drama of Alfred Jarry's *Ubu Roi* (1896), or Edward Gordon Craig's concept of the *Ubermarionette*, or in theatrical **surrealism**. By contrast, the **Epic Theatre** of Brecht and those who have used his techniques is concerned with the representation of the material world, not, as in Aristotle's terms, as a mimesis of the patterns of natural life, but as a representation of the social and political forces that shape that life.

The concept of 'mimesis' raises many questions for the student of drama and performance. We must decide whether drama is essentially an imitative process, and if so, how this is best achieved; or if drama creates its own world, what sort of world it is. If 'imitation' is the essence of drama, what should it be imitating and how? Furthermore, if we are concerned with imitating 'reality', do we mean more than 'surface' reality? Is mimesis what we mean by 'truth' in performance and, if so, what are we to make of forms of drama that seek to rediscover the symbolic acts of ritual, or create a communion with the audience? How do we interpret 'events', 'Happenings' or experimental physical and improvisatory theatre forms?

See also **impersonation**; **improvisation** *and* **naturalism**.

Motivation

The concept of 'motivation' has tended to dominate the naturalistic form of theatre and has profound implications for the ideas of **action** and **character**. It is the particulars of the motivation that become the issue, especially if we view plays as microcosmic parables of human behaviour. It may be valid to superimpose a social interactionist model on many of the artistic practices of the twentieth and twenty-first centuries, but what becomes apparent is that the theorists select their own interpretations of the dominant motivating factors in human existence.

The predominance of Stanislavsky's acting theories in the West has resulted in there being an emphasis on a *behavioural* interpretation of human affairs that stresses the importance of the past as a determining factor of our current behaviour. The American *Method* school and much improvisational theatre, both claiming roots in Stanislavsky's work, are associated with characters' introspections and those past experiences that have shaped their personalities and motivated their conduct. Each character carries around, as it were, a rag-bag of formative experiences. It is only comparatively recently that there has been a shift away from this idea towards a *cybernetic* model of behaviour, in which people are seen to modify their behaviour in response to constant feedback in an attempt to achieve their goals. Thus the 'Method' actor plays motivation and the 'cybernetic' actor plays intentions.

Robert Cohen (*Acting Power*, 1978, pp. 33–4) provides an excellent analogy of the difference between these two approaches to acting. He describes a situation in which a man is running towards a hut, chased by a bear. The 'motivational' interpretation is that the man is being caused to run by the bear, but the 'intentional' interpretation is that the man is running to safety. The implication is that if the man thinks more about the bear than the safety he may not get there. Thus, the **actor** had better determine, and follow, a course of action in line with a particular goal. The fact that behaviour is tactical or strategic obliges an actor to consider speech and physical action as something that must be carefully monitored in order to achieve a particular goal, and that must be modified in the light of success or failure. Other **characters** in the drama may become obstacles or resources in the drive towards particular ends and they may have to be bullied, cajoled or manipulated in some other way to enable the actor to achieve satisfaction for his or her character.

Emotion may be the outcome of some of a character's strategies and goals and this accords with Stanislavsky's idea that emotion should stem from a detailed rediscovery, through our own experience, of the path that leads to the expression of emotion. He wrote:

> Never seek to be jealous, or to make love, or to suffer for its own sake. All such feelings are the result of something that has gone before. Of the thing that goes before you should think as hard as you can. As for the result, it will produce itself. (*An Actor Prepares*, p. 41)

In all cases, emotion will be the logical outcome of a sequence of events, and through identification with these events the actor can find the appropriate presentation of emotion.

A character's motivation may well involve the employment of tactical emotion. In real life, people play games displaying emotions that can be 'read' and so that the 'reader' might act in a particular way. So in a play, for example,one character wants to make the another character feel pity and therefore will start to weep. An interactionist chain has been initiated: The first **character** cries for pity, the second gives pity, the first takes advantage of that pity and blames the second for what has happened, the second character defends him or her self by getting angry and the first leaves home ... which was precisely the long-term motivation and objective for which s/he needed justification.

If actors use the concept of motivation they have to ask 'why' a character is doing something, if they use the idea of 'intention' they must also ask 'what for?' If actors use the idea of strategy they have to examine the strategy and say what it is, especially in the light of feedback from interacting characters. Fundamental to all these questions is the belief that people want things and that their patterns of behaviour are a product of these wants. In terms of acting theory this means that actors draw on their own experiences and transpose this understanding to their fictional character.

If we consider the concepts of motivation and intention in relation to an entire play, we find that these constitute the most commonly accepted character indicator. This approach comes from Stanislavsky's idea of the 'super-objective', which he used to describe the logic of a character's behaviour as a causal pattern related to principles and goals. The idea is that each character in a play has a long-term objective that gives coherence to the behaviour displayed. A variety of obstacles will inhibit the achievement of the goals: these will include the goals of the other characters, the material world, the character's own nature and other **given circumstances**. Thus, the character is forced to adopt strategies to help overcome or circumvent the obstacles and these strategies will involve short-term objectives designed to over-come specific blocks on the path to the long-term 'super-objective'.

It is not necessarily implied that the character will achieve any of the objectives; indeed, he or she may well employ increasingly hopeless tactics to achieve an increasingly unattainable goal.

Whilst the concept of a long-term objective is fairly easy to grasp, the playing of short-term intentions or motivation requires the actor to be absolutely clear as to why his or her character is behaving in a cer-tain way. However, unlike 'real' people, the actor has the gift of fore-sight to shape the behaviour of a fictional character. In studying a play as a whole it is possible to map out the motivation of characters, and this process may involve allowing events from later in a play's action to inform the understanding of events towards the start of the play, in which a character's motivation may seem unclear or even incompre-hensible.

See also **action; character** *and* **naturalism.**

Naturalism

The concept of 'naturalism' underpins many of the ideas considered in this chapter and this is as good a reason as any for its inclusion here rather than in the chapter on 'Production Modes', where one might expect to find it. In fact, it would be perfectly possible to make a case for its inclusion in any of the main chapters and this merely illustrates the integrated nature and inter-relatedness that characterise what we call 'drama'. The main reason for the inclusion of naturalism at this point is that, although 'Naturalism' was a recognised nineteenth-century movement in the Arts, as far as drama is concerned it remains a dead concept unless some performative process is involved.

Naturalism in the theatre arose through the combination of a desire to create natural illusions in the Romantic dramas of the mid- to late nineteenth century and the advances in theatre technology that made this possible. We owe a great deal to the advances introduced by Georg, Duke of Saxe-Meiningen, who turned his interests towards the theatre in the late 1860s. He was particularly concerned with the pictorial and historical accuracy of his productions, intent on creating the illusion of reality in the physical groupings of his actors and the environment they inhabited, and the suggestion of life continuing beyond the frame of the stage. As the dramaturg remarks in Brecht's *Messingkauf Dialogues* (p. 22), 'Naturalist performances gave one the *illusion* of being at a real place.' This theatre of *imitation* led inevitably to a more natural style of acting as performers responded to their environment, and Stanislavsky commented that members of the Meiningen company were able to interact with each other rather than focus on the **audience**. Strindberg's Preface to *Miss Julie* explored this issue in relation to the predominant acting styles of the late nineteenth century, and in 1885 W. S. Gilbert (always anxious to satirise the latest artistic fashions) has one of his characters in *The Mikado* suggest that he is indulging in 'merely corroborative detail intended to give artistic verisimilitude to an otherwise bald and unconvincing narrative'.

In his discussion of Naturalism in the *Messingkauf Dialogues*, Brecht refers to Hauptmann, Tolstoy, Strindberg and Ibsen as the dramatists who had written 'naturalistic plays': to this we would need to add Chekhov as another dramatist who saw and responded to the possibilities offered by a theatre that could create the illusion of reality. Indeed, it was Stanislavsky's deployment of detail that bathed his actors in an atmosphere evoking the 'real' world, in his production of Chekhov's *The Seagull* at the Moscow Art Theatre in 1898, that so effectively demonstrated the potential of representing on stage the interaction between people and the spaces they inhabit. (This production is particularly well documented and makes a fascinating study.) In doing this he was influenced by contemporary developments in science, literature and the visual arts that stressed the effects of the environment on human behaviour. The Naturalist school of writers had enthusiastically embraced Darwin's theories of determinism introduced in *The Origin of Species* and sought to create environments in their plays that would explain and determine their characters' actions.

The settings created by Stanislavky's designer, Simov, were variations on the basic pattern of the '**box set**' that had been in use since the early years of the century. By joining together a series of canvas 'flats' and inserting panels containing doors, windows, fireplaces and other solid pieces, it had become possible to create a very accurate reconstruction of an interior. In this way, as a close examination of the stage directions of any play by Ibsen will show, the environment could convey a great deal of information about the tastes, economic condition and status of the characters. Furthermore, the box set encloses the actor within its walls with the assumption that there is an imaginary '**fourth wall**' on the side where the audience is placed. The characters are thus compelled to behave 'as if' they are inhabiting this 'real' space. We can see that this makes a totally different demand from, say, the wings and flats of Restoration theatre. This 'fourth wall' was so important to the performance style demanded by the director André Antoine (1858–1943) at the 'Théâtre Libre' in Paris in the 1880s, that he erected a fourth wall for rehearsals and only removed it for performances, so that the behaviour of the actors was as naturalistic as possible (see Chapter 4).

As is shown in the section on **acting style** (see also **actor/acting, mimesis**), there appears to have been a constant search for a more 'naturalistic' style of acting. Hamlet's advice to the players looks to insist on a more 'natural' style than the one it seeks to replace; Strindberg longed for actors who would turn their backs to the audience, Stanislavsky sought inner truth based on psychological understanding of a character's motivation. However, what gave a unique and innovative quality to the plays of the 'Naturalist' school was the attempt to create a stage language that approximated as nearly as possible to patterns and vocabulary of everyday speech, and to put those words in the mouths of characters who closely resembled in every detail the real people of everyday life. It is possible to argue that many of these qualities exist, for example, in the plays of Arthur Miller or Harold Pinter.

You are strongly advised to consult Edward Braun's excellent *The Director and the Stage* (1982), which is still, probably, the best guide to the work of directors and playwrights in the formative periods of naturalism, and to discuss the extent to which naturalism has remained the dominant mode in contemporary drama.

See also **action; character** *and* **motivation.**

Performance research

One of the most significant developments in the study of drama in recent years has been the acknowledgement by academic institutions that engagement in the practical process of creating performance constitutes a form of research. We owe much of the development of the concept of practical work in drama as 'research' to the Polish theatre director Jerzy Grotowski. He founded his 'Theatre Laboratory' in Opole in 1959 and it moved to Wroclaw in 1965, eventually being known as an 'Institute for Research into Acting'. Heavily influenced by Grotowski, the British director Peter Brook left the Royal Shakespeare Company in 1970 to establish his International Centre for Theatre Research, in Paris. Such developments led to the creation of the Centre for Performance Research in Wales (which has maintained many links with Polish theatre practice), and such projects as Practice as Research in Performance (PARIP) at the University of Bristol. A gradual acceptance of the validity of practical study in drama has also been reflected in academic publications such as the Text and Performance series from Macmillan or the Plays in Performance editions from the Bristol Classical Press, both of which replace the primacy of studying **texts** with a more integrated approach to the creation of theatre.

To some extent the basis of this work has always been understood by theatre practitioners but its introduction into academic discourse has raised many questions concerning methodology and validity. The ephemeral nature of drama and performance ensures that any form of documentation that aims to capture the essence of the process is problematic. Rehearsal diaries and reflective journals provide some means of analysing the work and there have been impressive published examples illustrating the work of leading directors, for example, much of Peter Brook's work has been carefully documented by those who worked with him. David Williams's *Peter Brook: A Theatrical Casebook* (1988) provides a detailed account of Brook's practice, and David Selbourne's *The Making of a Midsummer Night's Dream* (1982) documents what remains Brook's most famous and, possibly, most influential production. However, with the process of '**devising**' and the practical exploration of various texts becoming a recognised aspect of research, the urgency of finding more efficient forms of documentation using recent developments in sound, video, DVD and CD-ROM alongside written text has led to much discussion and experimentation. The problem is that the documentation may be so sophisticated that it becomes a performance itself.

Debate, therefore, centres around the complex layering of options offered by the potential of a variety of texts. As there is no equivalence between live practice and its documentation, there needs to be some relationship between the two modes if research is to carry weight and validity. A research document must, obviously, have its own autonomy if it is to be more than a supplement to the practice yet it is the evaluation of that practice that demonstrates how ideas and concepts have been tested, theories and proposals postulated and outcomes analysed.

See also **devising** *and* **Poor Theatre.**

Performative

Students and other readers may well feel entitled to some sense of confusion over the term and concept 'performative' because its definition and usage have become somewhat slippery. The concept originated in the field of Communication Studies in 1955 when the linguistics expert John Austin coined the use of the adjective 'performative' to point out that words are not solely used for describing things but also for doing things and effecting action and change. However, the term has since been used to describe and define a variety of activities and **texts** that have the qualities and potential for performance. Indeed, such reflective practitioners as Baz Kershaw (2007) have suggested that we, in the West, now live in a 'performative society' in which many aspects of our political, commercial, cultural and communal lives are manipulated and shaped by various kinds of 'performance.'

There would probably now be a consensus of opinion that a performative event demanded four components: a performer, a **text**, an **audience** and a context. The performer is a person whose expressive instrument is their own body; their 'performance' may be entirely unrehearsed and unscripted (see **cultural performance**) as in the telling of a joke or polished and prepared like a public reading. The **text** performed covers a similar range of formally structured and informal possibilities ranging from a poem, an extract from a written work or play to an oral text such as a remembered folk-tale, personal anecdote or saying. The key quality is that the text is repeatable in more or less the same form. As Grotowski discovered in his experiments with **paratheatre**, dispensing with an audience means dispensing with the concept of performance (see **Poor Theatre, paratheatre**) so an audience is essential if an event is said to be performative. Again, this may take many forms and may include apparently spontaneous gatherings to paying audiences and spectators at a sporting or theatrical event. To enable that audience to make meanings, however, there must be a context and this will be established by the attitudes and expectations brought by the audience together with the social, historical and aesthetic situations, ideas and **conventions** that influence the ways in which the audience interprets and understands what they see and hear.

Ideas of the 'performative society are explored in Baz Kershaw's *Theatre Ecologies: Environment and Performance Events* (2007) and in Helen Nicholson's *Theatre and Education* (2009).

Personification

This concept is often used in actor training and is based on two apparently opposite ideas. First, it derives from a term which suggests that plants, animals or natural forces have human characteristics and, second, from an actor's ability to represent such things on stage. In the first instance the process involves the non-human becoming humanized and in the second case the human actor pretends to be non-human. These activities exploit the dilemma of mankind's relationship with the natural world and suggest that drama may well have had its origins in rituals where humans costumed themselves as animals, or represented natural forces. In Medieval drama, such qualities as 'beauty,' 'strength', truth' or 'knowledge' were personified and 'vice figures' and angels personified ideas of evil and good emanating from the non-material world. In more recent drama and in actor training, the concept of personification has come to suggest the acquisition of characteristics that derive from any source other than the actor's own psyche. In such cases, as in 'comic' personification, there are elements of an attempt to conceal 'real' identity. This, of course, is part of the actor's perpetual paradox because the 'real' identity of the actor may be at odds with the character they are seeking to represent (see **impersonation)**

Ritual

It is frequently asserted that drama as we understand it had its origins in pagan or Christian ritual. However, in order to develop this argument, we need to understand the nature of ritual itself. Some form of ritual appears to permeate all societies and all ages within those societies and its study has attracted the attention of psychologists, sociologists, anthropologists and students of performance. The links between ritual and performance are considerable and it is generally agreed that there is a continuum which begins with individual behaviour, some of which may have ritual qualities, and which culminates in the 'high art' of the theatre of plays, opera and ballet.

As we have seen in our consideration of **character**, **motivation** and **impersonation**, human conduct frequently involves elements of performance and these private performances may well take on a ritual quality in the more sophisticated forms of play in childhood and in repetitive behaviour in adults. Once we have developed a habit of doing the same thing at the same time every week or even every day, we establish ritual patterns, which grow out of necessity but are shaped to make us feel comfortable and secure. Because of the feelings generated by such private rituals, the physical acts or speech acts take on an added layer of meaning: they may enhance our self-esteem, give us a sense of control, or enable us to shape time as we wish.

Societies are often built around social rituals, which have also grown out of socio-economic conditions and the nature of relationships. In Britain, for example, the 'Sunday Lunch' ritual, that once signalled the gathering of an entire family around the one substantial meal of meat that could be afforded in any week, has now given way to the 'Sunday Lunch in the pub' ritual, which still celebrates a sense of relaxed leisure but is more likely to involve fewer family members and to be more of a statement of being able to afford to 'eat out' and of the determination not to be bothered with the washing up or other pressing domestic issues in an increasingly pressured lifestyle. The fact that a particular menu is associated with this idea gives it an added sense of ritual: rituals involving special meals, often of deep significance, are common to many cultures. We can see, however, that rituals must adapt in order to have meaning in changing situations.

Some rituals do not translate across cultures, even if languages appear to. In some Middle Eastern societies, for example, it is common for visits to other people's homes to be frequently punctuated by a question-and-answer ritual which translates into English as 'How are you?' 'Very well, thank you'. In any Western gathering such constant repetition of this question and answer during a brief visit would seem patently absurd; however, not only has the literal translation failed to capture the spirit of the ritual, but also, in the *original* language, the words are simply signs that encode deeper meanings of friendship and mutual concern. You will no doubt be able to think of examples from your own experience of where words have now acquired a ritual rather than a literal function.

Social rituals are concerned with shared values and predictable and ordered patterns of behaviour. Some may remain within the confines of small groups and families but others may be more public. In such cases, rituals may take on more of the characteristics of performance. Many sexually driven rituals, such as attending a night-club, will involve special costumes, darkened rooms with evocative lighting, loud music, and dancing that includes a good deal of sexual display. In many primitive societies, such events would include a state of near-ecstasy in the participants and, possibly, the wearing of **masks** and elements of **shamanism**. Many religious traditions have used similar patterns of behaviour to express some sense of communion with the transcendent. Rituals have significance for the participants alone, except when they have evolved into ceremonies: you may wish to challenge this view but let us explore the more developed forms of social and cultural ritual a little further before we look at the concept of a ceremony.

A very familiar form of ritual is the frequently repeated Christian celebration of the Mass, or Communion. This ritual, commemorating the death of Christ through the communal eating of bread and drinking of wine, has caused huge controversy between different branches of the Church. Some see it as having purely symbolic meaning through a simple re-enactment of the 'Last Supper'; others consider that a literal transformation of the elements of bread and wine takes place; and yet others contend that, in some mysterious way, the ritual words, clothes and gestures ensure the presence of Christ and blessing of God. Some regard regular participation as essential, others see it as an option. Whatever view is taken, and whether the physical action includes watching and listening to the carefully developed and choreographed text of the liturgy, or simply sitting in a circle in silence, the ritual is universally felt by Christians to relate to the 'essence' of faith and to contain important elements of 'communion'. It is from the Mass and the services for Easter that medieval European drama is thought to have evolved (see **Mystery Play**); and it is significant that various theatre practitioners, who have sought to restore what they thought to be the essence of theatre, have turned to the concept of communion because they felt that audiences had become spectators, rather than participants in the ritual of theatre itself.

We can see that the clear assignment of roles, the wearing of costumes, the development of **text**, the symbolic acts, the designation of a special space, the use of the body and voice as expressive media, the intentions to perform, the shared agreements as to time and conduct, the willing use of the imagination, the use of music and the multi-layered meanings constructed by the participants are all features of drama.

There are, however, significant rituals that involve cultural rather than theatrical performance. These are ceremonies that allow a role for passive, or occasionally active, spectators: they, too, may involve considerable elements of display and many of the costumes, movements, masks or sounds may have original meanings that are lost. Ceremonies tend to reinforce cultural values, solidify social organisation or even stimulate political action; they also tend to remain rooted in history and the precise significance of some of the words, costumes and actions may well have been lost, even if they remain intrinsic to the ceremony. Many are associated with key moments of transition in life: birth, puberty, adulthood, marriage or death; they are rites of passage, but are ceremonies rather than pure rituals, because they all admit a degree of spectatorship. Initiation into some new state of being, or into membership of a new group, means that the duration of the ceremonial ritual is an 'in between' state: for example, during the marriage service, you are neither 'married' nor 'not married' until the conclusion of the service: you are in a state of transition. This betwixt and between state is known as 'liminal' and the concept of **liminality** has become one of the most frequently employed by students as a means of discussing the process of performance. We can see how this concept relates to theatrical performance, where, for instance, we may feel that the action during the period of the play is neither entirely 'real' nor entirely 'unreal'. We often, in fact, need to discuss precisely what state of being we do inhabit as we experience a ceremony or a play in performance.

Adherents of various faiths and cults have often celebrated their central myths through some kind of ceremonial re-enactment: examples would include the ceremonies related to the Ancient Egyptian dying and resurrecting God/Man, Osiris, and his later Greek equivalent, Dionysus;

the 'Mysteries' of Eleusis celebrating the myth of Demeter and her rescue of Persephone from the Underworld; or the spectacularly theatrical two-day celebrations of Easter that survive to this day on the Greek island of Corfu. In all such cases the sanctity of the subject makes the space for celebration 'sacred' and the role of the priest figure is central. The priest represents the people and through ritual behaviour mediates for them with the deities and symbolically takes on their lives. In Paul Allain's fascinating study of the Suzuki method of actor training, *The Art of Stillness* (2003), he assigns a similar role to the **actor** in a play:

> as self-appointed representatives, the performers play out human concerns and fears. They become partners with the **audience** in a social ritual in a shared 'sacred' space, where the presence of the gods is acknowledged by both parties, however individually these gods are perceived. (p. 5)

Such an approach to understanding the essence of the theatrical process lay at the root of many of Grotowski's ideas of **communion** (see Chapter 3) and the work he undertook during his '**paratheatrical**' period. They also inspired a number of attempts to rediscover and recover the ritual elements of drama that took place in the English-speaking theatre in the early years of the twentieth century. These are worth considering in some detail.

A number of factors appear to have given rise to the movement that we associate with the drama of W. B. Yeats, John Masefield, Gordon Bottomley and T. S. Eliot in the 1920s and 1930s. The first was undoubtedly the appearance of some new translations of Greek drama by Gilbert Murray (1866–1957), the brilliant young Professor of Greek whom G. B. Shaw used as the basis for his character Adolphus Cusins in *Major Barbara*. Although these verse translations would no longer be considered ideal for performance, in their day they attracted the interest of leading actors including Sybil Thorndyke, directors, choreographers, dance specialists and composers by their immediacy and accessibility as working scripts for a genre that had been the preserve of the study and the classroom for many centuries. Of particular interest were the ritual possibilities offered by the **chorus**: Gustav Holst's score for flutes, harp and voices for Euripides' *Alcestis* in Murray's translation remains one of the finest compositions of English theatre music, and the growing interest in choral speaking led to some bold experiments in the new drama schools.

The second factor was the influence of a group of Christian intellectuals that included J. R. R. Tolkein, C. S. Lewis, Dorothy L. Sayers and Charles Williams. Calling themselves 'the Inklings' because they believed that they had at least an inkling of the nature of God, this group had a specialised interest in **allegory** and a deep devotion to the rituals of the Catholic Church, which they viewed as a form of theatre. As a Christian reaction to rationalist materialism, they were part of a general revolt in literature against **naturalism** and **realism**. They, together with T. S. Eliot, W. B. Yeats and the group of poets known as the 'Georgians', argued for a return of verse as the natural mode of expression in **theatre language**, asserting that only verse is capable of handling the complex images and transcendent concepts which are the stuff of drama. (See K. Pickering, *Drama in the Cathedral*, 2001, for a full discussion of these issues.)

One of the major influences on the Georgian poets and dramatists was the publication in 1913 and 1916 of translations of Japanese '*Noh*' plays, by Ezra Pound and Ernest Fenellosa. This historic form of drama, involving complex rituals of performance, had been virtually unknown in the West and provided new perspectives on the use of space and stylised action. In order to experiment with such concepts as the ritual designation of the 'sacred space' for performance by the solemn unfurling of a stage cloth and the formalised verse dialogue, a number of playwrights sought out alternative venues for drama, or, as in the case of Masefield, built their own small, non-commercial theatres with 'open' stage areas or simple raised platforms as in the traditional Japanese theatre.

These movements towards a more ritualistic form of performance were given added impetus by the rediscovery of the power of medieval drama, led by the remarkable William Poel, who in 1901 staged the Morality Play *Everyman* for the first time since Early Tudor times. A succession of Medieval revivals of **Mystery Plays** followed and their flexible verse-forms, multi-focused staging, symbolic action and profound, spiritual insights made a telling impact on those searching for a drama that embraced communion and ritual. A further factor was the search for suitable staging conditions, which led to the use of churches, cathedrals, ruins, platforms, town squares and other 'non-theatrical' spaces for performance that related more closely to communities and enhanced the sense of celebration.

Most of the characteristics I have discussed are encapsulated in T. S. Eliot's remarkable play *Murder in the Cathedral*, written for performance at the Festival in Canterbury Cathedral in 1935, and this play rewards careful study. The 'Interlude' section where the **protagonist** Thomas Becket directly addresses the **audience**, contains the juxtaposition of rejoicing and mourning, celebration and mystery that seems to have its origins in re-enacted myth. We also find the heightened use of language – sometimes choric and incantatory – the stylised and symbolic action, the challenges to the conventions of **Naturalism**, the exploitation of an ancient form of theatre, the notion of communion and shared space and the spirit of festival that have informed many of the subsequent attempts to find a ritual form of drama. You will also encounter discussion of ritual ideas when considering the work of Artaud.

See also **action; actor-audience relationship; chorus; mask, paratheatre** *and* **Theatre of communion.**

Role/role play

The term 'role' now tends to signify the function of a **character** within a drama. Role play is used in a great deal of improvisatory work, including such techniques as **forum theatre** and training, but the original term came from the Ancient Greek and Roman theatre, where an actor's **text** and instructions were given on a parchment wound around a wooden roll. In that sense, the 'role' includes all the lines and actions of an actor, which, taken together, create a specific type (e.g. the villain, the lover). Most plays have both leading and supporting roles and it is the actor's task to build the role into a character, either through some kind of identification, imitation or 'inhabiting' of the part or, as in the case of Brecht, by a process of demonstration (see **alienation**).

The idea that an **actor** can unroll a parchment and adopt the role prescribed has not always characterised approaches to acting. Many actors have preferred to undertake roles that they think suit their own personality or physique, or even reflect their own lives. However, most recent acting demands a return to the Greek ideal even though there is a potential tension between the person of the actor and the role and *persona* (see **mask**) to be adopted. Questions as to the role of the actor in society, or the role of theatre itself (whether as a force for change or the preservation of the status quo), will affect the undertaking and adopting of a role in a play.

The work of Erwin Goffman is discussed in detail in the section on **frame analysis**. Goffman compares much human behaviour to theatre, and a concept of the roles that people play is key to understanding his ideas. Role play has been used as a training and educational technique because it enables trainees and students to make the imaginative leap necessary to explore situations that may emerge in life. In such contexts, 'role' has more of the meaning of 'type' and it is relatively easy to adopt a few typical behavioural characteristics to enable a 'role play' to function. This idea of 'role' is sometimes adopted in the theatre where, initially, the 'role' seems to demand no particular individual features but brings together several traditional properties and behaviours of a certain social class. In this case, the role serves to assist the creation of character because it is an intermediate state between the general **action** of the play and the specific behaviour, **motivation** and characteristics that the **actor** must eventually portray.

Shaman

Much recent discussion of acting has focused on the social dramas of the last hundred and fifty years or so and on the sense of the actor as a 'character' and social negotiator. If, however, we turn to more traditional dramatic forms in primitive cultures the **actor** takes on a quite different role: transcending humanity and becoming 'possessed'. Such possession works on a number of different levels but at its most profound it is the conduct of a shaman using his or her body as a medium for communication between the natural and supernatural worlds. In the theatre it is most associated with the wearing of **masks** and the consequent effect on performance. The role of shaman illustrates the nature of 'possession' behaviour most clearly. D. L. Browman and R. A. Schwarz define the term as referring to 'those persons who mediate relationships between man and the supernatural and intervene in specific cases of misfortune and illness to determine a cause and administer a cure' (Browman and Schwarz, *Spirits, Shamans and Stars*, p. 6).

The process of becoming a shaman is associated with ecstatic experience of trances, dreams and visions and with the direct teaching of shamanistic techniques, language, tribal myths and so on by senior shamans. The experience of an Australian aboriginal shamanistic initiation is described by Lommel:

> At sunset the shaman's soul meets somewhere the shadow of a dead ancestor. The shadow asks the soul whether it shall go with it. The shaman's soul answers yes.... Then they go on together, either at once into the kingdom of the dead or to a place in this world at which the spirits of the dead have gathered. ... The spirits begin to sing and dance.... When the dance is over the spirits release the shaman's soul and his helping spirit brings it back to his body. When the shaman wakes, his experiences with the spirits seem to him like a dream. From now on he thinks of nothing but the dances which he has seen and his soul keeps going back to the spirits to learn more and more about the dances. (Lommel, *Shamanism: The Beginning of Art*, 1967, pp. 138–9)

The association between shamanism and the wearing of masks is very common. The most frequently cited example is that of the Balinese festivals at which the ancestral gods are entertained and honoured. Occasionally at the rituals one of the human subjects will go into a trance and in that state will speak as though he were a god, giving answers to questions which the living put to him.

A comprehensive account of shamanishi use of masks is given by F. E. Williams in his *The Drama of the Orokolo* (1940). Williams describes the *hevehe* ritual cycle of the Elema tribe in New Guinea. This cycle, which takes many years to complete, includes a month-long dance of the masks. Each mask is a spirit with a name; the person wearing the mask is considered to be moved to dance, not by his own will, but by that of the spirit. There is a clear parallel to be drawn between such behaviour and the behaviour in our own society of people with clearly defined roles who have submitted themselves completely to those roles. Film of Nazi rallies, or experience of charismatic politicians or religious leaders, demonstrate how people can allow a mask to take over the responsibility for the logic of their behaviour. Williams notes that in the *hevehe* dances the dancer is aware of himself, but is not in control of his dance. He can thus be described as a conscious medium for his spirit, operating with two distinct kinds of logic. The same seems to be true of our charismatic figures. They can both observe their own charisma and submit to it like a medium.

The most common way for a person to become possessed by random and unsolicited thoughts is through dreaming, but access to this level of consciousness is frequently achieved through meditation or the taking of drugs. Its association with shamanism has been noted by Johnson in his book *Riding the Ox Home* (1982). He quotes the Red Indian shaman Lame Deer:

> We Sioux believe that there is something within us that controls us, something like a second person almost. We call it *nagi*, what other people might call soul, spirit or essence. One can't see it, feel it, or taste it, but that time on the hill ... I know it was inside of me. Then I felt the power surge through me like a flood. (John Fire Lame Deer and Richard Erdoes, *Lame Deer Seeker of Visions*, p. 16, quoted in *Riding the Ox Home*, p. 32)

There is considerable evidence to support the theory that through meditation, drugs or hypnosis people are able to tap deep forces within themselves, reaching a state of consciousness and behaviour more profound and engaging than is common. Whilst some discussion in the study of Theatre has been of the **actor** superimposing upon himself or herself perceived social practices, the possibility also arises of the **actor** being open to forces within the self that will bring about the transcending of his or her normal appearance. It has been argued (see R. Schechner, *Essays on Performance Theory*, and J. Grotowski, *Towards a Poor Theatre*) that it is this level of behaviour which provides the most vital attraction of theatre and that our actors are potentially our *shamans*. Certainly the idea of 'presence' does lead to the possibility of an actor being in a heightened state of being which we can share with him or her and thereby derive vicarious ecstasy.

See also **liminality**.

Soliloquy

When we consider the 'soliloquy' as opposed to the **aside** we have another form of direct address to the audience but, in this case, a much more extended monologue in which the character either is, or believes himself or herself to be, alone. Although there are some soliloquies in English medieval drama (such as some of the agonised contemplations of the best course of action in *Everyman*), the device was brought to perfection at the Rose Theatre by Marlowe and Shakespeare in the late sixteenth-century. The idea of actors standing alone on stage and thinking aloud about themselves was a crucial part of the emergence of the thinking self, which had a profound effect on the English psyche. This new-found liberation enabled people to question the hierarchies and institutions that seemed to deny the supremacy of the individual, and to enquire as to the very meaning of existence itself. Soliloquies such as those in Marlowe's *Dr Faustus* (*c.* 1588), Shakespeare's *Hamlet* or *Macbeth*, or Cyril Tourner's *The Atheist's Tragedy* (*c.*1611) are, in fact, an inner dialogue in which the character engages in moral debate or reasoning. They do, however, require a sense of intimacy with the audience even if that audience's presence is not actually acknowledged in the speaking of the words.

See also **conventions**.

Through line

See **action**.

Upstage

'Upstage' is a good example of a simple descriptive term that has become a concept. Originally, it denoted a position on the 'proscenium' stage (see **theatre form**) near to the rear wall or 'cyclorama'. Thus, a director's instruction to 'move upstage' would be clearly understood. Especially on a raked stage, the 'upstage' position enabled an **actor** to dominate the **action**. All lines could be delivered looking towards the **audience** and the position ensured that an actor could take in the entire scene visually. Once an actor moved upstage, his or her position was stronger than that of anyone else on stage. This may well be part of the intention of a production but, if an actor makes a habit of moving into the upstage position, placing others at a disadvantage and ensuring that they have to turn away from the audience to see the **character** or speak their lines, then the actor who has moved is said to have 'upstaged' them. This term has now become a metaphor for taking attention away from somebody and for ensuring, as in the theatre, that that person has to work harder to gain notice. It is generally considered to be an uncomfortable position to be in and to be the result of selfish behaviour.

Vocalisation

Roland Barthes once described the voice as 'the intimate signature of the actor', and it is the final stage in the communication of a written text to the **audience**. In our consideration of the **actor's** work I have tried to stress the organic nature of the process. The body, intellect and imagination must harmonise in response to the demands of the **text** or **director** in order to achieve communication with an audience. The actor's voice and speech are no exception and must not be thought of as separate from other elements of behaviour. Vocal 'centring' is akin to physical centring and both indicate a deep centre for the imagination and emotions. Muscular tension inhibits voice as well as action and, hence, communication. Emotional inhibition reveals itself vocally as well as physically and 'voice work' often involves a form of 'release'.

Stated very simply, what happens when we speak or 'vocalise' is that an impulse is sent from the motor cortex of the brain, stimulating our body to allow air to enter and leave it. As 'breath' the air plays on the vocal folds, which are situated in the larynx, creating oscillations which, in turn, cause the breath to vibrate. These vibrations are amplified in the resonating cavities of the pharynx, mouth and nose: the resultant sounds are articulated by the lips, teeth and tongue to create words. Additional resonance is achieved through all the hollow areas of the upper body including the chest and skull, and these are accessed through the conduction of sound through the skeleton and through sound waves that set up vibrations between one surface and another. The resonators provide the *tone* of the sound whilst the *pitch* is determined by the rate of the vibrations of the vocal folds (or cords, as they are somewhat confusingly called). There are many books, exercises and approaches concerned with the release of the voice, the increase of breath capacity and control, and achievement of better resonance. Many voice programmes of study now focus on Yoga, Tai Chi or Pilates (see K. Findlay and K. Pickering, *Preparing for your Diploma in Drama and Speech*, 2003) and most actor training is based on the acquisition of a sound breathing technique. This is by no means as recent a development as is often thought. Stanislavsky would not allow his students to use language until they had achieved resonance through humming and 'mooing' exercises.

It is easy for us to overlook the importance of voice to actors in earlier periods. In our concern for 'truth' and **motivation** we tend to concentrate on the **subtext**, but in the nineteenth century a powerful, euphonious elocutionary display was accepted as an integral part of an actor's performance. Critics on both sides of the Atlantic paid primary attention to an actor's voice and rivalled each other in graphic descriptions of vocal achievement. Working from contemporary sources, for example, Bogard, Moody and Meserve (Leech and Craik, *The Revels History of Drama in English*; vol. VII: *American Drama*) state that the actor William Forrest as Richelieu made the theatre walls tremble as he launched an ecclesiastical curse, and that when he played Lear his prayer to nature 'reverberated like a thunder storm'. It was only in the 1880s, however, that the physiology and function of the human voice began to be understood and in the last decade of the nineteenth century in Britain the study of 'elocution' and voice was introduced into the music academies, and a number of the drama schools still operating today were established with their curricula initially based on the 'correct' use of the voice.

Rather than simply remaining an instrument for the speaking of text, the voice has been explored in the modern theatre as having an expressive potential in its own right. Soundscapes created by the voice, singing in various modes, ritual chanting and non-verbal vocalisation are often used as aspects of **Physical Theatre** and as a means of release in the course of **improvisation.** Catherine Weate's comprehensive and accessible book *Classic Voice: Working with Actors on Vocal Style* (2009) provides the most up-to-date and stimulating guide to the use of voice in drama.

See also **chorus** *and* **ritual.**

Further Reading

Philip Auslander (1997) *From Acting to Performance: Essays in Modernism and Postmodernism* (London: Routledge).

Colin Counsell (ed.) (1996) *Signs of Performance: An Introduction to Twentieth-Century Theatre* (London: Routledge).

Peter Mudford (2000) *Making Theatre: From Text to Performance* (London: Athlone Press).

Kenneth Pickering and Mark Woolgar (2009) *Theatre Studies* (Basingstoke: Palgrave Macmillan).

Richard Schechner (2003) *Performance Theory* (London: Routledge).

Carol Simpson-Stern and Bruce Henderson (1993) *Performance: Text and Contexts* (New York: Longman).

Konstantin Stanislavsky (1950) *Stanislavsky on the Art of the Stage*, trans. David Magarshack (London: Faber & Faber).

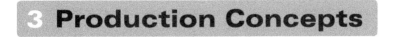 Production Concepts

In this chapter I shall be discussing concepts related to the production of plays, or what is sometimes called 'the realisation of text in performance'. The previous chapter explored some of the performing skills, traditions and requirements of drama but these all take place within the wider framework with which this chapter is concerned.

If you take part in, or attend, the production of any play, it soon becomes obvious that the practicalities are governed by a set of artistic principles. These may be part of an age-old tradition or may derive from the convictions of the director or theatre company. Whereas an attempt to produce a play by Shakespeare in an 'authentic' manner will impinge on decisions about staging, costume and the speaking of lines, a production designed chiefly to prick the consciences of the audience into action will be designed with an entirely different set of issues in mind. However, both productions will be underpinned by a number of basic beliefs about what Shakespeare termed 'the purpose of playing'.

For most of the twentieth century, the fundamental beliefs and concepts that shaped productions usually emanated from the director and it is inevitable that, in seeking to understand these concepts, it is necessary to consider the work of a number of influential directors. Much of the terminology and 'theory' of the modern stage comes from a relatively small number of twentieth-century directors or their disciples. This is mainly because such figures as Stanislavsky, Brecht, Grotowski or Brook gathered round themselves a group of actors who were anxious to embrace their principles. Ironically, perhaps, it was this growth of an 'ensemble' approach to acting that eventually led to a more 'actor-driven' way of working, so that the twenty-first century seems to belong to the empowered performer rather than to the prescriptive director.

There is considerable emphasis on the modern theatre in this chapter because its legacy in production modes is so diverse, and possibly indelible. However, many of the concepts embraced by directors and actors have their origins in an attempt to rediscover historic forms and approaches. Apart from the conscious attempt to apply the principles of Aristotle in classical dramaturgy, there were few, if any, manifestos or statements of key theoretical concepts of production prior to the twentieth century. To some extent, this is a reflection of the way in which the theatre of the past has actually worked. In the Elizabethan and Jacobean theatre of London, for example, the insatiable appetite of a relatively small population for new plays led to an astonishing level of productivity among playwrights. For theatre companies the overriding concern was to cater for popular taste in subject matter and performance style. By the late seventeenth and eighteenth centuries theatres were producing several different programmes in a week, and leading actors were committing upward of eighty roles to memory. Taste for spectacle and pictorial decoration demanded new inventions and new technologies. In all this 'production' there was little time to articulate, let alone write down and publish, a 'theory' of performance.

Those visionaries who have shaped the modern theatre ensured that there has probably never been a time when so great a variety of production modes have co-existed, and students should be aware that the range of options available to them is huge. This chapter should help you to consider, and take part in, the debates and concepts that dictate the way a production takes shape. That process is likely to be affected by philosophical, socio-political and aesthetic factors and a personal involvement in the process as practitioner or spectator should challenge you to make your own personal investigation into the rationale of a production.

Agit/Prop

This term is used to describe drama that aims to change an **audience**'s ideological viewpoint through theatrical 'agitation' and 'propaganda'. It is derived from the Department of Agitation and Propaganda established as part of the Central Committee Secretariat of the Communist Party in the Soviet Union in 1920. This department created 'consciousness-raising' 'Blue Blouse' theatre troupes to take information and entertainment into the countryside. Using a combination of Music Hall techniques, mass declamation from a **chorus** and documentary material in the form of a 'living newspaper', these troupes were emulated widely in Germany between 1924 and 1937 and may well have influenced the establishment of the Unity Theatre, with its strong Marxist leanings, in Britain in 1936. Techniques usually associated with Brecht and Piscator (see **alienation, Epic Theatre**) have characterised the work of Agit/Prop theatre companies in Britain, the USA and Europe and it would be accurate to describe Brecht's *Lehrstucke* (teaching pieces) as a sophisticated form of Agit/Prop.

In the United States the 'Living Newspaper' was created in 1935 as part of the Federal Theatre Project, and although this is often considered to be the forerunner of **documentary drama** it had many of the characteristics of Agit/Prop. Using many of the techniques developed by Piscator, the project attacked and exposed social injustice and deprivation until it was closed in 1939 for its alleged communist sympathies. However, the influence of the project was considerable and in the 1960s companies like the Bread and Puppet Theatre , the San Francisco Mime Troupe , El Teatro Campesio and the Free Southern Theatre all employed methods associated with Agit/Prop: apparently spontaneous set-up, direct address to the audience, the use of shocking statistics, to press home their message. Towards the end of the 1960s there was also a number of what Brockett (1997) describes as 'guerilla groups' who would mount unscheduled and frequently uninvited performances to provoke any gathering of people into a consideration of some topical and controversial issue.

The greatest single body of work in Agit/Prop, however, emerged in China during and just after the Cultural Revolution of 1965–70. Frequently adapting the form of the so called *Peking Opera* and relying heavily on the amateur contribution of troupes of peasants and factory workers, these plays exhorted an optimistic following of the party line and were presented in such venues as factory canteens and town squares, on raised platforms. The plays celebrated the achievements of industry and agriculture. In style they resembled much of the choric declamation of their earlier Soviet counterparts but they also included circus and operatic skills and the use of children (see Roger Howard, *Contemporary Chinese Theatre*, 1978).

By contrast, in the 1960s and 1970s Britain saw the establishment of several successful small-scale touring companies that visited 'alternative venues', exploring local political issues such as the collapse of industry and the rural economy or the absence of housing, and offering left-wing or Marxist viewpoints. The work of these companies probably now seems hopelessly idealistic and almost naïve in our more cynical age: 'bathed in a Marxist glow' as John Elsom (*Post War British Theatre*, 1976, pp. 151–3) puts it. But the plays were a genuine reflection of the rage and perplexity felt in response to the disintegration of whole industrial areas and the contempt shown by corporations towards the needs and concerns of individuals. The best known of these companies were, probably, Red Ladder (originally known as Agit/Prop Theatre), founded in 1968, and 7:84 founded by John McGrath in 1972, so named because 7 per cent of the then population of the UK owned 84 per cent of the wealth, a political comment in itself. 7:84's *The Cheviot, the Stag and the Black Black Oil* (1973), which was eventually televised, was an eloquent exposure of the disregard by the North Sea oil industry for the rural Scottish community. Other companies, including Pip Simmonds Company, Joint Stock, and Belt and Braces, all worked in similar ways, devising shows and using writers such as Steve Gooch or David Hare to develop scripts that grew out of particular situations, many of them subsequently published by the Pluto Press. The movement away from entirely **devised, documentary** pieces, using clowning, circus skills and other forms of direct attack on the audience, towards a more expansive yet Brechtian and considered style, is exemplified in David Hare's *Fanshen* (1976), developed with Joint Stock and their distinguished director Max Stafford Clark. This play, set in a Chinese village during a period of revolution, documents an historical event but establishes a universal debate on issues of social justice, and played at a number of more 'established' theatre venues.

The funding processes for a plethora of small-scale touring companies motivated by ideology and the general economic and aesthetic climate all changed sufficiently to bring about the demise of the Agit/Prop theatre in Britain. We must not overlook, however, the work of overtly Christian companies like Riding Lights, or the use of theatre as a means of advocating change in attitudes to the environment or to birth control in various parts of the world.

Contemporary, Postmodernist critics tend to be uncomfortable with the concept of Agit/Prop. As an art form it does not encourage layers of meaning to be constructed by the **audience**. It assumes a 'meta-narrative' rather than a random set of behaviours devoid of guiding principles and its purpose is transparently didactic. It is often seen as brief, trite and suitable for **street theatre**. It is assumed to occupy the popular end of the continuum of drama and entertainment but its messages have often been uncomfortable and powerful. The entire issue of **Postmodernism** and political drama is most interestingly discussed in Philip Auslander's book *From Acting to Performance* (1997), especially chapter 6, 'Towards a concept of the Political in Postmodern Theatre'.

See also **Epic Theatre** *and* **political theatre; theatre of testimony; verbatim theatre.**

Communion

See **Theatre of Communion.**

Community theatre/drama

The concept of community theatre or drama is defined somewhat differently on the two sides of the Atlantic. In the United States it is usually taken to mean non-professional drama generated by enthusiasts in a particular community. This activity may include the construction and maintenance of a local playhouse or theatre studio and may well attract and serve as an important outlet for local playwrights. In such community provision, considerable effort must focus on the raising of funds but the operation of local playhouses and amateur companies is often supported by professional theatre practitioners who contribute their time and expertise on a voluntary basis.

Community drama[1] in Europe may take many forms according to the community that is involved and the specific issues that are seen as a focus. One of the most interesting and significant examples of an entire community employing theatre as a means of a powerful collective statement and celebration takes place every four years in the Swiss town of Altdorf. The tradition began in 1898 when the 'people's assembly' of the town decided that they were determined to stage the play *William Tell*, written in 1804 by the neo-classical dramatist Friedrich Schiller. The production of this play, recounting a key event in the history of the Swiss, was seen to be so important that it was decided to build a playhouse for the first performance in the following year. Now, ever since that time, the Tellspielhaus (Tell Playhouse) has seen a new production of the play every four years using local community performers and a professional director. Recent publicity for a new production of the play suggests that it is has been, and continues to be, re-interpreted to respond to the 'spirit of the age' and to the differing expectations of audiences. The competition to play one of the major parts and the involvement of many members of the local population in aspects of the play make this a genuine piece of community theatre. A far better known example is that of the *Passion Play* presented every tenth year in the Bavarian town of Oberammergau since 1634 as a response to the population being spared from the plague. The event, as it now has become, is a major tourist attraction and has also resulted in the construction of a permanent theatre and the use of large numbers of amateur performers under professional direction. Passion Plays are undertaken by many church communities in both the United Kingdom and the United States, including a spectacular televised production at the Crystal Cathedral in California.

The motivation of communities to explore aspects of their history through theatre was a notable development in Britain during the second half of the twentieth century. The playwright, Ann Jellicoe, for example, spent time with local populations, listening to their stories, reading diaries, examining newspapers articles and minutes of meetings or looking at photographs and then moulding this material into performance using musicians, dancers and actors from the community. Projects of this kind have usually involved a small number of professional actors or directors together with writers or composers who work with a local population. The work has often been **site-specific** and has frequently explored significant developments in a community's industrial, economic or agricultural past. **Texts** have sometimes used the actual words spoken at meetings or other events and this has come to be known as **verbatim theatre**. Most frequently, productions have been characterised by the direct simplicity of the performance style and by the fact that many of the performers have rarely, if ever, participated in an event of theatre.

The continuing popularity of this form of drama was aptly demonstrated in 2009 by a project undertaken in the Kentish village of Ash. The local community had established a 'Heritage Group' with the intention of setting up an accessible archive of local history to preserve a considerable collection of historic documents, records, photographs and artefacts. As a means of publicising this project and following a successful application for funding the community decided to create a community play based on the records of the so-called 'Swing Riots' that had taken place in and around the village in the 1830s. In a period of economic deprivation and widespread unemployment for agricultural workers, local people had taken to smashing farm machinery and burning barns. These acts of vandalism and rebellion attracted the death penalty or deportation for those found guilty. Led by a professional director and writer and using the skills of a professional musician/composer, a very large proportion of the population of the village of all ages devised a 'promenade' **site-specific** play in which many of these incidents were re-enacted. Moving through the streets to the church, churchyard, pub and its garden and various other **found spaces** the audience was able to mingle with the actors, watch moments of high drama, talk to each other and enter into the *zeitgeist* of the 1830s. The play, which lasted for two hours, was given four performances in a single day and the audience was subdivided and 'colour coded' to allow the cast to lead them safely and effectively to each venue. As with many such community plays the success of the enterprise relied upon the pooling of useful and appropriate skills and the motivation of members of the public with little or no previous experience of performance. For many theatre companies the organisation of community plays has become an essential aspect of outreach and the fluctuating fortunes of regional theatres has provoked many to look at the wider community as a source of creative work.

See also **carnival; Applied drama; found space; site-specific; paratheatre; verbatim theatre.**

Constructivism

We associate this term with the work of the director Meyerhold (1874–1940), who had his early experience of theatre in Stanislavsky's Moscow Art Theatre. Like Piscator he was a Communist, but unlike Piscator most of his important work was carried out within a Communist state (see **Epic Theatre**).

It is worth noting here that the ideology of virtually all of the key theatre figures in the twentieth century had a democratising purpose and was partly didactic. Even Stanislavsky said in a speech to his company in 1898, 'What we are undertaking is not a simple private affair but a social task.... Our aim is to create the first intelligent, moral popular theatre and to this end we are dedicating our lives' (quoted in E. Braun, *The Theatre of Meyerhold*, p. 23). However, it would seem that this stated purpose was not so clear in practice and in 1899, while a member of Stanislavsky's company, Meyerhold wrote, 'We need to know *why* we are acting, *what* we are acting, and whom we are instructing or attacking through our performance ... to understand which society or section of society the author is for or against' (ibid.).

One of Meyerhold's arguments with Stanislavsky was that the Naturalistic theatre was necessarily conservative. He left the Moscow Art Theatre in 1902, but returned to run a studio theatre there in 1905. One of his objectives was to develop his ideas on 'stylisation'. He argued that the term was:

indivisibly tied up with the idea of convention, generalisation and symbol. To stylise a given period means to employ every possible means of expression in order to reveal the inner synthesis of that period or phenomenon, to bring about those hidden features which are deeply rooted in the style of any work of art. (p. 42)

Fundamentally, he was arguing that theatre should find the essence of the matter with which it was dealing and find symbols which expressed that essence. In staging terms, this had, for Meyerhold, to be a paring-down process, which readily associated with the socialist Puritanism in a post-revolutionary social context.

The artistic policy that was formulated to describe this 'essential' staging was Constructivism. Put simply, Constructivism was based on a socialist utilitarian principle that art should serve the people rather than elaborate on itself. Sheldon Cheney wrote in 1927:

The out-and-out Constructivists have announced that the stage setting must not only be stripped of every shred of adventitious decoration but must be conceived anti-decoratively.... The typical Constructivist setting may be described as a skeleton structure made up of the physically necessary means for acting ... an agglomeration of stairs, platforms, runways etc. ... stripped to their basic and structural forms, held together by plain scaffolding.... Every plank and part of it is tested by the rigid question of its functional use. It is the 'practicable' of the old pictorial scene plucked out of the picture, skeletonised and nailed together for safe usage. (*Theatre Arts Monthly*, November 1927, p. 557)

Meyerhold's personal interpretation of Constructivism led to some interesting experiments. He staged Ibsen's *A Doll's House* by propping up stock flattage back to front against the stage walls (1922). In *Earth Rampant* (1923) Meyerhold used utilitarian objects (cars, motor cycles, field telephones, lorries, a threshing machine and a field kitchen) and the one exception to the real objects was a gantry crane, which had to be made of wood because the stage floor was not strong enough to carry the weight of the real thing. This functional staging was complemented by **lighting** from actual searchlights placed in the auditorium, 'real' **costumes** and **actors** without **make-up**. *Earth Rampant* was dedicated to the Army, and from collections made at early performances an aeroplane was bought for the Army, which was given the name 'Meyerhold'. The play's celebratory nature was fully achieved at the Fifth Congress of the Comintern in Moscow in 1926, when a cast of 1500 took part, including infantry and horse cavalry, performing before an **audience** of 25,0000.

Meyerhold's Constructivism was clearly shaped by the enthusiasms of the post-revolutionary period; after a while, people tired of its constraints and of the jingoism associated with the sort of celebration that was described. Whilst maintaining the principle of art serving ideology, Meyerhold moved on to use many of the staging techniques which I shall discuss in relation to Piscator and Epic Theatre, employing multiple-staging, slides and film. Many other elements of his staging strategy are also of interest. One is his use of both individual actors and groups for their sculptural value and another is his use of props (see **properties**) in order to relate the minutiae of behaviour to general human issues. Both of these strategies were also to be used by Brecht (see Chapter 4).

Meyerhold referred to his actors as 'actor-tribunes', who acted 'not the situation itself, but what is concealed behind it and what it has to reveal for a specifically propagandist purpose' (in Braun, *The Theatre of Meyerhold*, p. 192). He continued, 'When the actor-tribune lifts the mask of the character he does not merely speak the lines ... he reveals the roots from which the lines have sprung.' The task demanded considerable technical clarity and pointing up of the actors' behaviour. This was helped by a process which Meyerhold called 'pre-acting', whereby according to Braun (ibid., p. 192), the actor employed 'mime before he spoke his lines in order to convey his true state of mind'. It can be seen that the slowing down of the acting and removal of the 'real' temporal and psychological context turn the actor into a kinetic sculptural form rather than a 'person'. The sort of impact deriving from the individual actor could also be achieved by the group. Meyerhold's most celebrated production was of Gogol's *The Government Inspector* (1926), in which *tableaux vivants* served to provide a visual comment and metaphoric amplification of the action of the central characters (see Chapter 2). The scenes were choreographed and orchestrated rather than directed. The performance has been described by Emmanuel Kaplan, who wrote the following with regard to the opening scene:

Introduction. Dark. Somewhere, slow quiet music begins to play. In the centre of the stage massive doors swing silently open of their own accord and a platform moves slowly forward towards the spectator, out of the gloom, out of the distance, out of the past – one senses this immediately, because it is contained in the music. The music swells and comes nearer, then suddenly on an abrupt chord – *sforzando* – the platform is flooded with light in unison with the music.

On the platform stand a table and a few chairs; candles burn; officials sit. The audience seems to crane forward towards the dark and gloomy age of Nicholas in order to see better what it was like in those days.

Suddenly, the music grows quiet – *subito piano* – gloomy like the period, like the colours of the setting: red furniture, red doors and red walls, green uniforms and green hanging lampshades: the colour scheme of government offices. The music is abruptly retarded and drawn out expectantly; everybody waits – on the stage and in the audience. Smoke rises from pipes and chibouks. The long stems 'cross out' the faces of the officials lit by the flickering candle flames; they are like fossilized monsters: crossed out and obliterated, once and for all. There they sit wreathed in a haze with only the shadows of their pipes flickering on their faces; and the music plays on slower and quieter as though flickering too, bearing them away from us, further and further into that irretrievable 'then'.

A pause – *fermata* – and then a voice: 'Gentlemen, I have invited you here to give you some unpleasant news ...' like Rossini in the Act one *stretto* with Doctor Bartholo and Don Basilio, only there the tempo is *presto*, whilst here it is very slow. Then suddenly, as though on a word of command, at a stroke of the conductor's baton, everyone stirs in agitation, pipes jump from lips, fists clench, heads swivel. The last syllable of 'revizor' (inspector) seems to tweak everybody. Now the word is hissed in a whisper: the whole word by some, just the consonants by others, and somewhere even a softly rolled 'r'. The word 'revizor' is divided musically into every conceivable intonation. The ensemble of suddenly startled officials blows up and dies away like a squall. Everyone freezes and falls silent; the guilty conscience rears up in alarm then hides its poisonous head again, like a serpent lying motionless, harbouring its deadly venom.

The dynamics of this perfectly fashioned musical introduction fluctuate constantly. The sudden *forte-fortissimo* of the Mayor's cry 'send for Lyapkin-Tyakpin!' The terrified officials spring up in all directions, hiding their guilty consciences as far away as possible – under the table, behind each other's backs, even behind the armchair where the Mayor was just sitting. It is like a dance-pantomime of fright. The District Physician begins to squeal on the letter 'i', first a long drawn-out whistle then jerkily on 'e' *staccato*, then the two 'notes' alternately rising and falling, whilst the next lines are 'embroidered' onto this background. In orchestral terms, it is like a piccolo with double bass *pizzicato*, just like the comic scenes in Rimsky-Korsakov's *May Night*. A sudden screech *glissando* from the Doctor and a new 'dance of terror' begins. The plastic pattern of the characters' movements corresponds to the rhythmical pattern of their voices. Their brief pauses seem to foretoken the dumb scene of the finale. (quoted in Braun, *The Theatre of Meyerhold*, pp. 221–2)

The use of props to point up the characters' inner emotions and as a cross-reference to general issues can also be seen from Meyerhold's production of Chekhov's 'vaudeville pieces' *The Bear*, *The Proposal* and *The Anniversary*, which he entitled *33 Swoons*. In *The Proposal*, Lomov and Natasha fought over a tray and a napkin whilst disputing the ownership of the meadows. In *The Anniversary*, the deputation of shareholders ironically present Chairman Shipuchin with a stuffed bear rather than an address and silver tankard (see *The Theatre of Meyerhold*, p. 260).

In the work of Meyerhold we have a clear example of an artist trying to share in and shape the evolution of a society, using as rationale for his staging the rationale of his political ideology. The fact that in the end Meyerhold was deemed to have deviated from the correct association, and was shot in prison, tends to indicate that to employ the criteria which he himself lived by underwrites tyranny rather than artistic expression. It might be argued, however, that the fault lies not in the principle of art serving ideology, but in the narrow perspective of political leaders.

Cruelty

See **Theatre of Cruelty**.

Director and directing

There has been a tendency in recent Drama and Theatre Studies for the subject to centre around the study of a disconnected series of 'theatre practitioners', most of whom were or are directors and many of whom first articulated some of the concepts mentioned in this book. This partial view of the work of directors has tended to obsure the extent to which, since the closing years of the nineteeth century, they have shaped not only the practice of actors, designers and playwrights but also the nature of discourse about drama. It is important, too, to grasp the inter-relatedness between the art of directing in the theatre and developments in other art forms: in poetry, literature, music, the visual arts and dance, for example and the fact that directors work within the context of political, philosophical and social change or ideologies and in the aftermath of previous practice and **conventions**.

It would probably be possible now to achieve almost complete agreement that the concept of a 'director' is of someone who takes total control of and ultimate responsibility for the artistic aspects of a production. This would include the shaping of a **text**, the casting and rehearsal of the play, decisions about staging, lighting, music and costuming in consultation with appropriate colleagues, and the **governing idea** for the entire production. By contrast, there would be little agreement as to how any one individual would reach this position of artistic power: unlike the **actor**, stage manager or scene designer, there is, as yet, no single recognised route for the would-be director to embark on training for his or her career. However some colleges and universities have relatively recently introduced options and short courses at undergraduate level and substantial graduate programmes for potential directors, the implication being that they should study something else or additional first. Many directors have, in fact, been actors or playwrights, often driven by convictions as to how they think drama should be presented. Some have established their own companies and simply set themselves up as directors and others have emerged from university drama societies or through the study and teaching of drama. What is clear is that in the 'modern theatre' the nature of drama in performance has been largely determined by directors; some dictatorial, some democratic, some cautious and some revolutionary. During the same period, the actor has largely gone from a position of supreme power to one of subservience, sometimes being little more than a puppet in the hands of a master, and it is only in comparatively recent times that the centrality of the actor has been re-asserted, partly because the primacy of the original text, over which directors have maintained control, has been challenged.

The concept of a director who is neither the playwright nor a leading actor in the production is relatively modern. Most scholars would date the advent of the 'director' from the work of Georg, Duke of Saxe-Meiningen, who took over the running of his court theatre in 1870. Fortunately, for those who wish to study the emergence of the director, there are three excellent sources: *Fifty Key Directors* edited by Shomit Mitter and Maria Shevtsova (2005) Edward Braun's *The Director and the Stage* (1982) and Toby Cole and Helen Krich Chinoy's *Directors on Directing* (1953) offer a rich fare of fact and interpretation. There are also many studies of individual directors listed in the Bibliography at the end of this book, and it is significant that many of the entries in this chapter deal with the work of influential directors who, by dint of their being able to stand outside their work and gain an overview, emerged as leading theorists of theatre practice. It is, indeed, partly through the body of literature created by directors during the twentieth century that the foundations for theoretical understanding of the processes of acting and directing in the modern theatre have been laid. Works by Stanislavsky, Brecht, Artaud, Grotowski, Brook, Boal or Barba, all of whom would be described as 'directors', have provided inspiration and challenge for generations of practitioners and helped to establish terminology, institutions, training courses and conferences. Their influence on university and college drama departments and on the design of new theatre spaces has been extensive and the ideas these books contain have been misrepresented or embraced in almost equal proportion.

Although there are dangers in seeking to achieve a total picture of the development of the concept of the director it is important to seek out strands of influence and contexts that have helped to fashion their work. Students may wish to ask, for instance, why a passion for realistic detail led to the English playwright T.W. Robertson's (1829–71) being nicknamed 'doorknobs Robertson' because of his insistence on accurate stage furniture and fittings or the playwright/librettist and director W.S. Gilbert (1836–1911) who was encouraged to take up playwriting by Robertson, to self-mockery in *The Mikado* where a character speaks of 'artistic verisimilitude'. How, we might ask, does this relate to the experiments of André Antoine (1858–1943) at the Théâtre Libre in Paris where, in an attempt to provoke a more realistic acting style, insisted on rehearsal with a **fourth wall** in place? We might then seek out links with the work of Stanislavsky (1863–1938) in his pursuit of 'truth' in acting and staging and ask why all these practitioners employed the **convention** of the fourth wall in an attempt to escape artificiality or why other playwrights including Strindberg, Ibsen, Chekhov, G.B. Shaw or Arthur Miller wrote within that convention. We might equally enquire as to why subsequent directors found both the 'realism' of acting and setting within the fourth wall restricting and why such concepts as Meyerhold's **Constructivism**, Piscator's and Brecht's **Epic Theatre**, Artaud's **Theatre of Cruelty** or Grotowski's **Poor Theatre** attempted to break down conventions and establish new horizons for theatre.

Records of the work of directors may take the form of journals kept by actors in their company (see, for example, the various studies of Peter Brook, and see **performance research**), but an invaluable source is the 'prompt copy' or *regiebuch* of a production in which the director plots the moves of characters and makes notes on lighting and sound cues and other physical aspects of a production. Directors vary considerably in their use of the 'prompt copy'; some, like the great Austrian director Max Reinhardt (1873–1943), recording every aspect of a production with meticulous detail and coming to rehearsals with a precise notion of how a scene would be played, whereas others, like the director and playwright Bertolt Brecht, appear to have allowed a scene to evolve, and to have used the prompt copy to record decisions made in rehearsal. In all cases, however, the prompt book will show the adaptations made to the script and will enable the stage manager to conduct rehearsals in the absence of the director and then take over the running of the production once the dress rehearsal is complete. The study of prompt copies and other evidence of working methods is only one means of understanding and preparing for the process of directing. There are many useful manuals on aspects of directing; of these, Katie Mitchell's *The Director's Craft: a handbook of the Theatre* (2008) and Mike Alfreds' *Different Every Night: Rehearsal and Performance Techniques for Actors and Directors* (2008) provide solid advice from two highly successful and respected contemporary directors. There is a most stimulating discussion of the dynamics between directors and actors in Richard Schechner's *Environmental Theatre* (1973) (see also **environmental theatre**).

Our knowledge of the antecedents of the modern concept of the 'director' are somewhat patchy. We know, for example, that in the Ancient Greek theatre the tragic dramatists directed their own works and frequently appeared in their own plays. The name *didaskalos* (teacher) implied that the author was the instructor not only of the performers during the rehearsal process but also of the **audience** through the performance itself. It appears that comic dramatists allowed someone else to direct their plays but we know little of their precise way of working. With the multiple and collaborative authorship of the **Mystery Play** cycles of medieval Europe and England the direction appears to have passed to 'pageant masters', of whom one, Jean Bouchet of Poitiers, achieved considerable recognition and success. We know that he staged a cycle of plays at Poitiers in 1508 and was still in demand as late as 1532. Outlining the duties of the pageant master or director, Bouchet listed the following: the erection of the staging and the placement of scenery and machines, finding persons to build and paint scenery and construct seating for the audience, ensuring that goods be delivered of high quality and in correct amounts, casting and rehearsing the actors, disciplining actors and establishing a scale of fines for those who fail in their responsibilities, acting some roles himself (women directors and actors were unknown at the time), assigning people to take money at the entrances, addressing the audience at the opening of the play and, after each intermission, giving a résumé of previous happenings and promising greater marvels to come! (see Oscar Brockett, *History of the Theatre*, 1995, p. 126). We can see that this list of duties includes those we might now assign to a producer. Clearly, however, the sheer complexity of a medieval cycle of plays would have demanded very careful oversight and artistic control, and, when this was vested in a single person, the results would have an impressive sense of unity.

A single person also seems to have directed the performances of the sixteenth-century **commedia dell'arte** troupes but this was often the leading performer. The productions were on a much smaller scale than the medieval Mystery Cycles: a troupe averaged about 10 members and the most respected member of the troupe would explain the action, characters and situations to the performers and acquire the **properties** before supervising rehearsals. In this case, because the 'plays' were largely improvised, the playwright was not a key figure.

However, in the public theatres of sixteenth- and seventeenth-century England, the playwright occupied a significant position in the production process. We have a vivid and memorable image of the rehearsal of a play (and of amateur drama) in Shakespeare's *A Midsummer Night's Dream* when a group of tradesmen and craftsmen meet to prepare a play for performance at court. The character of Peter Quince, who appears to have written the **script**, acts as 'teller': a non-acting member of the company who supervises the rehearsal and is the only person in possession of a complete script. The other actors only have their own parts written out together with their cues. In this situation, the 'teller' or director is in a unique position to guide the cast through their preparations. The involvement of playwrights in their own productions continued well into the seventeenth century: a visitor from overseas reported that 'in England, actors are daily instructed, as it were in a school, so that even the most eminent actors have to allow themselves to be taught their places by the dramatists' (see Leech and Craik, *The Revels History of Drama in English*, vol. III, 1975, p. 113). At some stage during the seventeenth century, however, more and more artistic control passed to the leading actor, who often was also a major shareholder in the company.

The tradition of 'Actor Managers' lasted well into the early twentieth century and the English theatre was largely shaped by such characters as Davenant, Garrick, Edmund and Charles Kean, and Irving, and it would be well worth your while to read Harold Pinter's descriptions of his early days as an actor when he worked for, and learned much from, the last of these Titans. His tribute to McMaster, the last of the great 'Actor Managers' (Harold Pinter, *Various Voices: Prose, Poetry, Politics 1948–1998*, 1998), is a superb evocation of the power and importance of such figures in the English-speaking theatre.

Research into the development of the concept of a 'director' reveals that the financial and artistic control have left both the playwright and the actor, and now reside with the producer and the director. (Until the middle years of the last century, these terms were synonymous, but we now use the word 'producer' to indicate 'management'.) **Actors** and directors now rarely own companies and are most likely to be employed by a management. However, the most interesting experiments in directing have often been undertaken by those who, dissatisfied with the status quo, have created their own companies or worked within an educational environment. There has also been a significant move by actors and playwrights to regain the ownership that many feel has been lost to all-powerful directors and managements. This has led to the creation of a number of collectives and groups dedicated to **devised** work.

See also **Agit/Prop; documentary drama** *and* **political theatre.**

Documentary drama

We tend to associate the concept of 'documentary drama' with the work of small-scale, 'politically active' theatre companies of the 1970s and 1980s, but its association with the rise of left-wing theatre can certainly be traced to the work of Piscator (1893–1966) in Weimar Germany after the First World War. His technique of using film and complex stage machinery to reflect contemporary events pioneered the direct and often naturalistic presentation of social issues that characterises documentary drama. In the United States in the 1930s, the Federal Theatre Project developed the 'Living Newspaper', which highlighted issues of public concern by dramatising them, until the government closed the project down in 1939. Since the extensive use of film documentary during the Second World War and the subsequent growth of television, the concept has tended to embrace work dealing with social issues but with fictional characters. Important examples of this development were Jeremy Sandford's *Cathy Come Home* (1966) and Alan Bleasedale's *Boys from the Black Stuff* (1985), both of which profoundly shocked television audiences. The French dramatist and philosopher Jean-Paul Sartre called documentary drama 'theatre of fact' and in his essay *Myth and Reality in Theatre* (1966) warns that 'the illusion may swallow the real'. However, it is important to remember that the most effective documentary drama has not only documented events, and thereby become a valid document in itself, but has often been based on careful research using documentary sources such as diaries, letters, contemporary accounts, court records and transcripts. The debate arises as to when this ceases to be drama and becomes mere imitation.

See also **Agit/Prop; verbatim theatre; theatre of testimony.**

Durational performance

When a director is planning a production or an audience is contemplating attending a performance the 'running time' of the play is considered to be a major issue. This information is also vital to those handling publicity or organising transport for groups who may wish to visit the theatre to see the production. However, in some cultural performances a more flexible attitude to time and duration pertains: audiences may arrive and leave at different times during the event or may join the spectators at various intervals, perhaps returning after a break for refreshment at a time of their own choosing. Although a 'starting time' and 'finishing time' may have been announced, these merely indicate the total duration of the action but they do not dictate a required time of arrival (after which doors may be closed) or when it is appropriate to leave.

By eliminating many of the conventions associated with the performances of drama some directors and theatre companies have created what are now termed 'durational' performances. The relative predictability of a play that begins and ends at a certain time has been replaced by a mode of performance that may be said to 'work' for audiences who arrive and leave at any time. This, of course, has profound repercussions for the structure of the 'play' and may rely on audiences creating meanings from apparently random activities or utterances. The jettisoning of such concepts as **plot, climax** or **denouement** means that more linear, spontaneous or image-filled **text** may be required and it is also likely that such durational performances may only take place once. The problem posed by durational performances is the significance of individual incidents. An absence of a **through line** will often lead to very differing audience experiences. There is a fascinating similarity here with the contrasting experiences of worshipers attending various forms of church service. In the Protestant tradition it is normal to announce a starting time for the congregation and the entire structure of the service is built around a mutually understood form that requires the active participation of the worshipper for an hour or so. However, in the Orthodox and to some extent in the Catholic traditions, worshippers may arrive at almost any time during a service and leave without causing offence. In these more 'durational' events' the audience/worshippers make active choices and the 'performers' are relatively unconcerned about their level of attention to a ritual that they will re-enact even if nobody else is present.

See also **Cultural Performance; ritual**

Environmental theatre

This term was introduced by an avant-garde theatre director and performance scholar from New York, Richard Schechner, to describe his concept of a new relationship between the stage and **audience** in which the major considerations were the distance or closeness that separated one from the other and a reduction of the distinction between them. Schechner aimed to transcend the separation between life and art by using spaces shared by **audience** and **actors** and by creating performances in **found spaces** rather than in conventional theatrical venues (see Chapter 4).

He developed these ideas with his own company, the Performance Group, which he founded in 1968, and in the same year he published six 'axioms' in which he sought to clarify the concept of 'Environmental theatre'. In his first axiom he maintained that all human events may be placed on a continuum, with 'Pure/Art' at the one extreme and 'Impure/Life' at the other. Traditional theatre was identified with 'Pure/Art' and then the continuum extended through environmental theatre, to Happenings (see **action, ritual**), and ended with public demonstrations, events and ceremonies. The second axiom involved the idea that in a performance all the space is used for performance and for the **audience**. Spectators, he maintained, were both 'watchers' and 'makers' of scenes in the way that bystanders in a street are part of a total picture even if they consider themselves to be only spectators of an event (see Chapter 5). Many subsequent experiments in *promenade* performances have used this idea (see **Mystery Play**). Third, an event can take place either in a 'transformed' space or in a **found space**. Thus, any space may be converted into an 'environment' and accepted as the location for a performance, and the production shaped to inhabit it. Fourth, Schechner insisted that 'focus is flexible and variable', and we can see this axiom at work in subsequent *Happenings* as well as in various recent outdoor and multiple-focus productions on scaffolding or in large, unconventional indoor spaces. Fifth, he insisted that all aspects of a production speak with their own language and that none is subservient to another or merely a support for the words. Finally, he argued that a **text** (see the introduction to Chapter 2) need 'be neither the starting point nor the goal of a production', in fact, he added, 'there may be no text at all'. In my discussions of **text, Physical Theatre** and aspects of staging we shall need to revisit some of Schechner's ideas but you should keep them in mind when considering your own personal practice and when confronting **conventions** that seem to assume only one possible type of performance or staging.

Schechner's productions with the Performance Group (which he left in 1980) are well worth researching for an insight into the development of **Postmodernist** ideas of theatre. He considered that the Polish Laboratory Theatre and the Living Theatre of New York (see James Roose-Evans, *Experimental Theatre*, 1970) were examples of 'environmental' practice (see the introduction to Chapter 2, **performance research, Theatre of Communion**). Schechner's work is documented in his *Environmental Theatre* (1973).

See also **community drama; site-specific**

Epic Theatre

In reaction to **Naturalism** there emerged an approach to production and to playwriting that has come to be known as Epic Theatre. It embraces many different styles, including the productions of Brecht, Meyerhold, Piscator and Joan Littlewood and the stylistic modes of **Expressionism, Epic** and **Constructivism**. In more recent times, the work of such companies as Red ladder or 7:84 and of playwrights such as Edward Bond, Peter Weiss and Peter Handke have come within its scope. Despite their many differences, these all share a common concern with an appeal to the minds and social consciences of the members of the **audience**. They are of interest to us because they offer alternative staging rationales to those of Stanislavsky and Antoine. The various theatre workers mentioned shared at least four basic attitudes: they were opposed to indulgence in theatricality for its own sake, they were opposed to the economic and political system of capitalism, they sought to emphasise the social and economic determinants of human behaviour and they wished to counter the tendency of the audiences to identify with the world and characters of the play.

The term 'Epic Theatre' was coined, in modern times, by Erwin Piscator (1893–1966) to describe a direct form of theatre which acknowledged its own artificiality, denying the audience an eavesdropping role, and using the actor to show not only the result, but the thought which created the result. Motive had to be transparent and clearly perceptible. Piscator had derived the term 'Epic' from the Aristotelian idea of a narrative unconstrained by the unities of time and place. By rejecting Naturalist imitations of real life and appealing to audience identification, he hoped to make it possible to analyse a social or political issue directly:

> In lieu of private themes, Piscator wrote, we had generalisations, in lieu of what was special, the typical, in lieu of accident, causality. Decorations gave way to constructiveness, Reason was on a par with Emotion, while sensuality was replaced by didacticism and fantasy by documentary reality. (Quoted by Willett, *The Theatre of Erwin Piscator*, p. 107)

The formative period of Piscator's work was between 1918 and 1933 in Germany when, in company with many young intellectuals, he had been appalled by the experience of the First World War. Socialism seemed to him to be the only appropriate response to the economic disarray and social malaise of the country. He formed a Communist theatre group, whose work was of an 'agit-prop' (see Agit/Prop) nature. The word derives from 'agitation' and 'propaganda', and the climactic lines from one of his early productions, *Russia's Day*, serve to illustrate the form of his communication:

VOICE OF THE RUSSIAN PROLETARIAT: Proletarians, into the struggle.
WORLD CAPITALISM: Hell, devil, plague.
THE GERMAN WORKER: Struggle, struggle, struggle.
VOICES (FROM ALL DIRECTIONS): Down with Soviet Russia!
THE GERMAN WORKER: All for Russia. All for Russia. Long live
Soviet Russia!

Whilst the play was more ideological than dramatic, the staging method, which used a map for scenery, heralded a scenic technique whose objective was to illustrate the plot and issues in the play rather than to localise a setting. The set became a counter-point to the action, a function which later was taken over in part by the use of projected slides and film. By announcing the content of a scene before it was played, much of the dramatic tension was removed, allowing the audience to focus on the meaning rather than the facts of each episode. In his *Despite All* (1925) there were 24 scenes, which were interspersed with documentary film. The play was a historical revue from the years 1914–19, the setting was merely a large revolve with a simple construction of steps and platforms, backed by a large projection screen. The final scene was a clear celebration of the Communist movement and 50 members of the Roter Frontkampferbund (a Communist paramilitary force) marched onto the scene and formed up waving eight enormous flags. This became a prototype for much of Piscator's work: a historical period dramatised in short scenes supported by documentary evidence, on a sparse set which relied on technology, with the intention of bringing art to the people and thereby explaining the meaning of history and the forces which shaped their lives.

The use of film was not new, but Piscator explored and exploited the medium for his own purpose of relating reality to fiction. He called his screen 'the theatre's fourth dimension' and argued that 'In this way the photographic image conducts the story, becomes its motive force, a piece of living scenery' (quoted in Willett, 1964, pp. 94–5). In *The Drunken Ship* (1926), Piscator used backing slides drawn by the cartoonist George Grosz, on three screens which both identified place and made comment. Thus a prison scene was played with the central character sitting on a chair on a bare stage. He was backed by a large slide showing a prison exercise yard, which was flanked by two other screens with slides of a grotesque warder on one side and a grotesque priest on the other. All the figures were very large and dwarfed the prisoner himself. Piscator referred to his use of slides as the 'literarisation of the theatre' and stated that he used film for three purposes: to instruct, for dramatic reasons, and as commentary.

According to Willet (p. 113), instructional film was documentary and historical, extending the subject matter in terms of time and space. He writes that dramatic film 'furthered the story and served the dialogue' and that commentary film 'pointed things out to the audience and emphasised the mood'.

The emphasis on film had a counterpart in the use of other technology and one of Piscator's principal devices was to have a stage of which some part could move. The revolve was commonplace, but a more ambitious device was the treadmill, on which an actor could walk against a background of moving and changing projected scenery, thus giving a sense of journeying, which was particularly suitable for his production of *Schweyk*, with its adventuring and picaresque central character. For that production Piscator used two parallel treadmills, each 55 feet long, crossing the full length of the stage.

No discussion of Epic Theatre can ignore the work of Bertolt Brecht (1896–1956). I have purposely left him until last in order to show that he was part of a larger artistic movement. My discussion will be brief because he has been written of so comprehensively in other sources, and I particularly recommend the reader to consult John Willett's books *The Theatre of Bertolt Brecht* and *Brecht on Theatre*. Probably the clearest statement that Brecht made about his objectives was in an essay called 'The Modern Theatre is the Epic Theatre' (in *Brecht on Theatre*, pp. 37–42). He compares his Epic Theatre with what he calls 'Dramatic Theatre' and creates a parallel analysis which identifies the 'shifts of accent' between the two.

The working method most often associated with this comparison is that of the 'distance' method of acting, through which the actor attempts to demonstrate rather than to impersonate his role (see **alienation**), commenting upon the character being portrayed and thereby revealing the relationship between motives and constraints. Discussion of this will be found in the section on acting in Chapter 2. But Brecht was also responsible for developing new staging techniques devoted to highlighting the real material causes and effects of human action. He often achieved this by means of a striking, but contradictory, central image. A good example of such an image is Mother Courage at the end of the play of that name, alone between the shafts of her cart on an otherwise empty stage. The whole action of the play has been building up to, and explaining the significance of, this stark image with which the audience leaves the theatre.

In his staging methods, Brecht was constantly searching for new ways of presenting vividly the contradictions of life under the capitalist system, or, as he put it, of making dialectics pleasurable. *The Good Person of Setzuan* illustrates the interplay of character and setting, contributing to the dialectical presentation of a contradictory situation. The setting is a tobacconist's shop and the central character's predicament is how to survive in business whilst remaining a compassionate human being. She can only resolve her contradictions by literally splitting in two: she adopts an alter ego, Shui Ta, the ruthless businessman. Once Shui Ta has set the business in order, by adopting the ruthless morality of the market forces, she can reappear as Shen Te, the good-hearted girl who has compassion for the sufferings of her fellows. The contradictory qualities of the commerce, which provides the means of both survival and exploitation, are reflected in the contradictory qualities of the two-in-one character. The audience is led towards an understanding of the play's issues through this paradox-in-action. The setting of the shop itself represents the essential contradiction.

In the work of both Meyerhold and Piscator, the **text** of the playwright was often distorted almost out of recognition to allow them to develop the staging forms and to make the ideological points that they wanted. Brecht, as both playwright and producer, was able to match his material and his methods more evenly. As a result of this, it is very difficult to study his plays satisfactorily without considering the appropriate performance methods. Over the four decades of his work in the theatre, his ideas were constantly developing and so it is only too easy to misapply the ideas of one period to a play written at a different time. One of the most celebrated of Brecht's suggestions was that the audiences in his theatre should be able to smoke and chat during the performance. This suggestion was made in the mid-twenties, when he wished to develop an informal atmosphere in which people could feel relaxed enough to ponder on the performance's issues. Round about the same time he was also thinking of the theatre in terms similar to sporting events. In 1926 he wrote an article called 'How to Apply the Principles of Good Sports Promotion to the Theatre'. The objective was to bring to the theatre the same perceptual approach as we bring to, say, a boxing match. The boxing promoter's aim is to reveal rather than disguise the contest, and the system of 'rounds' gives time for reflection and discussion. These approaches have to be compared with Brecht's quite conventional methods of staging with the Berliner Ensemble.

Perhaps the most characteristic attitude of Brecht towards staging was expressed in his statement to Mordecai Gorelik regarding the latter's production of *The Mother* in New York in 1935, in which he said:

Forget about settings ... Let's have a platform, and on this platform we'll put chairs, tables, partitions – whatever the actors need. For hanging a curtain give me a wooden pole or a metal bar; for hanging a picture a piece of wall. And I'll want a large projection screen ... Let it all be elegant, thin and fine, like Japanese banners, flimsy like Japanese kites and lanterns; let's be aware of the natural textures of wood and metal ... We'll place two grand pianos visibly at one side of the stage; the play must have the quality of a concert as well as that of a drama ... And we'll show the lighting units as they dim on and off, playing over the scene Quoted in Willett, *The Theatre of Bertolt Brecht*, p. 149)

The intention is clear. The staging must be functional and there must be no attempt at disguising the theatre. The qualities of texture and appearance must be observed. The occasion must be pleasurable. There must be the projection screen for the inevitable commentary and illustration. Brecht's work was not so stark as this implies, but it was always simple and direct.

The most striking characteristic of Brecht's staging method was his use of **properties**. A **character's** relationship with any object that he used had to be revealed by the way in which he used it. Willett tells us:

the jobs done by his characters, whether plucking a chicken or mending a motor tyre or scrubbing a man's back in the bath, always have to be done properly, as if they had a life-time's practice behind them. They could never be allowed to degenerate into 'business'; a botched up imitation of activities which to Brecht were at once beautiful and socially important. (Willett, *The Theatre of Bertolt Brecht*, p. 159)

The material world of objects was almost as intense as that of a Balzac novel. Though not so cluttered, the material world partly defined and illustrated the psychological world of the character. Use of properties indicated the character's economic basis, a point that is well illustrated by the way in which Brecht had Helene Weigel, as Mother Courage, bite a coin to see if it was genuine and then put it into a purse, which shut with a loud click. The incident was both amusing and illustrative of the character's situation and attitude.

Brecht has influenced modern theatre more than any other director or playwright. Epic Theatre has been developed and refined by a great many of the serious or innovatory playwrights since the war. His work has shown that political theatre does not need to rely on the over-simplifications of **Agit/Prop** to be effective, and his mastery of a style showing the interaction of people and objects on the stage has helped to inspire the work of directors as different as Mike Leigh, Max Stafford-Clark and Peter Brook.

Expressionism

The study of drama is a great deal more complex than understanding a series of historic 'isms', and if it remains at that level it rarely impinges in a creative way on personal practice. Expressionism is a good example of this dilemma. As a new and dominant concept of production and playwriting it had a very short life with a limited geographical spread, but its principles can inform our present practice and have influenced directors, designers and playwrights seeking an anti-realist approach. Expressionism is usually considered to have been a recognisable movement in the theatre in Germany and Austria between 1909 and the early 1920s. The term itself was introduced by the painter Hervé to describe a liberated style that focused on the outward expression of inner feelings. The first 'expressionist' production was probably Oscar Kokoschka's *Murderer, Hope of Women* in Vienna, in 1909, although it was labelled as such retrospectively.

Expressionism's main concern was the creation of images of the state of the 'inner self', a concept developed by Freud and Jung in the emerging schools of psychoanalysis in early twentieth-century Vienna. This approach remains the foundation of contemporary humanistic Arts therapies and the images produced often reveal considerable darkness, torment and disturbance. To experience the essence of Expressionism, which originated as a movement in the visual arts, it is a good idea to look at paintings, such as Edvard Munch's *The Scream*, or two significant films: Robert Wiene's *The Cabinet of Dr Caligari* (1919) and Fritz Lang's *Metropolis* (1926). Freud's *The Interpretation of Dreams* was published in 1900 and this remarkable book was also concerned with the creation of images that distort surface 'reality' in order to reach a deeper reality. We can see that dreamlike qualities are characteristic of Expressionist drama. Typically, a play would be presented with distorted and architecturally improbable settings, pools of light and deep, atmospheric shadows created by the recently developed and sophisticated electric spotlights; drab black, grey or white as the predominant 'colours' or else garish and clashing visual impacts. Acting would be emotionally charged, studiedly non-realistic, with staccato **vocalisations**, chanting and other forms of 'heightened' use of language. Facial expressions or **masks** might be grotesque, physical action mechanical or bizarre, the entire impact seeming arbitrary and subjective, and frequently dreamlike. Concepts of **plot**, narrative or grammar might appear to have collapsed in rebellion against a variety of forms of oppression and the inner experiences revealed were often of a tortured nature. The ghastly slaughter and mechanical fury of the First World War, resulting in mental illness and terrifying images for an entire generation, was evident in the staging of many of the plays.

We can see the characteristics of Expressionism most obviously in the plays of Georg Kaiser (1878–1945) and Ernst Toller (1893–1939). Kaiser's *From Morn to Midnight* (1916) established his use of an 'Everyman' **protagonist** searching for some meaning to life. He followed this with a trilogy of plays: *Coral* (1917), *Gas I* (1918) and *Gas II* (1920), which show an increasing sense of despair, and the world moving towards total destruction. A sense of disillusionment also permeates Toller's most famous plays *Man and the Masses* (1921) and *Hurrah, We Live* (1927) and these plays established Expressionism as a major style of production, particularly in the hands of Leopold Jessner (1878 1945), who became director of the Berlin State Theatre in 1919, and Jürgen Fehling (1890–1968), who sought to arouse the most intense emotional response in his audiences at the Berlin Volksbuhne. His production of *Man and the Masses* involved bankers dancing a foxtrot to the sound of jingling coins, wild dancing workers accompanied by a concertina and constantly shifting coloured lights. Such techniques not only had an impact on Piscator (see **Epic Theatre**) and Brecht but also provided a powerful and idiosyncratic theatre language for playwrights like the American Eugene O'Neill, whose play *The Emperor Jones* (1925) depicts an imaginary state ruled over by a dictatorial former criminal, and the Irish Sean O'Casey, who evokes the horror of trench warfare in *The Silver Tassie* (1928).

With the wisdom of hindsight we can see that the seeds of Expressionism were sown in the nineteenth century. Some scholars would now argue that the first play to show such characteristics was Buchner's *Woyzek* (1836), an unfinished and fragmentary piece that shows the gradual disintegration of a 'self'. The play was made into an opera, *Wozzek*, by the composer Alban Berg, and had its Berlin première in that form after 137 rehearsals, in 1925. Shocked audiences in Prague rioted the following year and the police were obliged to close the production. The economic dialogue and grotesque figures of Buchner's play were employed also by Wedekind in *Spring Awakening* (1891), and there are clearly elements of the concern with the repressed inner life, dreams and psychoanalysis in Strindberg's *To Damascus* (1898–1901), *The Dream Play* (1902) and *Ghost Sonata* (1907).

For further discussion of Expressionist drama, see Colin Counsell's example of reading a performance in *Signs of Performance* (1996), and J. L. Styan's *Modern Drama in Theory and Practice*, vol. 3: *Expressionism and Epic Theatre* (1980).

See also **Chorus**.

Forum theatre

The concept of 'Forum theatre' derives from the work of the contemporary Brazilian director and political activist Augusto Boal, and describes a technique employed by him as part of his wider concept of the 'Theatre of the Oppressed'. Boal has lived under a number of repressive and restricting political regimes and his theatre company has been involved in fighting for the rights and needs of 'oppressed' groups within such structures. He has also brought his work to Europe, where he has developed his therapeutic techniques, recognising that in supposedly more liberal circumstances, the *Cop-in-the-Head* is a more menacing agent than the actual *Cops*. His belief is that theatre can act as a form of empowerment and as an agent for personal and political change, and the process involved demands that spectators are transformed into *spect-actors*. He argues that many people have failed to take political action because they have retained 'cops in their head' long after their oppressors have ceased to have real power. For Boal, the cops in our heads have identities and a source in the external world of experience, all of which must be recognised before we can take effective action. In order to create a forum for examining the possibilities and strategies for change, he devised the participatory process for community action known as 'forum theatre' with his own theatre company.

In this technique, enactments by the company take place in any space that is suitable for spectators to gather, in a particular community that has encountered oppression. A scene is enacted in which the **protagonist** attempts, without success, to overcome the oppression relevant to that **audience**. Key to the next stage is the *joker*: a kind of master of ceremonies/**chorus** figure who directs the action. At the point where the protagonist has failed to overcome the specific oppression, the joker invites the spectators to replace the protagonist at any one point in the scene where they can imagine that an alternative course of **action** could result in a solution. The **scene** is then 'facilitated' by the joker, who sums up the essence of each proposed solution as the scene is played, many times, with alternative actions and interventions. A discourse is created and political action determined.

Boal's techniques demand great flexibility from actors. When I watched him working he was throwing a plastic water bottle to the actors and spectators, inviting them to create spontaneously some imaginary scenario. In his *joker system* developed with the Arena Stage company in Sao Paulo in the late 1960s and early 1970s, actors shifted roles and observed their characters in a form of **alienation**, employing direct address to the **audience** and using the concept of **gestus**. This ability to use theatre as an exploration of political possibilities has increasingly been exploited in the field of humanistic arts therapies and has some affinity with Moreno's psychodrama technique, in which clients are invited to act out their own personal dramas and postulate alternatives (see **improvisation**).

In forum theatre, the **actor** and spectator must operate in a situation of mutual trust and respect. It is tempting for companies who have neither the accurate knowledge of, nor the facility to research, the issues to create imitations that are insulting to audiences by their failure to enact the complexities of situations but, at its most potent, forum theatre can be energising and liberating.

Boal's ideas are set out in two important books: *The Theatre of the Oppressed* (1979) and *Games for Actors and Non-Actors* (1992). When, and only when these have been read, it is helpful to consult *Playing Boal: Theatre, Therapy, Activism* (1994), edited by M. Schutzman and J. Cohen-Cruz, which creates a theoretical framework for Boal's work. There are also valuable discussions of Boal in Phillip Auslander's *From Acting to Performance* (1997) and in *Modern Theories of Performance* (2001) by Jane Milling and Graham Ley.

See also **alienation; Epic Theatre; gestus; improvisation; applied drama; theatre of testimony; carnival** and **political drama**.

Governing idea

The 'governing idea' is the basic artistic concept, usually determined by the **director**, that shapes a production. The term is not used as frequently as it was and in the United States it is usually replaced by the term 'directorial concept'. However, the idea that a director or, sometimes, a designer will base an entire production on a particular artistic decision is still a major factor in live theatre. It could be argued that the concept of a governing idea is part of the wider trend in the British theatre of the late 1980s and early 1990s towards directors' and designers' theatre. There had been clear precedents in the early 1980s with, for example, two productions of new verse translations of plays by Molière set in modern society and using jazz music, but probably the most talked about and successful production of the early 1990s was not a new play but an **Expressionist** revival of J. B. Priestley's *An Inspector Calls*, directed by Stephen Daldry and designed by Ian McNeill. The play, sometimes seen as a rather dated piece of sermonising, seemed to benefit from a new governing idea, but Daldry himself was accused of imposing his aesthetic on this and on Sophie Tredwell's *Machinal* and Arnold Wesker's *The Kitchen*.

Actors also expressed some concern that the governing idea and design concept impeded their physical performance and inhibited full expression of their **characters**. There were similar reactions to the productions of plays and operas by Jonathan Miller, where a very strong and individualistic governing idea may have been interpreted as directorial arrogance. Such 'conceptual' productions as Miller's *The Tempest*, for which the governing idea was to present it as a parable about colonialism, did, however, give what Miller termed 'an after-life' to old pieces for a new generation. Contemporary theatre continues to provide many other examples of governing ideas, such as a recent Restoration play staged as if it were an episode of the TV series 'Footballers' Wives', and these may well provide stimulating new approaches to your practical work.

Physical Theatre

Writing in his programme notes for his play *The Dance of Death* in 1935, the poet and dramatist W. H. Auden said: 'Drama is essentially the art of the Body', and although we tend to think of Physical Theatre as a fairly recent form, elements of this concept can be found in the work of Meyerhold (1874–1939), Craig (1872–1966) or of the 'Group Theatre' in the London of the 1930s and 1940s. Physical Theatre is a recognition that the most basic essence of theatre is the human body in space, and this challenges the traditional primacy of the **text** and the spoken word. In *Towards a Poor Theatre*, Grotowski maintains that the actor is the one element without which theatre cannot be created, and his demanding physical training of his actors was designed to make the body an expressive and available instrument at the service of the play and its **director**. Taking this approach to a further point, modern Physical Theatre has devised drama that emanates from the physicality of the actors themselves.

Particularly in Britain, where there has been a long-established, classically text-based school of acting, the development in Physical Theatre since the 1980s has been a source of innovation and renewal. To some extent this has been reinforced by developments in contemporary dance, where choreographers and performers have extended the movement vocabulary to include almost all forms of human physical activity and have employed improvisatory techniques and modes of staging that focus on the body as the prime means of expression. The boundaries between dance and drama, already virtually non-existent in a number of Eastern cultural traditions, have been steadily demolished in the Western theatre. In addition we have seen the establishing of companies such as Théâtre de Complicité, whose founders trained with the great mime artist Jacques Lecoq in Paris and who have drawn inspiration from continental traditions of clowning, **commedia dell'arte**, mime and circus skills. Like Shared Experience, another company employing such skills, Théâtre de Complicité, has used non-dramatic texts, such as obscure novels, as its starting point and has woven a fabric of physical events and innovative acting styles around them, frequently employing settings of planks, levels, ropes, swings and collapsing objects to present a narrative without spoken language.

Poetic drama

This term is sometimes confusingly used as synonymous with 'verse drama' but it represents a far broader concept than drama that happens to be written in verse. Many plays have poetic qualities: they have their own internal rhythms, their orchestration of sounds, the use of striking motifs, images and metaphors and their ability to touch upon the transcendent. Plays may be as far removed from 'reality' as a sonnet is from everyday speech and yet still encompass essential truths and communicate powerful emotions. The poetic qualities may be such that, as in the plays of Chekhov, Howard Barker or Harold Pinter, the overall sense is of a 'stage poem' rather than a realistic narrative or simulation of actual life. Yet we do not doubt the accuracy of what is being evoked or fail to recognise it as an image with its own truth.

There have been two major attempts to generate a truly poetic theatre that are worth considering in some detail. The first centred around a group of Irish dramatists led by W. B. Yeats and Lady Gregory and later including J. M. Synge and Sean O'Casey. At the tiny Abbey Theatre in Dublin in the early years of the last century, this group worked to create a new poetic reality and a genuine national Irish drama. Writing in 1904, Yeats set out his principles to accompany his *Plays for Dancers* and it is worth reproducing them here because they encapsulate the essence of 'poetic theatre':

1. *Acting Style*: The actors must move, for the most part, slowly and quietly, and not very much, and there should be something in their movements decorative and rhythmical as if they were paintings in a freize ... we must get rid of everything that is restless, everything that draws attention from the sound of the voice.
2. *Character and mask*: There must be no realistic intrusion of the actor, who must wear a mask to make him abstract and impersonal.

The face of the speaker should be as much a work of art as the lines that he speaks or the costume he wears, that all may be as artificial as possible.

3. *Setting*: Poetic drama should have no realistic, or elaborate, but only a symbolic and decorative setting. A forest pattern and not a forest painting.

(NB: Yeats was especially admiring of the designs of Edward Gordon Craig.)

Although several other dramatists developed their own distinctive style of poetic drama, these ideas of Yeats give a good indication of the concerns that engaged both the Irish School and those who centred around the next major experiment in this aspect of drama: the 'Group Theatre' founded in London by the dancer Rupert Doone in the 1930s (see **Physical Theatre**). Poets including W. H. Auden, Christopher Isherwood, T. S. Eliot, Louis MacNeice and Stephen Spender aimed to challenge the norms of the commercial theatre with a style of per-formance and **theatre language**. As in Dublin, these dramatists were obliged to create their own venue for their experiments, seeking a non-realistic approach and debating the re-introduction of poetry into the theatre. Their work, which also embraced Radio Drama, con-centrated on the inner reality of the soul rather than on external real-ity: the idea of '**character**' was sometimes eliminated in favour of a series of stage figures who were symbols of states of mind. However, the body of the **actor** was seen as a potent means of communication. T. S. Eliot's important contribution to this movement, which he success-fully introduced into the commercial theatre, is discussed in Chapter 2. For a fascinating account of the Group Theatre's experiments, see Michel Sidnell's *Dances of Death* (1984), and for a succinct consideration of the Irish School, see J. L. Styan's *The English Stage* (1996).

Poor Theatre

The imagery of religion and belief in the need for 'holism' in life and the theatre are at the core of all of the **total theatre** pioneers. In more recent times the practices and process have tended to be inspired by the work of the Polish director Jerzy Grotowski, who died in 1999. In his 'Statement of Principles' (*Towards a Poor Theatre*, p. 256) Grotowski wrote:

Theatre – through the actor's technique, his art in which the living organism strives for higher motives – provides an opportunity for what could be called integration, the discarding of masks, the revealing of the real substance: a totality of physical and mental reaction.

Whilst his work evolved from fairly conventional staging methods to the point where he abandoned the whole notion of theatre, preferring to think in terms of a 'meeting', he consistently pursued the twin objectives embedded in the statement quoted above. The first objective was to strip down the barriers that inhibit communication, including the theatrical paraphernalia of staging and the **masks**, 'the daily mask of lies', behind which both **actor** and **audience** hide their sensitivity and vulnerability. The second objective was to take these exposed and receptive parties to a confrontation with their cultural myths in a communal 'trying out' of traditional values.

So far as staging is concerned, Grotowski reflected his 'inductive technique' or 'technique of elimination' in acting by the concept of the 'poor' theatre, which dispenses with the notion of theatre as a 'synthesis of disparate creative disciplines – literature, sculpture, painting, architecture, lighting, acting'. Grotowski accuses this 'synthetic' theatre of suffering from 'artistic kleptomania'. Whenever possible he reduced reliance on any element other than the **actor** himself, attempting to distil the theatrical experience to the core. For Grotowski that core must allow us to 'transcend our stereotyped vision, our conventional feelings, our standards of judgement' so that 'in a state of complete defencelessness we can "discover ourselves" and "entrust ourselves" to something we cannot name, but in which live Eros and Charitas' (*Towards a Poor Theatre*, p. 257). In other words, we discover the essence of our humanity.

Grotowski sought to put an end to the **actor/audience**, stage/auditorium separation. His audiences were witnesses to his actors' nakedness; the confrontation was to be an 'osmosis' and the stage was to be eliminated in favour of a 'chamber theatre'. The characteristics of such a theatre are that it permits the 'proper spectator/actor relationship for each type of performance', in which it is possible to 'embody the decision in physical arrangements'. Experiments with these principles led Grotowski to set *Kordian* (1962) in a psychiatric ward with the spectators sitting on and around the two-tiered beds as though they were patients. Marlowe's play *Dr Faustus* (1953) was set as though at a Last Supper. The spectator/guests were welcomed by Faustus and seated at two long refectory tables, while Faustus finally sat at a smaller table at one end, rather like the prior in a refectory. The action took place on the tables. For *The Constant Prince* (1965), the 'spectator-peepers' looked down over the wooden walls of a rectangular bear pit. The only staging element in the pit itself was a low oblong dais just long enough to take a man's body. Of *Akropolis*, Flaszen, Grotowski's literary adviser, wrote, 'it was decided that there would be no direct action between actors and spectators'. The actors were 'to be dead; the spectators represent those who are outside of the circle of initiates ... they are the living' (*Towards a Poor Theatre*, p. 63). The idea was that the separation, combined with the closeness of the spectators, gave the impression 'that the dead are born from a dream of the living'. The only material element present at the beginning of the piece was a large box with metallic junk piled on top of it: 'stovepipes of various lengths and widths, a wheelbarrow, a bathtub, nails, hammers ... Everything ... old, rusty ... picked up from a junkyard.' During the action of the performance all of these objects became elements in an evolving civilisation whose ultimate metaphor was the gas chamber. **Costumes** for *Akropolis* served not to identify characters or social groups, but to become metaphors for the torn human body. They were bags full of holes, the holes lined with material to suggest torn flesh. The spectators looked through the holes as though through the person's skin. This experimentation with space reached its final point when for *Apocalypsis cum Figuris* the space was completely undifferentiated and actors and audience shared a large empty hall.

In spite of the remarkable effects of this sort of drama and staging, for Grotowski a division still remained, identified by the idea of 'performance', which essentially denied the possibility of the fusion of appearance which he sought. Noting that true communication between human beings depended on an 'understanding that goes beyond the understanding of words' and that when that point was reached, concepts of performance and the theatre were no longer relevant, he decided that 'it was necessary to eliminate the notion of theatre' (an actor in front of a spectator) and that what remained was a 'notion of meeting'. The search for theatre became a search for what Grotowski calls 'active culture' (quoted in Mennen, 'Grotowski's Paratheatrical Projects', *The Drama Review*, 18 (4) 1976).

Like Artaud, Grotowski's imagery and point of reference are religious. Although he is an atheist he speaks of the 'holy' actor who 'sacrifices' his body. He writes:

> If the actor by setting himself a challenge publicly challenges others and through excess, profanation and outrageous sacrilege reveals himself by casting off his everyday mask, he makes it possible for the spectator to undertake a similar process of self-penetration.

If he does not exhibit his body, but annihilates it, burns it, frees it from every resistance to any psychic impulse, then he does not sell his body, but sacrifices it. He repeats the atonement, he is close to holiness. (*Towards a Poor Theatre*, p. 34)

It is not difficult to understand the sort of event and communication which Grotowski sought. He seemed to resent the spiritual monopoly which the church has claimed of man and sought to replace its moribund 'services' with his own penetrating and dynamic actor as the 'courtesan' actor who has accumulated skills to sell on behalf of a director/pimp. The spectators are more and more individuated in their relation to the myth, 'group identification with myth – the equation of personal, individual truth with universal truth is virtually impossible' (p. 23). The selling process itself is a barrier to the process of a 'sharing' communication which Grotowski sought. He also recognised the difficulty in making a profound communication across cultural barriers: 'The performance is *national* because it is a sincere and absolute search into *our* historical ego.'

The relation between Artaud and Grotowski is deceptively close. Grotowski did not read Artaud until long after he had begun his work and he denied most of the parallels that have been drawn between their work. Artaud was really only a man of inspirations which, according to Grotowski, were impossible to work in practice. His emphasis on puppetry would detract from the communion, and his staging form with the action around the audience would only change rather than destroy the audience/actor frontiers. His breathing techniques derived from the Cabala were based on a misunderstanding and were quite impractical.

The similarity which I wish to emphasise is their equal belief in the need to create a communion. The idea of 'communion', or at least the greater intimacy between audience and actor, was one of the greatest dynamics in the evolution of modern theatre. It was complemented by a desire to destroy the artificial theatricality of the stage. Whilst Grotowski and Artaud are most clearly identified with the movement, so too are a host of others, including such disparate names as Stanislavsky, Alan Ayckbourn and Bertholt Brecht.

Site specific

Writing in London's *The Evening Standard* in June 2009, the theatre critic Nick Curtis observed that 'While the West End groans with great performances and productions, site-specific and promenade shows are booming too'. Describing a variety of productions that involve taking the audience to a number of non-theatrical venues to see drama that, in some way, has grown organically from those spaces, Curtis remarks that it might be preferable to label this recent phenomenon 'immersive theatre'. The quality of site-specific theatre that provokes this suggestion is the usual close proximity of the audience to the action and the lack of provision for comfortable and distanced viewing. Many productions also take their audiences to a succession of venues related to the action of the play but make little, if any, distinction between a performance space and the viewing space. In some extreme forms of site-specific performances there is no designated, paying audience and a spontaneous group of spectators may be gathered as the performance progresses. In other situations, however, the apparently free-ranging audience is tightly controlled and the site itself closed to the general public.

The term 'site-specific' is sometimes mistakenly used to describe a drama that takes place in a **found space** (see **Environmental Theatre**) rather than taking place in a conventional theatrical space. This is to misunderstand the concept. For a piece to be 'site specific' it must, in some way be not only shaped by the space but have a profound association with it. Two recent examples will serve to illustrate this, both involving 'productions' that took place in London Underground (metro) stations. The first involved an audience that had assembled earlier and followed the company around a series of venues where small incidents from history that had taken place there were re-enacted (cf the Ash Community Play under **Community Drama**). This production culminated in part of an Underground station that had been used as a makeshift bomb shelter during the Second World War. No attempt was made to segregate the **audience** from the general public who continued to walk through the station going about their everyday lives. As the actors showed a scene of an event that took place there in the 1940s much of the drama of the performance derived from the uncertainty of passers by as to whether what they were witnessing was 'real' or not. However, the quality of that particular performance was that it was entirely 'specific' to the place in which it happened. No other space could have generated the same performance. Another production that also took place in an Underground station consisted largely of scenes acted on moving escalators. In this case, there was some advanced publicity that ensured that an audience of a kind might be present because they were aware that 'something was happening' but , again, much of the audience consisted of surprised members of the public unsure as to the nature of what they were witnessing. The entire performance was built around the particular design and features of a recently modernised station and escalator system that enabled the **action** to be seen from a large number of variable vantage points. The production could have 'worked' in no other space and was therefore 'site-specific'.

The abandonment of more conventional theatrical venues has it its roots in both economic and aesthetic considerations. Site-specific work can be seen as an attempt to take theatre to the community in the light of the community's reluctance to come to the theatre and, accordingly, may attract funding. Small-scale and experimental theatre companies which have few physical and financial resources may also find it viable to present site-specific productions in venues for which there is no hiring cost. For some directors however, site-specific work is seen as an escape from and creative alternative to the suffocating restrictions of the commercial theatre with its heavy reliance on 'commodity' productions with their associated merchandise and 'reality' TV shows. In some ways site-specific theatre is the most recent of a series of attempts to find a way to re-stimulate audiences and eschew what Peter Brook called 'The Deadly Theatre' (see **Empty Space**).

See also **Community Drama; Environmental Theatre** *and* **Found Space.**

Theatre of Communion

As Chapter 2 demonstrates, it has frequently been assumed that theatre has its origins in **ritual** rather than in demonstration or communication of the kind found in **Agit/Prop** or **Epic Theatre**. A **director** believing that the function of theatre is to unite the **audience** in the experience of a ritual of common affirmation will make very different choices in how to stage and present plays, from those of a director whose aims are those of political theatre or **Epic Theatre**. The possibilities open to directors wishing to create a 'theatre of communion' can best be outlined by reference to the work and theories of Antonin Artaud (see **Theatre of Cruelty**) and Jerzy Grotowski (see **Poor Theatre**).

Artaud, who was born in 1896 and died in 1948, was a French actor, writer and director who worked with Lugné-Poe, Charles Dullin and Jean-Louis Barrault. For much of his life he suffered from mental illness and the effects of drugs. He is best known for his theoretical collection *The Theatre and its Double* (1970). Whilst his ideas have had a profound influence on the theatre of the last seventy years, he was never able to achieve any great theatrical success himself. Artaud wrote in 1926:

> The illusion we are seeking to create has no bearing on the greater or lesser degree of verisimilitude of the action. By this very act, each show becomes a sort of event. The audience must feel a scene in

their lives is being acted out in front of them, a truly vital scene. In a word, we ask our audiences to join with us, inwardly, deeply.... Audiences must be thoroughly convinced we can make them cry out. (*Collected Works*, vol. 2, p. 18)

The idea that a theatrical performance has both a sense of community and communion has led to many practitioners using the term 'event' to describe what they have created. Central to this concept are the notions of interaction, joint celebration and shared values and the consideration of these have extended into an examination of **paratheatre, carnival** and **ritual.** For an introduction to these topics and indications of valuable sources see Pickering and Woolgar's *Theatre Studies* (2009).

See also ritual; paratheatre

Theatre of Cruelty

Artaud elaborated on his ambition for a sense of communion (see **Theatre of Communion**) in terms of both practice and rationale, evolving the concept of a 'Theatre of Cruelty'. The imagery he used is both religious and revolutionary. Religion and revolution both relate to absolute principles and to fundamental and frequently 'holistic' attitudes, and together they imply, at least in Artaud's terms, the discovery of new and purer socio-political and personal relationships. Artaud wished to reveal an 'occult equivalent' (*Collected Works*, 1968, p. 22) of the moribund religion of the time. He wanted to extirpate 'our world's lies, aimlessness, meanness and ... two-facedness' (ibid.). Believing that a 'real stage play upsets our sensual tranquility, releases our repressed sub-conscious, driving us to a kind of potential rebellion' (p. 19), he sought a new communion, a new **sign system**, and a new priesthood in the theatre to give form to his ideas and achieve his objectives.

The 'communion' element of Artaud's schemes was at the core of his beliefs. The audience was to be 'encircled' so that direct contact could be made. Seated in the centre of the action the **audience**, in swivel chairs, would change their focus according to the movement of the drama around the hall, which was to be similar architecturally to a 'holy place'. There was to be no vacuum in the audience's 'mind or sensitivity' (p. 84): their attention was to be persistent and persistently committed. 'Intensities of colour, light or sound ... vibrations and tremors, tonality of light ... tremoring gestures' were to fuse, to create discords and to envelop the whole space and people so that the experience was immediate and primal, 'as exactly localized as the circulation of blood through our veins' (p. 70).

Artaud sought 'true magic' and the 'hypnotically suggestive mood where the mind is affected by direct sensual pressure' (p. 84). However, the performance was not aimed to entice just the minds or the senses of the audience but their 'entire existence', plumbing and revealing 'the most secret recesses of the heart'. Artaud likenened the experience he sought to inspire to that of the snake which is charmed: 'I intend to do to the audience what snake-charmers do and to make them reach even the subtlest notions through their organism.' He had argued that it was not just the music that affected the snake, but the vibrations which its long body was contacting through the ground. It was this profound and complete experience which identified what Artaud meant by 'Theatre of Cruelty', a theatre in which the 'unconscious' was to be liberated and the individual's driving force revealed and recognised. It was to be 'cruel' in that it denied the audience a 'Peeping Tom' perspective, and forced them into a 'tangible laceration', a full and 'whole' commitment to the occasion:

> The theatre
> is the state
> the place
> the point
> Where we can get hold of man's anatomy and
> Through it heal and dominate life.
> ('*Aliéner l'acteur*', 12 May 1947, quoted in Esslin (1976), *Artaud*, p. 76)

These ideas of new **theatre language** and forms were confirmed for Artaud by the experience of watching a company of Balinese dancers, not in Bali, but in Paris in 1931. What particularly impressed him was the supremacy of movement and sound rather than verbal language. He saw in the dancers' behaviour the creation of a novel and essentially theatrical language. He wrote:

> by language I do not mean an idiom we fail to catch at first hearing, but precisely that kind of theatrical language foreign to every spoken language, where it seems a tremendous stage experience is recaptured, besides which our exclusively dialogue productions seem like so much stammering. (p. 39)

He wrote very precisely of his experience, speaking of

> those angular, sudden, jerky postures, those syncopated inflexions found at the back of the throat, those musical phrases cut short,

the sharded flights, rustling branches, hollow drum sounds, robot creaking ... a new bodily language no longer based on words but on signs. (p. 37)

The actors were like 'moving hieroglyphs', the whole appearance one of 'theatre **conventions**' with profound symbolic meaning too deep for 'logical discursive language'. Whilst it has been argued that Artaud was probably mistaken and the signs he perceived had more literal meaning than he realised, what is important is his stress on the concept of potential symbolic and metaphoric value of all elements of theatre.

This was not new: it may even be a necessary law of **perception**. When we see things, we can only understand them if they relate to our previous experience. We, therefore, continually place those things we see into a framework of meaning, and everything that we can see simultaneously and that appears to belong to the same event is placed within the same framework of perception. Therefore, all things on and around the stage are likely to be 'read' unless conventions of disattention are established which tell us not to consider certain elements, which are not designed for our perception at that moment. The most obvious attention/disattention convention in theatre is the use of stage **lighting** to focus on the desired action and place.

What was comparatively novel was the extra-intellectual, sensuous, but none the less precise nature of the **sign system**. Artaud was creating a 'total' environment, bringing about 'real' experiences. His aim, and it must be remembered that he never fully achieved this, was to discover and present an absolutely controlled system of symbolic experiences which would have exact sensory effects on his audiences. In order to achieve this he needed a high priest, a director who could orchestrate and choreograph a complex web of experiences for actor and audience.

What Artaud was seeking to remedy was man's partition of himself into body, mind and spirit and his separation from his fellow men. One of Artaud's immediate influences was the theatre of Bali, but he was also part of the general revolution away from the superficial and the vulgar, a revolution that he shared with Stanislavsky, Brecht, Grotowski and with almost every person working in the serious theatre, all of whom sought to inspire a new consciousness.

Whilst the Balinese dances had a striking effect on Artaud, more potent influences were Eastern mysticism and medicine, which seek to confront and treat the 'whole' person. In fact, he began to formulate acting techniques based on Chinese acupuncture points and on breathing methods derived from the Jewish Cabala.

He outlined the principles and techniques of acting in an article he called 'An Affective Athleticism'. Deriving his rationale from 'holistic' thought, Artaud developed two fundamental principles. One was that just as the athlete can command very isolated muscular action, the actor can identify very particular areas of his or her body to discover and convey emotion. In the article, Artaud only discusses the solar plexus, the small of the back, and the breasts, but suggests that as Chinese acupuncture recognises 380 pressure points, many of these must be available to provide the source of the actor's emotional behaviour. He argued: 'The secret is to irritate those pressure points as if the muscles were flayed' (*The Theatre and its Double*, pp. 94–5). Acupuncture points were not to be seen as just points on the body's surface, but as key points in the 'meridians' through which 'vital energy' passes, providing a network of channels throughout the body similar to the nervous system.

In developing his argument, Artaud noted the Chinese belief in pairs of opposites, most notably the *yin* and *yang*, which explain all human behaviour. An increase in one automatically leads to a decrease in its opposite. A balanced person is one in whom all of the opposites are in equilibrium. The art of acupuncture is to stimulate or decrease the body's 'vital energy' according to a person's needs. Artaud was arguing that in order to expose deep emotion the actor should learn to exploit acupuncture's 'points' through his own will.

Of Artaud's second principle, concerning the relationship between emotion and breathing, he wrote: 'All breathing has three measures, just as there are three basic principles in all creation and the figures that correspond to them can be found in breathing itself' (pp. 90–1). The three basic principles add a neutral state to the Chinese opposites so that in addition to 'male' and 'female' we have 'androgynous', or added to 'expanding' and 'attracting' we have 'balanced', and so on. In acting terms, the aim was to rediscover the breathing associated with 'every mental movement, every feeling' so that we can have access to the origin of emotion and thus convey it, thereby expressing the 'soul's flowing substantiality', creating what Artaud referred to as 'breathing tempi' – the source of the emotional flow of drama or 'passionate time'.

The end-product of this process is that the **audience** will lock into the breathing rhythms and subsequently the physical, emotional and spiritual tempi, merging with the actors and moving to a 'magical trance', the essence of 'divine theatre'.

It is important to note here that in spite of the mysticism and emotion, Artaud was still looking for a 'code' whereby his theatre could communicate. He spoke of 'breathing hieroglyphs' as his medium and scorned the primacy of verbal coding, but he identified the central need of all theatre to encode its meaning in such a way that the audience can share this meaning. Artaud's unique quality was that he sought a primal, innate and universal code as opposed to an abstract code of **conventions**, which has to be artificially created.

See also **conventions; perception; sign system; theatre language** and **vocalisation.**

Theatre of the Oppressed

See **forum theatre.**

Total theatre

Attempts to achieve the concept of 'total theatre' have inspired, tantalised, intrigued and, sometimes, eluded many of the significant practitioners of the modern theatre (see **Poor Theatre**).The German composer Richard Wagner (1813–83) dreamt of creating an art form that would embrace and integrate music, poetry, drama, lighting, décor and movement. In his attempt to create this *Gesamtkunstwerk* he may not have been entirely successful but he laid the foundations for later experiments in 'total theatre'. The term itself became popular in 1940s France when the director Jean-Louis Barrault (1910–94) achieved a successful production of Claudel's play The *Satin Slipper* that, because of its almost cosmic scale, had previously been thought unstageable. By 1943 Barrault had formulated his view that the **text** resembles an iceberg because only a small proportion is initially visible. The director's task, he argued, was to use all the theatre's resources in an imaginative way to expose the hidden portions of the text and thus complete it. Much influenced by Artaud (see **Theatre of Cruelty**), Barrault sought a synthesis of various production modes and in 1969 staged Rabelais's *Gargantua and Pantagruel* on a central platform with the audience all around. Such ambitions to create the sense of total theatre sometimes involved using as many theatrical resources as possible and sometimes were accompanied by a stripping bare of those resources to reveal what is elemental and vital. We see this particularly in the work of Erwin Piscator (see **Epic Theatre**). Perhaps the best indicator of the sort of theatrical event which Piscator was trying to achieve is the 'total theatre', that Gropius designed for him in 1927. Although the theatre was never built, the principles were clear. There was a rejection of a tiered seating arrangement such as obtained in conventional theatres, which Piscator saw as reflecting and reinforcing the class divisions in society. Through a system of three huge revolves, the space could be converted to provide thrust, arena and proscenium staging. Around and behind the auditorium there were seventeen projection points so that the audience could be completely surrounded. The overall aim was, according to Gropius (quoted in Willett, 1964, pp. 117–18), that of:

> building in mechanical and light-generated fields of force which can be shifted in all three spatial dimensions and by their components and their cubes of light permit the director to conjure up the dreamspaces of his imagination with infinite variability within the invisible network of coordinates imposed by the neutral, blacked-out auditorium. (p. 118)

The theatre was to be a place in which social relations were changed both by the piece presented and by the organisation of the theatre itself. Whilst Piscator was certainly innovative it is dangerous to emphasise this aspect of his work, for such emphasis detracts from his central ideological ambitions. His staging ideas were evolving experiments with the communication of a Marxist interpretation of events. Perhaps this is best illustrated with reference to his experimental work with **lighting**. One of the techniques he developed was the use of lighting sources behind and to the side of the stage which were in full view of the audience. His objective was to 'make things clear' or 'clarify facts'. One of his most radical works was *Salome* (1964). Hans Ulrich Schmuckle, who collaborated with Piscator, wrote of the work:

> One of Erwin Piscator's great problems was the stage floor. He eventually decided to transform it into yet another source of light ... he ... was watching the sunlight which shone into the aeroplane from the depths of the horizon. Waves of light flooded up through the cabin-windows from below. Yet there were no shadows to be seen on the passengers' face. Their faces were exceptionally clearly defined ... Later we tried to get the same effect with a transparent stage-floor made of glass. We laid lighting strips across the stage and inserted the sources of light underneath... By this means we were able to literally 'bathe' the characters in light. (Schmuckle, 'Erwin Piscator and the Stage', p. 21 of *Erwin Piscator, 1893–1966*, catalogue of Piscator's exhibition in 1979)

The point that Schmuckle iterates is that the technique served to undermine any illusionistic or decorative effect and focus on the action of the opera's meaning, not to appeal to the audience's pleasure in spectacle.

Piscator's working method was also radical. He developed his scenic ideas during the rehearsal process as he and the actors felt a need for a development of the scene's meaning or a structure which would support and amplify the action.

Both Brecht and Meyerhold (Brecht worked with Piscator intermittently during the 1920s) felt that, in the end, Piscator's emphasis on staging actually detracted from the ideological impact of the performance, and Meyerhold wrote in 1928 that he was 'on the wrong track' and that he 'had not grasped the problem'. In trying to create a revolutionary theatre he has focused on 'developing the *material* aspects of theatre technique' whereas he should have recognised the 'stage and theatre as a framework ... to which the actor's voice and gestures have to be accommodated' (Willett, p. 125) (see **Poor Theatre).**

The term 'total theatre' was taken up by the dramatist Peter Shaffer in the 1960s to describe the effect he was aiming to create in his play *The Royal Hunt of the Sun* (1964). In this spectacular piece, set in the conflict between the Spanish and the Incas in sixteenth-century Peru, we see the energy of sun-worship, religious allegory, huge masks, mime, dance, ritual chant and an environment rich in colour and light. Shaffer himself tried to 'convey the kind of excitement I believed could still be created out of total theatre' (quoted in Barnes, 1986, p. 225). A full discussion of Wagner's work and of very recent examples of total theatre is contained in Pickering and Woolgar's *Theatre Studies* (2009).

Further Reading

Paul Allain (ed.) with Georges Banu and Grzegorz Ziolkowski (2009) *Peter Brook with Grotowski: Theatre is just a Form* (Wrozlav: The Grotowski Insitutute).

Edward Braun (1982) *The Director and the Stage* (London: Methuen).

Toby Cole and Helen Krich Chinoy (1953) *Directors on Directing* (2nd edn, New York: Crown, 1970).

Lloyd Anton Frerer (1996) *Directing for the Stage* (New York: McGraw-Hill).

Jerzy Grotowski (1969) *Towards a Poor Theatre* (London: Methuen).

Robert Leach (2008) *Theatre Studies: the Basics* (London: Routledge).

James Roose-Evans (1989) *Experimental Theatre: From Stanislavsky to Peter Brook* (New York: Avon).

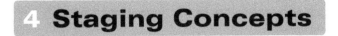 4 Staging Concepts

If a member of the public were to be asked for their definition of 'a stage' they would probably respond by describing some kind of elevated level or platform or, at the very least, a place that enabled them to watch performances in a degree of comfort. However, were the same question to be posed to a progressive theatre practitioner, critic or drama student, they would be more likely to use an expression like 'performance space' and insist that such a space enabled the performers to engage with or manipulate the perceptions of an audience. They might even suggest that a degree of discomfort for the audience could be an integral part of the experience. Almost certainly the most that we could all agree upon is that a stage is an area designated for the performers even if, at times, that space is shared with the spectators. The moment that a performer has created a space in which an act of performance takes place, a 'stage' comes into being.

In the title of this chapter I am using the term 'staging' as a verb, although there will be times when it will be used as a noun. Staging is the active process whereby a performance is provided with an appropriate environment. At certain periods during the history of theatre in the West, various permanent forms of staging have imposed a discipline and form on plays. In turn, these have affected the attitudes and expectations of audiences and influenced styles of performance. The ability to isolate an area and call it a stage has been transformed by developments in technology: a space can now be the only part illuminated in a larger room, or shaped to resemble almost anything – a house, a street, the inside of a huge mouth, a ship at sea, and so on. This has not always been the case; at times the audience has been clearly visible to the performers, or the environment has merely suggested another place through the use of agreed conventions or selected images. Rediscovering the dynamism and immediacy of ancient staging conventions has provided many modern theatre practitioners with stimuli for production styles and for the design and construction of flexible, permanent theatres incorporating as many historic forms as possible. In recent drama practice it is far more common for a director or company to consider what form of staging suits the demands of a particular play than it is for them to allow the shape and position of the stage to dictate the mode of performance. Hence, the demand for simple spaces that can be transformed into almost any form of stage and auditorium.

This chapter considers many of the features of various kinds of permanent performance space but it also embraces the process whereby a group of performers goes in search of a suitable environment or audience. Such a process will probably lead to spaces that have not been created specifically for performances but may simply and temporarily become a stage by the creation of drama. This is a far cry from the ritual unfolding of a cloth to denote the 'sacred space' for performance that preceded the Japanese *Noh* plays and was perpetuated in the 1920s and 1930s by those seeking to explore such conventions in a non-commercial theatre. Nevertheless, what these, and all approaches to staging have in common is that a space can be transformed not only by physical structures and scenography but by the nature of what takes place there and by the use of the imagination. Shakespeare, of course, discourses upon this aspect of theatre in the Prologue to his play *Henry V*, and it would be helpful to read this speech before embarking on this chapter:

Chorus
O for a muse of fire, that would ascend
The brightest heaven of invention:
A kingdom for a stage, princes to act,
And monarchs to behold the swelling scene.
Then should the warlike Harry, like himself,
Assume the port of Mars, and at his heels,
Leashed in like hounds, should famine, sword, and fire
Crouch for employment. But pardon, gentles all,
The flat unraisèd spirits that hath dared
On this unworthy scaffold to bring forth
So great an object. Can this cock-pit hold
The vasty fields of France? Or may we cram
Within this wooden O the very casques
That did affright the air at Agincourt?
O pardon: since a crookèd figure may
Attest in little place a million,
And let us, ciphers to this great account,
On your imaginary forces work.
Suppose within the girdle of these walls
Are now confined two mighty monarchies,
Whose high uprearèd and abutting fronts
The perilous narrow ocean parts asunder.

Piece out our imperfections with your thoughts:
Into a thousand parts divide one man,
And make imaginary puissance.
Think, when we talk of horses, that you see them,
Printing their proud hoofs i'th' receiving earth;
For 'tis your thoughts that now must deck our kings,
Carry them here and there, jumping o'er times,
Turning th'accomplishment of many years
Into an hourglass – for the which supply,
Admit me Chorus to this history,
Who Prologue-like your humble patience pray
Gently to hear, kindly to judge, our play.

(*Henry V*, Prologue, ll. 1–34)

Arena staging

See **theatre form.**

Box set

See **fourth wall.**

Constructivism

See Chapter 3.

Costume

The move from **Naturalism** to Symbolism, which was discernible in the European and American theatres during the closing years of the nineteenth century, had a considerable impact on the design and function of costume. The design of any production includes the human body moving in space, and nothing transforms the body so completely and variously as the wearing of clothes. Indeed, it may well be that in 'dressing up' we have one of our first experiences of drama, and throughout our lives the clothes we wear are part of the role we play and the impression of ourselves that we wish to project (see **frame analysis**). Many clothes are so personal to us that they virtually become an extension of our body, affecting the way we move, enhancing our **character**, changing our shape, enlarging the space we occupy, denoting our loyalty or reflecting our mood. Additionally, clothes are the most immediate symbol of changing fashion, and in some cases have become synonymous with the idea of fashion; they are recognisable as belonging to specific periods of history, geographical regions or nationalities, and are presumed to make a statement about the wearer.

In the theatre, costume not only embraces all the functions we have outlined, but is also part of a larger design scheme. It appears to be the one constant element in all forms and periods of theatre, for evidence suggests that in every type of drama, even when the stage was a bare platform or space on the ground, the choice of costume was a conscious artistic decision. This is because in dramatic action the performer is the focus of attention and careful thought must therefore be given to the visual impact of the body. The question of visibility is, however, one of the issues which affects theatre costume and sometimes changes the principles by which it must be designed in comparison with the clothes of everyday life. In the first instance, detail which is visible in the intimacy of a room may be lost in a theatre; accordingly, designs may need to be bolder and on a larger scale. At the same time, it is possible to simulate fine details with alternative techniques and materials – for example, the appearance of rich embroidery may be achieved by piping paint or drawing with felt-tipped pen, 'costly' jewellery can be constructed from nuts and bolts sprayed gold, and decoration of fabrics may be applied by stencil, paint spray or paint roller.

Under powerful stage **lighting** and at a distance, a range of fabrics different from those used for formal wear will produce better results. Loose woven materials such as hessian or calico, or those with a broken surface, like velour, velvet or rough wool, all take on richness and depth when made into stage costume. Such fabrics may be dyed, textured, cut, stuck or layered to produce an infinite number of shapes and effects, and stage designers are constantly experimenting with unusual and unexpected materials with which to enhance the human body.

Costume-making has become a highly specialised aspect of theatre design, although it is usual for the design to be executed by the set designer. Fortunately, the costume sketches from many past productions have survived and it is relatively easy to find illustrations which enable a student to trace the development of the art, at least during the past hundred and fifty years. A particularly rich source of costume design is found in the work of the group of artists who worked in Russia from the 1880s under the patronage first of Savva Mamontov and later of Diaghilev. Their contribution to the success of directors like Stanislavsky and Meyerhold or to the work of the leading choreographers and dancers of the day is very well documented in Edward

Braun's *The Theatre of Meyerhold*, and demonstrates an area in which both opera and dance have contributed to the development of the wider aspects of theatre.

Historical accuracy of costume has not always been considered of paramount importance, although at other times it has been the subject of much careful research. Whereas the productions of the mid-nineteenth century frequently employed absolute accuracy of dress and architecture down to the finest detail, illustrations from earlier periods show characters either dressed in contemporary costume or in a strange mixture of historic and modern attire. 'Modern dress' versions of older plays continue to excite rather special interest and are frequently accompanied by statements from the director anxious to point out the topicality or continuing relevance of the play. There are, of course, certain plays which appear to be firmly rooted in the social conditions or historic events of one particular period, but in recent years, quite apart from the frequent transmigration of Shakespeare to different times and places, Molière has had 1960s settings, Ibsen has been set in Scotland in the 1940s and Marlowe in futuristic dress.

One of the arguments for retaining some accuracy in the costume is that fashion extends to movement, posture, physical shape, language and manners, and that a production must leave the language unchanged. What happens then if we tamper with one of the details while others remain constant? Some designers and directors have attempted to solve this problem by making their costumes suggest rather than reproduce the style of a particular period whilst others, such as Jarry, have aimed for a style of costume that was somehow placed out of time. In a letter that Jarry wrote concerning the possible production of his play *Ubu Roi*, he asked that the costume be

> divorced as far as possible from local time or chronology (which will thus help to give the impression of something eternal): modern costumes, preferably, since the satire is modern, and shoddy ones, too, to make the play even more wretched and horrible. (*Selected Works*, p. 68)

An approach to costume which transcends the time element is to adopt a **convention** by dressing performers in certain traditional performance clothes such as those of clowns, Pierrots, or other characters originating in the **commedia dell'arte**, or in the top hat, white gloves and cane of the Music Hall; this technique was used most successfully in *O What a Lovely War*, the popular rock musical *Godspell* and Caryl Churchill's *Vinegar Tom*, to cite but three examples.

Another important consideration is the way in which costume establishes and extends **character**: the elaborate and outrageous dress of the 'fop' in Restoration comedy, the austerity of the puritan inquisitors in *The Crucible*, the short cloak of Henry II in *Curtmantle* or Osric's hat in *Hamlet* demand an understanding of the whole play before the designer can produce a suitable set of designs for a production. Many performers also find that they are greatly helped, even in early rehearsal, by being able to wear a key piece of costume.

Decorating the stage

The concept of decorating the stage may seem to imply the imposition of an external and, perhaps, trivial addition to a performance area. It is, however, more firmly linked to the idea of *décor*: a means of defining and shaping the stage environment. By the early years of the seventeenth century it was quite common for theatres to have a stock of what were termed *decoration* **sets** showing scenes such as gardens or the interior of churches or dungeons. This would enable the company to present almost any play using some of these selected environments. Indeed, it seems that some of the choices for **settings** were somewhat arbitrary and depended on what was in the stock. The first major form of stage decoration of which we have record is the use of *periaktoi*: triangular prisms with a scene painting on each of their three sides. Vitruvius (first century BC) describes the manner in which scenes in the Roman theatre were changed by revolving the *periaktoi*, in his treatise *De Architectura*. When this work was re-published in 1511, Italian Renaissance architects began to use *periaktoi* as **wings** to the stage, creating a sense of perspective and enabling a number of different scenes to be represented. Additional panels, which became known as *flats*, could be added at the sides and to the rear to increase the range of visual effects. These devices were introduced to England by the architect Inigo Jones (1573–1652) and employed in his designs for masques.

The gradual evolution of a 'picture frame' or '**proscenium**' in the theatre (see **theatre form**) greatly enhanced the opportunities for scenic decoration and by the nineteenth century the resident *scenic artist* would design and paint very large pieces of scenery for the manager. The main function of such scenery was to provide the actor with a painted background (we still use the expression *backdrop* to indicate a picture against which an action is played in real life) and to provide visual information about time and place. Scenic studios were set up to paint enormous stage cloths and flats and to provide scenery on demand; some such studios operated a form of mail order for standard scenic pieces and backdrops.

By the middle of the nineteenth century we get the distinct impression that the decoration of the stage had become more important than the actors. Playbills from the period list the exotic scenes and locations for each play and **melodrama** as if these features were the major attraction. Substantial pieces of music (see **incidental music**) were required to cover the lengthy scene changes and it is still possible to experience a hangover from these times when audiences applaud the scenery at the rise of the curtain. In some cases, the scenic design was a deliberate imitation of a famous painting, intended to be admired as a self-contained work of art. However, this mould was generally broken in the late nineteenth century with the coming of **Naturalism** and a predominating philosophy that attributed behaviour to the forces of environment, heredity, social pressures and the inner life of the psyche. Theatre was thus required to present these forces, especially the environment, in as much convincing detail as possible. A photographic realism was demanded and the stage became an integral part of the total conception of **character**. At this point, the responsibility for the visual impact of the stage shifted from the playwright, manager and scene painter to the designer (see **design concept**).

To some extent, the designer is still involved in decorating the stage because any production involves an audience looking at a relatively small area of space for a long and concentrated period. Such intense focus requires a degree of visual interest and, in the process of watching a play, the eye may become highly selective and critical. No part of the stage can be neutral when it is being observed: it invariably makes some kind of statement. Ideally the visual aspect of staging integrates with all the other elements of a production; it should never be considered in isolation.

There are a number of possible approaches to the concept of 'decorating the stage': (a) having a 'real' location in mind and adapting this to fit a particular physical space; (b) considering the **actors** and the events of the play and constructing an environment in which the **action** can best take place; (c) discovering a mood or theme and creating and shaping a space that reflects that; (d) creating a stage metaphor for the states of mind of the characters, as in **Expressionism**; or (e) conceiving the entire stage and auditorium as a single environment (see **environmental theatre**) or adopting the concept of the *found space* for performance. Once these initial decisions have been taken they must be followed by the selection of textures, colours, and objects such as furniture and props (see **properties**). In the modern theatre this also requires a considerable understanding of the effect of powerful stage **lighting** as well as a sensitive response to the particular **theatre form** in use. For example, the use of solid pieces of scenery will be very different on an 'arena stage' from that of a **proscenium** stage.

Design concept

Once the form, the actual physical space for performance, has been defined, the **director** and designer can set about transforming it into 'artistic space' as part of a unified concept. We owe much of the inspiration for modern design ideas to the writings of Gordon Craig (1872–1966), who insisted on the importance of seeing a production as a whole, and although some of his own designs were visionary rather than practical they set new standards in ways of thinking about the visual presentation of drama. In his most famous and influential book, *The Art of the Theatre* (1905), Craig writes in the form of a dialogue between a playgoer and a stage director. The playgoer has been attempting to define the nature of the art of theatre and the director replies:

> No; the art of the Theatre is neither the acting nor the play, it is not scene nor dance, but it consists of all the elements of which these things are composed: action, which is the very spirit of acting; words, which are the body of the play; line and colour, which are the very heart of the scene; rhythm, which is the very essence of the dance.
> (*The Art of the Theatre*, p. 102)

Craig is extending the idea of design to include far more than scenery, and drew on his friendship with Isadora Duncan, who did much to liberate dance from the rules of classical ballet, to formulate his belief that the arrangement of bodies in space can shape a performance as powerfully as a piece of scenery.

The options available to us in the modern theatre in determining what the audience will see are considerable and they constitute the set of decisions which follow the establishing of the chosen **theatre form** or space. We can change the shape of the stage space in a variety of ways as Craig demonstrated, and his designs always show the stage area transformed by **lighting**, scenic structure and live figures. By constructing and decorating certain types of scenery and by lighting appropriately the environment created, the stage can be made to precisely resemble somewhere else; alternatively we can provide sufficient visual clues for the setting to *suggest* another location. In other circumstances the designer may decide to provide a deliberately *distorted* representation of somewhere else in order that the audience views it with new interest, or so that a particular quality of the environment is highlighted. Fashions in scenic representation have changed, and compared with the early years of the twentieth century recent designs have tended less towards architectural or landscape accuracy and more towards economy and symbolic suggestion, but most designers are mainly concerned to create an image which makes its own statement. Such images may evoke a mood, a theme or an idea or, like the single tree in Beckett's *Waiting for Godot*, may remain essentially enigmatic yet organically linked to the nature of the play.

Various areas of the stage may be clearly defined by **lighting** or **setting** and one effect of this may be to divide the stage into a number of different parts, each with its own function. By dividing the stage horizontally the action can be made to move between two or more levels: such levels may be created with rostra, steps, ramps, scaffolding or even ladders or swings and in some theatres the facility exists for raising or lowering parts of the stage mechanically (see **stage machinery**). The division of the stage in this way is an ancient device and a good deal of speculation exists as to how, for example, the upper level of the Elizabethan playhouse was employed. The stage may also be divided vertically, each section representing a different place, so that characters move from one location to another, as they must have done in the simple journey in the medieval play of *Abraham and Isaac*; or various pre-set areas of the stage may be lit in rotation to show the action going on in several rooms or situations. In Brecht's *The Seven Deadly Sins*, the stage is divided vertically to allow the play to be acted and danced simultaneously, and a similar technique enables the director to show both the inside and outside of a house at the same time.

The introduction of various levels and special areas of the stage is not always a temporary arrangement imposed on a bare and level stage. Some theatre designers have insisted that certain permanent features be constructed in new theatres to provide, for example, a number of possible levels and locations for the action. Directors may find it extremely stimulating to work with the possibilities of such staging arrangements and may equally find inspiration in working in outdoor auditoria or in buildings such as warehouses or churches, which provide unusual stages.

So far I have examined the methods by which the shape of a stage may be modified according to the needs of the director; but the stage environment is also transformed by colour and texture. The colour of light used can create moods of tension, gloom or optimism; pools of shadow, shafts of bright light, large expanses of rich colour can all create a powerful image; or the director may elect to have his cast lit with constant bright and even light. Light from a lantern falls on the surfaces of the décor, and the effect will vary greatly depending on the materials and colours used in the scenic construction and decoration. In recent years there has been an enormous extension in the range of materials available to the designer: in addition to wood and canvas, lightweight synthetic materials which are both strong and versatile may now be used and there has been a particular advance in the recognition of the importance and impact of surface textures. This, coupled with several new techniques for the application of paints and dyes, has encouraged designers to create settings composed of bold and strikingly textured surfaces. Such experiments have produced environments in which the substance itself is the central feature and justification for the design; and some modern settings appear to be an exploration into the structural and aesthetic possibilities of mirrors, marbled blocks, rope, stainless steel, chrome, wire, moulded plastic and other substances. In other words, the material composing the actors' surroundings has become the subject of carefully considered, artistic choice.

A major problem facing the designer is the combination of the 'real' with the artificial. An **actor** entering a bare stage and telling a joke to the **audience** is simply that; but the same actor entering a stage that is shaped and painted to look like a room, in which he, as some fictitious character, lives, is a far more complex idea, especially if he then turns away from his interactions with other characters in the play and tells a joke to the *audience*. In a similar way there is a distinction between the walls of that room, which we know not to be made of plaster, and the furniture, which is as real as any in our own home. In some ways the effect of placing a natural object in an artificial environment is to sharpen the audience's awareness of the importance and function of that object, and this is particularly the case where a play shows characters whose personal property is particularly meaningful to them. The junk with which Aston surrounds himself in Harold Pinter's *The Caretaker* is not only a feature of the setting but an extension of his predicament and Brecht, who included several artificial theatrical devices in his productions, always insisted on absolute accuracy and reality in the stage **properties** used by the actors.

One of the objections that Appia (see **lighting**) had towards the scenic conventions of his day was that the surface on which the actor moved was always false:

> This painting which is supposed to represent everything is forced at the outset to renounce representing the ground ... there is no

possibility of relationship between the vertical flats of the set and the stage floor ... so the ground cannot be reproduced by painting. But that is precisely where the actor moves. (Cole and Chinoy, *Directors on Directing*, p. 139)

In an attempt to overcome this problem some designers have experimented with natural substances such as sand, earth or water as part of the stage setting: in the National Theatre's production of *The Creation*, for example, Adam and Eve emerged from a mound of clay, and in a production of Wallace Salter's *Crusade to Surly Bottoms* in Cardiff, the entire stage was covered with green turf and scrap metal.

Whatever ideas the designer and **director** may have concerning the staging of a play before rehearsals begin, it is quite possible that modifications may become necessary. In another production at Cardiff the designer had proposed a setting for *Macbeth* which consisted of a huge spiral ramp of textured wood supported on polished chrome columns. In the completed model the setting appeared to provide a whole range of performance possibilities and satisfied the need for those scenes in which the director wanted characters to appear 'above'. Once the set was constructed, however, the cast, who had been undertaking their early rehearsals on a level floor, found it quite impossible to move with any certainty on the ramp. The struggle to remain still or upright proved so physically exhausting that the cast insisted that the gradient of the ramp be lowered. On the other hand, the director found that the physical struggle was in itself productive and produced performances of great intensity and inventiveness. The modifications continued until after the dress rehearsal and formed an integral part of the evolution of the performance.

Adaptability on the part of designer and director is now seen as an essential quality if the creative process is to persist throughout the preparation for a production, and many theatre companies recognise the importance of the interplay between actor and environment. This has led some theorists to suggest that there must always be some physical risk involved as the performers struggle against human weakness to release latent energy. Performances in which actors run round precarious catwalks, swing from ropes, leap from towers, demonstrate astonishing feats of agility and acrobatics or retain uncomfortable poses for long periods have become part of the legacy of post-Artaudian theatre (see also **Theatre of Cruelty**).

The tendency towards more economic and adaptable forms of staging has received additional impetus from the emergence of hundreds of small-scale, experimental 'fringe' touring theatre groups in recent years. The demands of setting up in variable performance spaces, the economic necessity of quick 'get ins' and 'get outs' together with the fact that actors themselves often form their own stage-management crew, have all militated against elaborate settings and forced designers to construct portable 'minimal' scenery. Commercial theatres have also found that their budget, their approach to performance and the growth of their own 'lunch time' or studio theatres have restricted the scale on which scenery is built.

The one exception appears to be grand opera, which continues to demand lavish settings on a scale comparable with those of the late nineteenth century. Recent productions of *La Bohème* and *Aida* by English National Opera were both staged on massive 'realistic' sets, in which the performers resembled insects inhabiting a giant world; the spectacle was breathtaking but the visual and musical landscape relegated the human bodies, the so-called 'characters' of the drama, to almost marginal significance, and it is noticeable that many modern designers see their most exciting opportunities lying in the fields of opera and dance, in which the need for a forward-projected picture remains constant. More innovative design approaches have characterised many of the recent revivals of Baroque Opera. For instance, works by such composers as Handel and Purcell have been toured successfully with small casts and portable but carefully designed and effective sets by English Touring Opera.

When we first open a playtext, the *libretto* of an opera or the 'book' of a stage Musical, the suggested setting for the work is one of the earliest impressions we have of it. The writer's instructions may range from a brief indication of the location: 'a wood', 'a castle', etc., to a most elaborate description of the visual impact intended. Before the construction of 'scenery' became a normal part of theatrical presentation, the indications of the scene were often embedded in the text of the play so that the audience was asked to use its imagination to picture the setting. For example, the character called Rumour, who speaks the Prologue to Shakespeare's *Henry IV, Part 2*, asks us to imagine ourselves in 'this worm eaten hold of ragged stone' – Northumberland's castle. Theatre technology has advanced a great deal since Shakespeare's day and like all other forms of technology was accelerated enormously by the Industrial Revolution, so that since the nineteenth century playwrights have had an ever increasing range of **stage machinery, lighting** equipment, sound effects and constructional techniques at their disposal. Today the theatre is also able to employ sophisticated film techniques, computer-generated images and a wide range of digital technology. The cumulative effect has been for playwrights to conceive their plays in visual as well as aural terms, to include powerful visual images and, if they so wish, to simulate real life with greater accuracy.

See also **stage directions.**

Discovery

The concept of 'discovery' in a play is often associated with the large number of plays written for the London theatres in the late sixteenth and early seventeenth centuries. The most famous example is probably found in Shakespeare's *The Tempest* when, at the culmination of the **action**, Prospero 'discovers' the young lovers, Ferdinand and Miranda, 'playing chess'. Such **stage directions** have led to a great deal of scholarly debate concerning the precise way in which discoveries were handled. Some have speculated that in this scene, for example, Prospero simply draws aside a curtain or *arras* to reveal the young couple absorbed in their game of chess, and there seems to be considerable evidence that the *tiring house* – a room or space behind the acting area – may well have been equipped with a curtain that could be drawn aside to make a 'discovery space' for use in such instances. A play like Middleton's *Chaste Maid in Cheapside* (circa 1611), first performed at the Swan Theatre in London, which contains the stage direction. '*Enter Maudline and Moll, Shop being discovered*', clearly requires a small discovery space in which two players could suddenly be revealed to the audience. Such an area, neither quite 'on stage' nor yet 'off stage', might now be described as 'liminal' space (see **liminality**). From the information we have concerning the dimensions and construction of The Swan it would appear that the space would have been situated between the doors at the rear of the stage and would have been no more than 7 metres wide and 1 metre deep. This was quite probably a section of the *tiring house* but there is now extensive debate as to whether theatres were equipped with purpose-built discovery spaces. If you are interested in these debates you will find them in Volume 3 of Leech and Craik, *The Revels History of Drama in English* (1975) or Richard Leacroft's *The Development of the English Playhouse* (1988). Leacroft points out that the concept of 'discovery', that is, suddenly revealing a scene that is already in progress, was almost certainly employed in the medieval staging of Mystery or Morality Plays through the use of 'mansions' (see **Mystery Play**) and, again, was probably achieved by the use of some form of hanging or arras.

The modern director or designer has many more options and it is an interesting exercise to consider how the requirement for a discovery might be handled. The term is now used to describe any scene on which the curtain might rise or lights come up to 'discover' characters already on stage and, apparently, already engaged in conversation and/or activity. Turgenev's play *A Month in the Country* (1850), for example, has the curtain rise on an established game of cards. With the invention of electric stage lighting it became possible to effect many startling discoveries. By using a *gauze*, characters could seem to appear or disappear through apparently solid surfaces. The technique was widely used in melodrama but also in late nineteenth-century productions of Shakespeare. Tennessee Williams used the same effect in *The Glass Menagerie*. The concept of 'discovery' is not only a visual issue, although with sophisticated lighting or the projection of still or moving images, the possibilities are now almost infinite. The performance issue is that the actors must clearly establish the illusion that whatever it is they are doing has been going on for some while, and thus enrich the sense of a life outside the confines of the play.

Empty space

In 1969 the British Theatre director Peter Brook (see **Theatre of Cruelty, Theatre of Communion**) gave a series of four lectures subsequently published under the title *The Empty Space*. This book has established itself as one of the seminal works of the modern theatre. Its most frequently quoted and fundamental concept is:

> I take an empty space and call it a bare stage. A man walks across this empty space while someone else is watching him, and that is all that is needed for an act of theatre to be engaged.

Brook's formulation is typical of many attempts to state a lowest common factor for all theatre of all ages. Such reductions can be useful for their emphasis, which falls upon things done rather than said, actions rather than words, and upon the presence of the spectator. In stating the minimal act of theatre, Brook involves the idea of the *director* taking an empty space and transforming it into a stage, not by decoration or structures but by the nature of what takes place there and by the potential interaction of performer and spectator. For directors attempting to rediscover the eternal laws that govern the creation of theatre, space has a primal importance because it gives birth to forms and therefore has equal status with the **actor**.

For Brook, who was heavily influenced by Grotowski (see **Poor Theatre**), the shared space between actor and spectator was a means of establishing a sense of 'communion' and he fleshed out his ideas by describing four categories of theatre. The deadly theatre is dead through its own inertia and locked in conventions and clichés: one feels he had in mind here 'the bloody British theatre: insular, class-bound, text-bound and earth bound'. Such outbursts reflected Brook's impatience with the predictable and yet superficially experimental theatre that he saw around him. His second category is rough theatre – and would be best described as populist and vulgar; then there is immediate theatre, or what Brook liked to call the 'theatre of the vital spark'; and finally, holy theatre – a form of communion that is in search of secular ritual to replace the spiritual void. This Utopian and idealistic vision of a new function for theatre owed something to the theatre of ancient Japan, rediscovered in the 1920s and 1930s (see **Poetic Drama, ritual**), and led Brook to explore a variety of other Oriental forms of theatre that involved the ritual designation of an empty space for performance.

There are excellent discussions of Brook's work in Eyre and Wright's *Changing Stages* (2000) and in *Theatre is Just a Form* (Allain, 2009) cited in the bibliography of the previous chapter. There are also some useful thoughts on the concept of space in relation to Brook's ideas, in Gay McAuley's *Space in Performance* (1999).

Entrances

The concept of an 'entrance' in the theatre involves both an act and an aspect of physical staging. In his autobiographical *The Precarious Crust* (1971), Laurence Irving, whose father, mother, uncle and grandfather were all successful actors, describes his fascination, as a child, with watching actors 'waiting in the wings', preparing themselves for making an entrance and gathering their energy and focus for that moment of transformation when they stepped out 'in **character**' on to the acting area. The moment of entrance has always been significant for actors: Shakespeare alludes to it in the famous 'stage as metaphor' speech in *As You Like It*: 'All the world's a stage / And all the men and women merely players / They have their exits and their entrances'. Sir Henry Irving, Laurence Irving's grandfather, had an almost legendary entrance in the **melodrama** *The Bells* (1871) with the words 'It is I!' and accompanied by a great **gesture** that has been recorded in contemporary drawings. At that moment the entire audience applauded, and I have seen that tradition continued at the Leas Pavilion Theatre in Folkestone (at one time the oldest surviving 'rep' theatre in Britain) when the 'star' leading actor and manager of the company, Arthur Brough, who went on to become famous in the TV comedy *Are You Being Served?*, entered well into Act I of a play. (A more extensive description of this performance is given in Pickering and Woolgar's *Theatre Studies* (2009). It is still possible to see similar reactions to the entrance of a TV celebrity in a Pantomime.

Peter Barkworth, one of the most accomplished actors and teachers of acting of the latter half of the twentieth century, told how he once asked a new **director** how he wanted him to 'make his entrance'. The director replied 'Just come on.' But as I discovered when rehearsing with Peter Barkworth, he was capable of a seemingly infinite number of ways of entering, or of speaking a line, and the concept of an 'entrance' was integral to the building of an entire character and performance. The nature of an entrance by a performer will be dictated by many factors: **stage directions**, the structure of the stage and **setting**, the entire architecture of the performance venue, the style of the drama, or the physical characteristics of the **actor** and character, will all be contributing factors. The entrance may be accompanied by a drumroll, fanfare or *flourish* or it may be announced in the **dialogue**; a god may be lowered onto the stage by a *mechane* as in the Ancient Greek theatre (giving rise to the expression *deus ex machina*); an angel may descend into the acting area, as in the Church of the Annunciation in Florence in 1493 or as is still seen in the Spanish **Mystery Play** in the church of Santa María in Elche; a character may *fly in* as in *Peter Pan*, or shoot up onto the stage through a *star trap* (see **stage machinery**) as they did in the late eighteenth century. A character may enter *above*, as they clearly did in the Elizabethan theatre, or, like Tamburlaine in Marlowe's play of the same name, '*drawn in his chariot by the Kings of Trebizon and Soria, with bits in their mouths, reins in his left hand, and in his right hand a whip with which he scourgeth them*' (Part 2. Act IV, Sc. 3), or by complete contrast, simply 'walk across an **empty space**'.

McAuley (1999) describes a form of Balinese dance in which the moment of entrance is considerably extended to give added significance to the event. Each masked dancer appears from behind a curtain at the rear of the performance space, and the moment is prepared by music building to a climax and the curtain being shaken to draw attention to the unseen presence of the dancer, before it is finally opened to reveal the performer. A similar ritual significance is given to the actors of the ancient Japanese *Noh* plays (see **ritual**), in which each performer enters slowly via a long ramp that extends from the main acting area to a special location for the first sight of the characters, so that the **audience** has an opportunity to watch them before they engage in the drama itself. The moment of entrance of the **chorus** in the Ancient Greek theatre indicated the beginning of the play and, given the structure of the theatres, must have been a spectacular and complex process. In classical dramaturgy the unit of a **scene** is determined by the entrance of a new character (see **scene**), and not by a change of location.

The precise physical point of entrance to the stage is governed by its structure. Every experienced actor knows that, in any form of *end* staging (as opposed to 'arena staging'), the point for a strong entrance is upstage. For much of its history, the Western theatre has provided entrances to the stage in the form of doors in the rear wall. There appear to have been either two or three such doors in the *skene*, the permanent structure at the rear of the elevated acting area in the Greek theatre, from which the main actors could make their appearances; the chorus probably entered the *orchestra*, a central performance area, through an aisle known as the *parodos*, between the *skene* building and the *orchestra*. Elements of the Greek theatre remained constant in the Roman and Renaissance theatre and the evidence we have of the structure of Elizabethan theatres suggests that the two or three doors at the rear of the stage remained the principal means of access to the acting area.

Helen and Richard Leacroft (1984) maintain that by 1614, the second 'Globe Theatre' in London had at least four double doors and a '**discovery** space' at stage level and a first-level gallery with a further five openings. It is only by exploring the possible structure of Elizabethan theatres that you can make sense of such stage directions as '*Enter Oberon, the King of the Fairies, at one door, with his train; and Titania, the Queen, at another with hers*' (*A Midsummer Night's Dream*, Act II, Sc. 1). Preparing for such an entrance, Puck states 'Here comes Oberon', and this is one of many examples from sixteenth- and seventeenth-century plays that envisage the possibility of a long and impressive entrance onto the acting area from upstage. The same structure made processions and battle scenes fluid and simple by allowing individuals and groups to make frequent entrances and exits, constantly reappearing for short scenes and giving the impression of perpetual movement. It allowed characters to disappear quickly, and in the case of Marlowe's *Dr Faustus* or Shakespeare's *A Midsummer Night's Dream*, re-enter in a transformed state wearing cuckold's horns or the head of an ass.

With the advent in the seventeenth century of more architectural, perspective scenery constructed of screens or shutters that moved in grooves, or of *periaktoi* (see **decorating the stage**), the point of entry to the stage became radically changed. Actors performed on a forestage so that they could be seen and heard, while the painted **wings** and flats were confined to behind the **proscenium** arch. With this separation of actors and scenery, the entrances and exits were made through doors installed on either side of the **proscenium**. However, with the growing demand for spectacle, theatre managers and architects were inclined to remove the forestage and confine the action to behind the picture frame of the proscenium, thus making it necessary for entrances to be made from the wings. Actors resisted this move because it made the strong entrance more difficult, and some theatres retained the proscenium doors, but a new problem was not far away. With the introduction of the realistic **box set** in the latter part of the nineteenth century, the only practical entrances were the doors built into the canvas and wood flats of which the set was constructed, and this, again, changed the whole issue of entering the acting area and became an aspect of the realistic illusion (see **realism**).

Laurence Irving (1971) records that Martin Harvey was the first English director to break this convention, by having cast members enter through the auditorium in the 1920s. This was a period in which a number of ancient dramatic forms were being rediscovered (see **chorus, ritual**), and the restriction of the concept of the **fourth wall** needed to be broken. The concept of 'entrances' can only be fully comprehended when the problem of performing a play on a type of stage for which it was not originally written is encountered. (see **authenticity**) This is an important aspect of the perpetual link between plays, players and playhouses. Modern theatre practice has employed a variety of **theatre forms**, each requiring its own type of entrance. Some productions have involved the actors entering the shared space of an 'arena' stage and auditorium in full view of the audience and then sitting around the edge of the acting area and stepping into it when they were involved in a scene. In this use of **liminal** space the actors reconstruct the entire concept of an entrance because they remain visible throughout the performance. Characters also now often change costume in full view of the audience, providing what many may see as a less contrived style of performance and challenging the illusions of physical realism in favour of psychological depth.

See also **theatre form**.

Found space

In his book *Playwriting: a Complete Guide to Creating Theater* (1990) the American playwright and teacher Shelly Frome makes the somewhat unexpected suggestion that the process of writing a play should begin with a search for an inspirational space: a space that suggests myths and narratives of vital interest and significance to humanity. The concept of the 'found space' seems, in fact, to be as ancient as the concept of drama or performance although the term itself is relatively recent. (see **Environmental Theatre**) At some stage in many ancient societies a found space suitable for ritual or ritual/performance became also a sacred space and in this phenomenon we have the origins of theatre.

Records in Europe and the United States show that wherever there are actors there is a search for somewhere suitable to perform. The arrival of actors to the palace of Elsinore in Shakespeare's *Hamlet* or the rehearsal of the amateur actors in *A Midsummer Night's Dream* depend for their later success on finding a functional and convenient location for their work.

In more recent times, however, the found space has been employed as a deliberate alternative to the permanent theatre space. The use of non-theatrical venues for performance has been seen as liberating and may well constitute an act of outreach into the community. It may also form the basis of **site-specific** production and, indeed, the search for or discovery of challenging and fascinating locations can offer a starting point for the construction of **community plays, street theatre** or for a revitalisation of existing **texts**. The qualities of a found space must include the provision of a context for stories or action, a sense of organic unity with the performance and the sense that the space can be effectively shared between performers and audience/spectators.

Form

See **Theatre form.**

Fourth wall

The key question for the staging of any play is 'For what **audience** and to what effect?' All the choices that a **director** makes concerning the type of staging, styles of acting, **costumes, settings**, etc. follow from his or her response to this initial question. The variations in production style available to a modern director are almost infinite, but it is possible to identify various modes of theatre production and these will enable students to focus a discussion of staging problems by reference to concrete examples of the work of significant directors. An important category is the 'theatre of imitation', or Naturalist theatre, and there is an example of this in Stanislavsky's production of *The Seagull* (see **naturalism**). Stanislavsky's deployment of atmospheric detail bathed his actors in an environment that came as near as possible to evoking the real world in which the characters they were portraying lived and moved.

The settings designed by Stanislavsky's designer Simov were variations on the basic pattern of the '**box set**' which had been in use since the early years of the century. By joining together a series of canvas flats and inserting panels containing windows, doors, fireplaces and other solid pieces, designers had discovered that it was possible to create a very accurate reconstruction of an interior. In this way, not only could the play convey visually to its audience a great deal about the tastes and economic condition of the **characters**, but the **actors** portraying the characters were greatly helped by inhabiting an environment which gave realistic support to their performances. In a **box set**, the actors are enclosed within the walls of a setting and by assuming that there is an imaginary 'fourth wall' on the side where the audience is placed, they can re-create imaginatively the feeling of living in a real room. Among modern directors, André Antoine (1858–1943) was the most extreme exponent of the idea of the fourth wall:

> For a stage set to be original, striking, and authentic, it should first be built in accordance with something seen – whether a landscape or an interior. If it is an interior, it should be built with its four sides, its four walls, without worrying about the fourth wall, which will later disappear so as to enable the audience to see what is going on. (Cole and Chinoy, *Directors on Directing*, p. 95)

The development of these new staging techniques by Stanislavsky, Antoine and others was at first heralded as a move towards greater truth and vitality in the theatre. But the danger of theatre resembling life too closely is that it becomes merely an inert copy of it. The Russian director Nikolai Evreinov (1879–1950) argued that if Stanislavsky had followed his logic through when directing *The Three Sisters*, he would have rented a house in the suburbs of Moscow, 'the audience would have come under the pretext of looking for apartments and then looked through the keyhole or half-open door' (Styan, *Modern Drama in Theory and Practice*, vol. 3, p. 90). He was implying that Stanislavsky's theatre was barely theatre at all and involved its audience in the dangerous hypocrisy of pretending that the stage world was real and that the characters had independent existences. The end-product of such theatre could only be passive observation, sentimentality or, at worst, voyeurism. Though the audience members might feel sympathy for the characters portrayed, they would, he maintained, acquire no larger understanding of the way the world worked, nor discover any desire to change it.

See also **director.**

Lighting

Of all the inventions that changed the face of the theatre none was so influential as the introduction of first gas and, later, electric stage lighting. Gas was in use in British and European theatres from about 1817 onwards and this was gradually replaced by electricity during the 1880s. In subsequent years, lighting equipment has reached a very high level of sophistication but from the early years of the last century the control of intensity, direction, colour and quality of light has been seen as an integral part of the art of theatre.

When Shakespeare's mechanicals in *A Midsummer Night's Dream* are discussing how they will achieve the effect of moonlight for the meeting of Pyramus and Thisbe, the best they can suggest is that they leave open the casement window to allow the moon to shine into the chamber, or have a character carrying a lantern and thorn bush and bringing in a dog, to represent moonshine; yet we read that in Samuel Phelp's production of the play in 1853, moonlight and sunrise were 'exquisitely presented'. The imagery of the lantern, thorn and dog, no doubt understood by the original audiences, had been replaced with the moon shining to order, as the mechanicals had rather optimistically hoped! Much nineteenth-century lighting was concerned with special effects and lighting the set, and it was Appia who insisted that the lighting, rather than enhancing the bland flatness of the painted set, should create depth and shadow and provide an environment of light in which the actor should move. Another avant-garde theatre practitioner to investigate the artistic use of lighting was the poet and playwright Alfred Jarry (1873–1907) (see **absurdism/Theatre of the Absurd**) who attempted to counteract the tendency towards greater Naturalism in the theatre of his time by insisting that the actors should be as wooden and far from life as possible. In his essay 'On the Uselessness of Theatre in the Theatre', he began by proclaiming that two 'notoriously horrible things must be removed from the stage: sets and actors'. Instead he proposed that actors should be like puppets, wearing **masks** that are lit from below by footlights, which 'illumine the actor's body along the hypotenuse of a right-angled triangle, the actor's body forming one of the sides of the right angle' (*Selected Works*, p. 72). Jarry goes on to examine the effect of the footlights as if they were the eyes of the audience, although he suggests that they should be thought of as a 'single point of light situated at an indefinite distance, as if it were *behind* the **audience**'. In order to underline the potential that Jarry saw in the developing art of lighting, he states that actors should usually wear masks on which the play of light is particularly effective: 'With the old style of actor, masked only in a thinly applied make-up, each facial expression is raised to a power by colour and particularly by relief, and then to cubes and higher power by LIGHTING' (p. 72). Jarry does not make easy reading, partly because his ideas are presented in a highly idiosyncratic style and partly because he is writing in the context of modes of production which have died out. The footlights have gradually been rejected as a common means of ensuring that actors are well lit, mainly because of the changes in theatre forms which we have traced in this chapter. However, many of Jarry's ideas repay careful consideration for, like Appia, he saw the importance of creating a total environment and recognised that drama was shaped by very much more than the playtext.

When we consider what was attempted and achieved by playwrights, actor-managers and **directors** with new lighting facilities it is not surprising that a body of theoretical writing on the subject began to emerge. The new dimension in stage plays from the mid-nineteenth century onwards is recognisable both in popular **melodramas** and in the more serious, socially conscious plays of Tom Robertson, Ibsen or Strindberg. An example of the popular play built around scenic and lighting effects is Boucicault's *The Corsican Brothers* (1852), which was staged first by Charles Kean and later revived by Henry Irving. In both cases the famous leading **actor** played the part of both brothers, and a whole series of visions, appearances and disappearances and spectacular scenes were achieved by the use of machinery, gauzes and lighting. In Irving's production, 'sink and rise' scenery enabled the audience to see the vision one brother had of the other, while the 'Corsican trap' provided means whereby a ghost's head appeared slowly through the floor on one side of the stage and then the spectre gradually glided across the stage, rising from the ground (see **stage machinery**). Thousands of feet of gas piping, 30 gas men, 90 carpenters, 15 property men and tons of salt to create a snow scene were used in this production and it must have provided a nightmare for those concerned with continuity.

Ibsen certainly took advantage of the theatre's new technical capabilities and his plays *Brand* and *When We Dead Awaken* both call for spectacular mountain scenery with swirling clouds, snow or glaciers. But the plays of his middle period, which are the most frequently performed today made more subtle use of visual impact, particularly of the quality of light. The **stage directions** at the opening of these plays invariably refer to the light: *Ghosts* opens in 'a gloomy fjord landscape veiled by rain', *The Wild Duck* with 'brilliantly lit lamps and glowing coal fire', the first scene of *Rosmersholm* takes place at sunset, whereas *The Lady from the Sea* begins in 'morning light' but it is quite clearly specified that the sun 'shines in through the French windows'. The same technique of directing light with some precision enabled Ibsen to create perhaps his most moving lighting effect: the moment when the sun rises and streams in through the window on the dying Oswald at the end of *Ghosts* as he cries 'the sun, the sun'. Ibsen's work contains many other examples of effects made possible by hidden sources of light; where he stipulated that lamps light the interiors in which so many of his plays are set he was relying on the supplementary light from hidden lanterns to light the actors adequately, and he used light as a powerful image as well as a source of greater realism.

In subsequent years, finely controlled electric lighting has become one of the most important aspects of all live theatrical performances. Joan Littlewood, working with Theatre Workshop and Charles Chiltern in the 1960s, used a series of illuminating signboards onto which terrifying statistics flashed, in *O, What a Lovely War*, thus providing an ironic background to the sometimes comic action. Devices of this kind together with the idea of creating a uniquely shaped environment for the performers have been the result of much creative experiment, particularly in the rock/pop field, and since the impact of film and television these concepts have been seen as more appropriate employment of the theatre's technical resources than the simulation of 'real' interiors or landscapes.

Make-up

For many actors, dancers and singers the application of make-up is a vital part of the process of physical and mental preparation for performance, and without the mask of make-up they feel incomplete and exposed. The ritual of applying make-up may take a very long time: some complex designs can take many hours to complete and may require the assistance of a make-up artist to apply. Many performers, however, prefer to work on their own make-up as a means of focus and getting into **character**. The wearing of make-up is no longer seen as essential but it may involve encoding the face, as in the traditions of circus and Pierrots or the drama of ancient Japan, China and Sanskrit cultures. Or make-up may demand the wearing of prosthetic noses or facial characteristics, full body-paint or false hair. You may recall that Bottom in *A Midsummer Night's Dream* was concerned as to which beard he should wear for his role as Pyramus; similarly, the Tudor 'Interlude' of *Sir Thomas More* revolves around the use of a theatrical, false beard. However, the wearing of make-up may simply be a device for preserving the appearance of the face when viewed under immensely powerful lighting.

In the ancient Asian and Greek theatre performers wore white lead-based make-up (since discovered to have been very dangerous) with heavy, painted accents, or they wore masks. Western theatre make-up was originally oil-based and was known as *greasepaint*; it only became vital with the gradual development of oil, gas and electric lighting. Gas provided a much-needed control over the quality of light and in the mid- to late nineteenth century **actors** developed the art of applying elaborate make-up to be seen under the new visual conditions. Some created the habit of painting fixed expressions on their faces and it was largely against this absurdity that the playwright Strindberg raged in his Preface to *Miss Julie*:

> A word about make-up; which I dare not hope will be listened to by the ladies who prefer beauty to truth. But the actor might well ponder whether it is to his advantage to paint an abstract character upon his face which will remain sitting there like a mask. Imagine a gentleman dipping his finger into soot and drawing a line of bad temper between his eyes, and suppose that, wearing this permanently fierce expression, he were called upon to deliver a line smiling? How dreadful would be the result! And how is this false forehead, smooth as a billiard ball, to wrinkle when the old man gets really angry.
>
> In a modern psychological drama, where the subtler reactions should be mirrored in the face rather than in gesture and sound, it would surely be best to experiment with strong side lights on a small stage and with the actor wearing no make-up, or at best a minimum. (trans. Michael Meyer, p. 103)

Strindberg had already commented on the effect of the footlights on the appearance of faces and, in fact, a good deal of his advice has been absorbed into modern theatre practice: many, however, were not sure that they wanted a diet of 'psychological drama' and there was considerable resistance to some of his ideas.

Make-up completes the **costume** of an actor and enables physical features to be seen clearly at great distances and under powerful **lighting**. It ensures that the **audience** can see visual clues as to the actor's character, personality, age, race or general physical state. Even if an actor wishes to be seen exactly as he or she is, it may be necessary to wear make-up to compensate for the colour-draining effects of lighting, but it may be that the actor needs to change appearance altogether. Modern basic stage make-up consists of a foundation and some subtle colour-shadings. Grease paint has been replaced by *Pancake* as a foundation for the actor's basic skin colour: this is far more flexible and easy to apply than the traditional sticks of greasepaint and is conveniently supplied in small cases and applied with a damp sponge. Colour shadings of rouge, lipstick, liners, mascara and powder are applied with pencils and brushes and may be supplemented by synthetic hair, hair toners, glues and solvents. The tendency is to wear little or no make-up in intimate forms of theatre or, unless required for a total transformation, in outdoor theatre.

There are two basic concepts of 'make-up': *straight* and *character*. In the former the make-up highlights the actor's normal features so that they can be seen distinctly, but *character* make-up involves the transformation of the face and appearance to reveal age or attitude. This may be achieved by work on the nose, eyelashes, jawline, wrinkles, eye pouches, teeth, eyebrows, hair or beard; in some cases there may be hairpieces, wigs, scars or disfigurement. Where a make-up is highly complex it will be part of an overall **design concept**, but in every case, it must complement the costume and assist in the creation of character. One further use of make-up, particularly in melodrama and *Grand Guignol*, is the production of horrific effects such as blood and wounds: these require specialist knowledge for effective application and a production can be ruined by their inexpert handling.

One of the problems of literature concerning modern make-up is that it quickly goes out of date. If you wish to develop your own expertise you are strongly advised to consult a reputable supplier for guidance.

Properties

Properties, or 'props', as they are usually called, are any objects used or related to by the actors on a stage. It may seem strange to consider props as a key concept but when we remember that the tragedy of *Othello* eventually revolves around the possession of a handkerchief, or that in Ionesco's plays *The Chairs* and *The New Tenant* the entire stage is taken over by props, which become characters in their own right, we can see their profound significance. Properties are generally categorised as 'general props', such as objects standing around in a room, or as 'hand props', objects like fans, cigarette cases, canes or books carried and used by the **characters**. In some pieces of Physical Theatre, such as Théâtre de Complicité's *Street of Crocodiles*, the props become more like theatre machines with which the actors interact. This approach is familiar in the realm of 'stand-up comedy' and *slapstick*, where performers are well aware of the comic potential of ladders or planks. Staveacre (1987) devotes several chapters of his *Slapstick: The Illustrated Story* to demonstrating the central role played by props in the careers of Music Hall and early movie comics.

In other plays, such as Pinter's *The Dumb Waiter*, a working prop becomes a metaphor for the intrusion of forces from the outside world into the private world of the individual, whereas the sparce but significant props in the plays of Beckett distract the characters from worrying thoughts, or provide grim equivalents of comic routines.

In the late nineteenth- and early twentieth-century plays of social realism, accuracy of properties became a necessity. Stanislavsky's influence on the Actor's Studio developed a naturalist school of acting which can still be seen, for example, in the film performances of Marlon Brando, with its heavy dependence on using props. Brecht insisted that his stage props were real and not simulations. The physical process of working with and moving props was part of the comment on social situations.

One of the most discussed of props is the seagull in Chekhov's play of the same name (1896). Here, the object is clearly part of the stage symbolism within a naturalistic framework, although the precise nature of the symbol is never explained. The seagull itself must look real in order to become an *icon* for the audience, who, in turn, see it as a symbol for the disturbed figure of Nina, who says: 'I am a seagull.' Critics have seen iconic and symbolic aspects in many of the objects in the plays of Ibsen, and in a scene in Winsome Pinnock's play *Mules* (1996) we can see how the prop can still be employed as a central symbol for a governing idea when a coin is tossed onto the stage.

In order for actors to become comfortable with their 'props' and work with them it is often necessary for them to be available at an early stage. For this reason many theatre companies and theatre departments will maintain a store of certain basic props and these may, indeed, form the basis of newly devised work.

There are many source books for the making of props, but perhaps the most comprehensive is Mary Woollard, *An Illustrated Guide to Staging History* (1999).

Proscenium arch

See **Theatre form.**

Realism

Realism has been included in the chapter dealing with staging concepts because many of the results of embracing this particular concept are visual and involve various forms of physical construction. The idea that a work of art can ever re-create or present 'reality' is debatable. There are many perceptions as to what constitutes reality: some would see it as the concrete world of time and space that we perceive around us, and would argue that it is relatively easy to represent this on stage; others would maintain that reality is consciousness or some transcendent quality that can only be represented by images and metaphor. Some would take reality to be a dialectical view of the processes of social change, while others have viewed the ultimate reality as being nothingness. Many playwrights have attempted to capture realism through their use of language because they consider it to be a key organising principle of the mind while others have created a 'critical realism' that demonstrates a model of the world.

Students often find the differentiation between realism and **naturalism** difficult and, indeed, the terms are often used synonymously. Patrice Pavis (1998) dates Naturalism as an artistic movement around 1880–90 whereas he suggests that Realism emerged earlier, between 1830 and 1880. 'Realism' as a term was initially associated with the rejection of Classicism and Romanticism in painting and its followers advocated a faithful imitation of Nature. In literature, the movement of realism is seen in the works of novelists like Balzac, Zola and Stendhal, who attempted to provide an accurate representation of society. In all works of art that are concerned to show the life of mankind or of society, realistic representation attempts to create an accurate, objective and appropriate image of its subject, avoiding idealisation: as Pavis (1998) puts it, 'Realistic art presents iconic signs of the reality that inspires it' (p. 302). It is helpful to think of Naturalism as one kind of Realism. According to Brecht in the *Messingkauf Dialogues*, the 'naturalists' see the world differently from the 'realists': 'The naturalists depict men as if they were showing a tree to a passer-by. The realists depict men as if they were showing it to a gardener.' In practical theatre terms, Brecht's form of Realism, whilst acknowledging the fundamental unreality of theatre, seeks to demonstrate how things grow and change rather than how they appear, whereas Naturalism attempts the illusion of total imitation.

The most obvious implication of the growth of Realism in the theatre during the first half of the nineteenth century was the desire to construct scenery that provided a simulation of reality as a setting for the **action**. Developments in theatre technology, such as the facility to construct and paint huge canvas flats, the growing sophistication of **stage machinery**, the evolution of the **box set** and the introduction of gas **lighting**, with its greatly increased control, all contributed to the potential for creating pictures of reality within the frame of the **proscenium**. As the century progressed and practical doors and windows in the *set* replaced entrances from **wings** in interior **settings**, and functioning three-dimensional pieces of stage furniture created illusions of solid rooms, it became increasingly possible to present the lives of believable **characters** within their domestic environments. The English playwright T. W. Robertson, whose play *Caste* (1867) is sometimes credited with introducing a new form of Realism to the theatre, was known as 'door knobs Robertson' for his insistence on total accuracy for the **properties** and settings in his productions.

With the introduction of electric lighting (see **lighting**) it became possible to create an even more photographic realism in productions: the plays of Ibsen are dense with instructions for the quality, direction and colour of light, and this reflects the ability to simulate the source of 'natural' light and to use both on-stage lights and light entering the space through windows. You will encounter some of the results of such developments in Realism under the entry on the **fourth wall**, and it might be helpful to read or re-read this now. The debate concerning Realism has also been considerably widened by Marxist, formalist, structuralist and **Postmodernist** critics (see **theatre language**) and I need to touch upon them here.

Brecht was concerned to concentrate on the 'reality' of theatre rather than on the reality of appearances. He wanted 'no illusions about the power of illusion' and his stage designers were obliged to bear this in mind as they strove to create an 'epic realism'. In creating what I have earlier referred to as a 'critical Realism', based on the Marxist theory of knowledge, the theatre is not attempting to create a copy of reality but to provide an image of the **plot** that the **audience** can 'read' as showing the social mechanisms of reality. In this way, the theatre provides a means for the critical analysis of reality. In the language of Structuralism and **semiotics**, the stage does not, necessarily, provide photographic reproduction, but provides relevant **signs** in order to *signify* the world it is representing. A realistic production will enable its spectators to identify the reality being portrayed. Barthes (1963) warned against the slavish imitation of reality: 'The sign should be partly arbitrary, otherwise we fall into an art of expression, an art of essentialist illusion' (p. 55).

In order to present the kind of Realism on stage I have been discussing, it may well be necessary to find some form of *abstraction* of that reality through some kind of *stylisation*. Formalist criticism has largely discredited the idea that Realism involves a direct representation of the real, and the theatre constantly searches for means of engaging its spectators with a sense of what is real within the framework of a fiction. The question of Realism in the theatre has remained central to its function: because of the grim realism of some of the scenes, the anonymous writer of the **Mystery Plays** from York is often named as 'the York Realist' yet, thirty years before the end of the twentieth century, the director James Roose-Evans, imagining a return to theatre's pagan origins, was writing:

> Already the sex act has been performed on the New York stage, albeit off Broadway. It is but a matter of time before mice, snakes or rats are let loose among the audience; before the head of a real canary is chopped off during a production of Strindberg's *Miss Julie*. ... Quite soon we shall see, as in William Golding's *The Lord of the Flies*, a ritual pig-killing, a mass orgy and, finally – a human sacrifice. The wheel will have turned full circle. (*Experimental Theatre*, p. 145)

Those of us who now witness the plethora of 'reality' TV shows may well think that they constitute a form of human sacrifice!

Counsell and Wolf (2001) and Counsell (1996) contain useful discussions on theoretical aspects of Realism, whereas Brockett (1995) contains excellent illustrative material on the development of stage Realism. It is also important to read Strindberg's Preface to his play *Miss Julie*.

See also **acting styles; make-up** *and* **Naturalism.**

Scenography

The term 'scenography' is comparatively recent in usage, but the concept has been in use for a long time. In the United States, the single practitioner who designs scenery, **costume**, and **lighting** is sometimes called the *scenographer* and the director Meyerhold (see Chapter 3) used the term *scenology* to denote the study of all the elements that constitute a stage production: acting, dramaturgy, staging, lighting and stage-design.

However, the term 'scenography' has now become established not only as a description of the entire visual staging aspects of a production but also of its study as a discipline within Theatre and Performance Studies. Setting themselves free from the study of English Literature (see the introduction to Chapter 1), Drama, Theatre and Performance Studies have increasingly realised the inter-relatedness of aspects of performance. Central to this development have been the recognition that the history of the theatre shows that there has always been a profound relationship between the theatrical event, and scenographic and performance styles. In eighteenth-century England, especially under the influence of the actor Garrick and the scenographer Philippe-Jacques

Loutherbourg, the theatre was transformed from being a rhetorical event to being a pictorial experience. With the development of new construction techniques and the gradual introduction of more sophisticated **stage machinery** and forms of lighting, the ability to enhance the pictorial qualities of a production was greatly increased and the entire concept of a performance was modified.

At times, as in the late eighteenth century, the aim of the scenography has been to absorb the **audience** within the theatrical experience, and at other times it has provided a framework for a sense of detached observation of psychological realism. If you were to turn now to the entry under conventions you will see how a specific form of scenography affected the mode of delivery of certain lines; now it would be useful to compare this with the material under **entrances**. All these, together with many more of the issues discussed in this book, such as decorating the stage, **design concept** or **fourth wall**, are, in fact, aspects of scenography. You will find it a very useful exercise to use this book as a starting point and follow up other cited sources to research a specific period of theatre history, establishing the relationships between performance and scenographic elements. An excellent example of this form of scholarship is Christopher Baugh's *Garrick and Loutherbourg* (1993).

Set/setting

The term 'set' has different specific meanings in relation to theatre according to whether it is used as a noun or verb, but it is always related to the more general concept of 'setting'. A set is a structure or group of structures placed on a stage in order to create an environment for the play: David Welker (1969) suggests that a set can serve four basic functions: (a) it may constitute a machine for organising the arrangement and movement of the actors; (b) it may express the mood of the play; (c) it may give information about the locale and time of the play; or (d) it may be visually interesting in itself (p. 9). Throughout most of theatre history, the first of these functions has predominated but, if you research this issue more fully, you will find evidence that in the early nineteenth century, for example, (d) was in the ascendancy (see **decorating the stage**). During most periods, though, some sort of permanent or temporary structure has been erected on a stage.

We do, however, tend to associate the concept of a 'set' with the entire transformation of the stage by a number of possible means. A set may be composed of a variety of three-dimensional pieces: *rostra, platforms, stage-blocks, treads* (steps) or *ramps* intended to create different levels and used in conjunction with *drapes* (hanging curtains, usually black or grey) or *flats* (large canvas panels stretched over wooden frames). Such a set might also include free-standing pieces constructed to look solid, but actually made of papier mâché on a wire frame or of some synthetic material that can be easily moulded. It may gain much of its visual interest by being viewed, sometimes in silhouette, against the *cyclorama* (the rear wall of the stage). On the other hand, a set may be a variety of the '**box set**', the solid-looking interior constructed of flats *cleated* together: it may be symmetrical or it may be an *alcove* or *jog* set, the latter having an alcove at one side of the rear wall giving an 'off centre' appearance to the stage.

It is quite common for theatre companies to hire complete sets for productions because the construction and storage of sets is costly and complex. In many cases, a single set may suffice for an entire play, but in other productions, particularly musicals and pantomimes, audiences still enjoy a change of set for each **Act**. In the classical French theatre it was common to use only one set in order to comply with the Aristotelian unities of location, action and time. A set may be changed by having pieces *flown* (lowered or raised by ropes or wires on pulleys), *trucked* (mounted on wheels) or by the use of a *revolve* (see **stage machinery**). Sets are sometimes built so that they can simply be reversed, but some plays require that parts of the 'walls' be cut away or that several rooms be seen simultaneously. J. B. Priestley's *An Inspector Calls* demands that the same set be seen from different angles for each Act. However, in productions mounted on different types of staging from the original, major artistic and design decisions have to be made in relation to plays that make such specific demands. For example, many directors have found that the tension of Priestley's or Ibsen's plays makes them ideal for production 'In-the-Round' (see **Theatre in the Round**) but, in these circumstances, no set as such is possible.

The designer of a set is required to respond to the demands of the play, and these may be quite specific. Nevertheless, there invariably seems to be a choice between making a set more or less realistic in intention or making it, in some way, purely *representational*. At this point it might find it helpful to read the entry for **design concept** for a discussion of some of the options open to a modern stage designer. Experienced **directors** realise how important it is for a cast to be familiar with the dimensions, levels and **entrances** of a set, and for this reason any rehearsal space is marked out to indicate these features. For touring productions, the *get in* time when the stage crew can start erecting the set is crucial if it is to allow the actors some moments to familiarise themselves with a subtly different environment, and many actors still tell stories of the crew *striking* (taking down) the set during the last Act of a performance!

A decision to set a play in a certain time and place was, at one time, probably seen as the playwright's prerogative. From this decision emanates the design concept and performance style. The setting of a play provides much of the quality of the action: a court, a café, a prosperous house, a dingy flat, a woodland, an enchanted island, a church or a brothel all bring out different forms of behaviour, as do Tudor England, contemporary New York, 1930s Berlin or the Thirty Years War. Some plays that once had a 'contemporary setting' may many years later be seen as historic pieces: do we now give them a contemporary setting from today or set them in the context of their original creation? Such questions abound once we start making a new text from an existing work (see the introduction to Chapter 1).

Modern directors have tended to see the setting of a play as an aspect of the **governing idea** for a production rather than as a requirement of the playwright. Perhaps the most celebrated of such directors has been Jonathan Miller, who has made highly controversial but popular productions of opera by setting the **work** in a period and place totally different from the original, but arguing that such re-setting brings out the essence of the piece and gives it a fresh life, or 'after-life' as he likes to put it. A recent production of Marlowe's *Edward II* by a Hungarian company was a good example of this process. The production was mounted so that the entire **audience** sat around three sides of a space on the stage of a large theatre with a **proscenium**. They found themselves virtually in a butcher's shop with large carcasses of meat hanging from a rail of hooks and blood dripping onto the floor, which was 'hosed down' at intervals by the cast, who were dressed as butchers. In this setting, the underlying violence of the play and its depiction of corrupt politics and the use of power was made more shockingly 'real' than in any more 'historically accurate' production of the play I have ever seen (see **authenticity**). The setting had become a metaphor for the play's underlying themes and had communicated them powerfully. The proximity of the action and the sense of being unable to escape from the experience relates to my discussion of the **Theatre of Cruelty** and of the concept of 'communion' (see **Theatre of Communion**).

The most recent development for theatrical setting is in the field of digital imagery which may include soundscapes. This technology enables directors/designers to create entire environments without the need for construction. The use of multi-media creating both still and moving images has become the trademark of a number of contemporary directors, of whom, perhaps, Katie Mitchell has attracted the most critical attention.

There are many useful sources on the design and construction of sets but David Welker's *Theatrical Set Designs: The Basic Techniques* (1969) or Hendrik Baker's *Stage Management and Theatre Craft* (1981) are still the most accessible. However, students should supplement their reading of them with more recent books describing the use of synthetic materials.

Stage left/right

The terms 'Stage Left' or 'Stage Right' are examples of the many descriptions of positions on a stage. They only have currency when used for a 'proscenium' or some other kind of stage (see **theatre form**) where the entire **audience** is looking in more or less the same direction. The expression 'Stage Left' refers to the **actor**'s left when facing the audience and is abbreviated as SL or L. All such positions on stage are given in relation to an imaginary centre point known as 'Stage Centre' or 'Centre' (C), so 'Stage Left' is the extreme left-hand side of the stage in relation to Centre, whereas a point to the left further downstage is known as 'Down Left' (DL). A point roughly midway between Centre and Stage Left is known as 'Left of Centre' (LC) and a point in a similar position further downstage as 'Down Left of Centre' (DLC). Obviously, there are similar terms for various **upstage** positions and for those Stage Right. Towards the end of the nineteenth century, the prompter's box was moved from a central position in the orchestra pit facing the stage to a point behind the proscenium, Stage Left or Down Left. Ever since then, the Left-hand side of the stage has also been known as the 'Prompt Side' (P or PS) and the Right-hand side as 'Opposite Prompt' (OP).

All these terms and abbreviations have two main functions: first, they enable the playwright or the **director** to indicate where they wish an actor to stand, sit or move. The playwright may indicate this in the playtext and the director will record the required moves, using the abbreviations, in the *prompt copy*. During rehearsals, actors may mark their moves or 'blocking' in their **scripts**, and the stage manager or director will mark moves developed as a result of rehearsal in the *prompt copy*. Practices vary enormously. Some directors come to rehearsals with detailed 'blocking' of moves already decided, and impose these on the cast; others allow movements to evolve during rehearsal. Where moves are marked in the **text** of an 'acting edition' of a play, it is most likely that they were those used in a West End or Broadway production.

The second use for these terms is as a means of indicating the positions of the **entrances**, furniture and other key parts of the **set** that determine how the actors behave. They may be used to describe the positions of doors, windows, chairs, sofas, and once these have been set out in the initial **stage directions**, the **action** is shaped accordingly. The plays of Strindberg or Arthur Miller are good examples: the playwrights describe the **setting**, saying what features are Stage Left and so on, and then require that a **character** 'moves towards the sofa' or 'goes to the fridge'.

Some plays have survived from the early years of the nineteenth century showing the particular grooves in which the shutters should run to create a specific **scene**. These generally use the terminology of SL, C, etc.

With the growth of more flexible and intimate forms of staging, especially 'arena' staging and more experimental modes of production, the terms have become less frequently used. However, they are still vital in the Musical Theatre or in conducting a **lighting** rehearsal, and for many actors the concept of 'learning their moves' is still an essential part of their craft. Therefore, the terms we have been discussing remain common parlance among actors and directors as a means of communicating their intentions to each other.

Stage machinery

The use of mechanical devices to assist in the staging of plays appears to be almost as old as the Western theatre itself, and whenever *spectacle* has dominated the taste of audiences, stage machinery has been developed to assist in its creation. A complete history of the evolving of various forms of such machinery is well beyond the scope of this book but, fortunately, we can see working examples from one of the most productive periods of its history in the beautifully preserved baroque theatres of Cesky Krumlov, in the Czech Republic, and Gripshom or Drottingen in Sweden. To give but one example, the theatre in the castle at Cesky Krumlov can still display 13 basic decoration scenes, with the possibilities of many variations by the use of 11 fully functioning backdrops, 40 ground pieces and no fewer than 500 interchangeable **wings**, all of which are raised or lowered by mechanical means controlled by huge capstans mounted beneath the stage.

Stage machinery has three basic functions: moving scenery, moving actors or moving the stage itself. We may also add to that the achievement of special effects. Moving scenery has most usually been facilitated by the use of counterweighted ropes and pulleys, which enable large and heavy pieces to be raised or lowered within some sort of track. Similar principles have been used for heavy curtains. In many cases, the original winches and capstans have been replaced by electric power but the basic idea is unchanged and early stage machinery can still be seen in a number of British theatres, such as the oldest function-ing theatre, the Theatre Royal, at Margate.

As can be seen in the discussion of **entrances**, various mechanical means have been employed to enable **actors** to appear to fly or to be lowered onto the stage from a high point. The use of flying devices with a harness has become an established theatre practice and has often provided a means of ascension or a spectacular form of disappearance. By the eighteenth century, it was quite common for theatres to use the 'star trap': a star-shaped trap door in the stage floor, below which was mounted a lift that propelled an actor through the trap and onto the stage. Various other forms of trap door in the stage floor have also pro-vided the potential for sudden or unusual entrances and exits.

The nineteenth century saw the introduction of the revolving stage in both the Kabuki theatre of Japan and the theatres of Western Europe. This device particularly appealed to the creators of opera but is now quite a common feature in large playhouses. The device enables a cir-cular section in the centre of a stage to rotate, thereby changing any set that is mounted on it. The development of steam power also enabled French and English opera houses to be equipped with massive under-stage machinery that could tilt and rock sections of the stage or lift one section higher than another. This was remarkably effective in creat-ing the illusions of ships being tossed at sea or of earthquakes. Other devices, consisting of rollers mounted just beneath the stage level, ena-bled chariot races to take place on stage with horses galloping wildly but actually covering no ground. Lifts, revolves or mechanically trucked pieces of scenery are all widely used in today's theatre, but it is still the demand for spectacle that sees their most frequent employment.

If you find the topic and concept of 'stage machinery' fascinating there is no substitute for exploring a local theatre or consulting one of the many small published histories of former theatres. However, there is excellent guidance in Oscar Brockett's *History of the Theatre* in its lat-est edition and in the associated website to Pickering and Woolgar's *Theatre Studies*.

See also **decorating the stage; entrances; set/setting** *and* **wings.**

Street theatre

Street theatre takes place when a performer or group of performers goes in search of an **audience** in a non-theatrical, outdoor venue such as a street, public square or corner of a campus. It is probably one of the least documented forms of theatre but, as A. E. Green (1980) claims, one of the genuinely popular forms: 'It is my contention ... that only theatre which grows out of or exists for little aggregations of people – whether rural village or city street – can ever be popular in any useful sense' (in Bradby (ed.), *Performance and Politics in Popular Theatre*, p. 141). Various traditional, popular forms of drama, such as the Mummers' Plays, invariably seem to have taken place in the open air and depended on attracting an audience by their energy and immediacy. For this reason Nigel Forde (1986) claims that:

> Street theatre bears about the same relation to real theatre as kicking a dustbin does to symphonic music. Street theatre has to be loud, bright, coarse and over the top ... it is not indoor theatre taken outside and shouted with a silly hat on. (p. 97)

You will, no doubt, wish to question what Forde means by 'real theatre' but he does seem to capture both the essence and the specialised nature of Street theatre. It is aimed at 'non-theatrical' audiences and must be arresting if anyone is going to watch.

Street performers have probably always existed where there were towns and cities but theatre historians have suggested that it was the collapse of the Roman Empire that released a huge number of professional performers who had to seek their living in this way. Their descendants were the **commedia dell'arte**, the travelling players of Elizabethan England or some of the fringe theatre groups of more recent times. **Mystery Plays** were a form of street theatre in medieval England. During the twentieth and twenty-first centuries, street theatre has sometimes been thought to be synonymous with **Agit/Prop** and political theatre but this is a rather narrow perception. Since the 1970s there has been a less political and more aesthetic tone to much of the work. This may include single performers juggling, riding trick cycles or standing entirely still in the form of a statue sprayed with silver paint or making sudden appearances from inside a wooden box. Some of this work has been organised into Street Festivals and has taken on a celebratory, if still provocative, nature. This institutionalisation of the form can, however, seem at odds with its essential qualities.

Street Theatre was an important part of the *alternative* arts scene of 1960s New York, and its most famous exponent was Peter Schumann with his 'Bread and Puppet Theatre', who took Joan Littlewood's statement 'The world is full of theatre ... it's not in the theatre' as a challenge. Using giant puppets, an unpaid cast of between 15 and 100, and short plays or sketches on contemporary themes, he went into the streets of New York in a series of processions and performances. They would find whatever space seemed convenient and distribute bread to the audience who gathered round. More extreme modes of street theatre were undertaken by the director Yayoi Kusama in the late sixties. In pursuit of the potency of nudity she led a naked guerrilla raid on the Statue of Liberty, set up a nude crucifixion in Central Park with sex taking place at the foot of the cross, or invited audiences to join in a 'love-in'. More restrained but equally provocative forms of street theatre continue to be employed as a means of protest, and street performers remain as popular as ever in city centres.

It is well worth researching any local forms of traditional street theatre. For example, in areas of rural Kent the tradition of the *Hooden Horse* Play is still perpetuated by groups of young men who have no other connection with theatre, and new scripts continue to be written for their performances. For the most comprehensive account of street theatre in New York see Roose-Evans (1970).

See also **carnival; environmental theatre; theatre of testimony.**

Surrealism

Surrealism was one of the movements within the arts in the late nineteenth and early twentieth centuries that challenged established, orthodox notions of 'making sense' and constituted what we would now recognise as *modernism* and as an element of the *avant-garde*. Like so many of the intellectual movements we shall encounter, it had its epicentre in France. For the surrealists, conventional art seemed to support bourgeois culture and the dominant ideological and aesthetic order, so they aimed to produce works of art that defied common logical explanation and lay beyond those modes of making meaning employed by contemporary society. Surrealist artworks relied on the juxtaposition of unrelated and unexpected objects that appeared to have no cultural connection. The resulting works seemed inexplicable because they defied the critical tools with which meanings and interpretations were normally constructed. Surrealist art would mix spheres of meaning, bringing together objects from the 'real' world with those taken from dreams, fantasy, the unconscious and the subconscious: a painting of a fish in the middle of a **proscenium** stage, or of a sofa in the middle of a forest, for example. Objects detached from their normal context or function had then to be seen in a different way.

In 1924, Antonin Artaud (see **Theatre of Cruelty**) was appointed director of the newly established Bureau of Surrealist Enquiries in Paris. In the window hung a dress-shop dummy, and the public was invited to bring in their accounts of dreams and coincidences and any new ideas they might have had concerning art, fashion and politics. These were then typed and exhibited on the walls. In a typical challenge to the bourgeoisie, Artaud announced 'We need *disturbed* followers far more than we need active followers' (see De Botton, 2004, p. 299). In the same year as the establishment of the Bureau, André Breton produced his *First Manifesto*, in which surrealism is defined as:

> Pure psychic automatism by means of which we propose to express either verbally, in writing, or in some other fashion what really goes on in the mind. Dictation by the mind, unhampered by conscious control and having no aesthetic or moral goals. (p. 35)

The likely implications for drama and performance in this statement are obvious because the subconscious and unconscious mind provide the basis for some form of artistic truth. After his embracing of Communism in 1926, Breton sought to make a more militant kind of surrealism and, in his second *Manifesto* (1929), denounced many of the movement's adherents. However, we can trace the influence of surrealism and its precedent *dadaism* in the works of Alfred Jarry (see **lighting**), Guillaume Apollinaire, Jean Cocteau, Samuel Beckett and Tom Stoppard.

Guillaume Apollinaire (1880–1918) was an associate of most of the *avant-garde* writers and painters in the early years of the twentieth century and the main spokesman for *cubism*, but it was his play *The Breasts of Tiresias* (1903; revised and produced 1917) that most influenced the surrealist movement. In this extraordinary play, the female character Thérèse releases her breasts in the form of balloons, which float away, and leaves her husband to discover the means of producing children, of which he eventually produces over forty thousand. The drama epitomises Apollinaire's rejection of logic and his creation of a new form of expression through the combination of fantasy, tragedy, comedy, burlesque, physical theatre, music, dance, colour and light. Such ideas were taken up by the playwright and director Jean Cocteau (1892–1963) who, in addition to his work in a number of ballets and his collaboration with circus clowns, made a number of reworkings of myths. The most successful of these, *Antigone* (1922), *Orpheus* (1926) and *The Infernal Machine* (1934), all based on the Greek myths, included many surrealist elements.

The postmodernist philosopher Jean-François Lyotard (see **Postmodernism**) claimed that any avant-garde art plays a subversive role, and we can see this quality in the painting of Magritte, which was to inspire Tom Stoppard's play *After Magritte* (1970), and in the Theatre of the Absurd. Counsell (1996) points out that Magritte's painting of a pipe with the caption 'This is not a Pipe' emphasises that what we are perceiving is not a 'real' pipe but a painting of a pipe. In the same fashion, the drama of Beckett or Ionesco or any of the surrealist playwrights does not show a 'real' world, but a theatrical representation of a world.

Surrealism, with its willingness to make apparently random juxtapositions, has inspired a good deal of the *performance art* and various forms of contemporary dance emanating from the United States, which are now widely emulated.

You should explore the possibilities of surrealistic characteristics in your own performance work and think about its links with the concepts of 'loss of meaning' associated with **postmodernist** approaches to interpretation. Stern and Henderson (1993) provide some excellent examples of this way of thinking and working.

Symbolism

Unlike **surrealism** (above) symbolism is a concept that has probably always been a factor in drama although the nature of the discourse surrounding it has changed radically since the advent of **semiotics**, or *semiology* as it is now more commonly called, as a means of examining performance. Students may, in fact, find it helpful to read the entry on **semiotics** at this point. Peirce's statement that 'All words, sentences, books and other conventional signs are Symbols' (see Counsell and Wolf, 2001, p. 10) has ensured that any recent consideration of symbolism has the widest possible application. However, symbolism was also a recognisable anti-realist movement in the arts, with its origins in late nineteenth-century France. One of the most significant factors in the further development of the ideas of the symbol was the publication in 1900 of Freud's seminal work *The Interpretation of Dreams*. Freud demonstrated that, in dreams, the mind worked through symbols rather than through recognisable reality but that each symbol represented something of great significance. Taken to its logical conclusion, this idea suggests that inner realities are not represented by corresponding material objects and that there are profounder realities of mind and spirit lying beyond the physical realm.

Even before Freud, a group known as the 'Symbolists', taking their inspiration from the works of Edgar Allan Poe, Charles Baudelaire, Fyodor Dostoevsky and Richard Wagner, issued a *Manifesto* (1885) in which they asserted that profound truth could only be gleaned from subjectivity, spirituality and inexplicable inner and external forces. Such truth, they argued, could not be directly represented but was evoked through symbols, legends, myths and moods. Stéphane Mallarmé (1842–98), the movement's main spokesperson, considered that drama should be an evocation of the mystery of being, achieved through allusive and poetic language and a performance that utilised the minimum of appropriate atmospheric theatrical means in order to create something akin to a religious experience.

As with so many movements in the arts, it was not until the establishment of an independent theatre that many of the ideas of symbolism could be put into practice. The seventeen-year-old poet Paul Fort (1872–1962) set up the Théâtre d'Art and, frequently giving only one performance of each work (as sometimes now happens with **site-specific** pieces), presented a largely amateur range of productions ranging from new plays to adaptations of the Bible. When Fort abandoned this series of Symbolist ventures the work was taken over by Aurélien-Marie Lugné-Poe (1869–1940) at the Théâtre de l'Oeuvre, who set about mounting productions based on the principle that 'the word creates the décor', using minimalist **sets** composed of simple lines and colours painted on backdrops. Lugné-Poe was responsible for introducing the work of the Symbolist playwright Maurice Maeterlinck (1862–1949), and Jarry's play *Ubu Roi* (1896; see **Absurdism**), as well as working with Artaud.

The influence of these early experiments in Symbolist productions was considerable: the idea of the symbol as a code for reality and the construction of a symbolic language of theatre can be seen in the work of the designer Gordon Craig (see **design concept**), the lighting pioneer Appia (**see lighting**), the productions of Meyerhold (see **Constructivism**) and the plays of Ibsen, Chekhov, Strindberg, Yeats and Eliot (**see ritual, poetic drama**). If you wish to experience the essence of Symbolism you should explore Maeterlinck's short play *The Blind* or Strindberg's *Dream Play*. Working on these plays reveals how they were conceived as communicating their meanings through a series of symbols long before the nature of symbols was debated by semioticians. In *The Blind*, for example, the stage is filled with an unspecified number of blind people, who communicate mainly by groans and gasps. Dominating the 'skyline' is a silhouetted gallows from which hangs a corpse, and the play revolves around the gradual realisation of this ghastly presence as the actors literally grope their way to the discovery. The minimal action is dense with Symbolism, which you might wish to articulate after working on this or a similar play.

There is a useful discussion of aspects of Symbolism by Milling and Ley (2001) and the factual background of the Symbolist movement and its effects is admirably set out in Brockett (1995 or the latest edition).

Paul Allain and Jen Harvie's *The Routledge Companion to Theatre and Performance* (2006) contains some excellent and most helpful entries on Symbolism.

Theatre form

The form of the theatre building is the first thing a **director** must consider when begining to confront staging problems. At some periods in the history of Western theatre forms, a particular arrangement of stage and auditorium has predominated, at others a great variety of forms have co-existed. In the history of English theatre, two periods stand out as having been marked by the predominance of a particular theatre form: the Elizabethan age, when a *thrust stage* was common, jutting out into an **audience** that surrounded it on three sides, and the Victorian age, when the theatre was virtually divided into two separate rooms, stage and auditorium, separated by a proscenium arch.

The main difference between a thrust stage and a proscenium arch stage lies in the relationship established between the actors and their audience (see **actor/audience relationship**). On a thrust stage the actors inhabit the same space as the audience. They may therefore find it easy to address the audience directly. It is often maintained that the use of soliloquy in Elizabethan drama was particularly suited to thrust stages like that in the conjectured reconstruction of the Swan Theatre. On this kind of stage any scenic elements used need to be three-dimensional and practicable. There has been much discussion of the use made, on the Elizabethan stage, of the area between the two entrances in the back wall. In the masques that became popular at the English court in the first part of the seventeenth century, new Italian methods of providing spectacular backgrounds came into use, involving elaborate machinery for 'flying' scenery in and out. In the Restoration period (i.e. the years following 1660), new theatres were built to enable the use of perspective scenery, painted on backcloths and on flats placed at intervals on each side of the stage. But the scale of such theatres was much more intimate than the Elizabethan theatre had been; part of the stage remained thrust out into the auditorium and a door at the front of the stage on each side allowed for entrances and exits in close proximity to the audience. This was a theatre form in transition between the Elizabethan thrust stage and the proscenium arch stage, which was to predominate in the eighteenth and nineteenth centuries.

A proscenium arch stage is ideal for the creation of illusion and picture effects. Because the audience cannot see behind the surface of the proscenium it is possible to hide from view a great deal of **stage**

machinery, lighting equipment, constructional reinforcement and scenery, in preparation for several transformations of the stage picture. By the careful use of perspective, a designer can create the illusion of a larger space. Single flat surfaces can be painted to resemble buildings and landscapes or to make whatever visual statement the director desires. By cunning use of gauze and lighting, characters and scenes can be made to appear and disappear at will (see **discovery, decorating the stage**).

Such was the dominance achieved by the **proscenium** form by the end of the nineteenth century that it is still often referred to as the 'traditional' method of staging. This is misleading and inaccurate, for the period during which the proscenium arch was used to make a complete separation between stage and auditorium was a comparatively brief one. The proscenium arch itself is ancient; it was only during the late eighteenth and nineteenth centuries that theatres were built in such a way as to ensure that the audience's view of the entire stage was framed by this arch. The invention of first gas and then electric stage lighting, together with the innovation of darkening the auditorium for the performance, both enhanced the new sense of the **proscenium arch** as a barrier dividing actors from audience. The most extreme expression of this idea of a barrier was to be found in the staging methods of André Antoine (see **fourth wall**), who encouraged his actors and designers to think of the stage as just a room, from which the **fourth wall** had been removed to allow the audience to see inside.

In the twentieth and twenty-first centuries, especially since Gropius's work (see **total theatre**) theatre architects have tried to design flexible buildings which will allow for many different theatre forms under the same roof. The Royal National Theatre in London, for example, includes three auditoria; the Olivier has an *arena* stage, whose design borrows elements from both the Elizabethan thrust stage and the Ancient Greek open-air theatres; the Lyttleton has a *proscenium arch* stage, and the Cottesloe is a flexible space in which a number of different arrangements are possible: a stage may be constructed at one end of the auditorium, with part of the space used for tiered seating; or the whole space may be used for the dramatic action, with spectators looking down from the first and second galleries, which run right round the auditorium.

A number of flexible spaces like the Cottesloe have been built in recent years. They allow a director to vary the shape of this stage space for each new production, erecting a proscenium arch to frame the action if he so wishes, or seating an audience on three sides of a thrust stage or on both sides of a traverse stage. An example of such a building is the Manchester University Theatre.

The situation today, then, is one in which no single theatre form is predominant. Because of this, parallels can be drawn with the medieval period, when a variety of different theatre forms were also in use. As modern staging methods have become more flexible in recent years, so interest in medieval stages has grown, and it is for this reason that I shall conclude this discussion of theatre forms with a brief mention of four types of medieval stage. The great English cycle plays appear to have been performed on a number of different mobile stages or *pageants*, each one representing a particular location in the course of the cycle. Other plays were performed in *rounds*, which appear to have been common in western Europe during this period. Here the performance space consisted of a central *platea*, or acting area, with a number of raised structures around the edge. The audience crowded into the round with the actors and were kept in order by attendants, who would clear spaces for the actors and help direct the audience's attention.

A simpler, and very common form of staging was the *booth stage*, consisting of boards on a trestle with a curtain, behind which actors could change costumes and from which they could make a surprise entrance. Finally, many plays, like the Valenciennes Passion Play of 1547, were performed on a long stage in a town square, forming the central *platea* while behind it were ranged a sequence of *mansion*s or small, separate stage sets, representing different locations, from Heaven through to Hell's mouth. Most theatre histories deal with these and other forms of staging; a particularly interesting discussion of the subject is Richard Southern's book *The Seven Ages of Theatre* (1962), in which he emphasises the relevance of early theatre forms for understanding modern staging methods. One of the most fascinating and useful resources for the exploration of theatre form is the 'Theatron Project' led by the theatre historian Richard Beacham. His computer aided design (CAD) enables students to enter virtual theatre spaces through the internet.

Theatre in the Round

Another theatre form that has attracted revived interest in recent years is 'Theatre in the Round', in which the audience entirely surrounds the action. During the 1950s and 1960s, Stephen Joseph became Britain's leading exponent of this form of theatre and his book *New Theatre Forms* (1968) took on the force of a manifesto for all those who felt stifled by the dominance of permanent proscenium arch theatres. Joseph gathered round him **actors, directors** and playwrights who shared his enthusiasm, and in the small Library Theatre at Scarborough they carried out their experiments. A permanent Theatre in the Round at Stoke-on-Trent and the new theatre named in Stephen Joseph's memory at Scarborough, together with many other new buildings, such as the Manchester Royal Exchange, are a measure of his influence.

The central arena of a Theatre in the Round, which might be circular, square or many-sided, ensures that an **audience**, viewing from all sides, is always relatively near the **action**. **Entrances** and exits must be constructed through the auditorium and these, usually placed on opposite corners or sides, allow great fluidity of movement across the stage. The only background against which the actors perform is that of the spectators, and the actor and director have to discover ways in which they may all be meaningfully involved in the performance. Old rules about projection, the dominance of various parts of the stage, and the grouping of figures are no longer applicable, and because of the sight lines, the stage must be virtually free of décor.

Theatre space

Writing in 1970, the director and playwright James Roose-Evans said:

> The theatre must give the audience of today a new experience of space
> It is as necessary for us to re-discover a relationship with space, the
> space around us, as it is to explore outer space. We need to experi-
> ence afresh the height and depth and breadth of space, its intimacy and
> immensity. (p. 134)

This visionary theatre practitioner had wide experience of productions and he understood that to work on the text of a play quickly raises questions about the theatre space in which it is to be performed. No two theatres are exactly alike and over the centuries the size and shape of acting spaces has varied enormously, as also have the social connotations of the theatre as an institution. The depth and complexity of a good theatre performance is the result of a two-way influence: the theatre space influences our perception of the **text** and the text influences our perception of the space. To a person accustomed to seeing Shakespeare performed in a proscenium arch theatre, where the spaces for audience and for action are strictly separate, a performance in an assembly hall, warehouse or similar open space will seem very different. This has been the experience of visitors to the Edinburgh Festival. The influence also flows the other way: in an age when theatres were a convenient place for men to encounter prostitutes, the plays performed on stage were treated with some disdain, even plays now considered 'great'. Contrariwise, a play performed in the National Theatre acquires a certain status irrespective of its subject matter or dramatic merit.

Since much of the study of drama focuses on the play in performance, the space in which that performance takes place requires analysis as much as the **text** and the **conventions** of **acting**, costuming or setting. Certain characteristics of the performance space can be seen to hold good for almost any play, while others are more specific to particular periods or places. Among the generally valid, four can be distinguished by way of introduction. In the first place, a performance space is always defined by means of its limitations: it is separated off from the world of everyday reality that surrounds it. It is raised up or hollowed out or marked off in some other fashion and it is empty. This is as true for a purpose built theatre as it is for a **found space**. It presents itself as a space not yet filled with either objects or people. In the second place, this emptiness can be defined by reference to the purpose for which it is reserved. The purpose cannot be defined in one word because it is a double purpose, both concrete and imaginary, neither quality having a separable existence of its own, each existing by virtue of the other. It is *both* the physically defined, measurable area in which actors of flesh and blood can deploy their muscles, vocal cords, etc., and into which objects of various kinds may be introduced, *and* it is an imaginary space in which the laws of time, space and mass can be overruled. In the third place, this space possesses characteristics having a conventional or codified relation to the real world, both in its material aspects and in its social relations. An object, when it enters this space, will be understood to 're-present' something, as Quince explains to his actors in *A Midsummer Night's Dream*; it may, or may not, be a real object, but as soon as it enters the theatre space its function alters: it becomes representational. The same is true of social relations. The actor playing Macbeth may in fact hate the actor playing Macduff but when they confront one another on the stage they re-present a fight, they do not fight as they would in any other place outside the theatre. A fourth characteristic needs to be mentioned not because it is invariable, but because it is a characteristic always potentially present, whatever the type of theatre. This is the ceremonial or ludic quality. In Ancient Greece, in medieval Europe, and in many societies or subcultures scattered around the world today, theatre space was, and is, also a space reserved for devotional purposes or for public games, occasionally both at once. The place was thought of as a precinct or space especially inhabited by divine power. This is why it was empty. There was danger attached to entering the space and one only did so after complicated preparations and with an official seal of approval.

Of course theatre spaces change and develop. Among the many shaping influences upon them, one or other may predominate for a while but then another will reassert itself and bring about a return to earlier patterns. The recent history of the European theatre shows a theatre shaped chiefly by the demands of a public who wanted to be able to scrutinise one another (the horse-shoe shaped Italianate theatre), giving way to a theatre more suited to a convincing, even illusionistic depiction of reality (the late nineteenth-century proscenium arch theatre). This in turn has given way to a theatre in which the demands of the actor are the predominant shaping influence – either by establishing an open arena with a minimum of illusionistic equipment, as in the case of Peter Brook's or Jerzy Grotowski's theatres, or in the less extreme form of the thrust stages that are so common in theatres built during the last two decades.

Any act of theatre, however modest in means, involves a complex interplay of the various elements that have been identified: **stage directions** and **dialogue**, theatre technologies and social conventions, **sign systems** and the spaces in which they are deployed. In this book I have attempted to elaborate a method for studying each separate element in an appropriate manner while at the same time maintaining an overview of how each finds its place in the complete performance of a given play in a given theatre space. Particular help in exploring many different historic theatre forms may be found through the virtual world of digitally created images available on the web through the 'Theatron Project' (see **Theatre Form**).

See also **found space.**

Wings

Wings have been mentioned in many of the entries in this chapter because they have become an integral part of the traditions of theatre. The term refers both to the flats (very often painted) that are placed more or less parallel to a **proscenium arch**, masking the sides of the stage, or to the hidden stage area behind them from which **actors** can make their **entrances**. Wings were developed in the Italian theatres of the sixteenth century and could be swivelled, angled or stored in groups known as nests, where each painted wing could be removed to reveal another beneath in order to effect a change of **scene**. A further sophistication of this process involved the sliding of the wings in a series of grooves so that each could be removed quickly to reveal another vista. This involved the wings being mounted on trucks or chariots that could be controlled by a system of capstans and pulleys situated beneath the stage. One of the wonders of theatre became the experience of seeing a scene transformed before the eyes of the spectator. These techniques were introduced into England during the reign of James I by the architect Inigo Jones for use in his designs for court masques. As I have pointed out in a previous entry, there are a number of well-preserved theatres in which these devices are still operative (see **stage machinery**).

The idea of wings in grooves gradually died out as more flexible, symbolic and three-dimensional forms of scenery emerged towards the end of the nineteenth century, but the concept of *waiting in the wings* is a practical and emotional aspect of theatre that is likely to remain constant. There are a huge number of books concerning the history of stage construction, but a good overview of the development of a feature like wings can be obtained by perusing the illustrations of volumes such as Phyllis Hartnoll's *The Theatre: A Concise History* (1998) or Hendrik Baker's still classic book, *Stage Management and Theatre Craft* (1981).

See also **decorating the stage.**

Further Reading

Paul Allain and Jen Harvie (2006) *The Routledge Companion to Theatre and Performance* (London: Routledge).

Christopher Baugh (2005) *Theatre Performance and Technology* (Basingstoke: Palgrave Macmillan).

Phyllis Hartnoll (1998) *The Theatre: A Concise History*, 3rd edn (London: Thames & Hudson).

Chris Hoggett (2001) *Stage Crafts* (London: Heinemann).

Helen and Richard Leacroft (1984) *Theatre and Playhouse* (London: Methuen).

Gay McAuley (2000) *Space in Performance: Making Meaning in the Theatre* (Ann Arbor, MI: Michigan University Press).

5 Critical Concepts

This chapter is largely concerned with the experience of attending, watching and evaluating a theatrical performance or event. Its focus is on audiences, hermeneutics (that is: every aspect of the interpretation of text or verbal and non-verbal communication) and critical responses. Hopefully, this will help you in your attempt to become reflective practitioners. The chapter also includes reference to situations where there is no specific audience other than the participants in the drama itself. This will therefore, extend into areas of ritual and applied drama where the concept of 'performance' is largely irrelevant.

Comparatively little has been written about audiences, although the recent appearance of Helen Freshwater's admirable *Theatre and Audience* (2009) has begun to rectify that situation. Previously the most impressive pieces of the research into audiences have tended to concentrate on narrow periods of history. But anyone involved in the commercial production and consumption of drama knows that unless the responses of audiences and critics are constantly noted, their projects fail. More recent literature on the subject of audiences has tended to come from the field of Communication Studies where the concept of audience embraces all the media. However, many of the insights provided by this literature are of great value to students of drama.

The entries in this chapter make frequent reference to the 'making of meaning' by the audience. Modern critical theory has highlighted the point that it is only in the process of performance that meanings emerge, and that this can only happen if there is an audience. This standpoint amounts to a considerable empowerment of the audience because, if we accept it, the ultimate responsibility for a play's meaning and interpretation has passed from the playwright, director and actor to the audience.

Students of drama and performance are confronted with a bewildering array of critical theories that claim to help in facilitating responses and there are widely diverging views. For example, scholars disagree as to whether or not a performer can, in some sense, be considered as a member of the audience. So why use critical theory at all? I posed this question to Giles Auckland-Lewis, one of a new generation of thinkers, who is shaping the way we consider performance through his work at the Liverpool Institute for Performing Arts. This was his response:

> The answer is not that we can reject or forget our own emotional or intellectual responses to performance but rather that we can start to understand our responses and how the performances engender them for us. Theatre does not exist in a vacuum; it exists within cultures and societies and operates at many levels using codes, conventions and rules. Theoretical enquiry is not about telling us what is 'good' or 'bad' but rather it is about telling how theatre operates so that we can be empowered to make more valuable judgements ourselves, either as the producers or the consumers of theatre. In essence, theory, of whatever vintage, is really concerning itself with how theatre makes meaning or to be more accurate how we gain meaning from theatre. However, critical theory is not a neutral force. All theory has some ideological imperative behind it. The use of theory or rather the choice of theoretical position is a political one.

As with all other material in this book, it is vital to consider and debate the points made, attempting to identify value in a variety of viewpoints. The study of drama in performance is, in itself, rather like a theatre visit: ultimately, it is up to the student/spectator to make meanings. Some approaches may be thought to be outmoded just as they seem to become established, but I believe that there is sufficient enduring value in all the topics I have introduced here to make them worthwhile. Above all, I hope you will ask youself why you should ever bother to go to the theatre or attend a performance at all. Is it for escapism? Apparently not. Recently, for example, there was a drop of 30 per cent in the profits of one leading West End producer of Musicals and there was a reduction of 100,000 in London audiences for Commercial Theatre. On the other hand, there has been a perceptible increase in the popularity of plays exploring topical, political issues, for as Mark Espiner, co-artistic director of the Sound and Fury Theatre Company, has reminded us:

> From Aeschylus onwards, the theatre has scrutinized society and, in various ways, responded to lies and oppression, sometimes by operating subversively on the fringes under accusations of immorality. Once again, it's finding that its power isn't necessarily in escapism, nor restricted to the velveteen splendour of the stalls and upper circles. It's going public, looking for truth in the morass of everyday, everywhere theatricality, and it's implicating you.
> (*Guardian*, 22 May 2004)

Actor–audience relationship

The relationship between **actor** and **audience** is fundamental to the concept of drama and performance: both terms are virtually meaningless without the other. Grotowski (see **Theatre of Communion, Poor Theatre**) explored the possibility of removing all superfluous aspects of theatre in order to discover its true essence. In the process, he discovered that theatre 'cannot exist without the actor–spectator relationship of perceptual, "live" communion'. He went on to assert that 'This is an ancient, theoretical truth, of course, but when rigorously tested in practice it undermines most of our most usual ideas about theatre' (*Towards a Poor Theatre*, p. 19). At a later stage in the same book, Grotowski returned to the same fundamental concept. 'Can the theatre exist without an audience?' he asked. 'At least one spectator is needed to make it a performance', was his rejoinder. This led Grotowski to the conclusion (which readers would probably share) that 'We can thus define the theatre as "what takes place between spectator and actor"'. 'All the other things', he said, 'are supplementary – perhaps necessary, but supplementary' (pp. 32–3). When we consider the many concepts and aspects of performance we have encountered in this book we can see just how many of them Grotowski would have considered to be 'supplementary'. However, this process also demonstrates how central and *key* the concept of the 'actor/audience relationship' can be seen to be.

Before we explore this concept a little further let us focus on the terms *audience* and *spectator*. We tend to use the term 'audience' as a collective term for a body of people although we may well refer to a *member of the audience* as a single figure. In either case the term implies *listening* and students may be reminded of the seventeenth-century diarist Samuel Pepys, and his expression 'to *hear* a play'. Traditionally, audiences are associated with the ritual of theatre-going, and the term may well derive from a time when the actors were 'given a hearing' and when the spoken **text** was seen as paramount. The place for the attentive listeners is, of course, the *auditorium*. And the emphasis on listening implies the existence of a discourse. Recent performance studies tend to use the term *spectator*, emphasising the watching process and implying a similarity to sporting events. Those concerned with the arts as therapy even use the verb *to spectate* as a term to describe the activity carried out by the observer of a piece of art. The concept of the 'spectator' in the theatre is by no means new: Shakespeare has Hamlet refer to 'some barren quantity of spectators' in his famous advice to the players (see **actor**), and Brecht insisted that he wanted theatre audiences to behave more like the spectators at a boxing match, in his *Short Organum on Sport*.

The concept of the 'spectator' suggests, perhaps, a more vociferous and excitable relationship with the performer than does the word 'audience' but there have been plenty of examples of rowdy and intrusive audiences in the history of the theatre.

To some extent the actor/audience relationship depends on the size and design of theatre buildings. In the huge theatres of Ancient Greece the actors were a distant spectacle for many of the audience, whereas we have records of devils and demons running around and letting off firecrackers amongst medieval audiences. The actor in the Elizabethan theatre was virtually in the centre of an audience, who could comfortably feel near enough to overhear a soliloquy, yet with the growth of indoor theatres the bulk of the audience would be facing the actors in a single direction whilst a few maintained their right to sit at the sides of the stage. Only in the nineteenth century, with the advent of gas **lighting**, did the auditorium become darkened and eye contact between performers and the bulk of the audience become virtually impossible. With the abolition of the forestage and the rowdy *pit* and the introduction of *stalls* and the all-encompassing frame of the **proscenium arch** during the more decorous Victorian era the concept of an audience as a relatively passive body of listeners gained popularity and has persisted to the present. The experiments with a variety of theatre forms that have characterised the past sixty years or so have opened up many possibilities for the interplay of actor and audience. Grotowski described some of the approaches he employed with his Polish Laboratory Theatre, noting that: 'The essential concern is finding the proper spectator–actor relationship for each type of performance and embodying the decision in physical arrangements.' He then turned to the 'infinite variation of performer-audience relationships that is possible':

> The actors can play among the spectators, directly contacting the audience and giving it a passive role in the drama. Or the actors may build structures among the spectators and thus include them in the architecture of the action, subjecting them to a sense of the pressure and congestion and limitation of space. Or the actors may play among the spectators and ignore them, looking through them. The spectators may be separated from the actors – for example, by a high fence, over which their heads only protrude; from this radically slanted perspective, they look down on the actors as if watching animals in a ring, or like medical students watching an operation. Or (as in the production of *Dr Faustus*) the entire hall is used as a concrete place ... a refectory where Faustus entertains the spectators, who are guests at a baroque feast served on huge tables, offering episodes of his life.

We can see that the production mode, the use of space and the performance style all contribute to the actor/audience relationship, but another factor is the nature of the audience itself and of its expectations (see **audience**).

If we consider the forerunner of what we would now consider a typical, informed, 'middle-class' audience we might refer to the audience that gathered to watch Stanislavsky's production of Chekhov's *The Seagull* at the Moscow Art Theatre in 1898. Drawn from the Moscow intelligentsia, this group shared an interest in a new theatre that had only been open for a few months and that claimed by its name to be offering a new repertoire of high artistic standards for a broad audience – it was first known as the People's Art Theatre. They did not share the common religious beliefs of a medieval audience: some would have been atheists, some agnostics and some believers (see **audience**), but they did share a belief of a different kind: a belief that the latest developments in artistic style were important enough to merit serious, even reverential, consideration. Stanislavsky describes the play's first night as follows:

> I do not remember how we played. The first act was over. There was a gravelike silence. Knipper fainted on the stage. All of us could hardly keep our feet. In the throes of despair we began moving to our dressing rooms. Suddenly there was a roar in the auditorium and a shriek of joy or fright on the stage. Then there were the ovations to Lilina, who played Masha, and who had broken the ice with her last words which tore themselves from her heart, moans washed with tears. This it was that had held the audience mute for a time before it began to roar and thunder in mad ovation. (*My Life in Art*, p. 356)

This reaction suggests very clearly a collective state of mind of a group of people lost in rapt attention to what is being portrayed, awaking as it were from a dream at the end of the performance and taking some time to recapture the critical faculties, which then find expression in applause. This is an audience that does not expect to participate in the manner of a medieval audience, nor does it engage in other activities as a Restoration audience might have done. Instead, it comes for the pleasure of losing itself in a fictitious story presented with maximum **realism**. In order to increase this sensation, the lights in the auditorium are not left on as they were in the Restoration theatre, but everything is darkened, except the stage area, so that the audience appears to be observing a slice of real life that takes place as if unobserved, and whose agents never show that they realise they are being watched.

The audience, which became the model for many 'art' theatres all over the world in the twentieth century, is defined chiefly by its level of education and interest in a particular idea of art. The pleasure that its members expect to derive from a visit to the theatre will not always be accounted for simply by the extent to which the play absorbs them. It will also relate to a sense of being part of an élite group – those who know about and can follow the latest developments. But this social function is firmly subordinated to belief in the value of the work of art. Such an audience is prepared for a play that demands a lengthy attention span, presenting a single dramatic movement involving the same half dozen or so people and restricting itself to a single location, usually a drawing room similar to the one they have left behind in their own houses. The visit to the play flatters their belief that the most important events do indeed occur within their restricted caste and are located within their own special space: the four walls of the middle-class drawing room.

In his book *A Good Night Out*, John McGrath evokes a working-class audience that contrasts sharply with the middle-class audience we have just considered. Very amusingly, the author stresses the vitality, participation but unwillingness to pay attention that characterises a working-class audience unless it is sure that what is being presented really concerns it. Working in the theatre in Germany during the 1920s, the director playwright Bertolt Brecht was even more critical of the self-importance of the established middle-class theatre and sought to draw on the model of working-class entertainment:

> All those establishments with their excellent heating systems, their pretty lighting, their appetite for large sums of money, their imposing exteriors together with the entire business that goes on inside them [he wrote of the middle-class theatres], all this doesn't contain five penny-worth of fun. ('Emphasis on Sport' in Willett, *Brecht on Theatre*, p. 7)

His ideal audience was like the public at a boxing match – both passionately involved in the action and yet prepared to stand back and take a dispassionate view of the technique of the participants. In the Preface to *In the Jungle of Cities* (1923) Brecht addressed his audience in these terms: 'Don't worry your heads about the motives for the fight, concentrate on the stakes. Judge impartially the technique of the contenders and keep your eyes fixed on the finish.' Just as a boxer or a musician tries to show off his technique, so Brecht wanted the theatrical means and techniques to be plainly visible to the audience. From this followed all the familiar aspects of his production style: the half-curtain that did not attempt to hide the preparations going on behind; the use of very bright, even light from visible lighting rows; and an acting style that aimed to 'demonstrate' rather than 'incarnate'.

Brecht's view of the right relationship between **action** and audience was developed during the 1920s and early 1930s, a period when he was becoming convinced of the need to take sides in the political struggle then dividing Germany. In these circumstances, it seemed vital to prevent the audience from identifying itself in rapt, dreamlike attention with the action being portrayed. Instead, his model became the café or pub audience that McGrath later evoked. Such an audience not only remained detached and retained its independence of mind; it was also prepared to intervene if it disliked or disagreed with what was being presented for it on stage. Thus Brecht wrote a number of plays specifically for production in halls, schools or workers' clubs, which were designed to generate political discussion in their audiences. In Brecht's view, far from making theatre performance boring, this type of approach could reintroduce some of the fun that he had found missing in the middle-class theatre. He anticipated that his audience would experience a particular pleasure: that of discussing, learning, confronting new ideas:

> The theatre of the scientific age is able to make dialectics pleasurable. The surprises of development as it proceeds logically or by leaps and bounds, the instability of all states, the humour of contradictions, etc., these are enjoyments of the vitality of men, things and processes, and they heighten the art of living and the joy of living. ('Appendix to Short Organum', in Cole, *Playwrights on Playwriting*, p. 84)

A different kind of relationship between action and audience was envisaged by Jean Genet, when he wrote *The Blacks* (1959). It is one of the rare plays to go so far as to specify in so many words that it has been designed for performance before a particular audience:

> This play, written, I repeat, by a white man, is intended for a white audience, but if – which is unlikely – it is ever performed before a black audience, then a white person, male or female, should be invited every evening. The organizer of the show should welcome him formally, dress him in ceremonial costume and lead him to his seat, preferably in the front row of the stalls. The actors will play for him. A spotlight should be focussed upon this symbolic white throughout the performance. (Preface to the published edition, trans. Frechtman, 1960)

This shows an exceptionally sensitive attention on the part of a playwright to the function the audience performs in constructing a meaning for his play. The reason for his insistence on the presence of a white audience is that his play is not a story but a **ritual**; it does not describe events, it attacks attitudes. It is a ceremony for exorcising the European or white view of Africans or blacks. The ceremony is directed at the traditional white-skinned view of black skins as representing everything that is primitive, obscure, threatening, disgusting. The ceremony aims to realise as fully as possible this figment of the white imagination, in order, ultimately, to destroy it. Since it does not represent the reality of the blacks, but only the image imposed upon them by white people, it is essential to have a white audience. In other words, Genet requires a quality in his audience that is very like the quality of belief in a medieval audience. The images presented on stage only acquire their force as a result of the beliefs of the white audience. If we ask what kind of pleasure the white audience might be expected to derive from attending a performance of *The Blacks*, the answer must also be couched in something like religious terms. It is certainly not the pleasure of flattery or self-indulgence. It can only be described as the pleasure of seeing an indefensible myth undermined and exploded from within, and the sense of release that may come from recognising the evils embedded in one's own culture.

There is extensive discussion of the concept of **audience** in *Audiences* (1998) by Abercrombie and Longhurst and a comprehensive survey of attitudes to audiences and spectators in Pickering and Woolgar's *Theatre Studies* (2009).

See also **context/contextual studies.**

Analysis

As a student of drama you are likely to be required to undertake two forms of analysis: either the analysis of a performance or the analysis of a work of drama in the form of a written **text**. I shall be examining both in this entry.

In the 1970s and 1980s both Literary Criticism and Communication Studies embraced the development of *semiology*, or **semiotics**, as it is more frequently called, because it seemed to present an almost scientific mode of analysis, and I have made considerable reference to this kind of discourse. However, in more recent years, the limitations of this approach have been exposed, particularly because it appears to preclude that deep, intuitive form of analysis that an audience or, more consciously, a student, undertakes in response to the process of watching a play or other kind of performance. Analytical methods have increasingly relied on approaches from Sociology and Anthropology to do justice to the whole concept of a 'performance event' with its integrated elements and holistic experience.

In a wonderfully provocative entry under 'Performance Analysis' in his *Dictionary of the Theatre: Terms, Concepts and Analysis* (1998), the distinguished French drama theorist Patrice Pavis claims that 'Theatre people are rarely users of analysis, whether out of fear of discovery, a vague distrust of analysis or a lack of interest or time.' He goes on to assert that the result of this is that analysis is only carried out by small groups of 'experts'. He also wonders if, 'given the many different methods used in performance analysis if such a thing as a general method exists'. He does, nevertheless, concede that when he was teaching students, he found it necessary to devise a questionnaire to be answered immediately after a performance to enable them to undertake some informed type of analysis. There is a version of this questionnaire reproduced in Counsell and Wolf (2001) and you may find it helpful. However, throughout this book I have attempted to provide a series of conceptual tools under a number of general headings and, using the categories indicated by the chapters, it ought to be possible to devise a rather more sophisticated but equally accessible questionnaire of personal use. Let's consider some of the questions for which you might seek answers, under the main chapter headings and using some of the concepts we have discussed.

(1) The text
How did the performance relate to the structure and form of the work?
What dramatic techniques, such as flashbacks or montage, were employed and how?
How was the protagonist's journey or predicament conveyed?
How were the key stages in the plot handled?
How was dramatic irony used?
Did the distinctive 'voices' of the characters emerge and how was the language of the play presented and used?
Did a subtext emerge?
What was the play's genre and how did this determine the way in which it was performed?
If it was a devised piece, how did it differ in performance from a written text?
What kind of theatre language was evident?

(2) Performance techniques
What acting style, skills and approach were evident?

What forms of vocalisation or ritual were used?

How was the characterisation handled?

What specific devices (e.g. 'asides', 'improvisation') were evident and how did they affect the style of performance?

How were elements like music or mime employed?

Were there elements of 'Realism' or 'Naturalism' and, if not, what was the overall sense of the performance style?

(3) Production

Did you become aware of a governing idea?

Did the production employ some of the techniques of Epic Theatre or Physical Theatre, or attempt to be a piece of total theatre? If not, what fundamental approach did you detect?

How did the production attempt to address the audience?

Was its style 'poetic' or 'Expressionistic', or what other description would best sum up its totality? Justify any label you may give it.

How did the production 'realise' the intentions of the written work as you perceive them?

What kind of 'text' was created by the act of performance?

(4) Staging

How was the performance space employed?

What was the form of staging and why?

Where was the audience?

What forms of scenography were used?

Was there any use of stage machinery?

How did the lighting affect the environment and the actors?

What was the total design concept?

(5) Audience and critical reception

What were the predominant 'signs' and 'icons' in the performance and how did you 'read' them?

What was the relationship between the actors and spectators and how did the audience react?

Were you aware of 'intertextual' qualities?

Was authenticity an issue in the performance?

What meanings did you construct for the action of the play?

The various sections of this book should enable you to add further questions. The issues are, by no means, confined to the chapter on 'Performance' even though they are being drawn upon to analyse a performance event.

In conducting an analysis of a playtext I would suggest that initially students employ the seven basic steps that I developed in my book *Studying Modern Drama* (2003). They are: (1) recognise the **conventions**; (2) achieve a broad outline of the **action**; (3) define the **protagonist**'s predicament; (4) trace the main tensions and threats; (5) examine the world of the play and its social order; (6) imagine the play in performance; (7) draw the analysis together and pose some questions about the play.

Once this preliminary analysis of the entire **text** has been concluded you might then proceed to analyse smaller units such as **scenes**. This will facilitate close study of the **stage directions, motivation, dialogue** or **monologue**, together with an identification of such stages in the play as **exposition** or 'disclosure'. Although it is vital to retain a sense of the whole play and the context of any chosen unit, such close analysis of a small part also enables you to make an even closer analysis of key speeches. I would define a key speech as one that: (a) appears to sum up or deal with some of the central ideas of the play; (b) seems to mark a turning point in the action so that it can be traced back to that moment; (c) provokes particularly strong emotions in other characters or the audience – laughter or pity, for example; (d) reveals important aspects of a character's motives, goals or attitudes; (e) identifies an aspect of a protagonist's predicament.

Once such a speech has been identified it can subjected to closer analysis by: (a) identifying how the speech embodies a key concept or theme or marks an important moment in the play; (b) examining the speech characteristics of a character; (c) establishing the purpose for which language is being used; (d) exploring the relationship of the stage language to 'real' language.

Obviously, such consideration of a speech must involve an understanding of what constitutes a speech act (see **dialogue**), and should involve practical experimentation if at all possible. Each style and genre of written text invites, to some extent, its own kind of analysis and it is essential to return to the work as a whole before concluding the process because the fragmenting of the work into smaller units, however helpful, can distort the overall **structure** and the integration of disparate elements.

Wallis and Shepherd (2002) and Auckland-Lewis and Pickering (2004) both provide helpful models for the analysis of plays in performance and as playtexts.

See also **critic; negotiated meaning.**

Applied Drama

The concept of Applied Drama is included in this chapter dealing with critical reception because the approaches and activities described are normally intended solely for the benefit of the participants who constitute their own audience. Any audience involved in Applied Drama is, in fact, carefully selected and targeted and,where work generated may be shared with a group of interested spectators there is still the sense that drama is a vehicle and tool for some form of personal journey for the 'performers' and the onlookers are expected to play an active role in that journey.

Since the latter half of the twentieth century there has been an increasing application of the skills, methods of working and techniques of theatre in situations where learning, communication, personal growth and development, empowerment or conflict-resolution are desired. Using such techniques as **improvisation**, role play, 'hot seating', games, relaxation, story-telling or vocal work, facilitators (often initially trained in theatre or teaching) have applied their methods to a wide range of group situations. These have included prisons, self-help groups, schools, training groups for industry, therapy groups and small local communities. Much of the initial impetus for what is now collectively termed 'applied drama' came from the pioneering work of such practitioners as Peter Slade, Dorothy Heathcote and Gavin Bolton in Drama in Education which I have introduced under the entry for **improvisation.** Such thinkers promoted the use of drama as a means of learning and of personal and inter-personal development rather than as a performing art although they did not entirely abandon the concept of performance. Similar techniques were developed by Augusto Boal and his followers (see **forum theatre)** for use in places of conflict such as South Africa, Israel/Palestine or parts of South America. Other forms of applied drama may be used in **political drama, community theatre** and many non-traditional theatrical situations where people feel marginalised or dispossessed or where drama practitioners may engage in projects relating to aspects of social or cultural policy. Applied drama practitioners may also be required to interact with a wide range of practitioners from other fields of activity and it is recognised now that the work is essentially interdisciplinary.

One particular form of applied drama which requires specialist training beyond theatre but which draws heavily on the images and concepts of theatre is Transactional Analysis (TA). The basic assumption is that all human beings have a 'life script' and that through the development of a therapeutic relationship with a 'Gestalt' therapist (i.e. one who believes in the wholeness of things) clients can be led to recognise their 'life positions'. Such positions are dictated by an individual's 'ego state model' which Berne (1964: 23)) defines as 'a system of feelings accompanied by a related set of behaviour patterns'. To form these patterns, TA therapists believe that we all adopt the roles of Parent, Adult and Child at different times and in so doing we also establish life positions such as 'I'm OK' or 'I'm not OK' to enable us to survive in society.

Not all forms of 'dramatherapy' involve TA; some are based on a profound belief in the archetypes described by the psychiatrist Carl Gustav Jung (1865–1961) and will explore myth and story. Others will be based on an analysis of physical movement or resemble Boal's **forum theatre.** Recent developments embrace what is now known as 'reminiscence theatre', where groups and individuals make theatre through personal narrative, oral history and the sharing and enactment of memories. Work of this kind may well result in a written script and explore multicultural issues or inter-generational factors for older people and their carers. Such approaches are now used in a variety of care situations including day centres, residential homes and hospices.

Applied drama also includes the specialist techniques of 'Psychodrama' where groups explore fears and inhibitions, emotions and individual life situations in a safe and non-judgemental environment in which events and ideas are 'staged' and Sociodrama which is often employed in situations of collective trauma following disasters or war. There are recognised trainings for all these highly skilled techniques but they all demand and understanding of the basic concepts of drama.

Pickering's *Drama Improvised: A Handbook for Teachers and Therapists* (1997) provides a helpful survey of the development of Applied Drama together with practical suggestions and Helen Nicholson's *Theatre and Education* (2009) and *Applied Drama* (2005) explore the motivation and techniques of those involved in this kind of work. The drama therapies now have a substantial body of literature much of it published by Jessica Kingsley and some key texts are listed in the Bibliography.

See also **Improvisation; paratheatre; forum theatre; theatre of testimony.**

Audiences

The intellectual climate that affects an author may also be expected to shape the opinions of the audience, and the composition and assumptions of that audience form an essential element in the study of drama. The act of writing a play involves a commitment to communication with a public: all playwrights desire a public hearing for their work. However much they may shun publicity, disregard reviews or hate watching their plays performed, their aim is to provoke a confrontation of their ideas with a live audience. They may despise their public, or wish to shock them; more commonly, they will aim to please them; but whatever their attitude, their awareness of them will shape the way in which they write. Students of drama therefore need to be able to determine something of the playwright's attitude to the audience and of their ideological assumptions, as well as the social and economic conditions under which they live (see **zeitgeist**).

As an example, we can take some of Strindberg's remarks about his audience from a letter to Adolph Paul in 1907: '*Miss Julie* (without an intermission) has gone through its ordeal by fire and shown itself to be the kind of drama demanded by the impatient men of today: thorough but brief' (*Plays*, p. 3). Strindberg's sense of the 'impatient men' composing his audience was very different from George Etherege's idea of the people for whom he wrote *The Man of Mode*: members of fashionable society, who brought a far more casual attitude towards sex to the theatre. Etherege's audience was in no hurry; they could afford to listen with mild amusement to a lengthy prologue written by Sir Car Scroope, Baronet!

The study of audiences, and of playwrights' attitudes towards them, is thus the first step in re-creating any period play for a performance in the modern theatre. This emerges very clearly if we consider the problems of producing a play from the medieval period. In almost every important respect, the assumptions of the medieval audience were poles apart from those of contemporary theatre-goers. Let us imagine that we wish to stage *The Crucifixion* from the York Cycle. We shall use a translation which makes the language intelligible to a modern audience, but even so much of the force that the play originally held is likely to be lost when we consider the broad differences in audience assumption set out in the table overleaf.

Huge discrepancies can be seen to exist between the attitudes and expectations of the two audiences. It follows that before a meaningful performance of the play can take place, the audience must be transformed, made to shed some of its modern assumptions and 'play the part' of the medieval public. At a famous production of *The Passion*, a compilation by the National Theatre of medieval plays including the York *Crucifixion*, the director employed a variety of methods to induce something of this transformation in his audience. In the first place, he was clearly concerned by the discrepancy listed under (6) in the table. His solution was to use the Cottesloe auditorium, built as an open space resembling the courtyard of a late medieval inn. He cleared all the seats out and used every part of the space at some point in the action, thus ensuring that his audience moved around, sharing the space with the actors. Second, he drew the audience into the imaginative creation of the play's events at various points. For example, where the play dealt with the nativity of Christ, the cast distributed lighted candles to the

Comparison of medieval and modern audiences watching *The Mysteries*

Original audience	Modern audience
(1) Familiar with Christian symbols and liturgy.	(1) Not generally aware of Christian symbols or imagery.
(2) Mainly illiterate.	(2) Entirely literate and mainly 'well educated'.
(3) Very familiar with the words of the Bible story.	(3) Unlikely to be able to identify scriptural quotations or make cross references.
(4) Assumes that the subject matter is the most important event in world history.	(4) Sceptical, or doubting the truth of the historical event.
(5) Aware of theological and doctrinal points.	(5) Views the play as crudely realistic drama.
(6) Joins with the actors in celebrating redemption from sin.	(6) Watches the actors from comfortable, expensive seats in the auditorium.
(7) Either a cleric, soldier or manual worker on holiday.	(7) A middle-class, professional person who goes to theatres and buys drinks in the interval.
(8) Will be reminded of the need for regular church attendance.	(8) Regards the church as irrelevant except at weddings and funerals.
(9) Familiar with the story from visual representation in painting and sculpture – does not doubt Christ is God.	(9) Familiar with the rock-musical or a television play, both of which emphasise Christ's humanity.
(10) Used to acting that combines ritual qualities, verse-speaking and robust humour.	(10) Constantly exposed to 'realistic' acting on television.
(11) Regards life as part of a divine plan, largely inexplicable.	(11) Assumes rational, scientific explanations for everything.

audience, who then gathered round the scene of the birth at the centre of the floor space. By their action and positions, the audience found themselves contributing to the sacred significance of the scene. A very similar technique was employed at the Courtyard Theatre in their 2004 production of *The Mysteries*. The lack of a common belief among members of modern British society was, for the duration of the performance, over-ridden by the ceremonial force of the play's enactment of shared suffering and redemption.

The attempt to project oneself imaginatively into the situation of the original audience is part of the work of both student and director. Reviewers correctly identified this as one of the great achievements of the Royal Shakespeare Company's production *The Greeks*. Michael Coveny wrote:

> By telling a complete story, Mr Barton has achieved the astonishing *coup* of suggesting what it must have been like to sit with an audience in Athens and relate the narrative to what the playwrights assumed their customers knew. (*Financial Times*, 10 July 1979)

It is the knowledge of this assumption that enables us to understand a playwright's purpose and achievement. We need also to establish what is *unfamiliar* to a modern audience and try to present the plays in such a way that they become accessible and meaningful statements rather than interesting exercises in archaeology. Irving Wardle wrote of *The Greeks*: 'The story, addressed to a public coming fresh to the legends, is spell-binding' (*The Times*, 14 July 1979). What this production had successfully captured was the narrative dimension of Ancient Greek tragedy. It did this by refusing to allow its audience to treat the performance as after-dinner entertainment. Instead, it changed their expectations by performing three linked plays in the course of one day (as at the Ancient Greek drama festivals), beginning at 10.30 in the morning and continuing until 11.00 at night.

Much of the scholarship necessary to determine the conditions that prevailed when a play was first written depends on access to sources which may only be available to specialist researchers. Fortunately the trend in Drama Studies in recent years has resulted in scholarly editions of playtexts which bring together information from the various sources we have discussed, to give a clear picture of the factors that need to be borne in mind when planning a modern production. Such **texts** too are usually accurate and show precisely the changes and accumulations of **stage directions** made by successive generations of performers, printers and editors. It is important, therefore, to check that the **text** being used for any of the activities I have suggested represents the most recent scholarship available. This issue is addressed in more detail in the entry on **stage directions.**

I. Ang's *Desperately Seeking the Audience* (1991), D.McQuail's *Audience Analysis* (1997) and Helen Freshwater's *Theatre and Audience* (2009) are good examples of modern scholarship in relation to audiences.

Authenticity

The concept of authenticity covers a considerable range of experience and recent debate, performance theory, drama and theatre. The term itself may be used in a variety of contexts. Authenticity is central to existentialist philosophy and implies a state of mind that refuses to adopt comforting or protective beliefs. Such acts of 'bad faith' prevent the individual from confronting his or her own uniqueness in the world and from making the necessary but difficult choices that are an inevitable part of existence. Existentialists focus on the reality of living in the world rather than wishing to relate to any transcendent force. Significantly this attitude permeates much twentieth-century writing for the theatre particularly the **Theatre of the Absurd** and the plays of J.-P. Sartre (1905–1980) and Albert Camus(1913–1960).

The philosophical concept of authenticity also consciously or unconsciously underpins much discussion of approaches to acting and production. Grotowski, for example, placed great emphasis on the intense involvement, participation and truth to one's inner nature that characterised acting. For him an actor must be seen stripped naked of all artifice and reference to outside embellishments. Hence, an 'authentic' performance has come to mean something that ignores tradition and emanates solely from inner conviction and engagement with the **text** at a deep, organic level.

A rather narrower focus of the concept of authenticity has been part of a movement in the arts, particularly in music, dance and drama, to rediscover and reproduce original performance conditions and styles. During the twentieth and present centuries there have been a number of notable attempts to present plays in physical conditions which, as far as possible, resemble those that existed in the theatre when the play was written. The intention has been to preserve the playwright's original vision but it has also been discovered that the juxtaposition of ancient practice with modern expectations has had a most powerful effect. Perhaps the best example of this may be found by looking at the work of William Poel (1852–1934), who had a considerable influence on subsequent production styles.

Poel made his first appearance as a rather indifferent actor in 1876, but it was as a scholar and **director** that he inspired a generation of producers and playwrights. His major concern was with authenticity in performance, which naturally sprang from an insistence on using an accurate **text**. He was constantly seeking to rediscover original modes of staging, arguing that only by this means could an audience experience a play as the author intended. Many of Poel's ideas were seen as innovations in his day, though they may seem commonplace to us now. For example, writing of his 1901 production of *Everyman*, he claimed that it 'was the earliest instance in modern times of a return to the practice of characters approaching the stage through the auditorium', an idea that was taken up by Craig and Reinhardt. During the past century there have been so many changes in the theatre that few people would now think of this type of **entrance** as remarkable or as a return to the past; in order, therefore, to understand the impact of Poel, we need to see his work in the context of the theatre of his day, against which he was in revolt.

In order to achieve his aim of giving authentic productions of plays, Poel had to form his own production company because no commercial management was sympathetic. He chose to concentrate on what he considered to be the greatest drama written in English, that of the Tudor and Stuart period, and from 1894 to 1905 his 'Elizabethan Stage Society' mounted the first modern productions of Marlowe's *Dr Faustus* and Milton's *Samson Agonistes*, and the first production for four hundred years of *Everyman*. These, together with several Shakespearian plays, were performed in a variety of halls and courtyards and attracted considerable interest and critical acclaim.

We can see something of the nature of Poel's revolution by comparing an illustration of his staging of *Hamlet* in 1900 with a design for the same play by Hawes Craven used by the actor-manager Forbes-Robertson at the Lyceum Theatre only three years earlier in 1897. A photograph of Poel's production shows that it appears to be taking place on a reconstruction of an Elizabethan stage; by modern standards of research this is not a particularly accurate reconstruction but the intention is clear. There is no **proscenium arch** or row of footlights dividing the auditorium from the stage; the setting is non-representational and is obviously intended for use throughout the play. The characters, dressed in late Tudor or early Stuart costumes, dominate the picture. Poel's production looks small-scale, intimate and a little haphazard in grouping, but the interest is centred on the characters and what they are saying or doing. A row or two of uncomfortable-looking chairs suggest that this is not a modern commercial theatre but a hired hall and there seems to be little demand for sophisticated **lighting** effects. What Poel was trying to rediscover in such productions was the particular dynamic resulting from presenting a play in the type of theatre for which it was written. We can see that his *Hamlet* follows as many of the practices of the Elizabethan theatre as possible, including an absence of scenery. We also know that he regarded preserving the integrity of the original text to be as important as its mode of staging.

By contrast, an illustration of Hawes Craven's design comes from a painting of the designer's intentions. However, this illustration was included in the published version of *Hamlet* compiled by the actor-manager Forbes-Robertson to coincide with his production and we know from prompt copies left by Henry Irving when he used the same design, and from other illustrations made after the production, that this is how the stage would have appeared to members of the audience. The whole staging concept here is pictorial, designed to be seen through the frame of the proscenium arch. The sense of **Realism** is achieved by minutely detailed architecture and Gothic costumes; and the characters, almost dwarfed by the grandeur of the spectacle, employ gestures which seem to be part of the design. In order to achieve this picture, the actor-manager would have needed to employ elaborate late nineteenth-century theatre technology, and the overall impression is of Shakespeare reinterpreted to suit the tastes and expectations of Victorian theatre-goers.

Perhaps the most significant difference between the two productions I am considering here is the relationship between the **actors** and the **audience** (see **actor/audience relationship**). Poel was able to direct the play knowing that it would appear perfectly natural for the cast to address the audience directly and he could argue that this is what Shakespeare intended; on the other hand, for an actor to step from Hawes Craven's **setting** and speak directly to the audience would have seemed ridiculous and would have destroyed the illusion that the elaborate design was meant to create. Most nineteenth-century actor-managers were concerned with spectacle, and to some extent concern for the text of the play itself was secondary. George Bernard Shaw, one of the most trenchant critics of Lyceum productions, once lamented: 'How am I to praise this deed when my own art, the art of literature, is left shabby and ashamed amid the triumph of the arts of the painter and the actor?' (*Our Theatre in the Nineties*, vol. 1, p. 19). Poel felt convinced that Elizabethan drama could not be staged in the commercial theatre so dominated by the proscenium arch and 'realistic' scenery, because he claimed that 'the atmosphere of Elizabethan drama is created through the voice, that of modern drama through the sight' (*Monthly Letters*, p. 95).

In his search to rediscover the 'authentic' Shakespeare' Poel went to the earliest and most reliable sources for his information concerning the Elizabethan playhouse and the playtexts themselves. During the nineteenth century the plays had suffered a good deal of mutilation, partly on account of Victorian sensitivity to the more bawdy and explicit sexual aspects, and partly because actor-managers had attempted to reconcile the plays to the needs of the proscenium arch theatre: Poel therefore had no easy task. In order that famous actors could achieve startling scenic effects or dramatic **entrances** and exits for themselves, it was found necessary to alter the sequence of **scenes**, transpose locations of events and cut or add speeches. Evidence for this is widespread: a recently discovered wax-cylinder recording of Irving speaking a speech from *Henry VIII* reveals some extra lines inserted, and an examination of his prompt copy shows how these words were used to create a moving exit for the great actor as the curtain slowly fell. No wonder Shaw once remarked: 'Irving does not cut Shakespeare, he disembowels him!'

The acting edition of *Hamlet* from which the illustration I have discussed is taken shows how Forbes-Robertson adapted the play for his own purposes, cutting out any lines with sexual undertones and locating the action of the scenes differently. The scenes from Act II onwards are described as follows:

Act II
Scene 1.   Room of State in the Castle

Act III
Scene 1.   A Room of State in the Castle
Scene 2.   Another Room in the Same

Act IV
Scene 1.   The Orchard

Act V
Scene 1.   A Churchyard
Scene 2.   A Room in the Castle
Scene 3.   A Hall in the Castle

Justifying these changes and additions, Forbes-Robertson wrote in his Preface:

I have ventured to transfer the scenes taking place in the house of Polonius to the Castle of Elsinore in order to avoid as much as possible a change of scene, and to allow more scope and freedom of movement to the characters.

We must remember that scene-changing in the Victorian theatre was indeed something to be avoided, for it involved large numbers of stage-hands heaving on ropes and huge pulleys to send flats, **wings** and backdrops clanking noisily into position. But if Forbes-Robertson had taken Poel's solution and allowed a single open stage with a permanent setting to represent all the locations of the action and relied mainly on the text to set the scene, he would have avoided the problem altogether.

Scholarly research into playtexts and the acting conditions in past decades was very much in its infancy in the nineteenth century and actor-managers were faced with the problem of presenting to a public demanding spectacle, plays that were written for a type of theatre of which they were largely ignorant. The research in which Poel engaged enabled him to alert producers, directors and performers to the rich possibilities of ancient forms of staging. His work led to experiments with varying **actor–audience relationships**, **ritual** elements from Greek and medieval theatre, and modern plays specifically created to exploit new theatre spaces based on early models. Producers such as Granville-Barker began to insist on a careful and intelligent analysis of the text, a trend reflected in his famous *Prefaces*, and bold experiments in scenic design followed; there was a new impetus to the study of theatre history.

Catharsis

The concept of 'catharsis' is one of the most ancient, enduring and revisited in the whole of drama. Its literal medical meaning, taken from the Greek, is 'purgation' but Aristotle uses it in his *Poetics* to describe the total sensation experienced by the **audience** after feeling 'pity' and 'fear' from watching a **tragedy**. This purging of the emotions is further described in Aristotle's *Politics*, where he suggests that drama and music have the potential to take people out of themselves, possess them with an almost divine state and then return them cleansed and restored as if they had taken a purgative drug.

Critics invariably have difficulty with the concept of emotion: most prefer rational **analysis**, but the development of psychotherapy following the work of Freud has increasingly examined the emotional life of humans, its relationship to imagination and the arts, and the nature of the unconscious impulses that drive behaviour. The idea expressed in the *Politics* that the emotions can be purged 'orgiastically' is very close to modern psychotherapeutic methods of enabling patients to confront and organise their fears and emotions. Freud also recognised the need for children and adults to *play* in order to act out situations that disturb them, and that a vital aspect of such *play* was the repetition of tragic experience. For Freud and his followers, *play*, which often involved identifying with an imaginary person or situation and empathising with them, was a form of catharsis. Freudian psychology has, therefore, given us an insight into the nature of the cathartic experience.

Other attempts to explain the concept have focused on the feelings of audiences following their watching of a play. Freytag (1857) refers to the spectator feeling 'an intensification of vital power' after watching a tragedy because he or she senses a release from being involved in the suffering of the **hero**. On the other hand, Henn (1956) postulates a 'Reduction to Scale' theory that attributes catharsis to the realisation on the part of the audience that their suffering is minimal compared with that of the tragic figures in the play.

It can be argued that, if we focus on Aristotle's suggested emotions of 'pity' and 'fear', we can construct a model of catharsis based on the idea that tragedy achieves a balance between them. Pity moves us emotionally towards the sufferer whereas fear causes us to recoil: the resultant balance of these two impulses provides us with an ability to come to terms with the objects of our fears. A sense of identification with the suffering of the hero, a realisation that all must suffer and that even the most powerful can be brought down, are all embedded in the experience of catharsis. The fact that we may be prepared to witness the same tragedy over and over again, knowing full well that it will move, disturb, upset or anger us, is one of the most intriguing aspects of drama and clearly has to do with our emotional needs. You might wish to examine your own feelings and emotions following the performance of a play that you consider to be tragic. You should ask youself why you went and, perhaps more significantly, why you might go again. It is important to analyse your personal responses to the play and attempt to articulate a justification for presenting or witnessing something that focuses on suffering. Patrice Pavis (1998) provides a useful overview of historic attitudes to the concept of 'catharsis'.

See also **tragedy.**

Codes of communication

When we witness a performance, the meaning of the play presents itself to us as a totality. We do not ask whether this **lighting** effect or that movement serves to reinforce or to contradict a particular line of thought: we think alongside the performance, that is to say we construct a meaning as it goes along, responding to a whole variety of signs, which we do not necessarily separate out and disentangle from one another as the performance unfolds. But each movement, light, colour, sound that is presented on stage is the result of a choice by the **director** (or somebody on the production team) and it is necessary to find some way of categorising these different codes of signification (see **sign system**). No two structuralist critics of the theatre agree about how this is to be done, but in order to provide an example of how such a method operates we can suggest four basic and clearly differentiated codes:

(1) *The linguistic.* This includes the **dialogue** (or **monologue**) that is spoken and also words as they appear in any shape or form: projected onto a screen, written on the **set**, sung to music, represented as a 'text' mesage etc.

(2) *The perceptual.* This, a rather loose category, groups together anything that makes a direct impact upon the senses of the **audience**: sound, colours, images, movements, and all those elements that have a significance not filtered through language.

(3) *The socio-cultural.* The significance that will be attached to elements of both (1) and (2), above, will depend on **conventions** peculiar to specific societies and cultures. Hanging white sheets from the windows will be construed as signifying that a death has taken place (in Sweden), or that it is washing day (in Italy). For people working within their native culture and tradition, those kinds of associations will be taken for granted. Such conventions will operate at the level both of connotation and of denotation.

(4) *The theatrical.* More specific than the socio-cultural, and not necessarily recognised by every member of a socio-cultural group, are the theatrical conventions of codes of signification. These vary considerably, even with the same social and cultural tradition.

Of these four categories, only the first is included with any thoroughness in the printed **texts** of plays. As a result of this, the study of drama is bound to call upon creative and imaginative skill, as well as skills of a critical and analytical nature. This is evident as soon as we begin to analyse the speeches in a play. In order to be able to hear the voice with which they should be spoken, we require all sorts of information not contained in the **text**. For what survives of a play, once its original production has disappeared (or what exists of a play that has never been produced), is not **characters** or a story (although these can be reconstructed by the use of inference and imagination) but a sequence of speeches attributed to a set of names. These speeches are better described as *speech acts*. By 'speech act' is meant the **performative** function of speech, which is normally implied rather than stated (see **performative**). Most statements contain a function of this kind: they promise or threaten or enquire or command but often fail to include the explicit statement 'I promise', 'I threaten', etc. In order to bring these speech acts back to life in a performance, the performer has to attend not only to the statements themselves but also to the conditions in which they are uttered. Statements made by a character in a novel will also be affected by the conditions in which that character utters his words, but the novelist is able to provide a precise delineation of the circumstances of his choosing. The situation of the stage character is one of those elements of freedom and flexibility that necessitate a genuinely creative act on the part of the performer. For while certain circumstantial details are given by the playwright, others need to be found in the course of rehearsal and production work.

The conditions or circumstances that have to be considered by the performer are of two distinct kinds: the *material* conditions and the *imaginary* conditions. Material circumstances condition statements in a very obvious way: the words 'I am hungry' are spoken in a different voice when the character uttering them is rich and well fed from the voice that will be used by someone starving to death. In the theatre, material conditions of this kind have to be *materialised*, shown in concrete form, and the shape they take will depend on the scenic vocabulary and stage technology employed. Sometimes the form in which these conditions should be materialised is specified by the playwright. In *Endgame*, Beckett specifies that Nagg and Nell should be placed in dustbins, a situation which only too clearly conditions their statements about life, whether they are understood to rise above this degrading position, or thought of as merely 'talking rubbish'. In other cases the playwright could not possibly have suspected the material conditions in which the performer of his words is placed. In Peter Brook's now almost legendary 'white box' of a *Midsummer Night's Dream* in 1970, many of Oberon's lines were delivered while swinging on a trapeze.

The dustbins in *Endgame* or the trapeze in *A Midsummer Night's Dream* are both unusually concrete, non-metaphorical examples of conditioning. More common is the case where the performers themselves convey the imaginary situations that condition and define the meaning of the speeches. In a scene from Brecht's *Galileo*, we see the Pope at first expressing ideas quite sympathetic to Galileo. In the course of the scene he is dressed up in the papal regalia for a public audience: the more robes are put on him, the less able he is to resist the demands of the Cardinal Inquisitor, who wants to interrogate Galileo. In this case the change in an imaginary relationship is being presented to the audience by concrete, visual means; those of the papal regalia. Often, an essential condition which gives meaning to a statement is created simply by means of the attitudes and statements of other characters. In a celebrated scene from *The Man of Mode* (Act III, Scene 1), Harriet and young Bellair decide to put on a show of love for their respective parents, who are observing them. Their lines, taken out of context, do not read like a love scene at all. In the context provided by the presence of the onlookers they take on a different meaning. It is the peculiarity of theatre dialogue that what is important is not so much the statements themselves as the conditions in which they are uttered.

See also **deconstruction; negotiated meaning.**

Context and contextual studies

The study of drama involves a careful consideration of plays as potential pieces of live theatre, and we can only gain a comprehensive and balanced view of the meaning and nature of a play when we think about it in relation to performance. It follows therefore, that although their ultimate aims may be different, the kind of 'study' in which the **actor, director** or student engages is largely the same, for the idea of performance must always be present. Many school and university courses employ a different method, concentrating entirely upon literary analysis of the text, and students are never forced to test their ideas in the laboratory of real or possible performance. Such an approach may lead to one level of understanding but it fails to take into account many of the aspects of a play which only emerge in the theatre.

Many issues can and do affect the performance of a play: factors which may include the **acting style**, the nature of staging, the attitude of the **audience** and the topicality of the play. From a large number of such factors it is possible to discern two major strands. First there are those qualities indigenous to the play itself: the author's intentions discernible from the **text**, with its **characters** and **plot,** and (where these exist) in **stage directions** and an author's preface. It is important to acknowledge that some modern scholars doubt the importance or even existence of authors' intentions, but that argument has been firmly repudiated by the playwright David Hare in his *Obedience, Struggle and Revolt* (2005). Secondly, there are those qualities which the performers, playhouse and audience bring to the performance of a play. Clearly, when writing any play, the playwright may be influenced by the knowledge of who is to perform it and in what conditions, but if the play is not contemporary, we, who wish to perform the play again, are left to explore the links between the two sets of qualities we have mentioned.

To make these links, a play must be examined in the context of the theatre conditions that were current when it was first written. This leads us on to the whole question of the use of theatre history. Far too often, students assume that illustrations of Shakespeare's Globe or of medieval pageant wagons can do the same work as a modern production photograph. In fact these pieces of pictorial evidence raise as many questions as they answer, although the pursuit of such questions is often a fascinating and worthwhile task in its own right.

Before we can consider the importance of players and playhouses, we need to look at plays in the context of the social conditions and attitudes and the broader movements within the arts which existed at the time of their creation. Does this mean that a student of drama must also be a student of social and political history, the history of moral or religious beliefs, and of the arts? To the extent that drama both reflects and is capable of dealing seriously with some of these issues, the answer must be 'Yes.' Drama, the most public of all the arts, always involves people; either the imaginary characters of a play or the real people who give them substance and the real people who watch. Therefore any aspect of the human condition may become the business of the dramatists, the performer or the student of drama. This does not mean, however, that we should begin our study of a play with comprehensive research into the history of the period in which it was written. This mistake has adversely affected Drama Studies in the past, when, for example, students of Shakespeare have been asked to acquire an 'Elizabethan World View'. Obviously some knowledge of contemporary customs, fashions and attitudes is helpful because the dramatist peoples his play with characters who most frequently move, speak and think like his contemporaries; nevertheless an over-generalised view of a particular period is unlikely to be productive.

In establishing an appropriate method for gaining contextual information, the first principle must be that the play itself will reveal what is relevant. Instead of asking, 'What information about the author and his times is necessary for a full understanding of this play?' we should initially ask two questions: (1) What can we learn about the author and the social conditions and attitudes of his times *from* this play? (2) What are the relevant issues on which we require further information? Both these questions will help us to re-create imaginatively the conditions in which the play was first written and performed: a vital process if we hope to examine its 'afterlife'. This will not provide the complete picture, because we are setting aside for a moment the history of the theatre itself, but we often fool ourselves into thinking that a play is really about one set of issues because we are bringing our current beliefs and attitudes to bear upon it when, if we examine the play in its original context, it turns out to be about something quite different.

See also **zeitgeist.**

Critic

In Samuel Beckett's famous play *Waiting for Godot,* two characters, Didi and Gogo, pass time by insulting each other. This game comes to a climax with the word 'critic': the worst insult they can conceive! Hostility to the role of the critic in the theatre derives from the damage that they can do: on Broadway, and to some extent in the West End, a damning criticism in the press can bring about a production's demise, and you have probably experienced the sense of deflation and anger that accompanies the lukewarm reception of a production to which you have made a great commitment of emotional and artistic energy.

Once you are a member of a theatre **audience**, however, you are also a critic, because the process of watching drama is one of constant evaluation, albeit unconscious. The opinions you develop as you watch a play are based on your own set of criteria and tastes and recent approaches to critical theory have demonstrated that no two people actually see the same performance. Everyone will have *read* it differently from anyone else, including the person who may write and publish a review. This might lead you to ask if there is any point in there being critics.

However, good theatre critics can add significant new dimensions to our awareness of the art form, and create important records of performances. Theatre criticism brings what we see in the theatre into the wider public domain and is an inevitable part of a consumer-driven society. It also provides an invaluable indication as to what plays and performances are available, and will often inspire us to attend, or warn us to avoid, a particular production. Because such criticism exists it is also a strong economic factor in the life of the theatre. If we look at the prologues of many Restoration plays we can see the influence of (what were then largely verbal) critics on the aspirations and fortunes of playwrights.

Considering ourselves to be critics is an important aspect of theatre-going: whatever performance you have seen, something will remain in the memory, and even if you consider the production to have been 'bad' this will need qualifying and rationalising. You may find aspects of a production very satisfying: there may be an ingenious **set,** you may admire the **governing idea**, or directorial concept but might find one or more aspects of the performances unsatisfactory. You may feel that decisions about staging were inappropriate for the play or that the **acting style** failed to exploit the material, or lacked authenticity. In fact, if you were to go through this book now, listing the key concepts discussed, you would find that almost every one of them provided a point of criticism which could be applied to a play in performance. In this multiplicity of points it is helpful to have a few common viewpoints that audiences bring to the evaluation of a performed play. In her book *Theatre: A Way of Seeing* (1995), Milly Barranger suggests that there are four such viewpoints: human significance; social significance; artistic quality; and entertainment value. Let's briefly explore these. Theatre is a remarkable and unique medium in that it creates a relationship between us as human beings in the **audience** and the **actors** as **characters** in the fictive world of the stage. Plays explore what it means to be human in ordinary and extraordinary circumstances: we respond to the images created by the play, sometimes identifying with the predicaments and emotions experienced by the characters. We are confronted with the possibilities of fulfilment, loss, tragedy, relationships, tyranny, war, peace, love, the unexpected and undeserved, the inexplicable and the results of human actions and moral choices. We are led to an understanding of ourselves and of our potential or we are invited to question our motives and values in the light of what we see. Any critical evaluation of a performance will include reference to the richness or paucity of the experiences I have indicated.

Theatre is inextricably bound with society: it is a communal activity and reflects aspects of the community. Theatre-going can provide new perspectives on social, political and moral issues that affect the lives of nations and smaller groups. It is an opportunity to expose social injustice, mock authority, parody and shame sections of society and highlight contemporary issues. There is hardly a burning question that has not been the subject of recent drama and it is hardly remarkable that repressive regimes suppress performance. The balance with which a play production presents an issue, its avoidance of propaganda and its ability to establish discourse, will be criteria for evaluation.

Aesthetic judgements will stem from our experience and will grow in sophistication as we see more performances. However, we can also respond to the immediate. We know if we are engaged by a performance, and we can eventually say why. We know whether we can relax and make meanings from what we see rather than constantly being aware of the shortcomings of the acting or **setting.** We experience a sense of the integration of the aspects of the production if the visual, auditory and imagistic messages we receive seem complementary and part of a single statement. We can respond to the rhythm and shape of a production, its climaxes and suspense, its resolutions and special moments. Like Brecht, we can appreciate the skill of the performers and yet still be engaged with the issues of the play. We can applaud the strategies of the characters and yet be aware that they are the actions of a performer.

To what extent a production is 'entertaining' will depend on the genre but it is a mistake to assume that the sense of delight experienced in watching a farce or escapist piece of musical theatre is the only kind of entertainment. Any production should evoke an experience of rich satisfaction, even if this takes the form of catharsis or a mood of deep seriousness. Perhaps we are now too tolerant of inadequate productions that fail to entertain us in the real sense. In earlier centuries we would have expressed our dissatisfaction by calling out, walking out or going onto the stage! Every aspect of the gamut of emotions can be a part of the experience of theatre and you should expect your feelings as well as your ideas to be stimulated.

The role of the professional critic has frequently been ambivalent in relation to the makers of theatre. The most informed and influential critics can play a vital part in the maintenance of standards and the wider debate about the significance of drama. As long ago as 1968, John Russell Brown, one of the few individuals then to be holding a Professorial Chair in Drama, was making a plea for better and more informed criticism:

> If there is any form of writing about theatre that needs to be encouraged, I think it is extended, considered reviewing. Occasionally a critic can write about a single production twice or even three times, as it moves from one theatre to another. But if he could see it many times, keeping in touch with first impressions, and so compare one night's performance with another, and relate every detail of the production to every detail of the published text and, perhaps, to records of other productions; if he could assess an actor's performance in the light of his career as a whole, and compare the director's achievement with the designer's or the chief actor's; and if this critic had time to consider what the journalistic reviewers have said and what explanations of intentions the artists have published, and time to consider what the production has achieved in his own consciousness and to relate this to his personal view of others – then the critic might have found a full and careful way to study and criticize one theatrical experience. (*Drama*, 1968, p. 88)

This remarkable statement, coming from before the time when drama study spoke of 'codes' or **intertextuality** or of **audiences** 'making meanings', can provide drama and theatre students with a stimulating challenge, particularly as Professor Brown adds, 'As far as I know, this recipe has never been followed.' You are encouraged to read as much theatre criticism as possible to develop a vocabulary and range of concepts for your own evaluations.

Deconstruction

This concept was developed by the French philosopher Jacques Derrida in the 1960s as a term to describe the strategy of examining the *signs* or elements of language in isolation from other elements. In this process, also known as *poststructuralism*, the contradictions inherent within language are exposed. You will see the significance of this idea if this entry is read in conjunction with the entry on **theatre language**. Because of the development of the idea of there being a 'language' or **code of communication** in theatre, these critical examinations of the nature of language have come to have considerable significance for the entire concept of *reading* a performance.

Derrida's view of language was shaped by his understanding of the nature of knowledge, of how it is preserved and presented and how it acquires authority. As a consequence, his thinking was often directed towards texts and their interpretation and he came to the conclusion that no text can be sustained by a fixed body of knowledge and have an absolute and finite meaning awaiting our discovery. Thus, Derrida's work has called into question many conventional approaches to criticism and interpretation that seem to suggest that a *definitive* interpretation of any text can be said to exist. He, in fact, suggests that there is never a single or fixed meaning to any text but that meaning is constantly slipping and proliferating, and he terms this potential for multiple and shifting meanings *dissemination*. Meaning is in a constant state of flux because language that is used to express meaning, whether written or spoken, is invariably dependent upon related concepts: for example, we cannot think of 'good' without the concept of 'evil', we cannot wholly think of 'masculine' without, at least partially, thinking of 'feminine'. Language operates, Derrida contends, by silencing or negating the opposites to which it in fact refers. So texts are often about what they seem *not* to be about and in the process of 'deconstructing' a text we can find points where the otherness of what a work is about may become evident.

The term 'deconstruction' comes from Derrida's belief that in the West, knowledge is structured around a *centre*: this structuring process is rather subtle and does not, immediately, draw attention to itself. Any discourse refers to the *centre*, which both provides a focus and enables knowledge to be structured around a certain truth, or *logos*, that presents itself as beyond contention and as absolute (see **Postmodernism**). Traditional literary and dramatic texts have tended to reinforce these structures by claiming that there are definitive interpretations. This has often been done by claims that the author's intention is clearly understood and beyond debate. The academic disciplines have claimed a monopoly of the means whereby meanings can be recognised and knowledge preserved and presented. It is against such structures of authority that Derrida invites a deconstruction of the text by a consideration of all the related meanings and inbuilt contradictions that become evident. He insists that we examine the way in which meanings are structured around a centre and that we concede that meanings cannot be entirely contained but are always likely to diversify and diverge from their centre.

Although Derrida's work had an initial impact on literary theory, its implication for the study of drama as both text and performance rapidly became evident. For students and potential critics of drama, it is important to grasp the fundamental idea that meanings can be altered by external factors. Perception of the behaviour of characters will almost certainly be modified in the light of personal experiences, and interpretations will remain valid in spite of their constantly shifting nature. There is a particularly amusing and refreshing picture of the clash of traditional literary criticism with the new schools of 'structuralist' critics and academics in David Lodge's novel *Small World* (1984).

See also **negotiated meaning; codes of communication.**

Drama study

The study of drama in colleges and universities has undergone enormous change in recent years. Whereas drama may once have been an aspect of English or have established its own faculty, it may well now be part of an integrated undergraduate programme in Performing Arts, Liberal Studies, Gender Studies, Media, Communications Arts, or an aspect of a course in Image Studies involving film, dance and visual arts.

With the advent of modular degrees with credit-rated units, it is often possible to take a single unit on an aspect of drama or performance without a broader course involving theatre skills or theatre history. There have also been significant and essential developments in courses focusing on areas of drama that have been neglected in a largely conservative, male-dominated and Euro-centric subject: thus there are now modules that encourage the study of post-colonial, feminist or gay and lesbian theatre and drama. Courses where these types of plays appear place the study of drama within the context of political, cultural and social change. Consequently we have seen the emergence of what have essentially become new genres, like 'queer drama', 'theatre of apartheid' or 'theatre of protest'. An example of a play that features in one university's course attempting to address sexual politics through Drama is David Mamet's *Oleanna*. This play considers the power conflict between the sexes, through scenes showing the conversations between a male lecturer and his female student.

Other modules involving the study of drama are drawn from the broad spectrum of Cultural and Critical Studies. Such titles as 'Drama Theory and Criticism' or 'Analysis of Dramatic Texts' enable students to apply literary and critical theory to plays and, in some cases, performance. This has enabled teachers and students to evolve their own vocabulary and approach for the specific analysis of works for the theatre. It should be noted that it is useful to be able to place plays in some sort of historical perspective in order to understand them as not only affected by prevailing attitudes in society or in critical theory but also subject to the constant possibility of performance.

This book provides the opportunity for students to cross-reference their particular topic of interest and, in the process, help demolish the artificial barriers that are sometimes erected between various approaches to and aspects of the study of Drama. In the introduction to the book I have outlined the emergence of Performance Studies as potentially hostile to, but in fact complementary to, Drama and Theatre Studies. A constant awareness that we are considering a potential 'event' should underpin all attitudes to study in our emerging discipline.

Drama has often been studied with a view to extracting and discussing the philosophy of its author; but it is not so easy to extract a line of thought from the speeches of a play. For the speeches are seldom intended to be taken at face value, but rather, should be understood within the context of a total situation. An author who has suffered particularly in this respect is Molière. Volumes of criticism have been devoted to a study of this author's thought and to elucidating the philosophies of the different **characters** of his plays. But Tartuffe's famous statement that 'il y a des accommodements avec le ciel' is not interesting as a philosophical proposition. It is interesting as the kind of thing a man will say when he is trying to play the saintly celibate but is in fact aflame with a lust he can neither deny nor control. Similarly, the statements made by Alceste and Oronte in the discussion of the sonnet (*Le Misanthrope*, Act I) are in themselves too extreme to be foundations of philosophy.

Their interest lies in the context. This shows that the protestations made by the two men are quite out of proportion to the rather trivial occasion. If taken separately and out of context, both the statements of Alceste and those of Oronte seem absurdly extreme. But taken in their place in the **scene** as Molière wrote it, each character's statements are explained by the extremism of the other and the point of the scene can be appreciated, i.e. to extract comedy from the contrast between the man who believes that one should always say exactly what one thinks, and the one with the opposite attitude, who maintains that one should always flatter and deceive.

So a play can be seen to function more by presenting a number of conflicting ideas than by developing a single philosophy. In studying plays, we find that we have to pay attention to a number of different 'voices'. It is not simply a matter, as in a novel, of assessing the author's meaning. The task is to be attentive to all the different voices in a play. Among these different voices we can sometimes even distinguish the voice of the public. When Winnie, in Beckett's play *Happy Days*, recalls a bystander looking at her and asking,

> What's the idea? he says – stuck up to her diddies in the bleeding ground – coarse Fellows – What does it mean? he says – What's it meant to mean?

the natural response of the average observer is being built into the fabric of the **dialogue**.

If we look only at the printed word of the playtext, we encounter another interesting problem for the study of drama. This has to do with the action of character in literature. Much dramatic criticism treats characters in the theatre as if they were similar to characters in a novel. But the novelist does not rely solely on dialogue. He or she is able to provide a wealth of information concerning the character's thoughts, dreams, upbringing, ancestry, and can even tell us things that the characters themselves do not know. But a 'character' in a playtext is literally only a set of disconnected speeches set down against a name. The one factor giving unity to the character is the actor who portrays him or her. This **actor** must find a **mask, costume**, voice, way of moving, etc. that integrate all the things set down for the character to say. If any privileged information of the kind supplied by the novelist is to be conveyed to the **audience**, then it must be by other **characters** speaking about other characters behind their back, and such information is always suspect – an **audience** will wait for characters to confirm from their behaviour the truth or otherwise of the assertions made about them When Polonius tells Ophelia that Hamlet is going mad, we do not immediately believe him, but wait to see how Hamlet will behave. In this situation, a novelist would be able to tell us *both* what Polonius thought *and* what was really going on in Hamlet's mind. But the dramatist has voluntarily limited himself to the perspective of his characters, choosing to speak through their voice alone.

The unity of character that the actor must supply is as complex as the unity of people in real life. The best playwrights are those whose lines allow the actor to build into the unity of a role some of the contradictory movements of characters in real life. In doing this, he or she is assisted by the nature of dramatic development, which is not linear but tabular. That is to say that the audience perceives the character as a series of images, situations, relationships. In each separate scene, the character's behaviour is governed by a particular logic of aims and achievements or frustrations, but this logic may change from scene to scene. At the extreme, each new scene may be designed specifically to establish discontinuities of character. This is the case in Brecht's *The Good Person of Setzuan*, in which the central character is exposed to pressures of so contradictory a nature that she splits in half, 'becoming' two different characters, the kindly Shen Te and the ruthless Shui Ta.

Tabular development is simply one aspect of a particular set of dramatic **conventions**. All the speeches contained in a playtext have been set down with the assumption of certain precisely defined conventions for mimetic and representational **actions** by the actor. Broad differences of convention are easy enough to spot. Shakespeare would clearly have constructed his speeches differently if he had written for the late nineteenth-century **proscenium arch** stage. Part of the task of students will be to rediscover these performance conventions and to fill in the subtler details that are not immediately apparent. This does not mean they have to be lavish in following original conventions. A Shakespeare season by the Theatre du Soleil has shown that by employing some of the conventions of *Kabuki* theatre, Shakespeare's characters can be made to come to life in surprising ways. But the purpose of understanding the original conventions will be partly to decide how far they can or should be followed in production.

See also **authenticity**; **praxis**; **contextual studies**; *zeitgeist*.

Ideology

An ideology is a set of beliefs that may be evident in the work of a playwright, actor or director but will be equally present in an audience. Where there is a generally shared ideology a theatrical event may be a form of celebration of common beliefs and values but the ideology of a play or its presentation may be at odds with parts of an audience and cause disquiet or even riot. At its most obvious, ideologically driven drama will take the form of **agit/prop** but there are many plays, such as those adopting an existentialist viewpoint (see **authenticity**) that also have a strong ideological platform.

However, 'ideology' is a central concept to the relatively recent discipline of 'Cultural Studies' that has an interface with theatre and performance. Discourse in the field of critical theory has very often centred on the very particular view of ideology held by Marxist thinkers. For most people an ideology is simply a grouping of ideas and beliefs which constitutes a politically neutral position but for the Marxist critic ideology is anything but neutral or passive: it is a highly political concept concerned with the whole issue of power and control. For Karl Marx (1818–83) and his followers, ideology involves distortion, concealment and the masking of reality. It is about the construction and the maintenance of power that enables one group to perpetuate its dominance over another. Marxist critics of theatre like Raymond Williams (1921–88) regarded all cultural **texts** as political, offering partial images of the world and society. For Brecht and other Marxist playwrights, drama and theatre were part of the battle ground for the class struggle and the site of power and potential control.

Interculturalism

Interculturalism when applied to drama and theatre involves the blending of material from different cultural traditions in an attempt to understand other ways of living and doing. This activity has usually consisted of the exploration of **performance styles**, **forms**, **texts** and practices from a wide range of ethnic groups and cultures. The intended outcome of this process is usually the creation of new performance work that draws upon multiple cultural influences.

The most celebrated practitioners in intercultural theatre in recent times have been Peter Brook (b.1925) and Eugenio Barba (b.1936). Brook founded the International Centre for Theatre Research in 1970 and began a series of experiments in which he sought to draw upon performance traditions and situations from many ancient and contemporary sources. He and his company toured remote rural communities in Africa and Australia, shaping productions to the expectations and conditions he discovered. Through improvisation and the use of masks he also created a number of productions that drew upon ancient texts. These included *Orghast in Persepolis* (1971) which utilised the 'lost'

Persian language Avesta, *The Conference of the Birds* (1979) based on a Sufi poem and the work of Sufi musicians an the huge *Mahabharata* (1985) derived from an Indian epic.

The Indian sub-continent has provided considerable impetus to experiments in interculturalism, partly because its colonial history has produced a blend of cultural influences. Western literature and drama were taken to a part of the world already rich in performance and literary traditions. Ancient dance forms and techniques together with important legends and poems have been preserved and they influenced such practitioners as Grotowski. Now they form the basis of performance work for immigrant populations in the West and the enrichment of Western approaches to dance and drama.

Eugenio Barba, who established an International School of **Theatre Anthropology** demonstrates a concern to create methods of actor-training derived from multicultural sources. Perhaps his most notable achievement was the creation of an intercultural performance *Theatrum Mundi* ('Theatre of the World') in 1982.

Students interested in this area of work would do well to begin with *The Intercultural Performance Reader* (1996) edited by Patris Pavis.

Intertextuality

I am going to begin this entry by providing a very obvious but striking example of what is meant by 'intertextuality'. Eugene O'Neill's play *Desire under the Elms* (1924) is set in and around a New England farmhouse in the 1850s and is concerned with greed, lust, conflict between father and son, and infanticide. As many a programme note has pointed out, it has the form and feeling of a Greek **tragedy**, and the playwright went on to make his own version of the Orestes myth in his later play *Mourning becomes Electra* (1931). The dialogue of *Desire Under the Elms* is dense with biblical quotations and idiom yet also relies on the repetition of the song 'I'm going to California'. So the **text** of the play makes constant reference to other texts and we become aware of a kind of recycling that makes new meanings and forms and yet is never, in fact, a replication of an earlier text.

The concept of 'intertextuality' had its origins in France in the 1960s and owed a good deal to Roland Barthes's idea of the text as a *network*. His view was that the writer no longer occupied an exclusive, central role in the production of a text but that the text came about by drawing on a network of discourses and writings that were already circulating in some form. Thus, as we have seen in the example I gave, certain myths and legends constantly reappear in various forms and it seems as though, consciously or otherwise, we compare any play we see or are involved in with films, TV programmes, novels or other plays. So, the idea that **texts** have their meaning largely in relation to other texts is the basis of the concept we are discussing. Consider the following statement by Barthes from his essay 'Theory of the Text' and then scan the work of a particular playwright for examples of what is being described:

> Any text is a new tissue of past citations. Bits of code, formulae, rhythmic models, fragments of social languages, etc. pass into the text and are redistributed within it, for there is always language before and around the text.

The works of Harold Pinter or Sarah Kane's play *Crave* (1998), for example, are rich with incidences of intertextuality. For further discussion see also Robert Young (ed.), *Untying the Text* (1981).

See also **codes of communication; postmodernism** and **introduction to Chapter 2.**

Intervention theatre

Intervention theatre is a form of Applied Drama and takes its definition from the fact that the process in which a teacher, leader or facilitator becomes involved in a situation to bring about some form of learning, change of attitude or behaviour, the resolution of conflict or crisis or to move that situation forward in some way is known as an 'intervention'. Intervention Theatre is an educational tool in the broadest sense and invariably depends on the creation of a non-threatening environment. Therapists and teachers will often 'intervene' with clients or pupils on a one-to-one basis but the most common form of Intervention Theatre is for a small number of performers to work with a group sharing some common problem or concern in order to bring about change. The performers may use role-play to demonstrate to and involve the participants or they may use other performance skills such as **improvisation** or **devising** to create situations where issues can be explored. Situations in which Intervention Theatre has been used with considerable success have included young offenders' units, prisons, areas of social deprivation and a variety of workplaces. Issues have ranged from alcohol or substance abuse, juvenile crime, knife crime and gambling addition to industrial relations and the development of management and leadership skills. Some of the projects have been on a large scale: of these, a televised project in which the Birmingham Royal Ballet involved a group of disaffected young people in a performance of *Romeo and Juliet* or the work of a University Drama Department in Northern Ireland with a group addicted to car theft have enjoyed a high profile. On the other hand, small groups of actors offering their services to companies in order to bring about better working practices have been of no less value.

Useful discussion and examples on Intervention Theatre are provided by Tim Prentki and Sheila Preston (eds) in their *The Applied Theatre Reader* (2008).

See also **applied theatre; improvisation; forum theatre; theatre of testimony.**

Liminality

The concept of 'liminality' has become central to the study of drama in performance and is best explored through a number of examples. Imagine that you are taking part in a project that involves visiting some old people's homes in order to undertake some research for a documentary play. You persuade some of the residents to come together and share their memories orally. The *personal narratives* that result would be a form of what is termed 'cultural performance': often very moving and gripping and, sometimes, helped by the prompting of the listeners. But would this form of performance be private or public? To some extent, these personal memories would be private and informal and yet they would probably have an element of the public presentation about them. Had they simply arisen during a conversation over a cup of tea in the kitchen, they would have been entirely private; but had there been an invited audience, they would have been public. The fact is, they were neither: they occupied a border land between the two; they inhabited a threshold or *limen* and were, therefore, 'liminal'.

Anthropologists have often associated this state of liminality with rites of passage in various societies. A simple example is a wedding, in which, during the actual course of the ceremony, the couple is neither married nor unmarried. The fact that the ceremony is also associated with having a **script, costume, ritual form**, and **incidental music** together with precise **roles** and an **audience** within the structure of a type of 'staging' emphasises that we employ many theatrical devices to facilitate such life-changing rites and to enhance the betwixt and between state we describe as 'liminal'. A particular point at which Anthropology and Performance Studies intersect is their common interest in the phenomenon of the **shaman** (see Chapter 2). During the rite of passage through which the potential shaman passes there is a substantial period in which he is, in essence, neither dead nor alive. In this liminal phase, the person is neither totally possessed by the spirit of the shaman nor totally himself.

The profound significance of this concept for drama may now be obvious and you may recall that I referred to the 'discovery space' as being neither on stage nor off stage and therefore 'liminal'. Think of how an actor may approach the mastery and presentation of a character. Like the **shaman**, the **actor** is, in some sense, *possessed* by another person and is, therefore, no longer the person you and I might meet in the bar. Yet neither is that person wholly someone else: if they were, they might well abdicate control of the performance. The actor must constantly experiment with liminality but is only one of the many elements of theatre that does so. It could be argued that the entire experience of going to see a play is 'liminal': it is not in *real* time yet not entirely removed from it; the *reality* of any situation in a theatre is both fact and fiction and the **dialogue** we hear is sometimes so *real* that we accept it as having been created at that moment, still knowing that it is artificial. The state of liminality from which theatre is built runs contrary to our Western habit of insisting on binary oppositions in so much of our discourse and thinking. Many borders are, in fact, blurred and the liminal zone is a rich source for our imagination and creativity.

If you wish to explore these ideas further you will find helpful sections in Stern and Henderson (1993).

Negotiated meaning

This concept is taken from what is generally known as 'critical theory' and owes much to attempts by the Marxist thinker Stuart Hall (b.1942) to describe what takes place when a discourse, in the form of a performance, is entered into with an **audience**. In an important article in the *British Culture Studies Journal* (1973) Hall identified three phases of the performance process: encoding meaning, programme as meaningful discourse and decoding. In the first phase a director and performer will translate the raw **text** into a theatrical event employing design, performance conventions and ideological constructions. In the second phase, the performance or 'programme' takes place and becomes a meaningful discourse with the audience and is open to be 'read' in many ways. In the third phase, the audience, bringing all their ideological standpoints and aesthetic expectations and prejudices, 'decode' the performance and create meanings. They may accept the intentions and encoding systems of the producers of the performance or may make a contrary reading. However, the most likely outcome is that the audience will enter into a 'negotiated meaning', accepting some elements and rejecting others.

See also **codes of communication; ideology; sign system.**

Paratheatre

The concept of paratheatre is mainly associated with work undertaken during and emanating from the concluding phase in the career of the twentieth-century Polish theatre practitioner Jerzy Grotowski (see **Poor Theatre**). In his Laboratory Theatre experiments Grotowski had progressively sought to eliminate what he saw as the unnecessary clutter of the commercial theatre in an attempt to rediscover and redefine the art form's essence. His focus had concentrated on the actor in a simple shared space with an audience and he had explored ways of breaking down the barriers between them. However, he eventually abandoned the underlying idea of 'theatre' with its notions of 'performer' and audience, in order to seek a theatre 'beyond theatre': a 'paratheatre' where there was no purpose-built auditorium or concept of performer and spectator. In order to achieve this he set up a series of projects that existed solely for the benefit of the participants. Such activities as his 'Mountain Project' involved the exploration of communal rituals and of the nature of the 'self' and, accordingly, many of Grotowki's critics considered that he was seeking an interface with therapy and religious mysticism. What Grotowski termed 'active culture' extended to modes of communal participation that demanded the same immense seriousness, asceticism, total focus and concentration from its participants that he had always demanded from his actors.

See also **Applied Drama**.

Perception

When we attend and respond to a theatre performance we are employing our powers of 'perception': the process whereby sensory experience is transformed and organised. A percept may be formed by many stimuli and a skilled theatre practitioner will realise this sufficiently to be able to manipulate the perceptions of an **audience**. At one time, the understanding of perception was considered to be the province of philosophy, largely because it impinged on theories concerning the sources and validity of human knowledge. Some philosophers have asked whether a real, physical world actually exists independently of human experience and, if it does, how we can verify the truth concerning existence. Obviously, such questions investigate the reliability of experiences that come to us via the sense organs, as do our experiences in the theatre. What **directors** are able to exploit is the fact that, through technology, **audiences** can be made to see and hear what is selected for them. When we are in the theatre, **actions** and events are framed as someone else has determined: emphases are made, things hidden from view, sounds magnified or distorted. *Gestalt* psychologists have pointed out that we tend to perceive things as wholes and not as small parts or components: we receive and perceive a performance in similar fashion.

Postmodernism

In Chekhov's *The Cherry Orchard* (1904): a play that reflects the loss of confidence and certainty in fragmenting Russian society, one of the characters interposes into some desultory conversation the question: 'Have you read Nietzsche?' This philosopher (who died in 1900) is sometimes credited with being the forerunner of that set of ideas we now know in the West as 'Postmodernism'. With his famous assertion in *Thus Spake Zarathustra*, 'this old God liveth no more. He is dead indeed' (p. 231), and his belief that 'there are no facts, only interpretations', Nietzsche had articulated the sense of uncertainty that we can trace in the drama, music, poetry and art of the early twentieth century. The concept of modernity or modernism was really created by the attitudes of the Renaissance, and brought to its summit in the eighteenth-century Enlightenment. It was based on the belief that humankind could provide a rational, scientific explanation for everything within a Divinely ordained Universe, and that this certainty could be expressed in reliable language. Faith and science were an issue of some divergence and there were various beliefs about the relationship between the two, ranging from the hostile to the complementary. Nevertheless, a sense of order, confidence and certainty was reflected in drama and literature. With Postmodernism, however, no such certainties exist, and this set of ideas, which we now largely associate with the twentieth-century French philosophers Jacques Derrida, Jean-François Lyotard, Michel Foucault and Jean Baudrillard, has been particularly prominent since the 1980s and has had profound implications for the study of drama, and for philosophy, aesthetics, religion, history and various forms of literary criticism.

We can already see the seeds of doubt and loss of faith, together with the increasing secularisation of modernity, in the almost prophetic work of the nineteenth-century English poet and critic Matthew Arnold, and it is significant that the vision in his poem *Dover Beach* (1867) of the 'Sea of Faith' became the title of a television series in the 1980s dealing with the collapse of conventional Christian belief:

> But now I only hear
> Its melancholy; long withdrawing roar,

Retreating to the breath
Of the night wind, down the vast edges drear
And naked shingles of the world.

Similar images of a bleak and desolate landscape and a sense of dis-integration have reappeared in the music of Elgar, the poetry of T. S. Eliot or the drama of Samuel Beckett and Harold Pinter in a century that witnessed humankind constantly invoking science and technology to descend into a new kind of barbarism.

The first characteristic of Postmodernism then, is a sense of loss of meaning. For the postmodernist there is no verifiable certainty other than immediate sensory experience and there is no 'grand narrative', or what Lyotard terms *Meta-Narrative*, that explains existence or gives it a purpose. In short, there is *nothing* outside of human life to provide a scale of values, sense of destiny, or set of rules for living. Baudrillard reckons that postmodernity is largely a product of the age of mass media and that we live in a world of images. It is interesting to note that at least one leading British university drama department has added the words 'Image Studies' to its title. These images have, of course, been created by ourselves, so in no way do they provide an external expla-nation of anything from which we can derive a sense of over-riding 'meaning'. Even science, Baudrillard maintains, is 'just the name we attach to certain modes of explanation' (Sarup, 1993).

Given that there is no external set of values to which we can relate, it follows that, for Postmodernism, there is no hierarchy of human activity, and an absence of any form of discrimination between what is profound or trivial, of high artistic value or of merely populist appeal. The postmodern world is rather like the experience of commut-ing from London by train surrounded by newspapers that juxtapose tragic world events with the marital affairs of footballers, reviews of opera, and advertisements for cars; there is no sense of discrimination or irony, whilst mobile phones make any form of personal interac-tion impossible. Cultural activity is placed by the postmodernist critic on a continuum rather than in a hierarchy. There is no 'great' work of art as opposed to 'popular' art. Karaoke is as significant as cho-ral singing but is simply the product of different cultural influences. Thus, for instance, the discipline of 'Theatre Studies' has given way to the relatively new field of 'Performance Studies', drawing heavily on Anthropology, and similarly, the more traditional 'Theology' has given way to 'Religious Studies'.

Both these examples lead us to another of the key issues in the con-cept of 'postmodernism', and that is the indeterminacy of language and the unreliability of the **text** or of anything that is meant to communicate meaning. This relates to the wider epistemological concern of Postmodernism: the perception about what we can know and how we can know it. Traditionally, for instance, it had always been assumed that a text could be analysed in such a way as to reveal the meanings or insights that it was intending to convey; such a belief lies at the root of much traditional study of drama and literature. However, Derrida has attacked such assumptions, arguing that 'there is nothing beyond the text', and alongside other *structuralist* and *poststructuralist* critics has emphasised an approach that insists that any 'reader's' interaction with a text is a form of *discourse* from which the original author is absent. This is particularly troubling for the notion of written history because the postmodernist would consider that while the events described may have generated the written text, at best that text tells the reader something about the political and cultural views of the author, and more significantly, the interpretation of the text reveals a great deal about the political and cultural influences of the reader. Postmodern approaches to the text also include an awareness of the way that any one text may relate to other texts. This **intertextuality** is, in fact, quite common; there are, for example, many texts that relate thematically, structurally or in direct quotation to the *Bible*.

How, then, can we determine the 'truth'? It seems to be possible that language refers to nothing outside itself, and that we, as 'readers' make meanings to such an extent that Roland Barthes expressed the concept of the 'Death of the Author'. These are areas of debate in which you must engage.

A further important and essential element of postmodernism is the deeply suspicious and antagonistic attitude towards institutions and aspects of the Establishment. These are seen as instruments of control: Foucault and Derrida, in particular, view the world as a place in which humans are largely engaged in the business of attempting to exercise power over each other. In the view of many recent thinkers this would include the institution of the mainstream, commercial theatre. The playwright Howard Barker (1989) reckoned that 'the authoritarian art form is the Musical'. You may care to debate this. Even language is viewed as a means of control and manipulation because it so often claims to contain the truth when, in fact, it is concerned with domination and power over those who are asked to believe. Whether it be the various forms of the media or the teachings of a particular religious Faith, those claiming to know the truth dominate those who listen, read and believe. The constant attempts of one section of society or of one individual to achieve dominance over another is part of the vision of an essentially violent world portrayed by the postmodernists, a world concerned with oppression and the preservation of the self.

The idea that 'power and knowledge directly imply one another' (Foucault) raises once again the question of how we can know, and what is the purpose of knowing. Derrida uses the term *logos* as a key concept in his thinking. We traditionally associate the *logos* with the opening words of St John's Gospel, where it is translated as 'The Word'. More recent translations of the *Bible* use such expressions as 'the Idea'. For postmodernists, the term implies the founding principle in any discourse, which is beyond interrogation and from which all claims and formulations in that discourse derive their status as *truth*.

This entry is a brief summary of some of the key concepts relating to Postmodernism and it is worth my adding that you should not feel intimidated by some of the terminology employed. Some reading in the field of Postmodernism can seem impenetrable and obscure and it is important to remember, for example, that Richard Eyre and Nicholas Wright (*Changing Stages*, 2000) were able to write one of the finest books on Modern Drama without ever employing the language of Postmodernism. You may, indeed, find yourself siding with the famous linguist and philosopher Noam Chomsky who said 'Postmodernism?: I don't know what that means. But I suspect it's a scam thought up by intellectuals to keep themselves employed!' (reported in *New Internationalist* Oct. 2009).

There are a number of suggestions for further reading at the end of the chapter, and you may find Counsell (1996) and Marsen's *Communication Studies* (2006) especially helpful in seeing the relevance of the ideas of Postmodernism to a study of drama.

Praxis

The concept of 'praxis' forms the underlying philosophy of this entire book because it expresses an indissoluble link between learning and its practical application. This concept has its origins in Eastern Orthodox theology which teaches that 'faith' is not simply a set of beliefs and religious observances but that it constitutes ideas that must be converted into action. In a similar fashion 'drama' and 'performance' are not merely 'subjects' or a body of theoretical knowledge: they are activities in which human beings engage, albeit with skills reinforced by knowledge and understanding. At the point of praxis the practitioner is not conscious of theoretical considerations but this does not preclude praxis from being a learning situation. In recent years this has led to the development of the concept of 'practice as research' and the self-criticism and analysis that follows praxis creates what has come to be known as 'the reflective practitioner': a term increasingly employed to describe the intended learning outcomes of courses of training for performers. In the study of drama any form of theory that is divorced from practice, either real or potential has little meaning and less value.

Reception

This term and concept have fairly wide applications in the fields of drama, theatre and literature. Most recently, the concept has been used to imply the study and significance of *how* a work, or body of work, is received. For example, almost every student is aware of Shakespeare and can probably name some of his plays. Students will invariably have access to relatively inexpensive copies of his 'Complete Works' and individual plays. It is far less likely that drama students will be familiar with the work of the Elizabethan contemporary of Shakespeare, John Lyly and it is even more unlikely that they will be able to obtain an inexpensive copy of his 'Complete Works'. However, in his time, Lyly's works were far better known than Shakepeare's and, indeed, were the first plays to be published and reprinted many times during a playwright's lifetime It is only the subsequent 'reception' of these works that has determined their continued popularity. Lyly went out of fashion and favour, probably because he remained a Roman Catholic and his writings became identified with the royalist cause after the revolution that led to the execution of the king. Literary criticism took a more puritan line in later centuries and the works of Lyly, so famous and influential in their day, virtually disappeared whereas the works of Shakespeare, published after his death, gradually became recognized as having qualities to ensure their survival and popularity.

In the theatre, we may take 'reception' to also mean the **audience's** reaction to a play in performance. The many elements that make up a performance provide the spectators with an aesthetic experience and an array of images and the individual members of any audience will find their responses shaped by aspects of cultural conditioning, personal taste or moral stance on the one hand, and collective dynamics on the other. Audiences may be shocked, as they were by Osborne's *Look Back in Anger*, Edward Bond's *Saved* or Sarah Kane's *Blasted*; they may equally be baffled, as they were, and still are, by Beckett's *Waiting for Godot*, Pinter's *The Dumb Waiter* or one of Kaprow's *Happenings*, but they may wish to distinguish between the substance of the play and the quality of performance. Both the historical details of reception of plays in the past and the **analysis** of whatever is seen in the theatre today are part of the study of drama.

Brecht insisted, by coining the term *spectator art*, that the business of going to the theatre involved active and critical rather than comfortable and passive consumption of the play. This process involves relating the experiences of the **characters** portrayed to the personal experiences of the audience, and understanding that the audience is bringing diverse personal perspectives to the performance. Patrice Pavis (1998) provides an extensive discussion of the various 'codes of reception' that are employed by an audience and he distinguishes between the Psychological, Ideological and Aesthetic–Ideological codes. You may find it helpful to draw up your own set of principles and factors that seem to affect the way in which a play is received. What is known as 'Reception Theory' is a critical movement that insists that the historical context is the horizon against which any literary or dramatic **text** is considered. This may be a somewhat limiting activity but it does provide a useful antidote to the attitude that a work does not relate to its period and circumstances of authorship.

Semiotics/theatre

Semiotics is the study of signs and of **sign systems** and derives from the Greek word *semeion*. Drama and Performance Studies have drawn on literary and communications theory to make deductions about the role of signs in the theatre (see **theatre language**), and some scholars have preferred to use the term *semiology* in order to imply a precise science. The most important issue to grasp is that signs have a crucial role in the construction or reconstruction of meaning because they are an element of language: the means whereby we mediate all facets of social life and practice. They are arranged by codes and employed in discourses but have no fixed meaning: the interpretation of the sign system depends on the social context of those who use them, and their interaction with each other.

The foundations of semiotics were established by the linguistic theories of Ferdinand de Saussure (1857–1913). His lectures, *Cours de Linguistique Générale* (1916), published posthumously, set out to demonstrate that spoken language is not simply a linear sequence like pearls on a necklace but is both a *system* and a *structure*. Various points on the string relate to other points and exist within an entire network of relationships with other possible points. Developing this further, the American philosopher and pragmatist C. S. Peirce (1834–1914) conceived 'semiotics' as an interdisciplinary subject in which sign systems and structures could be analysed in philosophical, psychological, sociological and linguistic terms. The development of semiotics was greatly influenced by the

French philosopher Roland Barthes (1915–80), who extended the idea that almost anything can be a sign capable of providing meaning or *signification* and that this has particular relevance to the **analysis** of the arts and aspects of human behaviour.

Because semiotics is the study of signs it is the sign itself that the semiologist must examine. In the terminology of semiotics, signs operate within a *culture*. Although the primary focus of study is the **text**, it is the *reader* (or audience in the case of theatre) who creates meaning and significance by bringing values and emotional reactions. Semiologists see an important link between the reading and ideology of the reader, and, following Peirce, they may identify an *icon* (a sign that resembles the object being described), an *index* (which has a direct link between itself and its object), and a *symbol* (which has no direct resemblance to, or with, an object but is accepted, like words, to stand for something). I have drawn on some of this terminology throughout this book, demonstrating how it applies to the act of theatre and of performance (see **sign system**). There is some evidence that the limitations of a semiotic approach are being recognised but it provides one of many useful analytical tools. Elam's *The Semiotics of Theatre and Drama* (1980) remains a most helpful support and McCauley (1999) examines the problems of using linguistic models in the study and analysis of drama.

See also **codes of communication**.

Sign system

The various new approaches to literary criticism that are discussed under such entries as **codes of communication** and **theatre language** serve to remind us that any approach to theatre must somehow take account of the variety of different sign systems through which the theatre communicates. The idea of the sign system has been developed by Structuralist critics, especially Roland Barthes, to show that we are perpetually 'reading' messages in the objects that surround us, but they are messages not communicated in words. Almost everything around us, from traffic lights to the latest dress fashion, conveys a meaning to us, or rather, offers us a specific set of coded signs which we interpret, often subconsciously. In the theatre, it is clear that **costume** does not convey the same sort of message, nor does it communicate in the same way as speech. But the spectator certainly interprets it, or attaches a meaning to it, whether consciously or subconsciously. The world of costume constitutes a 'sign system', by means of which meanings can be constructed, meanings which may either denote (i.e. state explicitly) or connote (i.e. suggest by means of association). The same is true of all aspects of theatre production. **Lighting, sets, properties**, actions, dances, music, sound effects are all separate sign systems available to the actors and producer/**director** in the construction of a performance.

Text

It may seem strange to return to a further, brief, consideration of text in this section but it has to be remembered that a play has two kinds of life: one in a written form that is available for a level of consideration and another through the synthesis achieved in the minds of the **audience** in witnessing a performance. Whether or not we wish to think of the audience member as someone who is *reading* a performance, we still have to find a way of describing that blend of signs, rhythms, sounds, symbols, images, words and movements that we call a *play*. And we still need to recognise that texts can be generated, and not necessarily written down, as part of the process of being human. Evidence for the demise of the text-based play is flimsy: the text may well be the personal narratives of Palestinians and Israeli army *refusniks*, in a recent 'performance' in Trafalgar Square, or the diary of a sailor on board a British warship, but the ordered format of language for performance has an obstinate habit of remaining a vital art form with deep cultural roots.

Theatre Anthropology

The concept of Theatre Anthropology has come to mean the comparative study of the ways in which performers from differing cultural backgrounds and traditions execute their craft. More specifically it has involved Western scholars and practitioners in exploring performance practices from Asia in an attempt to discover mutual underlying principles and develop **intercultural** performances. In recent years this process has not only involved the careful observation of traditional and ancient performance modes in Asia but also the consideration of some ancient texts that set out the complex multiple possibilities of physical movement for performance developed in that culture.

The greatest impetus for activity in Theatre Anthropology was the founding of The International School for Theatre Anthropology in 1979 by the Italian theatre practitioner Eugenio Barba, who is usually credited with having initially defined the nature of the subject (see **Interculturalism**). Barba centred his discussions on what he termed the 'pre-expressive behaviour' of performers and sought to find the principles that preceded the act of performance. His analysis, therefore, was concerned with training, approaches, physical development and techniques. Although such investigations may be said to be still ongoing, Barba identified certain core issues that seemed to him to constitute a common strand between diverse performance traditions; they included the ways in which the human body is both amplified and dilated in terms of space and energy; the employment of techniques that push the body's capabilities well beyond those needed for normal daily living; the physical principle of 'opposition' that lies behind the potential for movement and what he called 'the inconsistent inconsistency' of performance modes where communication is through commonly understood codes, as in various established dance forms.

Together with the scholar Nicola Savarese, Barba set out many of the issues he had explored in *A Dictionary of Theatre Anthropology* (1991) and in his fascinating *The Paper Canoe: A Guide to Theatre Anthropology* (1994).

See also **dramaturgy of the actor.**

Theatre of testimony

The theatre of testimony is a concept developed by Loren Kruger (1999) to describe and define the use of theatre as a form of resistance during the years of apartheid in South Africa and especially in the 1970s and 80s. It is so named because it represented a means of testifying to uncomfortable truths. Initiated by such plays as *Sizwe Banzi Is Dead* (1972) by Athol Fugard, John Kani and Winston Ntshona and establishing itself as a major form of protest with the production of *Woza Albert!* by Percy Mtwa, Mbongeni Ngema and Barney Simon at the Market Theatre in Johannesburg in 1981, the theatre of testimony challenged the injustice of such factors as the pass laws, prison conditions, workers' rights and the condition of women in society.

The presentational form of testimonial theatre drew on techniques from Brecht, Grotowski and Joan Littlewood's East London 'Theatre Workshop' and included direct address to the audience, physical and verbal comedy, the adoption of multiple roles by the actors and the use of minimal **props.** Many of the scripts were **actor-generated** through **improvisation** often included personal narratives and **verbatim theatre**.

Some scholars, notably Mda (1993), have sought to draw a distinction between 'protest theatre' typified by the plays presented at the Market theatre and which aimed to disturb the consciences of the **audience** and 'theatre for resistance' generated by such playwrights as Maishe Maponya and more usually staged in township situations, which openly aimed to rally the oppressed to active opposition against injustice (see **Forum Theatre**).

Students will see the inter-relatedness of drama study from this brief discussion of 'Theatre of Testimony'. Aspects of such concepts as **Political Theatre, Epic Theatre; Forum Theatre, Verbatim Theatre, Agit/Prop** or **Documentary** all may be subsumed in this concept alone and this is not to mention any discussion of techniques for performance or the creation of **text**, all of which are a part of other concepts mentioned in this book. Furthermore, we can see that a concept initially articulated to describe a movement in South Africa could now equally be applied to drama dealing with other more recent contexts where prejudice, economic forces, social deprivation, sexual orientation, faith, gender, race or accident of birth are still the root cause of injustice.

The entire field of theatre as an instrument of protest and search for human dignity and justice is admirably surveyed in Paul Rae's *Theatre and Human Rights* (2009).

Zeitgeist

This concept was developed by the German philosopher Georg Hegel (1770–1831) to convey the idea of the 'spirit of the age' or 'spirit of the times'. It is a particularly useful concept for the student of drama and performance because it is an appreciation of the *zeitgeist* at the period of writing of a work that enables us to interrogate a **text** with understanding. Furthermore, it is the *zeitgeist* that will help determine the nature of any subsequent production of that work. There are many examples of this latter fact, ranging from a recent setting of Shakespeare's *A Midsummer Night's Dream* in a nightclub where drugs are freely available to the production of a Restoration play as if it were an episode in the TV drama *Footballers' Wives*. Future drama students will need to understand the *zeitgeist* currently present in our society in order to appreciate the **texts** and performances being produced now. Similarly, their attempts to give such texts new life in performance will be affected by their *zeitgeist*. The *zeitgeist* is an essential area of investigation in **contextual studies**.

See also **ideology**.

Further reading

Peter Buse (2001) *Drama and Theory: Critical Approaches to Modern British Drama* (Manchester: Manchester University Press).

Colin Counsell and Laurie Wolf (eds) (2001) *Performance Analysis: An Introductory Coursebook* (London: Routledge).

Helen Freshwater (2009) *Theatre and Audience* (Basingstoke: Palgrave Macmillan).

John Gassner and Ralph Allen (eds) (1992) *Theatre and Drama in the Making* (New York: Applause).

Loren Kruger (1999) *The Drama of South Africa* (London:Routledge).

Jane Milling and Graham Ley (2001) *Modern Theories of Performance* (Basingstoke: Palgrave Macmillan).

Kenneth Pickering (2003) *Studying Modern Drama* (Basingstoke: Palgrave Macmillan).

Bibliography

Abercrombie, N. and Longhurst, B., *Audiences* (London: Sage, 1998).

Allain, P., *The Art of Stillness* (New York and Basingstoke: Palgrave Macmillan, 2003).

Allain, P. and Harvie, J., *The Routledge Companion to Theatre and Performance* (London: Routledge, 2006).

Allain, P. Banu, G. and Ziolkowski, G. (eds) *Peter Brook and Grotowski: Theatre is Just Form* (Wroclaw: The Grotowski Institute: 2009).

Alfreds, M., *Different Every Night: Rehearsal and Peformance Techniques for Actors* (London: Nick Hern Books, 2008).

Ang, I., *Desperately Seeking the Audience* (London: Routledge, 1991).

Anon., *Edward the Third* in E. Sams (ed.), *Shakespeare's Edward III* (New Haven and London: Yale University Press 1996).

Archer, W., *Playmaking* (Boston, MA: Maynard, 1912).

Aristotle, *Poetics*, in T. S. Dorsch, *Classical Literacy Criticism* (Harmondsworth: Penguin, 1983).

Arnott, P., *Public Performance in the Greek Theatre* (London: Routledge, 1985).

Artaud, A., *Collected Works*, trans. V. Corti (London: Calder & Boyars, 1968).

Artaud, A., *The Theatre and its Double* (London: Calder & Boyars, 1970).

Auckland-Lewis, G. and Pickering, K., *Thinking about Plays* (London: Dramatic Lines, 2004).

Auerbach, E., *Mimesis: The Representation of Reality in Western Literature* (Princeton, NJ: Princeton University Press, 1946).

Auslander, P., *From Acting to Performance* (London: Routledge, 1997).

Austin, J. L., *How We Do Things with Words* (Cambridge, MA: Harvard University Press, 1962).

Ayckbourn, A., *The Crafty Art of Playmaking* (London: Faber & Faber, 2002).

Baker, H., *Stage Management and Theatre Craft* (Colwall, Malvern: Garnet Miller, 1981).

Barker, H., *Arguments for a Theatre* (Manchester: Manchester University Press, 1989).

Barba, E., *The Paper Canoe: A Guide to Theatre Anthropology* (London: Routledge, 1994).

Barba, E. and Savarese, N.,(eds) *A Dictionary of Theatre Anthropology* (London: Routledge, 1991).

Barkworth, P., *About Acting* (London: Methuen, 1999).

Barnes, P., *A Companion to Post War British Theatre* (London: Croom Helm, 1986).

Barranger, M., *Theatre: A Way of Seeing* (Belmont: Wadsworth, 1995).

Barroll, J.L., Leggatt, A., Hosley, R. and Kernan, A., *The Revels History of Drama in English: Vol. III. 1576–1613* (London: Methuen, 1973).

Barthes, R., *Sur Racine* (Paris: Seuilh, 1963).

Baugh, C., *Garrick and Loutherbourg* (Cambridge: Chadwyck-Healey, 1993).

Benedetti, R., *The Actor at Work* (New Jersey: Prentice Hall, 1994).

Bermel, A., *Artaud's Theatre of Cruelty* (London: Methuen, 2001).

Berne, E., *The Games People Play: the Psychology of Human Relationships* (London: Penguin, 1964).

Boal, A., *Theatre of the Oppressed* (London: Pluto Press, 1979).

Boal, A., *Games for Actors and Non-Actors* (London: Routledge, 1992).

Bradby, D. (ed.), *Performance and Politics in Popular Theatre* (Cambridge: Cambridge University Press, 1980).

Bradley, A. C., *Shakespearean Tragedy* (London: Macmillan, 1904).

Braun, E., *The Theatre of Meyerhold* (London: Methuen, 1979).

Braun, E., *The Director and the Stage* (London: Methuen, 1982).

Brecht, B., *The Messingkauf Dialogues*, trans. J. Willett (London: Methuen, 1979).

Brecht, B., 'In the Jungle of Cities' in *Collected Plays*, trans. J. Willett, vol. I, part iv (London: Methuen, 1980).

Bristol, M., *Carnival and Theatre* (London: Methuen, 1985).

Brockett, O., *History of the Theatre* (Boston, MA: Allyn & Bacon, 1995).

Brook, P., *The Empty Space* (Harmondsworth: Penguin, 1972).

Brook, P., *The Shifting Point* (London: Methuen, 1988).

Brown, J. Russell, *Drama* (London: Heinemann, 1968).

Brownan, D. L. and Schwartz, R. A., *Spirits, Shamans and Stars* (The Hague: Mouton, 1979).

Buse, P., *Drama and Theory: Critical Approaches to Modern British Drama* (Manchester: Manchester University Press, 2001).

Butler, C., *Postmodernism: A Very Short Introduction* (Oxford: Oxford University Press, 2002).

Carlson, M., *Performance: A Critical Introduction*, 2nd edn (London: Routledge, 2004).

Chan, M., *Music in the Theatre of Ben Jonson* (Oxford: Clarendon Press, 1980).

Cohen, R., *Acting Power* (Palo Alto, CA: Mayfield, 1978).

Cole, T., *Playwrights on Playwriting* (New York: Hill & Wang, 1960).

Cole, T. and Chinoy, H., *Directors on Directing* (1953; New York: Crown, 1970).

Counsell, C., *Signs of Performance* (London: Routledge, 1996).

Counsell, C. and Wolf, L. (eds), *Performance Analysis* (London: Routledge, 2001).

Craig, E. G., *The Art of the Theatre* (London: Foulis, 1905).

Davies, A., *Other Theatres: The Development of Alternative and Experimental Theatre in Britain* (Basingstoke: Macmillan, 1987).

Davis, J., *Farce* (London: Methuen, 1979).

De Botton, A., *Status Anxiety* (London: Hamish Hamilton, 2004).

Delsarte, F., *Delsarte System of Oratory* (New York: Werner, 1893).

Elam, K., *The Semiotics of Theatre and Drama* (London: Methuen, 1980).

Elsom, J., *Post War British Theatre* (London: Routledge & Kegan Paul, 1976).

Esslin, M., *The Theatre of the Absurd* (Harmondsworth: Penguin, 1961).

Esslin, M., *Artaud* (London: Fontana, 1976).

Eyre, R. and Wright, N., *Changing Stages* (London: Routledge, 2000).

Findlay, K. and Pickering, K., *Preparing for your Diploma in Drama and Speech* (London: Dramatic Lines, 2003).

Forde, N., *Theatrecraft* (London: MARC, 1986).

Freak, T. and Gandy, P., *The Jesus Mysteries* (London: Thorsons, 1999).

Freshwater, H., *Theatre and Audience* (Basingstoke: Palgrave Macmillan, 2009).

Freytag, G., *Die Technik des Dramas* (Darmstadt: Wissenschaftliche Birckgesellschaft, 1857).

Frohnsdorff, M. and Pickering, K., *(Great Neglected Speeches from the Elizbabethan Stage* (Brighton: Pen Press, 2010).

Frome, S., *Playwriting: A Complete Guide to Creating Theater* (North Carolina: Mc Farland,1990).

Frye, N., *The Anatomy of Criticism* (London: Macmillan, 1957).

Gassner, J. and Allen, R. (eds), *Theatre and Drama in the Making* (New York: Applause, 1992).

Genet, J., *The Blacks* (London: Faber, 1960).

Goffman, E., *The Presentation of Self in Everyday Life* (Harmondsworth: Penguin, 1969).

Goffman, E., *Frame Analysis* (Harmondsworth: Peregrine, 1975).

Gordon, M., *The Comic Routines of the Commedia dell'Arte* (New York: P.A.J. Publications, 1983).

Grotowski, J., *Towards a Poor Theatre* (London: Methuen, 1969).

Gurr, A., *The Shakespearean Stage, 1574–1642*, 2nd edn (Cambridge: Cambridge University Press, 1980).

Hammond, W. and Steward, D. (eds), *Verbatim, Verbatim: Techniques in Contemporary Documentary Theatre* (London: Oberon, 2007).

Hartnoll, P., *The Theatre: A Concise History* (London: Thames & Hudson, 1998).

Hayman, R., *Techniques of Acting* (London: Methuen, 1969).

Heaton, V., *The Oberammergau Passion Play* (London: Robert Hale, 1983).

Henn, T. R., *The Harvest of Tragedy* (London: Methuen, 1956).

Hilton, J., *New Directions in Performance* (Basingstoke: Macmillan, 1987).

Hodgson, J. and Richards, E., *Improvisation* (London: Eyre Methuen, 1963).

Hodgson, T., *The Batsford Dictuonary of Drama* (London: Batsford, 1988).

Howard, R., *Contemporary Chinese Theatre* (London: Heinemann, 1978).

Innes, C., *Avant Garde Theatre, 1892–1992* (London: Routledge, 1993).

Irving, L., *The Precarious Crust* (London: Chatto & Windus, 1971).

Itzin, C., *Stages in the Revolution* (London: Methuen, 1980).

Jarry, A., *Selected Works* (London: Methuen, 1965).

Jellicoe, A., *Community Plays: How to Put them On* (London: Methuen, 1987).

Kershaw, B., *Theatre Ecologies: Environment and Performance Events* (Cambridge: Cambriidge University Press, 2007).

Johnson, W., *Riding the Ox Home* (London: Rider, 1982).

Johnstone, K., *Improvisation* (London: Eyre Methuen, 1981).

Joint Association of Classical Teachers, *The World of Athens* (Cambridge: Cambridge University Press, 1984).

Joseph, B., *Elizabethan Acting* (Oxford: Oxford University Press, 1951).

Joseph, S., *New Theatre Forms* (London: Pitman, 1968).

Kelleher, J., *Theatre and Politics* (Basingstoke: Palgrave Macmillan, 2009).

Kellerman, P. F., *Sociodrama and Collective Trauma* (London: Jessica Kingsley, 2007).

Kruger, L., *The Drama of South Africa: Plays, Pageants and Publics since 1910* (London: Routledge, 1999).

Lacey, S., *British Realist Theatre: The New Wave in its Context, 1956–1965* (London: Routledge, 1995).

Leach, R., *Theatre Studies: the Basics* (London: Routledge, 2008).

Leacroft, R., *The Development of the English Playhouse* (London: Methuen, 1988).

Leech, C. and Craik, T. (eds), *The Revels History of Drama in English*, vol. III (London: Methuen, 1975).

Leggatt, A., *Jacobean Public Theatre* (London: Routledge, 1992).

Lennard, J. and Luckhurst, M., *The Drama Handbook* (Oxford: Oxford University Press, 2002).

Lodge, D., *Small World* (Harmondsworth: Penguin, 1984).

Lommel, A., *Shamanism: The Beginning of Art* (New York: McGraw-Hill, 1967).

Marsen, S., *Communication Studies* (Basingstoke: Palgrave Macmillan, 2006).

McAuley, G., *Space in Performance* (Ann Arbor, MI: Michigan: University Press, 1999).

McGrath, J., *A Good Night Out* (London: Methuen, 1981).

McQuail, D., *Audience Analysis* (London: Sage, 1997).

Mda, Z., *When People Play People* (Johannesburg: Witwartersrand University Press, 1993).

Milling, J. and Ley, G., *Modern Theories of Performance* (Basingstoke: Palgrave Macmillan, 2001).

Mitchell, K., *The Director's Craft: A Handbook of Theatre* (London: Routledge, 2008).

Mitter, S. and Shevtsova, M. (eds), *Fifty Key Directors* (London: Routledge, 2005).

More, T., *The Planets Within* (New York: Lindisfarne Press, 1980).

Mudford, P., *Making Theatre: From Text to Performance* (London: Athlone Press, 2000).

Nelson, R., *Play Within the Play* (Boston, MA: Yale University Press, 1958).

Nicholson, H., *Applied Drama: The Gift of Theatre* (Basingstoke: Palgrave Macmillan, 2005).

Nicholson, H., *Theatre and Education* (Basingstoke: Palgrave Macmillan, 2009).

Nietzsche, F., trans. A. Tille, *Thus Spake Zarathustra*, (London: Dent, 1957).

Oddey, A., *Devising Theatre* (London: Routledge, 1994).

Orgel, S., *Impersonations: The Performance of Gender in Shakespeare's England* (Cambridge: Cambridge University Press, 1996).

Pavis, P. (ed.) *The Intercultural Performance Reader* (London: Routledge,1996).

Pavis, P., *Dictionary of the Theatre: Terms, Concepts and Analysis* (Buffalo, NY: University of Toronto Press, 1998).

Pavis, P., trans. D. Williams, *Analyzing Performance: Theater, Dance and Film* (Ann Arbor, MI: University of Michigan Press, 2004).

Pickering, K., *Drama Improvised* (Colwall, Malvern: Garnet Miller, 1997).

Pickering, K., *Drama in the Cathedral* (Colwall, Malvern: Garnet Miller, 2001).

Pickering, K., *Studying Modern Drama* (Basingstoke: Palgrave Macmillan, 2003).

Pickering, K. and Woolgar, M., *Theatre Studies* (Basingstoke: Palgrave Macmillan, 2009).

Pinter, H., *Various Voices: Prose, Poetry, Politics, 1948–1998* (London: Faber & Faber, 1998).

Pool, W., *Monthly Letters* (London: Werner Laurie, 1929).

Potter, R., *The English Morality Play* (London: Routledge, 1975).

Prentki, T. and Preston,S. (eds), *The Applied Theatre Reader* (Abingdon, UK and New York: Routledge, 2008).

Rae, P., *Theatre and Human Rights* (Basingstoke: Palgrave Macmillan, 2009).

Rayner, A., *Drama and the Phenomenology of Action* (Ann Arbor, MI: Michigan University Press, 1994).

Read, A., *Theatre and Everyday Life* (London: Routledge, 1993).

Richardson, C. and Johnson, J., *Medieval Drama* (Basingstoke: Macmillan, 1991).

Righter, A., *Shakespeare and the Idea of the Play* (Harmondsworth: Penguin, 1967).

Rolfe, B., *Behind the Mask* (Oakland, CA: Persona, 1977).

Roose-Evans, J., *Experimental Theatre* (New York: Avon, 1970).

Saint-Denis, M., *Theatre: The Rediscovery of Style* (New York: Theatre Arts, 1960).

Salinger, L., *Shakespeare and the Traditions of Comedy* (Cambridge: Cambridge University Press, 1974).

Sarup, M., *An Introductory Guide to Postmodernism and Poststructuralism* (Atlanta, GA: University of Georgia, 1993).

Schechner, R., *Environmental Theatre* (New York: Hawthorn, 1973).

Schechner, R., *Between Theatre and Anthropology* (Philadelphia: University Press, 1985).

Schechner, R., *Performance Theory* (London: Routledge, 1988).

Schechner, R., *By Means of Performance* (New York: Drama Books, 1990).

Schutzman, M. and Cohen-Cruz, J. (eds), *Playing Boal* (London: Routledge, 1994).

Schweitzer, P., *Reminiscence Theatre* (London: Jessica Kingsley: 2006).

Selbourne, D., *The Making of 'A Midsummer Night's Dream'* (London: Methuen, 1982).

Senelick, L., *The Chekhov Theatre: A Century of the Plays in Performance* (Cambridge: Cambridge University Press, 1997).

Shaw, G. B., *Our Theatre in the Nineties* (London: Constable, 1932).

Shklovski, K., *Russian Formalist Criticism* (Reis: University of Nebraska, 1968).

Sidnell, M., *Dances of Death* (London: Faber, 1984).

Sierz, A., *In-Yer-Face Theatre: British Drama Today* (London: Faber, 2001).

Slade, P., *Child Drama* (London: London University Press, 1954).

Southern, R., *The Seven Ages of Theatre* (London: Faber 1962).

Spolin, V., *Improvisation for the Theatre* (London: Pitman, 1963).

Stanislavsky, C., *Building a Character* (1950; London: Methuen, 1968).

Stanislavsky, C., *My Life in Art* (1924; London: Methuen, 1980).

Stanislavsky, C., *An Actor Prepares* (1936; London: Methuen, 1980).

Stanislavsky, C., *Creating a Role* (1961; London: Methuen, 1981).

Stavenacre, T., *Slapstick* (London: Angus, 1987).

Stern, C. and Henderson, B., *Performance, Texts and Contexts* (New York: Longman, 1993).

Strindberg, A., *Notes for an Effective Play* (Stockholm: Berniers, 1902).

Strindberg, A., *Plays*, trans. M. Meyer (London: Eyre Methuen, 1976).

Styan, J., *Modern Drama in Theory and Practice*, vol. 3: *Expressions and Epic Theatre* (Cambridge: Cambridge University Press, 1980).

Styan, J., *The English Stage* (Cambridge: Cambridge University Press, 1996).

Taylor, J. R., *Anger and After* (Harmondsworth: Penguin, 1962).

Taylor, J. R., *The Rise and Fall of the Well-Made Play* (London: Methuen, 1967).

Turner, V., *From Ritual to Theatre* (New York: PAJ, 1982).

Turner, V., *Eugenio Barba* (London: Routledge).

Tydeman, W., *The Theatre in the Middle Ages: Western European Stage Conditions, c. 800–1576* (Cambridge: Cambridge University Press, 1978).

Wallis, M. and Shepherd, S., *Studying Plays* (London: Edward Arnold, 2002).

Watson, J. and Hill, A., *A Dictionary of Communication and Media Studies* (London: Edward Arnold, 1984).

Weate, C., *Classic Voice: Working with Actors on Vocal Style* (London: Oberon, 2009).

Webster, R., *Studying Literacy Theory* (London: Edward Arnold, 1990).

Weiss, S. and Wesley, K., *Postmodernism and its Critics* (Alabama University website, 2002).

Welker, D., *Theatrical Set Designs: The Basic Techniques* (Boston, MA: Allyn & Bacon, 1969).

Willett, J., *Brecht on Theatre* (London: Methuen, 1964).

Willett, J., *The Theatre of Bertolt Brecht* (London: Methuen, 1977).

Willett, J., *The Theatre of Erwin Piscator* (London: Methuen, 1978).

Williams, D., *Peter Brook: A Theatrical Casebook* (London: Methuen, 1988).

Williams, F. E., *The Drama of Orokolo* (London: Oxford University Press, 1940).

Williams, R., *Modern Tragedy* (London: Chatto & Windus, 1966).

Williams, R., *Keywords* (London: Fontana, 1981).

Woollard, M., *An Illustrated Guide to Staging History* (Colwall, Malvern: Garnet Miller, 1999).

Wraight, A.D., *Christopher Marlowe and Edward Alleyn* (London: Adam Hart, 1993).

Young, R. (ed.), *Untying the Text* (London: Routledge, 1981).

Index

Note: This index should be used in conjunction with the Contents pages which provide page references for all key terms. **Bold** numbers indicate where a major definition is offered.

283